OSCAR WILDE

OSCAR WILDE

A Collection of Critical Essays

Edited by
Jonathan Freedman

Prentice Hall, Upper Saddle River, New Jersey 07458

Library of Congress Cataloging-in-Publication Data

Oscar Wilde : a collection of critical essays / edited by Jonathan
    Freedman.
        p.   cm. — (New century views)
    Includes bibliographical references.
    ISBN 0–13–146044–7
    1. Wilde, Oscar, 1854–1900—Criticism and interpretation.
I. Freedman, Jonathan.   II. Series.
PR5824.083   1996
828'.809—dc20   95–12411
                                                            CIP

Acquisitions editor: Tony English
Editorial/production supervision
    and interior design: Mary McDonald
Cover design: Karen Salzbach
Buyer: Mary Ann Gloriande

© 1996 by Prentice-Hall, Inc.
Simon & Schuster/A Viacom Company
Upper Saddle River, New Jersey 07458

Printed in the United States of America
10   9   8   7   6   5   4   3   2   1

ISBN 0-13-146044-7

Prentice-Hall International (UK) Limited, *London*
Prentice-Hall of Australia Pty. Limited, *Sydney*
Prentice-Hall Canada Inc., *Toronto*
Prentice-Hall Hispanoamericana, S.A., *Mexico*
Prentice-Hall of India Private Limited, *New Delhi*
Prentice-Hall of Japan, Inc., *Tokyo*
Simon & Schuster Asia Pte. Ltd., *Singapore*
Editora Prentice-Hall do Brasil, Ltda., *Rio de Janeiro*

Contents

Introduction: On Oscar Wildes

Jonathan Freedman

There has been no figure of the past century so insistently multiple as Oscar Wilde. Even for a generation of polymaths—he was two years older than George Bernard Shaw, one year younger than John Maynard Keynes—Wilde proved uniquely various, pouring all his many selves into both his extravagant public life and his slender but equally diverse *oeuvre*. Dandy and bourgeois; author of fairy tales, drawing room comedies, and self-consciously decadent fictions; nationalist without a nation; socialist without portfolio or program; editor of a mass-market fashion magazine and committed critic of the marketplace; thoroughgoing ironist and self-created (if undeniably courageous) martyr; theorist of the artificial and sentimentalist supreme: There are so many Wildes that one loses track of them as one tries to tote them up.

But as many biographical Oscar Wildes as there have been, an even greater number circulated in popular culture from the earliest days of his career to its infamous end. Wilde first achieved notoriety while still an undergraduate at Oxford through George DuMaurier's *Punch* cartoons of languid, lily-toting aesthetes, one of whom looked like him and many of whom quoted his *bon mots* and epigrams. His celebrity was amplified by Gilbert and Sullivan's immensely popular operetta, *Patience*, as well as the numerous pamphlets, parodies, and lampoons avidly consumed by a booming mass audience in both England and America. ("Oscar Wilde the ass-thete" was one of the kinder appellations Wilde found attached to himself during his 1882 American tour.) Later, Wilde became even more notorious as the author of *Dorian Gray*, a work far more successful in suggesting the effect of depravity than in delivering the depraved goods but which nevertheless came to symbolize the literary movement of "decadence" and the slogan (not fully apposite to Wilde, though he echoed it frequently enough) of "art for art's sake." And this process climaxed when, after his trials, and indeed, after his life, Wilde was designated as the paramount and quite literal embodiment of an entirely new social category—the "homosexual" or, in the term of the time, the "degenerate."

The same process has been performed by literary critics, at least until recently. Ass-thete or aesthete, gay saint or *poète maudit*: These were the roles Wilde played in classrooms and criticism for most of the twentieth century. A few serious accounts of his work could be found, particularly in the later days of the New Criticism; but it was largely for his flamboyant life and as Exhibit A of "deca-

1

dence" that Wilde was considered. The predecessor of this collection is an excellent case in point. In 1969, *Twentieth Century Views* added Oscar Wilde to its list in a volume of essays edited by the distinguished scholar of Anglo-Irish modernism, Richard Ellmann. That book contained 23 selections, among them condescending remarks from Yeats's autobiographies; Pater's edgy review of *Dorian;* André Gide's famous account of meeting Wilde and Alfred Douglas in North Africa; stringent critiques from Auden and Mary McCarthy and more sympathetic commentary from Thomas Mann and Borges; fine poems by Hart Crane, Brendan Behan, and John Betjeman and a not-so-fine poem by Douglas. A few essays took Wilde's example and *oeuvre* seriously, the best being Ellmann's essay on *Salomé*— one sign of the crucial role Ellmann played in the rise of Wilde studies (his contribution to this volume is another). But even these essays frequently strike a note of astonishment that the ineffable Oscar should be the subject of serious commentary at all.

In the twenty-odd years since, however, an abundance of new, more extensive and more trenchant responses to Wilde has emerged, circulating with increasing force in the past decade. Indeed, in that time Wilde has emerged from the taint of scandal, obscurity, and light-weightedness to become a crucial object of (and incitement to) critical practice. The sheer copiousness of this more recent commentary suggests Wilde's hold on the cultural imagination, both within and beyond the academy. The editor of this volume, for example, has had the benefit of consulting two plays and three novels (including a mystery in which Wilde, during his American tour, teams up with a Western sheriff to solve a murder); Ellmann's biography; an anthology of criticism edited by Regenia Gagnier, herself the author of an excellent book on Wilde and his culture; and no fewer than 336 entries in the MLA bibliography.

Reasons for this recent proliferation of critical works are doubtless as profuse as the criticism itself, but all surely suggest the uncanny appositeness of Wilde to the concerns and obsessions of our own *fin-de-siècle* moment. Wilde's art and life alike turned on three issues that have emerged, in the past twenty-five years, as among the most crucial in contemporary criticism: the nature of sexuality, particularly the reshaping of male desire in an irrevocably homophobic culture; the relation between the culture industry and mass society; and the vicissitudes of representation itself. Wilde, that is to say, may not only turn out to be our contemporary; recent critics are discovering—and asserting—that we are his.

Wilde does so, we might speculate, not because of a near-preternatural prescience but because of his unique ability to provoke, challenge, and critique the very categories of thought we bring to bear on his work. Nowhere is this truer than in the most frequently invoked venue in which Wilde has been placed by partisans and antagonists alike: that of homosexuality. Both because Wilde was himself defined by the institutions of dominant culture as one of the prime examples of that new sexual typology and because of his subsequent canonization by gay male culture, late nineteenth- and early twentieth-century discourses on homosexuality have largely been forged with reference to Wilde. When Max

Nordau set out in 1892 to define the archetypal "degenerate," for example, he cited Wilde as his prime example; so too did numerous preachers and a sensational yellow press. But the same set of identifications, given a different spin to be sure, proved central to the efforts of twentieth-century gay men to establish an affirmative identity for "the homosexual"; in these efforts, too, Wilde has served as both warrant and exemplar. After his trial—during which the name of the love that dare not speak its name was shouted out loud for the first time by a sensation-mongering press—and even more powerfully after his imprisonment, Wilde was celebrated by a nascent gay male community as hero, martyr, and role model. And much of the subsequent writing in the service of creating a distinctive gay male culture takes Wilde as its central object. From Gide's memoir through Susan Sontag's famous essay on that prime category of gay taste, camp, through Wayne Koestenbaum's essay on the birth of gay reading, Wilde has served as both the source and the reference point for a distinctive gay male poetics and hermeneutics.

But the very centrality of Wilde to the discourse on gay male sexuality has proved problematic, not only for Wilde but also for that discourse itself. Wilde's very canonization has established models of identity that many gay men are currently contesting. Although for some the categories of "dandy" and "martyr" that circulate around Wilde remain central to gay male identity, for others the very persistence of those categories reflects the vicissitudes of race, class, and of homophobia internalized under the sign of victimization. More recently, critics have used Wilde to investigate the relation between the birth of "the homosexual" as a conceptual ideal-type and the *fin-de-siècle* reformulation of masculinity itself. Following Foucault but moving beyond him, they ask what the relation might be between Wilde's understanding of masculine desire and the simultaneous policing and promoting of male desire that characterize the late nineteenth and early twentieth centuries.

Whatever else we can say about his relation to gay male desire, then, one thing remains clear: Wilde serves as a marker for homophobes and homophiles alike of the possibilities of desire "between men" in a way that Wilde himself would have found thoroughly engaging. But even placing Wilde in this more capacious framework fails to do justice to the extensiveness and generosity of his identities and concerns. Wilde's interest in redefining same-sex desire is supplemented by a yet more ample vision of the factiousness of both gender and sexuality. For Wilde's destabilizing play with the conventions and categories of gendered identity reveals that notion, too, as a species of performance or play: One adopts identities as a man or a woman with all the serious frivolity with which one dresses (or cross-dresses) for dinner. And in reckoning with this awareness, Wilde's male characters frequently lag behind his women: What Dorian must learn from Lord Henry, Lady Bracknell has already known from the beginning. This is one of the reasons, it seems to me, that from the moment of his trial, when a number of women bombarded the court with appeals for mercy, through the period immediately after his death, when (as Richard Dellamora shows) writers like Willa

Cather and Katherine Mansfield found Wilde an inspiration for new visions of sexuality, imagination, and the body, to the present day, when some of Wilde's most insightful critics have proved to be women—Susan Sontag, Regenia Gagnier, Katharine Worth, Eve Kosofsky Sedgwick, and Rachel Bowlby—Wilde has found attentive readers of every gender and sex, every ideological position and political disposition.

The point, then, is not that Wilde shouldn't be considered under the sign of recent investigations of masculinity and sexuality; to the contrary, Wilde himself shaped the way we think about those issues so thoroughly that it's impossible to treat them without reference to him. But when one places Wilde's witty, paradoxical, and complex formulations in the midst of our own complex understanding of these issues, he challenges the categories we use to think about them. Indeed, he makes it impossible for us to think about him in terms of *just* those categories, pressing us to come up with new ones and critiquing us when we do. The phenomenon we observe in sexual politics is seen even more clearly with those of class and nation: just as Wilde volatilized firm demarcations of gendered identity, so he did those of caste and nationality. As that outsider of outsiders, an Irishman in England—as the son, in fact, of an Irish revolutionary poet, known as "Speranza"—Wilde made his way in the British social world by outsnobbing the aristocracy, dramatizing and problematizing the fictions of class and country as fully as he did those of sex and gender. As far as his own national and political self-identification goes, Wilde always identified himself as *other*—but in a highly qualified and complicated way. "I am not English; I'm Irish—which is quite another thing," Wilde stated in 1894, in an interview in the highbrow *Pall Mall Gazette*. The salient point to be made about his comment is not only that he saw himself in terms of a nation that didn't then exist, but also that he defined that identity as "another thing" without specifying further what that thing might be. Wilde, among his other attributes, may be profitably considered as a prophet of the postcolonial; and it is a further tribute to his prescience that when so considered he adumbrates the issues of ambivalence and hybridity that stand at the center of contemporary writing on postcoloniality.

Yet Wilde's identification of himself under the sign of all-purpose otherness should not blind us—it certainly didn't blind Wilde—to the ways he maneuvered within the coordinates of the English class system, or at least within a segment of that system. By this I don't mean that Wilde made a number of stabs at high bourgeois respectability, although he did; rather, I mean to suggest that he functioned within what some theorists refer to as a "new class"—those who produce and consume information rather than goods, services, or even capital itself. Wilde's entire career was circumscribed, in fact, by knowledge-producing and consuming institutions both within and without the mass market economy: the university; the booming mass magazines and their auxiliary, advertising—including both those that initially publicized him, like *Punch*, and those that later employed him, like *Woman's World;* and the publishing industry, to which Wilde contributed not only works of imagination but also those of criticism, commentary, and controversy. Indeed,

Wilde learned (at first giddily, thereafter tragically) that within such a world, one's very being could be transformed into a marketable good—a piece of information, an object of publicity, gossip, and revilement, all in the interests of selling more papers.

Wilde not only maneuvered within this world, he understood fully its coordinates and principles, and commented relentlessly, if ironically, upon its possibilities and failings. Much of Wilde's writing demands to be read as an attempt to come to terms with a newly forming public sphere in which symbolic encodings take preeminence over the real—that world we call "postmodern" but which Wilde's experience suggests came into being in the late nineteenth and early twentieth centuries. Wilde's most brilliant epigrams and essays testify to his response to the institutions that govern such a world, and hence speak with uncanny accuracy to our own. As Katharine Worth felicitously puts it, it is as if Wilde had set depth charges in his writing, timed to go off at our moment, not his own.

"If the poor only had profiles there would be no difficulty in solving the problem of poverty," Wilde wrote in 1894: It has taken political theorists a hundred years to catch up with his vision of the making and unmaking of social policy in a thoroughly aestheticized, media-mediated public sphere. "In old days men had the rack. Now they have the press. That is an improvement, certainly. But still, it is very bad, and wrong, and demoralising." This aphorism, from Wilde's wonderful essay *The Soul of Man under Socialism*, is uncannily prescient as well as devastatingly funny in its understanding of the continuity between primitive forms of social control and our more recent varieties. Indeed, Wilde's understanding of the mutual enmeshment of celebrity, politics, and journalism (which is hardly original to him) and of the uses of this volatile admixture as a means of social control (which *is*) reads with amazing accuracy at the current moment. In light of Woody Allen, O. J. Simpson, and recent presidential campaigns, some of Wilde's most famous words achieve a new explosiveness—one which beggars any commentary I might offer on them: *"The fact is, the public have an insatiable curiosity to know everything, except what is worth knowing.* Journalism, conscious of this, and having tradesmanlike habits, supplies their demands. In centuries before ours the public nailed journalists to the pump. This was quite hideous. In this century journalists have nailed their own eyes to the keyhole. That is much worse."

As with sexual politics and the politics of class, so too with literary criticism—and, more generally, with the theory of representation itself. In magnificent essays like *The Critic as Artist, The Decay of Lying,* and *The Truth of Masks*—not to mention such works as *The Importance of Being Earnest*—Wilde reworked the predominant critical idioms of his day, refashioning Matthew Arnold's heavily moralized critical emphasis on "seeing the object as in itself it truly is," and Walter Pater's delicate revision of Arnold, which sought to privilege the sensations of the individual critic, into the bold assertion that the critic's job is to see the object as it is *not*. Asserting the priority of the interpreted over the natural and of the imaginative critic over the minutely faithful one, Wilde argued that criticism is as creative a form as the art it seeks to assess, and that the critic's touching will to read the world in Arnoldian clarity and forthrightedness was best diverted to an appreciation of the role language plays in establishing social, cultural, and imaginative production. As such, Wilde seems to have anticipated many of the doctrines of contemporary literary theory. Roland Barthes, for example, may be read as a deeply Wildean critic, one who both constructed and interpreted himself under the sign of textual desire. Wildean as well are the arguments of American critics Harold Bloom and Geoffrey Hartman for the creative aspects of the critical act. And Wilde's work anticipates, as Joel Fineman brilliantly suggests, many of the central tenets of *both* deconstruction and analytic philosophy.

But it would be just as problematic, it seems to me, to read Wilde as foretelling the directions of contemporary theory as it would be to deify him as the first gay man or reify him as a resolute Irish revolutionary. Here, too, Wilde anticipates the concerns of our moment, but in such a way as to complicate the ways that we have come to think about them. What makes Wilde both so salient and so resistant to contemporary Anglo-American theory is that, like current criticism, he focuses in theory and practice on the nature of the linguistic act, but in such a way as to underline simultaneously the two understandings of language that divide contemporary critics: the vision of language as an arbitrary system and that which sees it as a social artifact. For Wilde, words were on the one hand always already absurd, artificed, part of a contrived, conventional system; yet they are also and by that same logic always already socially sedimented and culturally contumacious.

Thus, to cite one particularly powerful moment in *The Importance of Being Earnest*, Gwendolen and Cecily's wit-battle turns at one crucial point (as does everything else in that play) on the question of language:

Cecily:	Do you suggest, Miss Fairfax, that I entrapped Ernest into an engagement? How dare you? This is no time for wearing the shallow mask of manners. When I see a spade I call it a spade.
Gwendolen:	(*Satirically*) I am glad to say that I have never seen a spade. It is obvious that our social spheres have been widely different.

The satire here runs in a number of different directions, but all of them turn on the question of what it means to call a thing by the name appropriate to it. Cecily insists, Arnoldianly enough, on seeing things as they are and calling them by their proper name. Gwendolen undoes Cecily by out-literalizing her, turning her trope for truth-telling into the thing itself—the spade Cecily has metaphorically invoked in the service of speaking plainly—thereby mocking her assertion of both the transparency of ordinary language and of the notion of genuine affect existing beyond linguistic encodings. But Gwendolen's satirical inversion of the figurative and the literal exposes, unbeknownst to her, the shaping of language by background, by social experience, and (in a word) by class. The satire thus extends from Cecily, who is reproved for being a naive literalist, to Gwendolen herself, who is shown to be a snobbish prig; and by that very same logic, the critique extends itself even further, beyond the footlights, to the theatrical audience itself—a citified, bourgeois audience that has little more direct experience of actual spades than do these two figures on the stage before them. Wherever you turn, Wilde is suggesting, you see the artificiality and the sociality of language. You see language both as an autonomous system and as a socially established one; this complicated vision calls into question both a naive reliance on the plain meaning of words and an equally unquestioning reliance on a social position that enables you to use them any way you like.

The crossroads of these two visions of language, of fiction, and of art is a particularly dangerous intersection in contemporary criticism: It is where theorists of culture, form, language, gender, and ideology all meet, lurching into each other with all the grace of bumper cars at an amusement park. And it is Wilde's particularly unsettling genius to occupy simultaneously (at least) three or four of those vehicles. This makes the task of approaching Wilde from any of the theoretical positions dominant at our particular moment problematic—all the more so because he insists on questioning assumptions fundamental to all of them. (Wilde makes it no easier to be a complacently materialist critic than he does to be a self-satisfied formalist.) Further muddling the matter, Wilde's awareness of the power of social institutions to constrict as well as construct means that his work fits uncomfortably, at best, into the discursive demands and canonizing tendencies of the Anglo-American academy. What else can one say about a writer who claimed that "a truth ceases to be true when more than one person believes in it" except that one anthologizes his critics with a certain hesitancy?

Luckily, the contributions to this volume are so varied that it is doubtful that Wilde would find any of them anything but unerringly true. While some perspectives must perforce remain unrepresented, I have made an effort to include many different critical approaches to Wilde, ranging from the New Critical through the deconstructive, materialist, gay-themed and the resolutely unclassifiable and eclectic. Readers in search of a single "take" (or even several "takes") on Wilde may find the resulting effect somewhat perplexing, but Wilde himself offers the best defense of this method in his marvelous essay *The Critic as Artist*. It is true that what Wilde means by "criticism" is surely different from what many of the contributors to this volume mean by it. But the urge behind criticism in Wilde's sense of the word surely animates all the critics anthologized herein: the desire to remake the world in the most powerful of all ways, by renaming it. Or as Wilde himself puts it, in what I hope is a suitable epigraph for the essays that follow: "When man acts he is a puppet. When he describes he is a poet." And it hardly needs to be added that Wilde's renewed relevance to our era proves what the etymology of the word "poet" suggests: Each act of description that constitutes the critic's *poesis* is itself an act of making, of creation in the strongest sense of the term; and the ramifications of that making are as socially puissant as they are intellectually unpredictable.

The descriptions—the renamings—of Wilde that follow place him, his works, and his legacy in a number of different contexts and suggest a number of different relations among them, very much in the manner of Wilde himself, who, as many critics have suggested, was quite concerned with shaping audience's response. The book leads off with a series of essays on Wilde's performance as a subversive presence in the public sphere, what we today might want to call a public intellectual. These essays focus on Wilde's works of literary criticism, ethics, and politics and, more generally, on Wilde as a self-promoting but also undeniably effective presence in the world of public discussion and debate both during his life and after his death. The first is Susan Sontag's "Notes on 'Camp,' " published in 1965. That essay represents perhaps the most famous attempt to bring the aesthetics of gay taste to bear on the cultural world beyond gay male subculture. It is significant that Sontag's prime example of "camp"—that definitively undefinable category of aesthetic response hovering between parody and affirmation, self-mockery and critique, satire and innocence—is Wilde, because Wilde's understanding of the high seriousness of the trivial and his ethical appreciation of the artificial remain perhaps his most important influence on gay male culture itself. But it is also crucial because that attitude has moved through that culture into the social world at large—not only into the world of high cultural production, that is to say, but also into the parodic world of mass and popular culture, where "camp" itself has become a byword through the intervention of Sontag's essay. Although "Notes on 'Camp' " dates to the 1960s, it has found its best readership in the later years of the century; in a thoroughly Wildean fashion, it created the very readership that it has found.

Wilde's relation to the public sphere is also the subject of Richard Ellmann's "The Critic as Artist as Wilde." Although Ellmann's essay focuses on literary criticism—this piece served as the introduction to his collection of Wilde's literary essays—it nevertheless traces the ways Wilde's self-representation merged with his critical and imaginative endeavor to do powerful work in the sphere of ethics as well as that of aesthetics. Ethics and transgressivity are the subject of Jonathan Dollimore's 1988 essay "Different Desires: Subjectivity and Transgression in Wilde and Gide," in which Wilde's career-long endeavor to subvert the structures of subjectivity central to his cultural moment is assessed in both its positive and negative guises. The fate of Wilde's intervention in the cultural politics of his time is Regenia Gagnier's subject too; she places Wilde in the context of the critique of the mass market central to the work of so-called Victorian sages like Thomas Carlyle and Matthew Arnold to suggest how adroitly Wilde plays out the paradoxical position of the high-culture artist addressing a cultural sphere governed by the logic of the mass. And Lawrence Danson concludes this section by suggesting how Wilde's essay "The Portrait of Mr. W. H." uses the question of the authorship of Shakespeare's sonnets to construct a viable position for his own authorial endeavor.

The collection then turns to Wilde's drama. Richard Dellamora traces the various uses Wilde finds for the feminine in *Salomé,* a play written for Sarah Bernhardt, then at the height of her fame, but denied a license on the grounds of blasphemy and not performed until 1896 in Paris. Criticism of the play has, for the most part, emphasized either its role in importing the thematics of French "decadence" or the psychoanalytic valences of its imagery of castration; Dellamora stresses instead the play's deployment of a hyper-empowered woman within the context of both male homosexual and lesbian desire. The next essays skip over Wilde's society dramas (readers interested in criticism of these relatively underappreciated works, as well as more on *Salomé*, should consult Katharine Worth's *Oscar Wilde*), and turn to the work that is generally conceded to be his most successful single achievement, *The Importance of Being Earnest*. Joseph Loewenstein places *Earnest*—and Wilde's paradoxical hymn to earnestlessness—in the contexts of French society drama and Sophoclean tragedy, both of which are simultaneously parodied and fulfilled by Wilde's endlessly inventive text. Katharine Worth, in an essay from the volume I mentioned above, reads the play as a theatrical text, suggesting as well its influence on the theater of the absurd. And the late Joel Fineman uses an account of the pun in *Earnest* to suggest how Wilde's wordplay works in the context of the concerns with reference and representation that shape both philosophy and literary theory of the twentieth century.

The volume concludes with five essays on Wilde's most notorious work, *The Picture of Dorian Gray*, and the directions it points to, both in Wilde's own life and his critical afterlife. Jeff Nunokawa discusses the ways *Earnest* and *Dorian* depend on a non-European other defined by the West's Orientalizing imagination for their exploration of the possibilities of art and desire. Ed Cohen's "Writing Gone Wilde" represents one of the first and most sustained readings of the novel through the lens of newer theories of masculinity, homosexuality, and desire. Rachel Bowlby considers *Dorian* under the sign of consumerism, suggesting links between the doctrines of aestheticism and the rise of a consumer culture and its ancillary art, advertising. Eve Kosofsky Sedgwick's bravura reading of Wilde and Nietzsche investigates the imaginative and literary concomitants of a transgressive (or "queer") understanding of sexuality, the body, and art. Wayne Koestenbaum suggests how Wilde's last published work, *The Ballad of Reading Goal*, serves as the origin of a distinctively gay style and strategy of reading. And the volume concludes with some of Wilde's own apothegms on all the subjects considered by his critics—imagination, desire, sexuality, consumption, transgressivity, subversion, subjectivity, masculinity, femininity, advertising—for Wilde himself serves not only as his own best reader and interpreter, but as the best critic of his own critical reception.

Notes on "Camp"

Susan Sontag

Many things in the world have not been named; and many things, even if they have been named, have never been described. One of these is the sensibility—unmistakably modern, a variant of sophistication but hardly identical with it—that goes by the cult name of "Camp."

A sensibility (as distinct from an idea) is one of the hardest things to talk about; but there are special reasons why Camp, in particular, has never been discussed. It is not a natural mode of sensibility, if there be any such. Indeed the essence of Camp is its love of the unnatural: of artifice and exaggeration. And Camp is esoteric—something of a private code, a badge of identity even, among small urban cliques. Apart from a lazy two-page sketch in Christopher Isherwood's novel *The World in the Evening* (1954), it has hardly broken into print. To talk about Camp is therefore to betray it. If the betrayal can be defended, it will be for the edification it provides, or the dignity of the conflict it resolves. For myself, I plead the goal of self-edification, and the goad of a sharp conflict in my own sensibility. I am strongly drawn to Camp, and almost as strongly offended by it. That is why I want to talk about it, and why I can. For no one who wholeheartedly shares in a given sensibility can analyze it; he can only, whatever his intention, exhibit it. To name a sensibility, to draw its contours and to recount its history, requires a deep sympathy modified by revulsion.

Though I am speaking about sensibility only—and about a sensibility that, among other things, converts the serious into the frivolous—these are grave matters. Most people think of sensibility or taste as the realm of purely subjective preferences, those mysterious attractions, mainly sensual, that have not been brought under the sovereignty of reason. They *allow* that considerations of taste play a part in their reactions to people and to works of art. But this attitude is naïve. And even worse. To patronize the faculty of taste is to patronize oneself. For taste governs every free—as opposed to rote—human response. Nothing is more decisive. There is taste in people, visual taste, taste in emotion—and there is taste in acts, taste in morality. Intelligence, as well, is really a kind of taste: taste in ideas. (One of the facts to be reckoned with is that taste tends to develop very unevenly. It's rare that the same person has good visual taste *and* good taste in people and taste in ideas.)

Taste has no system and no proofs. But there is something like a logic of taste: the consistent sensibility which underlies and gives rise to a certain taste. A sensibility is almost, but not quite, ineffable. Any sensibility which can be crammed into the mold of a system, or handled with the rough tools of proof, is no longer a sensibility at all. It has hardened into an idea. . . .

To snare a sensibility in words, especially one that is alive and powerful,[1] one must be tentative and nimble. The form of jottings, rather than an essay (with its claim to a linear, consecutive argument), seemed more appropriate for getting down something of this particular fugitive sensibility. It's embarrassing to be solemn and treatise-like about Camp. One runs the risk of having, oneself, produced a very inferior piece of Camp.

These notes are for Oscar Wilde.

"One should either be a work of art, or wear a work of art."
  —Phrases & Philosophies for the Use of the Young

1. To start very generally: Camp is a certain mode of aestheticism. It is *one* way of seeing the world as an aesthetic phenomenon. That way, the way of Camp, is not in terms of beauty, but in terms of the degree of artifice, of stylization.

2. To emphasize style is to slight content, or to introduce an attitude which is neutral with respect to content. It goes without saying that the Camp sensibility is disengaged, depoliticized—or at least apolitical.

3. Not only is there a Camp vision, a Camp way of looking at things. Camp is as well a quality discoverable in objects and the behavior of persons. There are "campy" movies, clothes, furniture, popular songs, novels, people, buildings. . . . This distinction is important. True, the Camp eye has the power to transform experience. But not everything can be seen as Camp. It's not *all* in the eye of the beholder.

4. Random examples of items which are part of the canon of Camp:

Zuleika Dobson
Tiffany lamps
Scopitone films
The Brown Derby restaurant on Sunset Boulevard in LA
The Enquirer, headlines and stories
Aubrey Beardsley drawings
Swan Lake
Bellini's operas
Visconti's direction of *Salome* and *'Tis Pity She's a Whore*
certain turn-of-the-century picture postcards
Schoedsack's *King Kong*

---

[1]The sensibility of an era is not only its most decisive, but also its most perishable, aspect. One may capture the ideas (intellectual history) and the behavior (social history) of an epoch without ever touching upon the sensibility or taste which informed those ideas, that behavior. Rare are those historical studies—like Huizinga on the late Middle Ages, Febvre on 16th century France—which do tell us something about the sensibility of the period.

the Cuban pop singer La Lupe
Lynn Ward's novel in woodcuts, *God's Man*
the old Flash Gordon comics
women's clothes of the twenties (feather boas, fringed and beaded dresses, etc.)
the novels of Ronald Firbank and Ivy Compton-Burnett
stag movies seen without lust

5. Camp taste has an affinity for certain arts rather than others. Clothes, furniture, all the elements of visual décor, for instance, make up a large part of Camp. For Camp art is often decorative art, emphasizing texture, sensuous surface, and style at the expense of content. Concert music, though, because it is contentless, is rarely Camp. It offers no opportunity, say, for a contrast between silly or extravagant content and rich form. . . . Sometimes whole art forms become saturated with Camp. Classical ballet, opera, movies have seemed so for a long time. In the last two years, popular music (post rock-'n'-roll, what the French call yé yé) has been annexed. And movie criticism (like lists of "The 10 Best Bad Movies I Have Seen") is probably the greatest popularizer of Camp taste today, because most people still go to the movies in a high-spirited and unpretentious way.

6. There is a sense in which it is correct to say: "It's too good to be Camp." Or "too important," not marginal enough. (More on this later.) Thus, the personality and many of the works of Jean Cocteau are Camp, but not those of André Gide; the operas of Richard Strauss, but not those of Wagner; concoctions of Tin Pan Alley and Liverpool, but not jazz. Many examples of Camp are things which, from a "serious" point of view, are either bad art or kitsch. Not all, though. Not only is Camp not necessarily bad art, but some art which can be approached as Camp (example: the major films of Louis Feuillade) merits the most serious admiration and study.

"The more we study Art, the less we care for Nature."
                                        —*The Decay of Lying*

7. All Camp objects, and persons, contain a large element of artifice. Nothing in nature can be campy. . . . Rural Camp is still man-made, and most campy objects are urban. (Yet, they often have a serenity—or a naïveté—which is the equivalent of pastoral. A great deal of Camp suggests Empson's phrase, "urban pastoral.")

8. Camp is a vision of the world in terms of style—but a particular kind of style. It is the love of the exaggerated, the "off," of things-being-what-they-are-not. The best example is in Art Nouveau, the most typical and fully developed Camp style. Art Nouveau objects, typically, convert one thing into something else: the lighting fixtures in the form of flowering plants, the living room which is really a grotto. A remarkable example: the Paris Métro entrances designed by Hector Guimard in the late 1890s in the shape of cast-iron orchid stalks.

9. As a taste in persons, Camp responds particularly to the markedly attenuated and to the strongly exaggerated. The androgyne is certainly one of the great images of Camp sensibility. Examples: the swooning, slim, sinuous figures of pre-

Raphaelite painting and poetry; the thin, flowing, sexless bodies in Art Nouveau prints and posters, presented in relief on lamps and ashtrays; the haunting androgynous vacancy behind the perfect beauty of Greta Garbo. Here, Camp taste draws on a mostly unacknowledged truth of taste: the most refined form of sexual attractiveness (as well as the most refined form of sexual pleasure) consists in going against the grain of one's sex. What is most beautiful in virile men is something feminine; what is most beautiful in feminine women is something masculine. . . . Allied to the Camp taste for the androgynous is something that seems quite different but isn't: a relish for the exaggeration of sexual characteristics and personality mannerisms. For obvious reasons, the best examples that can be cited are movie stars. The corny flamboyant femaleness of Jayne Mansfield, Gina Lollobrigida, Jane Russell, Virginia Mayo; the exaggerated he-man-ness of Steve Reeves, Victor Mature. The great stylists of temperament and mannerism, like Bette Davis, Barbara Stanwyck, Tallulah Bankhead, Edwige Feuillière.

10. Camp sees everything in quotation marks. It's not a lamp, but a "lamp"; not a woman, but a "woman." To perceive Camp in objects and persons is to understand Being-as-Playing-a-Role. It is the farthest extension, in sensibility, of the metaphor of life as theater.

11. Camp is the triumph of the epicene style. (The convertibility of "man" and "woman," "person" and "thing.") But all style, that is, artifice, is, ultimately, epicene. Life is not stylish. Neither is nature.

12. The question isn't, "Why travesty, impersonation, theatricality?" The question is, rather, "When does travesty, impersonation, theatricality acquire the special flavor of Camp?" Why is the atmosphere of Shakespeare's comedies (*As You Like It*, etc.) not epicene, while that of *Der Rosenkavalier* is?

13. The dividing line seems to fall in the 18th century; there the origins of Camp taste are to be found (Gothic novels, Chinoiserie, caricature, artificial ruins, and so forth). But the relation to nature was quite different then. In the 18th century, people of taste either patronized nature (Strawberry Hill) or attempted to remake it into something artificial (Versailles). They also indefatigably patronized the past. Today's Camp taste effaces nature, or else contradicts it outright. And the relation of Camp taste to the past is extremely sentimental.

14. A pocket history of Camp might, of course, begin farther back—with the mannerist artists like Pontormo, Rosso, and Caravaggio, or the extraordinarily theatrical painting of Georges de La Tour, or Euphuism (Lyly, etc.) in literature. Still, the soundest starting point seems to be the late 17th and early 18th century, because of that period's extraordinary feeling for artifice, for surface, for symmetry; its taste for the picturesque and the thrilling, its elegant conventions for representing instant feeling and the total presence of character—the epigram and the rhymed couplet (in words), the flourish (in gesture and in music). The late 17th and early 18th century is the great period of Camp: Pope, Congreve, Walpole, etc., but not Swift; les précieux in France; the rococo churches of Munich; Pergolesi. Somewhat later: much of Mozart. But in the 19th century, what had been distributed throughout all of high culture now becomes a special taste; it takes on over-

tones of the acute, the esoteric, the perverse. Confining the story to England alone, we see Camp continuing wanly through 19th century aestheticism (Burne-Jones, Pater, Ruskin, Tennyson), emerging full-blown with the Art Nouveau movement in the visual and decorative arts, and finding its conscious ideologists in such "wits" as Wilde and Firbank.

15. Of course, to say all these things are Camp is not to argue they are simply that. A full analysis of Art Nouveau, for instance, would scarcely equate it with Camp. But such an analysis cannot ignore what in Art Nouveau allows it to be experienced as Camp. Art Nouveau is full of "content," even of a political-moral sort; it was a revolutionary movement in the arts, spurred on by a utopian vision (somewhere between William Morris and the Bauhaus group) of an organic politics and taste. Yet there is also a feature of the Art Nouveau objects which suggests a disengaged, unserious, "aesthete's" vision. This tells us something important about Art Nouveau—and about what the lens of Camp, which blocks out content, is.

16. Thus, the Camp sensibility is one that is alive to a double sense in which some things can be taken. But this is not the familiar split-level construction of a literal meaning, on the one hand, and a symbolic meaning, on the other. It is the difference, rather, between the thing as meaning something, anything, and the thing as pure artifice.

17. This comes out clearly in the vulgar use of the word Camp as a verb, "to camp," something that people do. To camp is a mode of seduction—one which employs flamboyant mannerisms susceptible of a double interpretation: gestures full of duplicity, with a witty meaning for cognoscenti and another, more impersonal, for outsiders. Equally and by extension, when the word becomes a noun, when a person or a thing is "a camp," a duplicity is involved. Behind the "straight" public sense in which something can be taken, one has found a private zany experience of the thing.

"To be natural is such a very difficult pose to keep up."
—*An Ideal Husband*

18. One must distinguish between naïve and deliberate Camp. Pure Camp is always naïve. Camp which knows itself to be Camp ("camping") is usually less satisfying.

19. The pure examples of Camp are unintentional; they are dead serious. The Art Nouveau craftsman who makes a lamp with a snake coiled around it is not kidding, nor is he trying to be charming. He is saying, in all earnestness: Voilà! the Orient! Genuine Camp—for instance, the numbers devised for the Warner Brothers musicals of the early thirties (*42nd Street*; *The Golddiggers of 1933*; . . . *of 1935*; . . . *of 1937*; etc.) by Busby Berkeley—does not *mean* to be funny. Camping—say, the plays of Noel Coward—does. It seems unlikely that much of the traditional opera repertoire could be such satisfying Camp if the melodramatic absurdities of most opera plots had not been taken seriously by their composers. One doesn't need to know the artist's private intentions. The work tells all.

(Compare a typical 19th century opera with Samuel Barber's *Vanessa*, a piece of manufactured, calculated Camp, and the difference is clear.)

20. Probably, intending to be campy is always harmful. The perfection of *Trouble in Paradise* and *The Maltese Falcon*, among the greatest Camp movies ever made, comes from the effortless smooth way in which tone is maintained. This is not so with such famous would-be Camp films of the fifties as *All About Eve* and *Beat the Devil*. These more recent movies have their fine moments, but the first is so slick and the second so hysterical; they want so badly to be campy that they're continually losing the beat. . . . Perhaps, though, it is not so much a question of the unintended effect versus the conscious intention, as of the delicate relation between parody and self-parody in Camp. The films of Hitchcock are a showcase for this problem. When self-parody lacks ebullience but instead reveals (even sporadically) a contempt for one's themes and one's materials—as in *To Catch a Thief, Rear Window, North by Northwest*—the results are forced and heavy-handed, rarely Camp. Successful Camp—a movie like Carné's *Drôle de Drame;* the film performances of Mae West and Edward Everett Horton; portions of the Goon Show—even when it reveals self-parody, reeks of self-love.

21. So, again, Camp rests on innocence. That means Camp discloses innocence, but also, when it can, corrupts it. Objects, being objects, don't change when they are singled out by the Camp vision. Persons, however, respond to their audiences. Persons begin "camping": Mae West, Bea Lillie, La Lupe, Tallulah Bankhead in *Lifeboat*, Bette Davis in *All About Eve*. (Persons can even be induced to camp without their knowing it. Consider the way Fellini got Anita Ekberg to parody herself in *La Dolce Vita*.)

22. Considered a little less strictly, Camp is either completely naïve or else wholly conscious (when one plays at being campy). An example of the latter: Wilde's epigrams themselves.

> "It's absurd to divide people into good and bad. People are either charming or tedious."
> —*Lady Windermere's Fan*

23. In naïve, or pure, Camp, the essential element is seriousness, a seriousness that fails. Of course, not all seriousness that fails can be redeemed as Camp. Only that which has the proper mixture of the exaggerated, the fantastic, the passionate, and the naïve.

24. When something is just bad (rather than Camp), it's often because it is too mediocre in its ambition. The artist hasn't attempted to do anything really outlandish. ("It's too much," "It's too fantastic," "It's not to be believed," are standard phrases of Camp enthusiasm.)

25. The hallmark of Camp is the spirit of extravagance. Camp is a woman walking around in a dress made of three million feathers. Camp is the paintings of Carlo Crivelli, with their real jewels and *trompe-l'oeil* insects and cracks in the masonry. Camp is the outrageous aestheticism of Sternberg's six American movies with Dietrich, all six, but especially the last, *The Devil Is a Woman*. . . . In Camp there is often something *démesuré* in the quality of the ambition, not only in the

style of the work itself. Gaudí's lurid and beautiful buildings in Barcelona are Camp not only because of their style but because they reveal—most notably in the Cathedral of the Sagrada Familia—the ambition on the part of one man to do what it takes a generation, a whole culture to accomplish.

26. Camp is art that proposes itself seriously, but cannot be taken altogether seriously because it is "too much." *Titus Andronicus* and *Strange Interlude* are almost Camp, or could be played as Camp. The public manner and rhetoric of de Gaulle, often, are pure Camp.

27. A work can come close to Camp, but not make it, because it succeeds. Eisenstein's films are seldom Camp because, despite all exaggeration, they do succeed (dramatically) without surplus. If they were a little more "off," they could be great Camp—particularly *Ivan the Terrible I & II*. The same for Blake's drawings and paintings, weird and mannered as they are. They aren't Camp; though Art Nouveau, influenced by Blake, is.

What is extravagant in an inconsistent or an unpassionate way is not Camp. Neither can anything be Camp that does not seem to spring from an irrepressible, a virtually uncontrolled sensibility. Without passion, one gets pseudo-Camp— what is merely decorative, safe, in a word, chic. On the barren edge of Camp lie a number of attractive things: the sleek fantasies of Dali, the haute couture preciosity of Albicocco's *The Girl with the Golden Eyes*. But the two things—Camp and preciosity—must not be confused.

28. Again, Camp is the attempt to do something extraordinary. But extraordinary in the sense, often, of being special, glamorous. (The curved line, the extravagant gesture.) Not extraordinary merely in the sense of effort. Ripley's Believe-It-Or-Not items are rarely campy. These items, either natural oddities (the two-headed rooster, the eggplant in the shape of a cross) or else the products of immense labor (the man who walked from here to China on his hands, the woman who engraved the New Testament on the head of a pin), lack the visual reward— the glamour, the theatricality—that marks off certain extravagances as Camp.

29. The reason a movie like *On the Beach*, books like *Winesburg, Ohio* and *For Whom the Bell Tolls* are bad to the point of being laughable, but not bad to the point of being enjoyable, is that they are too dogged and pretentious. They lack fantasy. There is Camp in such bad movies as *The Prodigal* and *Samson and Delilah*, the series of Italian color spectacles featuring the super-hero Maciste, numerous Japanese science fiction films (*Rodan, The Mysterians, The H-Man*) because, in their relative unpretentiousness and vulgarity, they are more extreme and irresponsible in their fantasy—and therefore touching and quite enjoyable.

30. Of course, the canon of Camp can change. Time has a great deal to do with it. Time may enhance what seems simply dogged or lacking in fantasy now because we are too close to it, because it resembles too closely our own everyday fantasies, the fantastic nature of which we don't perceive. We are better able to enjoy a fantasy as fantasy when it is not our own.

31. This is why so many of the objects prized by Camp taste are old-fashioned, out-of-date, *démodé*. It's not a love of the old as such. It's simply that the process

of aging or deterioration provides the necessary detachment—or arouses a necessary sympathy. When the theme is important, and contemporary, the failure of a work of art may make us indignant. Time can change that. Time liberates the work of art from moral relevance, delivering it over to the Camp sensibility. . . . Another effect: time contracts the sphere of banality. (Banality is, strictly speaking, always a category of the contemporary.) What was banal can, with the passage of time, become fantastic. Many people who listen with delight to the style of Rudy Vallee revived by the English pop group, The Temperance Seven, would have been driven up the wall by Rudy Vallee in his heyday.

Thus, things are campy, not when they become old—but when we become less involved in them, and can enjoy, instead of be frustrated by, the failure of the attempt. But the effect of time is unpredictable. Maybe "method" acting (James Dean, Rod Steiger, Warren Beatty) will seem as Camp some day as Ruby Keeler's does now—or as Sarah Bernhardt's does, in the films she made at the end of her career. And maybe not.

32. Camp is the glorification of "character." The statement is of no importance—except, of course, to the person (Loie Fuller, Gaudí, Cecil B. De Mille, Crivelli, de Gaulle, etc.) who makes it. What the Camp eye appreciates is the unity, the force of the person. In every move the aging Martha Graham makes she's being Martha Graham, etc., etc. . . . This is clear in the case of the great serious idol of Camp taste, Greta Garbo. Garbo's incompetence (at the least, lack of depth) as an *actress* enhances her beauty. She's always herself.

33. What Camp taste responds to is "instant character" (this is, of course, very 18th century); and, conversely, what it is not stirred by is the sense of the development of character. Character is understood as a state of continual incandescence—a person being one, very intense thing. This attitude toward character is a key element of the theatricalization of experience embodied in the Camp sensibility. And it helps account for the fact that opera and ballet are experienced as such rich treasures of Camp, for neither of these forms can easily do justice to the complexity of human nature. Wherever there is development of character, Camp is reduced. Among operas, for example, *La Traviata* (which has some small development of character) is less campy than *Il Trovatore* (which has none).

> "Life is too important a thing ever to talk seriously about it."
> —*Vera, or The Nihilists*

34. Camp taste turns its back on the good-bad axis of ordinary aesthetic judgment. Camp doesn't reverse things. It doesn't argue that the good is bad, or the bad is good. What it does is to offer for art (and life) a different—a supplementary—set of standards.

35. Ordinarily we value a work of art because of the seriousness and dignity of what it achieves. We value it because it succeeds—in being what it is and, presumably, in fulfilling the intention that lies behind it. We assume a proper, that is to say, straightforward relation between intention and performance. By such standards, we appraise *The Iliad*, Aristophanes' plays, The Art of the Fugue,

Middlemarch, the paintings of Rembrandt, Chartres, the poetry of Donne, *The Divine Comedy*, Beethoven's quartets, and—among people—Socrates, Jesus, St. Francis, Napoleon, Savonarola. In short, the pantheon of high culture: truth, beauty, and seriousness.

36. But there are other creative sensibilities besides the seriousness (both tragic and comic) of high culture and of the high style of evaluating people. And one cheats oneself, as a human being, if one has respect only for the style of high culture, whatever else one may do or feel on the sly.

For instance, there is the kind of seriousness whose trademark is anguish, cruelty, derangement. Here we do accept a disparity between intention and result. I am speaking, obviously, of a style of personal existence as well as of a style in art; but the examples had best come from art. Think of Bosch, Sade, Rimbaud, Jarry, Kafka, Artaud, think of most of the important works of art of the 20th century, that is, art whose goal is not that of creating harmonies but of overstraining the medium and introducing more and more violent, and unresolvable, subject-matter. This sensibility also insists on the principle that an *oeuvre* in the old sense (again, in art, but also in life) is not possible. Only "fragments" are possible. . . . Clearly, different standards apply here than to traditional high culture. Something is good not because it is achieved, but because another kind of truth about the human situation, another experience of what it is to be human—in short, another valid sensibility—is being revealed.

And third among the great creative sensibilities is Camp: the sensibility of failed seriousness, of the theatricalization of experience. Camp refuses both the harmonies of traditional seriousness, and the risks of fully identifying with extreme states of feeling.

37. The first sensibility, that of high culture, is basically moralistic. The second sensibility, that of extreme states of feeling, represented in much contemporary "avant-garde" art, gains power by a tension between moral and aesthetic passion. The third, Camp, is wholly aesthetic.

38. Camp is the consistently aesthetic experience of the world. It incarnates a victory of "style" over "content," "aesthetics" over "morality," of irony over tragedy.

39. Camp and tragedy are antitheses. There is seriousness in Camp (seriousness in the degree of the artist's involvement) and, often, pathos. The excruciating is also one of the tonalities of Camp; it is the quality of excruciation in much of Henry James (for instance, *The Europeans*, *The Awkward Age*, *The Wings of the Dove*) that is responsible for the large element of Camp in his writings. But there is never, never tragedy.

40. Style is everything. Genet's ideas, for instance, are very Camp. Genet's statement that "the only criterion of an act is its elegance"[2] is virtually interchangeable, as a statement, with Wilde's "in matters of great importance, the vital element is not sincerity, but style." But what counts, finally, is the style in which ideas

---

[2]Sartre's gloss on this in *Saint Genet* is: "Elegance is the quality of conduct which transforms the greatest amount of being into appearing."

are held. The ideas about morality and politics in, say, *Lady Windermere's Fan* and in *Major Barbara* are Camp, but not just because of the nature of the ideas themselves. It is those ideas, held in a special playful way. The Camp ideas in *Our Lady of the Flowers* are maintained too grimly, and the writing itself is too successfully elevated and serious, for Genet's books to be Camp.

41. The whole point of Camp is to dethrone the serious. Camp is playful, antiserious. More precisely, Camp involves a new, more complex relation to "the serious." One can be serious about the frivolous, frivolous about the serious.

42. One is drawn to Camp when one realizes that "sincerity" is not enough. Sincerity can be simple philistinism, intellectual narrowness.

43. The traditional means for going beyond straight seriousness—irony, satire—seem feeble today, inadequate to the culturally oversaturated medium in which contemporary sensibility is schooled. Camp introduces a new standard: artifice as an ideal, theatricality.

44. Camp proposes a comic vision of the world. But not a bitter or polemical comedy. If tragedy is an experience of hyperinvolvement, comedy is an experience of underinvolvement, of detachment.

> "I adore simple pleasures, they are the last refuge of the complex."
> —*A Woman of No Importance*

45. Detachment is the prerogative of an elite; and as the dandy is the 19th century's surrogate for the aristocrat in matters of culture, so Camp is the modern dandyism. Camp is the answer to the problem: how to be a dandy in the age of mass culture.

46. The dandy was overbred. His posture was disdain, or else *ennui*. He sought rare sensations, undefiled by mass appreciation. (Models: Des Esseintes in Huysmans' *A Rebours, Marius the Epicurean,* Valéry's *Monsieur Teste*.) He was dedicated to "good taste."

The connoisseur of Camp has found more ingenious pleasures. Not in Latin poetry and rare wines and velvet jackets, but in the coarsest, commonest pleasures, in the arts of the masses. Mere use does not defile the objects of his pleasure, since he learns to possess them in a rare way. Camp—Dandyism in the age of mass culture—makes no distinction between the unique object and the mass-produced object. Camp taste transcends the nausea of the replica.

47. Wilde himself is a transitional figure. The man who, when he first came to London, sported a velvet beret, lace shirts, velveteen knee-breeches and black silk stockings, could never depart too far in his life from the pleasures of the old-style dandy; this conservatism is reflected in *The Picture of Dorian Gray*. But many of his attitudes suggest something more modern. It was Wilde who formulated an important element of the Camp sensibility—the equivalence of all objects—when he announced his intention of "living up" to his blue-and-white china, or declared that a doorknob could be as admirable as a painting. When he proclaimed the importance of the necktie, the boutonniere, the chair, Wilde was anticipating the democratic *esprit* of Camp.

48. The old-style dandy hated vulgarity. The new-style dandy, the lover of Camp, appreciates vulgarity. Where the dandy would be continually offended or bored, the connoisseur of Camp is continually amused, delighted. The dandy held a perfumed handkerchief to his nostrils and was liable to swoon; the connoisseur of Camp sniffs the stink and prides himself on his strong nerves.

49. It is a feat, of course. A feat goaded on, in the last analysis, by the threat of boredom. The relation between boredom and Camp taste cannot be overestimated. Camp taste is by its nature possible only in affluent societies, in societies or circles capable of experiencing the psychopathology of affluence.

> "What is abnormal in Life stands in normal relations to Art. It is the only thing in Life that stands in normal relations to Art."
> —*A Few Maxims for the Instruction of the Over-Educated*

50. Aristocracy is a position vis-à-vis culture (as well as vis-à-vis power), and the history of Camp taste is part of the history of snob taste. But since no authentic aristocrats in the old sense exist today to sponsor special tastes, who is the bearer of this taste? Answer: an improvised self-elected class, mainly homosexuals, who constitute themselves as aristocrats of taste.

51. The peculiar relation between Camp taste and homosexuality has to be explained. While it's not true that Camp taste *is* homosexual taste, there is no doubt a peculiar affinity and overlap. Not all liberals are Jews, but Jews have shown a peculiar affinity for liberal and reformist causes. So, not all homosexuals have Camp taste. But homosexuals, by and large, constitute the vanguard—and the most articulate audience—of Camp. (The analogy is not frivolously chosen. Jews and homosexuals are the outstanding creative minorities in contemporary urban culture. Creative, that is, in the truest sense: they are creators of sensibilities. The two pioneering forces of modern sensibility are Jewish moral seriousness and homosexual aestheticism and irony.)

52. The reason for the flourishing of the aristocratic posture among homosexuals also seems to parallel the Jewish case. For every sensibility is self-serving to the group that promotes it. Jewish liberalism is a gesture of self-legitimization. So is Camp taste, which definitely has something propagandistic about it. Needless to say, the propaganda operates in exactly the opposite direction. The Jews pinned their hopes for integrating into modern society on promoting the moral sense. Homosexuals have pinned their integration into society on promoting the aesthetic sense. Camp is a solvent of morality. It neutralizes moral indignation, sponsors playfulness.

53. Nevertheless, even though homosexuals have been its vanguard, Camp taste is much more than homosexual taste. Obviously, its metaphor of life as theater is peculiarly suited as a justification and projection of a certain aspect of the situation of homosexuals. (The Camp insistence on not being "serious," on playing, also connects with the homosexual's desire to remain youthful.) Yet one feels that if homosexuals hadn't more or less invented Camp, someone else would. For the aristocratic posture with relation to culture cannot die, though it may persist only

in increasingly arbitrary and ingenious ways. Camp is (to repeat) the relation to style in a time in which the adoption of style—as such—has become altogether questionable. (In the modern era, each new style, unless frankly anachronistic, has come on the scene as an anti-style.)

> "One must have a heart of stone to read the death of Little Nell without laughing."
> —*In conversation*

54. The experiences of Camp are based on the great discovery that the sensibility of high culture has no monopoly upon refinement. Camp asserts that good taste is not simply good taste; that there exists, indeed, a good taste of bad taste. (Genet talks about this in *Our Lady of the Flowers*.) The discovery of the good taste of bad taste can be very liberating. The man who insists on high and serious pleasures is depriving himself of pleasure; he continually restricts what he can enjoy; in the constant exercise of his good taste he will eventually price himself out of the market, so to speak. Here Camp taste supervenes upon good taste as a daring and witty hedonism. It makes the man of good taste cheerful, where before he ran the risk of being chronically frustrated. It is good for the digestion.

55. Camp taste is, above all, a mode of enjoyment, of appreciation—not judgment. Camp is generous. It wants to enjoy. It only seems like malice, cynicism. (Or, if it is cynicism, it's not a ruthless but a sweet cynicism.) Camp taste doesn't propose that it is in bad taste to be serious; it doesn't sneer at someone who succeeds in being seriously dramatic. What it does is to find the success in certain passionate failures.

56. Camp taste is a kind of love, love for human nature. It relishes, rather than judges, the little triumphs and awkward intensities of "character." . . . Camp taste identifies with what it is enjoying. People who share this sensibility are not laughing at the thing they label as "a camp," they're enjoying it. Camp is a *tender* feeling.

(Here, one may compare Camp with much of Pop Art, which—when it is not just Camp—embodies an attitude that is related, but still very different. Pop Art is more flat and more dry, more serious, more detached, ultimately nihilistic.)

57. Camp taste nourishes itself on the love that has gone into certain objects and personal styles. The absence of this love is the reason why such kitsch items as *Peyton Place* (the book) and the Tishman Building aren't Camp.

58. The ultimate Camp statement: it's good *because* it's awful. . . . Of course, one can't always say that. Only under certain conditions, those which I've tried to sketch in these notes.

The Critic as Artist as Wilde

Richard Ellmann

Wilde is the one writer of the Nineties whom everyone still reads, or more precisely, has read. The mixture of frivolity and pathos in his career continues to arrest us. That career displays its self-conjugation in Wilde's own terms of "The Critic as Artist."

In 1914 Henry James could complain that there was not enough criticism about to give novelists their bearings, while T. S. Eliot and Saul Bellow have since regretted, for different reasons and in different tones of voice, that there is now too much. The obtrusive place of the critic today can be related to a methodological emphasis which is conspicuous in other disciplines as well. But Wilde was one of the first to see that the exaltation of the artist required a concomitant exaltation of the critic. If art was to have a special train, the critic must keep some seats reserved on it.

Wilde reached this conclusion by way of two others. The first is that criticism plays a vital role in the creative process. If this sounds like T. S. Eliot admonishing Matthew Arnold, Wilde had expressed it, also as an admonition to Arnold, almost thirty years before. The second is that criticism is an independent branch of literature with its own procedures. "I am always amused," says Wilde, "by the silly vanity of those writers and artists of our day who seem to imagine that the primary function of the critic is to chatter about their second-rate work." And he complains that "The poor reviewers are apparently reduced to be the reporters of the police-court of literature, the chroniclers of the doings of the habitual criminals of art." In protesting the independence of criticism, Wilde sounds like an ancestral Northrop Frye or Roland Barthes. These portentous comparisons do indeed claim virtue by association, and such claims may be broadened. André Gide found Nietzsche less exciting because he had read Wilde, and Thomas Mann in one of his last essays remarks almost with chagrin on how many of Nietzsche's aphorisms might have been expressed by Wilde, and how many of Wilde's by Nietzsche. What I think can be urged for Wilde then, is that for his own reasons and in his own way he laid the basis for many critical positions which are still debated in much the same terms, and which we like to attribute to more ponderous names.

When Wilde formulated his theories the public was more hostile to criticism than it is now, and Wilde was flaunting his iconoclasm, his contempt for the unconsidered and so uncritical pieties of his age. This in fact was his mode: not to speak for the Victorians, or for the prematurely old writers who dithered that they were the end of an era, as if they must expire with the 1800s. Wilde proposed to speak for the young, with even excessive eagerness. His own age was always a little embarrassing for him, because he had already spent three years at Trinity College, Dublin, when he went up to Oxford. He was not above a little deception on this score. In 1877, when he was twenty-three, he sent a poem to Gladstone with a letter saying, "I am little more than a boy." And in a poem written that year he spoke of his "boyish passion" and described himself as "one who scarce has seen some twenty summers." This line, in turn, he repeated in his poem "The Sphinx," finished when he was forty. Even in court he injudiciously testified he was two years younger than he was, so that he sounds a little like Falstaff shouting to Bardolph during the robbery, "They hate us youth." Wilde's mode was calculated juvenescence, and the characters in his books are always being warned by shrewder characters of the danger of listening to people older than themselves. To help reduce that danger, Wilde's characters are invariably parentless. The closest kin allowed is an aunt.

Like Stendhal, Wilde thought of himself as a voice of the age to be, rather than of the one that was fading. Yet like anyone else writing criticism in the nineteenth century, he had to come to terms with the age that had been, and especially with everybody's parent, Matthew Arnold. Wilde sought Arnold's approbation for his first book, *Poems*, in 1881, which he sent with a letter stressing their shared Oxonian connections. These extended, though he wisely did not enforce the claim, to their both having won the Newdigate. Actually their prize-winning poems offer a contrast of manners, Arnold's being just as determined to appear older as Wilde's younger than his years. Arnold replied politely.

But by 1881 Arnold was genuinely old, and seven years later, in 1888, he was dead. Wilde's only book of criticism, *Intentions*, was written during the three years following Arnold's death and published in 1891, as if to take over that critical burden and express what Arnold had failed to say. Yeats thought the book "wonderful" and Walter Pater handsomely praised it for carrying on, "more perhaps than any other writer, the brilliant critical work of Matthew Arnold." Pater's encomium is a reminder, however, not to ignore *him*. There are not two but three critical phases in the late nineteenth century, with Pater transitional between Arnold and Wilde.

In 1864, lecturing from the Oxford Chair of Poetry on "The Function of Criticism at the Present Time," Arnold declared—to everyone's lasting memory—that the "aim of criticism is to see the object as in itself it really is." This statement went with his demand for "disinterested curiosity" as the mark of the critic; its inadvertent effect was to put the critic on his knees before the work he was discussing. Not everyone enjoyed this position. Nine years later Walter Pater wrote his preface to *Studies in the History of the Renaissance*. Pretending to agree with Arnold's definition of the aim of criticism, he quoted it, then added, "the first step towards seeing one's object as it really is, is to know one's impression as it really is, to discriminate it, to realise it distinctly." But Pater's corollary subtly altered the original proposition; it shifted the center of attention from the rock of the object to the winds of the perceiver's sensations. It made the critic's own work more important as well as more subjective. If observation is still the word, the critic looks within himself as often as out upon the object.

Wilde had been Pater's disciple, and in *Intentions* eighteen years later he tweaks Arnold's nose with the essay which in its first published form was entitled, "The True Function and Value of Criticism: with Some Remarks on the Importance of Doing Nothing." Here Wilde rounded on Arnold by asserting that the aim of criticism is to see the object as it really is not. This aim might seem to justify the highly personal criticism of Ruskin and Pater, and Wilde uses them as examples; his contention goes beyond their practice, however; he wishes to free critics from subordination, to grant them a larger share in the production of literature. While he does not forbid them to explain a book, they might prefer, he said, to deepen a book's mystery. (This purpose is amusing but out of date now; who could deepen the mystery of *Finnegan's Wake*?) At any rate, their context would be different from that of the creative artist. For just as the artist claimed independence of received experience (Picasso tells us that art is "what nature is not"), so the critic claimed independence of received books. "The highest criticism," according to Wilde, "is the record of one's own soul." More closely he explained that the critic must have all literature in his mind and see particular works in that perspective rather than in isolation. Thus he, and we as well,

> shall be able to realise, not merely our own lives, but the collective spirit of the race, and so to make ourselves absolutely modern, in the true meaning of the word modernity. For he to whom the present is the only thing that is present, knows nothing of the age in which he lives. To realise the nineteenth century, one must realise every century that has preceded it and that has contributed to its making.

Through knowledge the critic might become more creative than the creative artist, a paradox which has been expressed with more solemnity by Norman Podhoretz about literature of the present day.

Wilde reached these formulations of his aesthetic ideas late in his short life. They were latent, however, in his earliest known essay, "The Rise of Historical Criticism," which he wrote as a university exercise. While praising historians for their scrupulousness, Wilde finds the core of history to be the wish not merely to paint a picture, but to investigate laws and tendencies. He celebrates those historians who impose dominion upon fact instead of surrendering to it. Later he was to say much more boldly, "The one duty we owe to history is to rewrite it," and to praise Herodotus as father not of history but of lies. It is part of his larger conception that the one duty (or better, whim) we owe nature, reality, or the world, is to reconstruct it.

When Wilde turned to literary as distinguished from historical criticism, he at first was content to follow Pater. Wilde was won by Pater's espousal of gemlike flames and of high temperatures both in words and in life. Next to him Arnold sounded chilly, never so Victorian as when he was cogently criticizing

Victorianism. That word "impression," with which Pater sought to unlock everything, became a favorite word in both Wilde and later in Arthur Symons, and was only arrested by Yeats in the late 1890s because he could not bear so much impermanence and insisted on a metaphysical basis—the *Anima Mundi*—for transitory moods. Like the word "absurd" today, though without a systematic philosophy behind it, the word "impression" agitated against pat assumptions and preconceptions.

Pater's vocabulary shapes the initial poem of Wilde's book of verse, published when he was twenty-five. This poem "Hélas!" encapsulates much of Wilde's temperament, but with Pater's coloring:

> To drift with every passion till my soul
> Is a stringed lute on which all winds can play,
> Is it for this that I have given away
> Mine ancient wisdom, and austere control?
> Methinks my life is a twice-written scroll
> Scrawled over on some boyish holiday
> With idle songs for pipe and virelay
> Which do but mar the secret of the whole.
> Surely there was a time I might have trod
> The sunlit heights, and from life's dissonance
> Struck one clear chord to reach the ears of God:
> Is that time dead? lo! with a little rod
> I did but touch the honey of romance—
> And must I lose a soul's inheritance?

To call the Poem "Hélas!," to sigh in a foreign language, alerts us that the confession to follow will luxuriate in its penitence. The Biblical archaisms which occur later offer compunction suitably perfumed. "To drift" may well put us off as weak; on the other hand, "to drift with every passion" is not so bad. As its image of passivity, the poem offers "a stringed lute on which all winds can play." For the romantics the Aeolian harp was a favorable image because it harmonized man and nature. Here the winds are winds of temptation, rather than gusts of Lake Country air. The rhetorical question which begins, "Is it for this?" sounds reproachful enough, yet the phrases "ancient wisdom" and "austere control"—self-congratulatory since Wilde never had either—are so vague as to constitute a stately but equally unenergetic alternative to drifting.

The word "drift" comes down from Oxford in the 1870s. It occupies a prominent position in Pater's *Studies in the History of the Renaissance*, and specifically in the notorious conclusion to that book. This "Conclusion" was included in the edition of 1873, but omitted in 1877, when Wilde was at Oxford, on the ground that it "might possibly mislead" the young, who accordingly thronged to be misled by the first edition. It was the boldest thing Pater ever wrote; he drew upon the scientific work of his day to deny the integrity of objects. Physical life is now recognized, he says, to be a concurrence of forces rather than a group of things; the mind has no fixities either. He hits upon a metaphor of liquidity such as William

James and Bergson were to adopt a little later in characterizing consciousness as a river or stream; Pater says more balefully that consciousness is a whirlpool, an image which later both Yeats and Pound relished. In our physical life, Pater grants, we sometimes feel momentarily at rest; in our consciousness, however, altering the whirlpool image, he finds "nothing but the race of the mid-stream, a drift of momentary acts of sight and passion and thought." To drift is not so wanton, then, as inevitable. To guide our drifting we should rely not on sights or thoughts, in Pater's view, but on "great passions." "Only be sure it is passion," he puts in as a caveat. He urges his readers to recognize that "not the fruit of experience, but experience itself, is the goal." "Our one hope lies in getting as many pulsations as possible into the given time." This attempt to render experience in terms of quantitatively measurable pulsations sounds a little like *Principles of Literary Criticism*, but Pater's tone is not like Richards'; he plays on the flute for the young to follow him.

When Pater at last decided to reprint this "Conclusion" (in 1888), he toned it down a little. In *Marius the Epicurean* (1885), also later, the word "drift" is again prominent, but this time is pejorative instead of merely descriptive. To suit his later and more decorous manner, Pater, in reviewing *Dorian Gray*, complained of the book's "dainty Epicurean theory" because, he said:

> A true Epicureanism aims at a complete though harmonious development of man's entire organism. To lose the moral sense therefore, for instance, the sense of sin and righteousness . . . is to lose, or lower, organisation, to become less complex, to pass from a higher to a lower degree of development.

The letting-go, as well as the drawing-back, of Pater are both evident in Wilde; his work celebrates both impulses, balancing or disporting with them. In a letter of March 1887, written four years before "Hélas!," he informs an Oxford friend:

> I have got rather keen on Masonry lately and believe in it awfully—in fact would be awfully sorry to have to give it up in case I secede from the Protestant Heresy. I now breakfast with Father Parkinson, go to St. Aloysius, talk sentimental religion to Dunlop and altogether am caught in the fowler's snare, in the wiles of the Scarlet Woman—I may go over in the vac. I have dreams of a visit to Newman, of the holy sacrament in a new Church, and of a quiet and peace afterwards in my soul. I need not say, though, that I shift with every breath of thought and am weaker and more self-deceiving than ever.
>
> If I *could hope* that the Church would wake in me some earnestness and purity I would go over *as a luxury*, if for no better reasons. But I can hardly hope it would, and to go over to Rome would be to sacrifice and give up my two great gods "Money and Ambition."

In this letter Wilde testifies playfully to the same yearning to be earnest that he shows in "Hélas!" and then mocks in his later comedy. He is half-converted to Catholicism, half to Masonry—that these two groups cannot bear each other does not prevent their being equally attractive to him; they have parity as new areas of sensation, to be enjoyed willfully and passingly. If, as Wilde announced later, "the best way to resist temptation is to yield to it," the reason is that having done so, one may pass on to the next and the next, and in this concourse one may keep a residual freedom by not lingering with any single temptation long.

During the four years between writing this letter and writing "Hélas!," Wilde had put aside both Catholicism and Masonry. In his sonnet he has in mind chiefly his formal education as contrasted with his romantic self-indulgence. A classicist by training, Wilde considered Hellenism to be the more basic side of his nature, overlaid, but only as a palimpsest conceals the original, by a more modern mode. He berates himself, gently. His new life is made up of "idle songs for pipe and virelay," a self-accusation which only concedes frivolity, not depravity. Moreover, it is artistic frivolity, a further mitigation. Wilde remembered Pater's comment in the same "Conclusion" that "the wisest" instead of living spend their lives in "art and song." If it is wrong to drift, and Wilde hedges a little, then it is less wrong to drift gracefully. A "boyish holiday" is also not the most offensive way to spend one's time, especially if one likes boys.

The sestet of the poem restates the issue, with new dashes of metaphor. The poet then asks histrionically, "Is that time dead?" He won't say for sure, but again he sweetens his offense: he has but touched with Jonathan's rod the honey of romance. The last question is not so much despairing as hopeful. Wilde felt he was superior to both classical and romantic modes, because he could manipulate both: he said in his essay on the English renaissance that this variability was the strength of the new movement in letters to which he belonged. He thought he had physiological as well as artistic support for his method, because "the desire of any very intensified emotion [is] to be relieved by some emotion that is its opposite." He shifts therefore from foot to foot in other poems besides "Hélas!" "The Sphinx" begins with a fascinated invocation of the sphinx and ends with a strident rejection of her. Wilde summarizes his state or rather his flow of mind in a letter:

> Sometime you will find, even as I have found, that there is no such thing as a romantic experience; there are romantic memories, and there is the desire of romance—that is all. Our most fiery moments of ecstasy are merely shadows of what somewhere else we have felt, or of what we long some day to feel. So at least it seems to me. And, strangely enough, what comes of all this is a curious mixture of ardour and of indifference. I myself would sacrifice everything for a new experience, and I know there is no such thing as a new experience at all. I think I would more readily die for what I do not believe in than for what I hold to be true. I would go to the stake for a sensation and be a sceptic to the last! Only one thing remains infinitely fascinating to me, the mystery of moods. To be master of these moods is exquisite, to be mastered by them more exquisite still. Sometimes I think that the artistic life is a long and lovely suicide, and am not sorry that it is so.

Life then is a willed deliquescence, or more exactly, a progressive surrender of the self to all the temptations appropriate to it.

What Wilde needed was not to avoid the precious occasions of evil in "Hélas!" but to approach more enterprising ones. Yet after his *Poems* appeared in 1881 he was at check for almost six years. He kept busy; he went on a lecture tour for a whole year to America; he returned to England and went lecturing on; he tried unsuccessfully for a post as school inspector such as Matthew Arnold had; erratically still, he married in 1884 and took up husbanding, begetting two children born in 1885 and 1886. Then in 1887 Wilde began the publications by which he is known. He wrote a volume of stories, and one of fairy tales, then one of criticism, then five plays, besides editing from 1887 to 1889 a magazine, *Woman's World*—a patrician equivalent of the A & P *Woman's Day*. It would seem that something roused him from the pseudo-consolidation of marriage and lectures, which were dilettantism for him, to genuine consolidation which seemed dilettantism to others.

This something appears in the original version of *The Picture of Dorian Gray*, published in *Lippincott's Magazine*. Wilde emphasizes more there than in the final version the murder of the painter Basil Hallward by Dorian; it is the turning-point in Dorian's experience, a plunge from insinuations of criminal tendency to crime itself. The murder at once protects the secret of his double life and vents his revulsion against the man who wants him innocent still. In *Lippincott's* Wilde specifies: "It was on the 7th of November, the eve of his own thirty-second birthday, as he often remembered afterwards. . . ." Then when the novel was published as a book, Wilde altered this date: "It was on the ninth of November, the eve of his own thirty-eighth birthday, as he often remembered afterwards."

Altering Dorian's age would be gratuitous if Wilde had not attached significance to his own thirty-second year which began in 1886. The passage must have been autobiographical, and such a conjecture receives support from Robert Ross, who boasted that it was he, at the age of seventeen, who in 1886 first seduced Wilde to homosexual practices. Wilde evidently considered this sudden alteration of his life a pivotal matter, to be recast as Dorian's murder of Hallward. He himself moved from pasteboard marriage to the expression of long latent proclivities, at some remove from the "ancient wisdom" and "austere control" to which he had earlier laid claim as his basic nature. Respectability, always an enemy, was destroyed in his own house. The first work which came out of the new Wilde was, appropriately, "Lord Arthur Savile's Crime," in which murder is comically enacted and successfully concealed.

From late in the year 1886 then, Wilde was able to think of himself, if he wanted to, as criminal. Up to that time he could always consider himself an innocent misunderstood; now he lived in such a way as to confirm suspicions. Instead of challenging Victorian society only by words, he acted in such a way as to create scandal. Indiscreet by nature, he was indiscreet also by conviction, and he waged his war somewhat openly. He sensed that his new life was a source of literary effect. As he wrote later of Thomas Wainewright: "His crimes seem to have had an important effect upon his art. They gave a strong personality to his style, a quality that his early work certainly lacked." He returned to this idea: "One can fancy an intense personality being created out of sin," and in "The Soul of Man Under Socialism," he thought that "Crime . . . under certain conditions, may be said to have created individualism." In "The Portrait of Mr. W. H." (1889), he made Shakespeare's sonnets depend upon a similarly forbidden love affair, with an actor the same age as Ross. Thomas Mann's Mario Kröger speaks of a banker who discovers his literary talent by committing a serious crime for which he is put in prison. The artist-criminal is implicit in romantic and symbolistic theories of art, but Wilde anticipates the explicitness on this subject of both Mann and Gide, as he does that of Cavafy in "Their Beginning" or of Auden in *About the House*:

> Time has taught you
> > how much inspiration
> your vices brought you. . . .

Wilde might have discounted the sinfulness of his conduct and applied to himself his own epigram: "Wickedness is a myth invented by good people to account for the curious attractiveness of others." But he was quite content to think of himself as sinful.

He now succeeded in relating his new discoveries about himself to aesthetic theory. His only formal book of criticism, *Intentions*, has the same secret spring as his later plays and stories. Ostensibly he generally says that the spheres of art and of ethics are absolutely distinct and separate. But occasionally, overtly or covertly, he states that for the artist crime does pay, by instilling itself in his content and affecting his form. Each of the four essays that make up *Intentions* is to some degree subversive, as if to demonstrate that the intentions of the artist are not strictly honorable. The first and the last, "The Decay of Lying" and "The Truth of Masks," celebrate art for rejecting truths, faces, and all that paraphernalia in favor of lies and masks. Wilde doesn't do this in the romantic way of extolling the imagination, for while he uses that word he is a little chary of it; the imagination is itself too natural, too involuntary, for his view of art. He prefers lying because it sounds more willful, because it is no outpouring of the self, but a conscious effort to mislead. "All fine imaginative work," Wilde affirms, "is self-conscious and deliberate. A great poet sings because he chooses to sing." On the other hand, "if one tells the truth, one is sure, sooner or later, to be found out!" "All bad poetry springs from genuine feeling." Wilde celebrates art not in the name of Ariel, as the romantics would, but in the name of Ananias.

He finds art to have two basic energies, both of them subversive. One asserts its magnificent isolation from experience, its unreality, its sterility. He would concur with Nabokov that art is a kind of trick played on nature, an *illicit* creation by man. "All art is entirely useless," Wilde declares. "Art never expresses anything but itself." "Nothing that actually occurs is of the smallest importance." Form determines content, not content form, a point which Auden also sometimes affirms and which is often assumed by symbolists. With this theory Wilde turns Taine upon his head; the age does not determine what its art should be, rather it is art which gives the age its character. So far from responding to questions posed by the epoch, art offers answers before questions have been asked. "It is the ages that are her symbols." Life, straggling after art, seizes upon forms in art to express itself, so that life imitates art rather than art life. ". . . This unfortunate aphorism about Art holding the mirror up to Nature, is," according to Wilde, "deliberately said by Hamlet in order to convince the bystanders of his absolute insanity in all art-matters." If art be a mirror, we look into it to see—a mask. But more precisely, art is no mirror; it is a "mist of words," "a veil."

Sometimes the veil is pierced. This indifferent conferral of forms upon life by art may have unexpected consequences which implicate art instead of isolating it. In "The Decay of Lying" Wilde speaks of "silly boys who, after reading the adventures of Jack Sheppard or Dick Turpin, pillage the stalls of unfortunate applewomen, break into sweetshops at night, and alarm old gentlemen who are returning home from the city by leaping out on them in suburban lanes, with black masks and unloaded revolvers." In *Dorian Gray* the effect is more sinister; Dorian declares he has been poisoned by a book, and while Lord Henry assures him that art is too aloof to influence anybody, Dorian is felt to be right. Art may then transmit criminal impulses to its audience. Like Whitman, Wilde could and did say, "Nor will my poems do good only, they will do just as much evil, perhaps more."

The artist may be criminal and instill his work with criminality. Wilde's second essay in *Intentions* is "Pen Pencil and Poison." He uses Thomas Wainewright as the type of the artist. We need not expect to find a beautiful soul; Wainewright was instead "a forger of no mean or ordinary capabilities, and . . . a subtle and secret poisoner almost without rival in this or any age." Among his interesting tastes, Wainewright had "that curious love of green, which in individuals is always the sign of a subtle artistic temperament, and in nations is said to denote a laxity, if not a decadence of morals." When a friend reproached him with a murder, he shrugged his shoulders and gave an answer that Susan Sontag would call camp: "Yes; it was a dreadful thing to do, but she had very thick ankles." Wilde concludes that "the fact of a man being a poisoner is nothing against his prose," and "there is no essential incongruity between crime and culture." Wainewright's criminal career turns out to be strictly relevant to his art, fortifying it and giving it character. The quality of that art it is too early to judge, Wilde says, but he clearly believes that Wainewright's personality achieves sufficient criminality to have great artistic promise.

"The Critic as Artist" is the most ambitious of the essays in *Intentions*. It too conveys the notion that art undermines things as they are. The critic is the artist's accomplice in crime, or even masterminds the plot in which they are mutually engaged. Criticism overcomes the tendency of creation to repeat itself; it helps the artist discover unused possibilities. For at bottom, Wilde says, criticism is self-consciousness; it enables us to put our most recent phase at a distance and so go on to another. It disengages us so we may reengage ourselves in a new way.

From this argument Wilde proceeds to find criticism and self-consciousness to be as necessary as sin. "What is termed Sin is an essential element of progress"; without it, he holds, the world would stagnate or grow old or become colorless.

> By its curiosity [there is Arnold's word with Wilde's meaning] Sin increases the experience of the race. Through its intensified assertion of individualism it saves us from monotony of type. In its rejection of the current notions about morality, it is one with the highest ethics.

By a dexterous transvaluation of words, Wilde makes good and evil exchange places. Even socially sin is far more useful than martyrdom, he says, since it is self-expressive rather than self-repressive. The goal of man is the liberation of personality; when the day of true culture comes, sin will be impossible because the soul will be able to transform

> into elements of a richer experience, or a finer susceptibility, or a newer mode of thought, acts or passions that with the common would be commonplace, or with the uneducated ignoble, or with the shameful vile. Is this dangerous? Yes; it is dangerous— all ideas, as I told you, are so.

What muddies this point of view in Wilde is his looking back to conventional meanings of words like sin, ignoble, and shameful. He is not so ready as Nietzsche to transvaluate these, though he does reshuffle them. His private equation is that sin is the perception of new and dangerous possibilities in action as self-consciousness is in thought and criticism is in art. He espouses individualism, and he encourages society to make individualism more complete than it can be now, and for this reason he sponsors socialism as a communal egotism, like the society made up of separate but equal works of art.

Meantime, before socialism, what should be thought of the criminal impulses of the artist? Increasingly in his later writings, Wilde spreads the guilt from the artist to all men. If we are all insincere, masked, and lying, then the artist is prototype rather than exception. If all the sheep are black, then the artist cannot be blamed for not being white. Such an exculpation is implied in three of Wilde's plays after *Salomé—Lady Windermere's Fan, A Woman of No Importance, An Ideal Husband.* Wilde allows his characters to be found guilty, but no guiltier than others, and more courageous in their wrongdoing.

Even as he defends them, he allows them to be mildly punished. Half-consciously, Wilde was preparing himself for another abrupt shift in his experience, such as he had made in 1886. It would be false to say that Wilde wanted to go to prison, yet the notion had frequently crossed his mind. He had always associated himself with the *poètes maudits*, always considered obloquy a certificate of literary merit. In "The Soul of Man under Socialism" he had opposed suffering, yet acknowledged that the Russian novelists had rediscovered a great medieval theme, the realization of man through suffering. More particularly, in a review of a new book of poems by Wilfrid Scawen Blunt in 1889, he began: "Prison has had an admirable effect on Mr. Wilfrid Blunt as a poet." It was like the effect of crime on Wainewright. Blunt had been merely witty and affected earlier, now his work had more depth. "Mr. Balfour must be praised," Wilde says jestingly, since "by sending Mr. Blunt to gaol . . . [he] has converted a clever rhymer into an earnest and deep-thinking poet." Six years later, just before his own disgrace, Wilde wrote in "The Soul of Man under Socialism," "After all, even in prison a man can be quite free." These hints indicate that Wilde was prepared, or thought he was, for trial and prison, and expected he would derive artistic profit from them. He had no idea of running away, even on a boyish holiday, whatever his friends might say. Instead he accepted imperial authority as readily as Christ had done—a precedent he discovered for himself, though hardly the first or last in hot water to do so. Blunt's poems written in prison were called *In Vinculis*, and Wilde's letter to Douglas from prison, which we know by Ross's title as *De Profundis*, was originally entitled by Wilde *Epistola: In Carcere et Vinculis.*

Hélas! Wilde's literary career was not transmogrified by prison as he hoped, but his experiences there, which were so much worse than he anticipated, gave him his final theme. *"La prison m'a complètement changé,"* he said to Gide at Berneval; *"je comptais sur elle pour cela."* As before, he made no effort to exonerate himself by saying that his sins were venial or not sins at all. Defenses of homosexual or "Uranian" love were common enough at this period; he did not make them. But he reached for the main implication of his disgrace through a double negative; though men thought he was unlike them, he was *not*. He was a genuine scapegoat.

This ultimate conception of himself was never put into an essay, but it is involved in his *De Profundis* letter to Douglas, and in *The Ballad of Reading Gaol*. Both are predictably full of imagery of Christ. Before this Wilde had depreciated pity as a motive in art; now he embraced it. The hero of his poem is a man who has murdered his mistress and is about to be hanged for his crime. Wilde identifies himself closely with this prisoner. The poem's tenor is that the prisoners are humanity, all of whom are felons:

> Yet each man kills the thing he loves,
>   By each let this be heard,
> Some do it with a bitter look,
>   Some with a flattering word,
> The coward does it with a kiss,
>   The brave man with a sword! . . .
>
> Some love too little, some too long,
>   Some sell, and others buy;
> Some do the deed with many tears,
>   And some without a sigh:
> For each man kills the thing he loves,
>   Yet each man does not die.

This poem was chosen for the *Oxford Book of Modern Verse* by Yeats, but he removed what he regarded as the commentary, including these stanzas. His effort to improve the poem evokes sympathy; it must be said, however, that whatever the quality of the bare narrative that Yeats prints, for Wilde—as for D. H. Lawrence and most readers—the commentary was the excessive and yet determining part of the poem. During the six years before his imprisonment he had demonstrated first that the artist was basically and usefully criminal, and second that criminality was not confined to artists, but was to be found as commonly among members of the Cabinet. Where most men pretend to a virtue they don't have, the artist, fully aware of his own sins, takes on those they don't acknowledge. The purpose of sin has subtly shifted in Wilde's mind—it is no longer a means for the artist of extending the boundaries of action, it is a means for him to focus and enshrine guilt. He has the courage, exceptional among men, of looking into the heart of things and finding there not brotherly love so much as murder, not self-love so much as suicide. In recognizing the universality of guilt he is like Christ; in revealing his own culpability he plays the role of his own Judas. Wilde, who had written in one of his poems that we are ourselves "the lips betraying and the life betrayed," had in fact brought about his own conviction. The result was that he was remarried to the society from which he had divorced himself; he was no outcast, for he accepted and even sought the punishment which other men, equally guilty, would only submit to vicariously through him, just as all the prisoners suffer with the doomed murderer. By means of submission and suffering he gives his life a new purpose, and writes over the palimpsest once again.

In this concern with social role Wilde has clearly moved away from Pater, and perhaps we can conceive of him as moving toward another writer, Jean Genet. Genet is of course ferocious and remorseless in a way that Wilde was not, and makes much less concession to the world. But the two men share an insistence on their own criminality and on a possible sanction for it. The comparison with Christ has been irresistible for both. As Genet says in *Thief's Journal*:

> Let us ignore the theologians. "Taking upon Himself the sins of the world" means exactly this: experiencing potentially and in their effects all sins; it means having subscribed to evil. Every creator must thus shoulder—the expression seems feeble—must make his own, to the point of knowing it to be his substance, circulating in his arteries, the evil given by him, which his heroes choose freely.

Wilde in *De Profundis* remembered having remarked to Gide that "there was nothing that . . . Christ had said that could not be transferred immediately into the sphere of Art, and there find its complete fulfillment." And again, Genet speaks like Wilde of the courage required to do wrong, saying: "If he has courage, the guilty man decides to be what crime has made him." He wishes to obtain "the recognition of evil." Both writers envisage a regeneration which can come only from total assumption of their proclivities and their lot; as Genet puts it:

> I shall destroy appearances, the casings will burn away and one evening I shall appear there, in the palm of your hand, quiet and pure, like a glass statuette. You will see me. Round about me there will be nothing left.

Wilde summons for this sacred moment a red rose growing from the hanged man's mouth, a white one from his heart. He had terrified André Gide by trying to persuade that strictly reared young man to authorize evil, as to some extent in the *acte gratuit* Gide did, and it is just such authorization that Genet asserts with more fierceness than Wilde.

In his criticism and in his work generally, Wilde balanced two ideas which, we have observed, look contradictory. One is that art is disengaged from actual life, the other that it is deeply incriminated with it. The first point of view is sometimes taken by Yeats, though only to qualify it, the second without qualification

by Genet. That art is sterile, and that it is infectious, are attitudes not beyond reconciliation. Wilde never formulated their union, but he implied something like
this: by its creation of beauty art reproaches the world, calling attention to the
world's faults through their very omission; so the sterility of art is an affront or a
parable. Art may also outrage the world by flouting its laws or by picturing indul-
gently their violation. Or art may seduce the world by making it follow an example which seems bad but is discovered to be better than it seems. In these various
ways the artist forces the world toward self-recognition with at least a tinge of
self-redemption.

Yet this ethical or almost ethical view of art coexists in Wilde with its own can-
celation. He could write *Salomé* with one hand, dwelling upon incest and
necrophilia, and show them as self-defeated, punished by execution and remorse.
With the other hand, he could dissolve by the critical intellect all notions of sin and
guilt. He does so in *The Importance of Being Earnest*, which is all insouciance
where *Salomé* is all incrimination. In *The Importance of Being Earnest* sins which
are presented as accursed in *Salomé* and unnameable in *Dorian Gray* are translated into a different key, and appear as Algernon's inordinate and selfish craving
for—cucumber sandwiches. The substitution of mild gluttony for fearsome lech-
ery renders all vice harmless. There *is* a wicked brother, but he is just our old
friend Algernon. The double life which is so serious a matter for Dorian or for The
Ideal Husband, becomes a harmless Bunburying, or playing Jack in the country
and Ernest in town. In the earlier, four-act version of the play, Wilde even parodied punishment, by having a bailiff come to take Jack to Holloway Prison (as
Wilde himself was soon to be taken) not for homosexuality, but for running up
food bills at the Savoy. Jack is disinclined, he says, to be imprisoned in the suburbs
for dining in town, and makes out a check. The notion of expiation is also mocked;
as Cecily observes: "They have been eating muffins. That looks like repentance."
Finally, the theme of regeneration is parodied in the efforts of Ernest and Jack to
be baptized. (By the way, in the earlier version Prism is also about to be baptized,
and someone comments, "To be born again would be of considerable advantage to
her.") The ceremonial unmasking at the play's end, which had meant death for
Dorian Gray, leaves everyone bare-faced for a new puppet show, that of matri-
mony. Yet amusing as it all is, much of the comedy derives from Wilde's own sense
of the realities of what are being mocked. He was in only momentary refuge from
his more usual cycle which ran from scapegrace to scapegoat.

During his stay in prison Wilde took up the regeneration theme in *De
Profundis* and after being freed he resumed it in *The Ballad of Reading Gaol.* But
he was too self-critical not to find the notion of rebirth a little preposterous. When
his friends complained of his resuming old habits, he said, "A patriot put in prison
for loving his country, loves his country, and a poet in prison for loving boys, loves
boys." But to write about himself as unredeemed, unpunished, unreborn, to claim
that his sins were nothing, that his form of love was more noble than most other
people's, that what had happened to him was the result merely of legal obtuseness,
was impossible for Wilde. So long as he had been a scapegrace the door to comedy

was still open; once having accepted the role of scapegoat the door was closed. He conceived of a new play, but it was in his earlier mode and he could not write it. Cramped to one myth, and that somber and depleted, Wilde could not extricate himself. There was nothing to do but die, which accordingly he did. But not without one final assertion of a past enthusiasm: he was converted to Catholicism the night before his death.

Different Desires: Subjectivity and Transgression in Wilde and Gide

Jonathan Dollimore

In Blidah, Algeria, in January 1895 André Gide is in the hall of a hotel, about to leave. His glance falls on the slate which announces the names of new guests: "suddenly my heart gave a leap; the two last names . . . were those of Oscar Wilde and Lord Alfred Douglas."[1] Acting on his first impulse, Gide "erases" his own name from the slate and leaves for the station. Twice thereafter Gide writes about the incident, unsure why he left so abruptly; first in his *Oscar Wilde* (1901), then in *Si le grain ne meurt* (*If It Die*, 1920, 1926). It may, he reflects, have been a feeling of *mauvaise honte* or of embarrassment: Wilde was becoming notorious and his company compromising. But also he was severely depressed, and at such times "I feel ashamed of myself, disown, repudiate myself."[2] Whatever the case, on his way to the station he decides that his leaving was cowardly and so returns. The consequent meeting with Wilde was to precipitate a transformation in Gide's life and subsequent writing.

Gide's reluctance to meet Wilde certainly had something to do with previous meetings in Paris four years earlier in 1891; they had seen a great deal of each other across several occasions, and biographers agree that this was one of the most important events in Gide's life. But these meetings had left Gide feeling ambivalent toward the older man, and it is interesting that not only does Gide say nothing in *If It Die* about Wilde's obvious and deep influence upon him in Paris in 1891, but, according to Jean Delay, in the manuscript of Gide's journal the pages corresponding to that period—November to December 1891—are torn out.[3]

Undoubtedly Gide was deeply disturbed by Wilde, and not surprisingly, since Gide's remarks in his letters of that time suggest that Wilde was intent on undermining the younger man's self-identity, rooted as it was in a Protestant ethic and high bourgeois moral rigor and repression that generated a kind of conformity to which Wilde was, notoriously, opposed. Wilde wanted to encourage Gide to trans-

First published in *Genders* 2 (1988). Reprinted with permission of the author.

Thanks to Joseph Bristow for his comments on an earlier draft of this paper.

[1]André Gide, *If It Die* (1920; private edition 1926), trans. Dorothy Bussy (Harmondsworth: Penguin, 1977), p. 271.
[2]Ibid., pp. 271, 273.
[3]Jean Delay, *The Youth of André Gide*, abridged and trans. J. Guicharnaud (Chicago and London: University of Chicago Press, 1956–57), p. 290.

gress. It may be that he wanted to reenact in Gide the creative liberation—which included strong criminal identification—which his own exploration of transgressive desire had produced nine years earlier. (Wilde's major writing, including that which constitutes his transgressive aesthetic, dates from 1886, when, according to Robert Ross, he first practiced homosexuality.)[4] But first Wilde had to undermine that lawful sense of self which kept Gide transfixed within the law. So Wilde tried to decenter or demoralize Gide—"demoralize" in the sense of liberate from moral constraint rather than to dispirit; or, rather, to dispirit precisely in the sense of to liberate from a morality anchored in the very notion of spirit. ("Demoralize" was a term Gide remembers Wilde using in just this sense, one which, for Gide, recalled Flaubert.) Hence, perhaps, those most revealing of remarks by Gide to Valéry at this time (December 4, 1891): "Wilde is religiously contriving to kill what remains of my soul, because he says that in order to know an essence, one must eliminate it: he wants me to miss my soul. The measure of a thing is the effort made to destroy it. Each thing is made up only of its emptiness." And in another letter of the same month: "Please forgive my silence: since Wilde, I hardly exist anymore."[5] And in unpublished notes for this time he declares that Wilde was "always trying to instil into you *a sanction for evil.*"[6] So, despite his intentions to the contrary, Wilde at that time seems indeed to have dispirited Gide in the conventional sense. Yet perhaps the contrary intention was partly successful; on January 1, 1892 Gide writes: "Wilde, I think, did me nothing but harm. In his company I had lost the habit of thinking. I had more varied emotions, but had forgotten how to bring order into them."[7] In fact, Gide reacted, says Delay, in accordance with his Protestant instincts, reaffirming a moral conviction inseparable from an essentialist conception of self (cf. *Journal*, December 29, 1891: "O Lord keep me from evil. May my soul again be proud"). Even so, this meeting with Wilde is to be counted as one of the most important events in Gide's life: "for the first time he found himself confronted with a man who was able to bring about, within him, a transmutation of all values—in other words, a revolution."[8] Richard Ellmann concurs with this judgment and suggests further that Wilde's attempt to "authorize evil" in Gide supplies much of the subject of *The Immoralist* and *The Counterfeiters*, the former work containing a character, Ménalque, who is based upon Wilde.[9]

It is against the background and the importance of that earlier meeting, together with the ambivalence toward Wilde which it generated in Gide, that we return to that further encounter in Algeria four years later. If anything, the ambivalence

[4]Richard Ellmann, ed., *The Artist as Critic: Critical Writings of Oscar Wilde* (1968: London: W. H. Allen, 1970), p. xviii.

[5]J. Guicharnaud, trans., *Correspondence 1890–1942, André Gide—Paul Valéry* (1955), cited here from the abridged version, *Self-Portraits: The Gide/Valéry Letters* (Chicago and London: University of Chicago Press, 1966), pp. 90, 92.

[6]Delay, *Youth*, p. 291.

[7]André Gide, *Journals*, 4 vols. (New York: Alfred A. Knopf, 1947–51).

[8]Delay, *Youth*, pp. 289–90, 291, 295.

[9]Richard Ellmann, ed., *Oscar Wilde: A Collection of Critical Essays* (Englewood Cliffs, N.J.: Prentice-Hall, 1969), p. 4.

seems even stronger; in a letter to his mother Gide describes Wilde as a terrifying man, a "most dangerous product of modern civilization" who had already depraved Douglas *right down to the marrow.*"[10] A few days later Gide meets them again in Algiers, a city which Wilde declares his intention to demoralize.[11] It is here that there occurs the event which was to change Gide's life and radically influence his subsequent work, an event for which the entire narrative of *If It Die* seems to have been preparing. He is taken by Wilde to a café. It is there that "in the half-open doorway, there suddenly appeared a marvellous youth. He stood there for a time, leaning with his raised elbow against the door-jamb, and outlined on the dark background of the night." The youth joins them; his name is Mohammed; he is a musician; he plays the flute. Listening to that music, "you forgot the time and place, and who you were."[12] This is not the first time Gide has experienced this sensation of forgetting. Africa increasingly attracts him in this respect;[13] there he feels liberated and the burden of an oppressive sense of self is dissolved: "I laid aside anxieties, constraints, solicitudes, and as my will evaporated, I felt myself becoming porous as a beehive."[14] Now, as they leave the café, Wilde turns to Gide and asks him if he desires the musician. Gide writes: "how dark the alley was! I thought my heart would fail me; and what a dreadful effort of courage it needed to answer: 'yes,' and with what a choking voice!" (Delay points out that the word "courage" is here transvalued by Gide; earlier he had felt courage was needed for self-discipline, whereas now it is the strength to transgress.)[15]

Wilde arranges something with their guide, rejoins Gide, and then begins laughing: "a resounding laugh, more of triumph than of pleasure, an interminable, uncontrollable, insolent laugh . . . it was the amusement of a child and a devil." Gide spends the night with Mohammed: "my joy was unbounded, and I cannot imagine it greater, even if love had been added." Though not his first homosexual experience, it confirmed his (homo)sexual "nature," what, he says, was "normal" for him. Even more defiantly Gide declares that, although he had achieved "the summit of pleasure five times" with Mohammed, "I revived my ecstasy many more times, and back in my hotel room I relived its echoes until morning"[16] (this passage was one of those omitted from some English editions). At this suitably climactic moment we postpone further consideration of Gide and turn to the antiessentialist, transgressive aesthetic which Wilde was advocating and which played so important a part in Gide's liberation or corruption, depending on one's point of view. And I want to begin with an indispensable dimension of that aesthetic: one for which Wilde is yet hardly remembered, or, for some of his admirers, one which is actively forgotten; namely, his advocacy of socialism.

---

[10]Quoted from Delay, *Youth*, p. 391 (my italics).
[11]André Gide, *Oscar Wilde*, trans. Bernard Frechtman (New York: Philosophical Library, 1949).
[12]Gide, *If It Die*, pp. 280, 281.
[13]Ibid., pp. 236–37, 247–49, 251, 252, 255, 258–59.
[14]Ibid., p. 264.
[15]Delay, *Youth*, p. 394.
[16]Gide, *If It Die*, pp. 282, 284–85.

Wilde begins his *The Soul of Man under Socialism* (1891) by asserting that a socialism based on sympathy alone is useless; what is needed is to *"try and recon-struct society on such a basis that poverty will be impossible."* It is precisely because Christ made no attempt to reconstruct society that he had to resort to pain and suffering as the exemplary mode of self-realization. The alternative is the socialist commitment to transforming the material conditions which create and perpetuate suffering. One might add that, if the notion of redemption through suffering has been a familiar theme within English studies, this only goes to remind us of the extent to which, in the twentieth century, criticism has worked in effect as a displaced theology or as a vehicle for an acquiescent quasi-religious humanism. So Wilde's terse assertion in 1891 that "pain is not the ultimate mode of perfection. It is merely provisional and a protest"[17] may still be an appropriate response to those who fetishize suffering in the name, not of Christ, but of the tragic vision and the human condition (sainthood without God, as Camus once put it).

Wilde also dismisses the related pieties, that humankind learns wisdom through suffering, and that suffering humanizes. On the contrary, "misery and poverty are so absolutely degrading, and exercise such a paralysing effect over the nature of men, that no class is ever really conscious of its suffering. They have to be told of it by other people, and they often entirely disbelieve them." Against those who were beginning to talk of the dignity of manual labor, Wilde insists that most of that too is absolutely degrading. Each of these repudiations suggests that Wilde was fully aware of how exploitation is crucially a question of ideological mystification as well as of outright coercion: "to the thinker, the most tragic fact in the whole of the French Revolution is not that Marie Antoinette was killed for being a queen, but that the starved peasant of the Vendée voluntarily went out to die for the hideous cause of feudalism." Ideology reaches into experience and identity, reemerging as "voluntary" self-oppression. But it is also the ruling ideology which prevents the rulers themselves from seeing that it is not sin that produces crime but starvation, and that the punishment of the criminal escalates rather than diminishes crime and also brutalizes the society which administers it even more than the criminal who receives it.[18]

There is much more in this essay, but I have summarized enough to show that it exemplifies a tough materialism; in modern parlance one might call it antihumanist, not least because for Wilde a radical socialist program is inseparable from a critique of those ideologies of subjectivity which seek redemption in and through the individual. A case in point would be Dickens's treatment of Stephen Blackpool in *Hard Times* (Wilde made a point of disliking Dickens); another might be Arnold's assertion in *Culture and Anarchy:* "Religion says: 'The Kingdom of God is within you'; and culture, in like manner, places human per-

---

[17]Oscar Wilde, *The Soul of Man under Socialism* (1891), reprinted in Ellmann, ed., *The Artist as Critic*, pp. 256 (his italics), 286–88, 288.
[18]Ibid., pp. 259, 268, 260, 267.

fection in an *internal* condition, in the growth and predominance of our humanity proper."[19] But isn't a category like antihumanism entirely inappropriate, given
Wilde's celebration of individualism? The term itself, antihumanism, is not worth
fighting over; I have introduced it only as a preliminary indication of just how different is Wilde's concept of the individual from that which has prevailed in idealist culture generally and English studies in particular. It is this difference which
the next section considers.

Individualism

In Wilde's writing, individualism is less to do with a human essence, Arnold's
inner condition, than a dynamic social potential, one which implies a radical possibility of freedom "latent and potential in mankind generally." Thus individualism
as Wilde conceives it generates a "disobedience [which] in the eyes of anyone who
has read history, is man's original virtue. It is through disobedience that progress
has been made, through disobedience and through rebellion."[20] Under certain
conditions there comes to be a close relationship between crime and individualism, the one generating the other.[21] Already, then, Wilde's notion of individualism
is inseparable from transgressive desire and a transgressive aesthetic. Hence, of
course, his attack on public opinion, mediocrity, and conventional morality, all of
which forbid both the desire and the aesthetic.[22]

The public which Wilde scorns is that which seeks to police culture; which is
against cultural difference; which reacts to the aesthetically unconventional by
charging it with being either grossly unintelligible or grossly immoral. Far from
reflecting or prescribing for the true nature or essence of man, individualism will
generate the cultural difference and diversity which conventional morality, orthodox opinion, and essentialist ideology disavow. Wilde affirms the principle of differentiation to which all life grows and insists that selfishness is not living as one
wishes to live, but asking others to live as one wishes to live, trying to create "an
absolute uniformity of type." And unselfishness not only recognizes cultural diversity and difference but enjoys them. Individualism as an affirmation of cultural as
well as personal difference is therefore fundamentally opposed to that "immoral
ideal of uniformity of type and conformity to rule which is so prevalent everywhere, and is perhaps most obnoxious in England."[23]

---

[19]Matthew Arnold, *Culture and Anarchy* (1869; London: Smith Elder, 1891), p. 8.

[20]Wilde, *The Soul of Man under Socialism*, pp. 261, 258.

[21]Wilde reiterates this elsewhere: see Oscar Wilde, "Pen, Pencil and Poison" (1889), in Ellmann,
ed., *The Artist as Critic*, p. 338; "The Critic as Artist" (1890), in ibid., p. 360. Cf. Ellmann's formulation of Wilde's position: "since the established social structure confines the individual, the artist must
of necessity ally himself with the criminal classes" (ibid., p. 3).

[22]See also Wilde, "The Critic as Artist," p. 341; Wilde, *The Soul of Man under Socialism*, pp.
271–74.

[23]Wilde, *The Soul of Man under Socialism*, pp. 273, 284–85, 286.

Uniformity of type and conformity to rule: Wilde despises these imperatives not only in individuals but as attributes of class and ruling ideologies. Wilde's Irish identity is a crucial factor in his oppositional stances, and it is instructive to consider in this connection a piece written two years earlier, in 1889, where he addresses England's exploitation and repression of Ireland. "Mr Froude's Blue Book" is a review of J. A. Froude's novel, *The Two Chiefs of Dunboy*. In the eighteenth century, says Wilde, England tried to rule Ireland "with an insolence that was intensified by race-hatred and religious prejudice"; in the nineteenth, with "a stupidity . . . aggravated by good intentions." Froude's picture of Ireland belongs to the earlier period, and yet to read Wilde's review now makes one wonder what if anything has changed in Tory "thinking" except that possibly now the one vision holds for both Ireland and the mainland:

> Resolute government, that shallow shibboleth of those who do not understand how complex a thing the art of government is, is [Froude's] posthumous panacea for past evils. His hero, Colonel Goring, has the words Law and Order ever on his lips, meaning by the one the enforcement of unjust legislation, and implying by the other the suppression of every fine natural aspiration. That the government should enforce iniquity, and the governed submit to it, seems to be to Mr. Froude, as it certainly is to many others, the true ideal of political science. . . . Colonel Goring . . . Mr. Froude's cure for Ireland . . . is a "*Police* at any price" man.[24]

Individualism joins with socialism to abolish other kinds of conformity, including, says Wilde, family life and marriage, each being unacceptable because rooted in and perpetuating the ideology of property.[25] Individualism is both desire for a radical personal freedom and a desire for society itself to be radically different, the first being inseparable from the second. So Wilde's concept of the individual is crucially different from that sense of the concept which signifies the private, experientially self-sufficient, autonomous, bourgeois subject; indeed, for Wilde, "Personal experience is a most vicious and limited circle" and "to know anything about oneself one must know all about others."[26] Typically, within idealist culture, the experience of an essential subjectivity is inseparable from knowledge of that notorious transhistorical category, human nature. This is Wilde on human nature: "the only thing that one really knows about human nature is that it changes. Change is the one quality we can predicate of it."[27] To those who then say that socialism is incompatible with human nature and therefore impractical, Wilde replies by rejecting practicality itself as presupposing and endorsing both the existing social conditions and the concept of human nature as fixed, each of which suppositions socialism would contest: "it is exactly the existing conditions that one objects to . . . [they] will be done away

[24]Oscar Wilde, "Mr. Froude's Blue Book" (1889), in Ellmann, ed., *The Artist as Critic*, pp. 136–37.
[25]Wilde, *The Soul of Man under Socialism*, p. 265.
[26]Oscar Wilde, "The Decay of Lying" (1889), in Ellmann, ed., *The Artist as Critic*, p. 310, and "The Critic as Artist," p. 382.
[27]Wilde, *The Soul of Man under Socialism*, p. 284.

with, and human nature will change."[28] Elsewhere Wilde accepts that there is *something* like human nature, but, far from being the source of our most profound being, it is actually ordinary and boring, the least interesting thing about us. It is where we differ from each other that is of definitive value.[29]

Art versus Life

The key concepts in Wilde's aesthetic are protean and shifting, not least because they are paradoxically and facetiously deployed. When, for example, he speaks of life—"poor, probable, uninteresting human life"[30]—or reality as that to which art is opposed, he means different things at different times. One of the most interesting and significant referents of concepts like life and reality, as Wilde uses them, is the prevailing social order. Even nature, conceived as the opposite of culture and art, retains a social dimension,[31] especially when it signifies ideological mystification of the social. That is why Wilde calls being natural a "pose," and an objectionable one at that, precisely because it seeks to mystify the social as natural.[32]

Nature and reality signify a prevailing order which art ignores and which the critic negates, subverts, and transgresses. Thus, for example, the person of culture is concerned to give "an accurate description of what has never occurred," while the critic sees "the object as in itself it really is not"[33] (Wilde is here inverting the proposition which opens Arnold's famous essay, "The function of criticism at the present time"). Not surprisingly, then, criticism and art are aligned with individualism against a prevailing social order; a passage which indicates this is also important in indicating the basis of Wilde's aesthetic of transgressive desire: "Art is Individualism and Individualism is *a disturbing and disintegrating force*. There lies its immense value. For what it seeks to disturb is monotony of type, slavery of custom, tyranny of habit."[34] Art is also self-conscious and critical; in fact, "self-consciousness and the critical spirit are one."[35] And art, like individualism, is oriented toward the realm of transgressive desire: "What is abnormal in Life stands in normal relations to Art. It is the only thing in Life that stands in normal relations to Art."[36] One who inhabits that realm, "the cultured and fascinating liar," is both an object and source of desire.[37] The liar is important because he or she contradicts

[28]Ibid., p. 284.
[29]Wilde, "The Decay of Lying," p. 297.
[30]Ibid., p. 305.
[31]For example, Wilde, "The Critic as Artist," pp. 394, 399.
[32]Oscar Wilde, *The Picture of Dorian Gray* (1890–91; Harmondsworth: Penguin, 1949), p. 10.
[33]Wilde, "The Critic as Artist," pp. 343, 368.
[34]Wilde, *The Soul of Man under Socialism*, p. 272 (my italics).
[35]Wilde, "The Critic as Artist," p. 356.
[36]Oscar Wilde, "A Few Maxims for the Instruction of the Overeducated," *The Complete Works*, with introduction by Vyvyan Holland (London and Glasgow: Collins, 1948), p. 1203.
[37]Wilde, "The Decay of Lying," pp. 292, 305.

not just conventional morality, but its sustaining origin, "truth." So art runs to meet the liar, kissing his "false beautiful lips, knowing that he alone is in possession of the great secret of all her manifestations, the secret that Truth is entirely and absolutely a matter of style." Truth, the epistemological legitimation of the real, is rhetorically subordinated to its antitheses—appearance, style, the lie—and thereby simultaneously both appropriated and devalued. Reality, also necessarily devalued and demystified by the loss of truth, must imitate art, while life must meekly follow the liar.[38]

Further, life is at best an energy which can only find expression through the forms that art offers it. But form is another slippery and protean category in Wilde's aesthetic. In one sense Wilde is a proto-structuralist: "Form is the beginning of things. . . . The Creeds are believed, not because they are rational, but because they are repeated. . . . Form is everything. . . . Do you wish to love? Use Love's Litany, and the words will create the yearning from which the world fancies that they spring."[39] Here form is virtually synonymous with culture. Moreover, it is a passage in which Wilde recognizes the priority of the social and the cultural in determining meaning, even in determining desire. So for Wilde, although desire is deeply at odds with society in its existing forms, it does not exist as a presocial authenticity; it is within and in-formed by the very culture which it also transgresses.

Transgression and the Sense of Self

Returning now to Gide, we are in a position to contrast his essentialism with Wilde's antiessentialism, a contrast which epitomizes one of the most important differences within the modern history of transgression. In a way that perhaps corresponds to his ambivalence toward Wilde, Gide had both submitted to and resisted the latter's attempts to undermine his sense of self. Both the submission and the resistance are crucial for Gide's subsequent development as a writer and, through Gide's influence, for modern literature. The submission is apparent enough in the confirmation of his homosexual desire and the way this alters his life and work. In 1924 he published *Corydon*, a courageous defense of homosexuality which he later declared to be his most important book (*Journal*, October 19, 1942). In *Corydon* he did not just demand tolerance for homosexuality but also insisted that it was not contrary to nature but intrinsically natural; that heterosexuality prevails merely because of convention; that historically homosexuality is associated with great artistic and intellectual achievement, while heterosexuality is indicative of decadence. About these provocative and suspect claims I have only the space to observe that the fury they generated in the majority of commentators is as significant as Gide's reasons for making them in the first place. Two years later Gide published the

[38]Ibid., p. 305.
[39]Wilde, "The Critic as Artist," p. 399.

equally controversial commercial edition of *If It Die,* which, as already indicated, contained, for that time, astonishingly explicit accounts of his homosexuality, and for which, predictably, Gide was savagely castigated. Much later still, Gide was to write to Ramon Fernandez, confirming that "sexual non-conformity is the first key to my works"; the experience of his own deviant desire leads him first to attack sexual conformity and then "all other sphinxes of conformity," suspecting them to be "the brothers and cousins of the first."[40]

But Gide—having with Wilde both allowed and encouraged the subversion of an identity which had hitherto successfully, albeit precariously, repressed desire— does not then substitute for it the decentered subjectivity which animates Wilde's aesthetic; on the contrary, he reconstitutes himself as an essentially new self. Michel in *The Immoralist* (1902) corresponds in some measure to Gide in Algiers (while, as earlier remarked, another character in that novel, Ménalque, is probably based on Wilde). For Michel, as for Gide, transgression does not lead to a relinquishing of self but to a totally new sense of self. Michel throws off the culture and learning which up to that point had been his whole life in order to find himself: that "authentic creature that had lain hidden beneath . . . whom the Gospel had repudiated, whom everything about me—books, masters, parents, and I myself had begun by attempting to suppress. . . . Thenceforward I despised the secondary creature, the creature who was due to teaching, whom education had painted on the surface." He composes a new series of lectures in which he shows "culture, born of life, as the destroyer of life." The true value of life is bound up with individual uniqueness: "the part in each of us that we feel is different from other people is the part that is rare, the part that makes our special value."[41]

Whereas for Wilde transgressive desire leads to a relinquishing of the essential self, for Gide it leads to a discovery of the authentic self. As he writes in *If It Die,* it was at that time in Algiers that "I was beginning to discover myself—and in myself the tables of a new law."[42] And he writes to his mother on February 2, 1895: "I'm unable to write a line or a sentence so long as I'm not in *complete possession* (that is, WITH FULL KNOWLEDGE) of myself. I should like very submissively to follow nature—the unconscious, which is within myself and must be *true.*"[43] Here again there is the indirect yet passionate insistence on the naturalness, the authenticity of his deviant desire. With that wilful integrity—itself a kind of perversity?—rooted in Protestantism, Gide not only appropriates dominant concepts (the normal, the natural) to legitimate his own deviation but goes so far as to claim a sanction for deviation in the teachings of Christ.[44] (In his journal for 1893 [detached pages] he wrote: "Christ's saying is just as true in art: 'Whoever will save his life [his personality] shall lose it.' " He later declared, after reading Nietzsche's *Thus Spake Zarathustra,* that

[40]Delay, *Youth,* p. 438.
[41]André Gide, *The Immoralist* (1902; Harmondsworth: Penguin, 1960), pp. 51, 90, 100.
[42]Gide, *If It Die,* p. 298.
[43]Delay, *Youth,* p. 396.
[44]Gide, *If It Die,* p. 299.

it was to this that Protestantism led, "to the greatest liberation.")[45] Delay contends, plausibly, that some of the great Gidean themes, especially those entailing transgression, can be found in the rebellious letters that he wrote to his mother in March 1895, letters inspired by his self-affirmation as a homosexual.[46]

It would be difficult to overestimate the importance, in the recent history of Western culture, of transgression in the name of an essential self which is the origin and arbiter of the true, the real, and the moral, that is, the three main domains of knowledge in Western culture: the epistemological, the ontological, and the ethical. Its importance within the domain of sexuality and within discourses which intersect with sexuality is becoming increasingly apparent, but it has been central also in liberation movements which have not primarily been identified with either of these. This, finally, is Gide in 1921:

> The borrowed truths are the ones to which one clings most tenaciously, and all the more so since they remain foreign to our intimate self. It takes much more precaution to deliver one's own message, much more boldness and prudence, than to sign up with and add one's voice to an already existing party. . . . I believed that it is above all to oneself that it is important to remain faithful.[47]

Paradox and Perversity

The contrast between Gide and Wilde is striking: not only are Wilde's conceptions of subjectivity and desire antiessentialist but so too—and consequently—is his advocacy of transgression. Deviant desire reacts against, disrupts, and displaces from within; rather than seeking to escape the repressive ordering of sexuality, Wilde reinscribes himself within and relentlessly inverts the binaries upon which that ordering depends. Inversion, rather than Gide's escape into a pre- or trans-social reality, defines Wilde's transgressive aesthetic. In Gide, transgression is in the name of a desire and identity rooted in the natural, the sincere, and the authentic; Wilde's transgressive aesthetic is the reverse: *in*sincerity, *in*authenticity, and *un*naturalness become the liberating attributes of decentered identity and desire, and inversion becomes central to Wilde's expression of this aesthetic, as can be seen from a selection of his *Phrases and Philosophies for the Use of the Young* (1894):

> If one tells the truth, one is sure, sooner or later, to be found out.
> Only the shallow know themselves.
> To be premature is to be perfect.
> It is only the superficial qualities that last. Man's deeper nature is soon found out.
> To love oneself is the beginning of a lifelong romance.[48]

[45]Delay, *Youth*, p. 467.
[46]Ibid., p. 407.
[47]Gide, *Journals*, p. 338. Cf. ibid., pp. 371–76.
[48]Oscar Wilde, *Phrases and Philosophies for the Use of the Young* (1894), in Ellmann, ed., *The Artist as Critic*, pp. 433–34.

In Wilde's writings a noncentered or dispersed desire is both the impetus for a subversive inversion *and* what is released by it. Perhaps the most general inversion operating in his work reverses that most dominating of binaries, nature/culture; more specifically, the attributes on the left are substituted for those on the right:

X	for	Y
surface		depth
lying		truth
change		stasis
difference		essence
persona/role		essential self
abnormal		normal
insincerity		sincerity
style/artifice		authenticity
facetious		serious
narcissism		maturity

For Michel in *The Immoralist* and to an extent for Gide himself, desire may be proscribed, but this does not affect its authenticity; if anything, it confirms it. In a sense, then, deviant desire is legitimated in terms of culture's opposite, nature, or, in a different but related move, in terms of something which is precultural or *always more than* cultural. Gide shares with the dominant culture an investment in the Y column above; he appropriates its categories *from* the dominant *for* the subordinate. In contrast, for Wilde transgressive desire is both rooted in culture and the impetus for affirming different/alternative kinds of culture. So what in Gide's conception of transgression might seem a limitation or even a confusion— namely, that the desire which culture outlaws is itself thoroughly cultural—in fact facilitates one of the most disturbing of all forms of transgression: the outlaw turns up as inlaw; more specifically, that which society forbids Wilde reinstates through and within some of its most cherished and central cultural categories—art, the aesthetic, art criticism, individualism. At the same time as he appropriates those categories he also transvalues them through inversion, thus making them now signify those binary exclusions (the X column) by which the dominant culture knows itself (thus abnormality is not just the opposite, but *the necessarily always present* antithesis of normality). It is an uncompromising inversion, this being the (perversely) appropriate strategy for a transgressive desire which is of its "nature," according to this culture, an inversion.

But inversion has a specific as well as a general target: as can be seen from the *Phrases and Philosophies* just quoted, Wilde seeks to subvert those dominant categories which signify *subjective depth.* Such categories (the Y column) are precisely those which ideologically identify (interpellate?) the mature adult individual, which confer or ideologically coerce identity. And they too operate in terms of binary contrast: the individual knows what he—I choose the masculine pronoun deliberately[49]—is in contrast to what he definitely is not or should not be. In

---

[49] The attacks on Wilde after his trial frequently reveal that it is masculinity which felt most under threat from him and which demanded revenge.

Wilde's inversions, the excluded inferior term returns as the *now superior* term of a related series of binaries. Some further examples of Wilde's subversion of subjective depth are:

> A little sincerity is a dangerous thing, and a great deal is absolutely fatal.[50]
> All bad poetry springs from genuine feeling.[51]
> In matters of grave importance, style, not sincerity, is the *vital* thing.[52]
> Only shallow people . . . do not judge by appearances.[53]
> Insincerity . . . is merely a method by which we can multiply our personalities. Such . . . was Dorian Gray's opinion. He used to wonder at the shallow psychology of those who conceived the Ego in man as a thing simple, permanent, reliable, and of one essence. To him man was a being with myriad lives and myriad sensations, a complex, multiform creature.[54]

At work here is a transgressive desire which makes its opposition felt as a disruptive reaction upon, and inversion of, the categories of subjective depth which hold in place the dominant order which proscribes that desire.

The Decentered Subject and the Question of the Postmodern

Wilde's transgressive aesthetic relates to at least three aspects of contemporary theoretical debates: first, the dispute about whether the inversion of binary opposites subverts or, on the contrary, reinforces the order which those binaries uphold; second, the political importance—or irrelevance—of decentering the subject; third, postmodernism and one of its more controversial criteria: the so-called disappearance of the depth model, especially the model of a deep human subjectivity. Since the three issues closely relate to each other, I shall take them together.

It might be said that Wildean inversion disturbed nothing; by merely reversing the terms of the binary, inversion remains within its limiting framework: the world turned upside down can only be righted, not changed. Moreover, the argument might continue, Wilde's paradoxes are superficial in the pejorative sense of being inconsequential, of making no difference. But we should remember that in the first of the three trials involving Wilde in 1895 he was cross-examined on his *Phrases and Philosophies*, the implication of opposing counsel being that they, along with *Dorian Gray*, were "calculated to subvert morality and encourage unnatural vice."[55] There is a sense in which evidence cannot get more material than this, and it remains so whatever our retrospective judgment about the crassness of the thinking behind such a view.

[50]Wilde, "The Critic as Artist," p. 393.
[51]Ibid., p. 398.
[52]Oscar Wilde, *The Importance of Being Earnest* (1894–99). ed. R. Jackson (London: Ernest Benn, 1980), p. 83 (my italics).
[53]Wilde, *The Picture of Dorian Gray*, p. 29.
[54]Ibid., pp. 158–59.
[55]H. M. Hyde, *Oscar Wilde: A Biography* (1976; London: Methuen, 1982), p. 271.

One of the many reasons why people thought as they did was to do with the perceived connections between Wilde's aesthetic transgression and his sexual transgression. It is not only that at this time the word "inversion" was being used for the first time to define a specific kind of deviant sexuality and deviant person (the two things now being indissociable), but also that, in producing the homosexual as a species of being rather than, as before, seeing sodomy as an aberration of behavior,[56] society now regarded homosexuality as rooted in a person's identity; this sin might pervade all aspects of an individual's being, and its expression might become correspondingly the more insidious and subversive. Hence in part the animosity and hysteria directed at Wilde during and after his trial.

After he had been found guilty of homosexual offences and sentenced to two years' imprisonment with hard labor, the editorial of the London *Evening News* subjected him to a vicious and revealing homophobic attack. He had, it claimed, tried to subvert the "wholesome, manly, simple ideals of English life"; moreover, his "abominable vices . . . were the natural outcome of his diseased intellectual condition." The editorial also saw Wilde as the leader of a likeminded but younger subculture in London.[57] The view expressed here was, and indeed remains, for some, a commonplace: sexual deviation is symptomatic of a much wider cultural deterioration and/or subversion. There is an important sense in which Wilde confirmed and exploited this connection between discursive and sexual perversion: "What the paradox was to me in the sphere of thought, perversity became to me in the sphere of passion."[58] This feared crossover between discursive and sexual perversion has sanctioned terrible brutalities against homosexuals, at the same time,

---

[56]Michel Foucault, *The History of Sexuality*, vol. 1: *An Introduction* (1978; New York: Vintage Books, 1980), p. 43.

[57]H. M. Hyde, *The Trials of Oscar Wilde* (London: William Hodge, 1948), p. 12.

[58]Oscar Wilde, *De Profundis* (1897), in *The Letters of Oscar Wilde* (London: Rupert Hart-Davis, 1962); cited from the abridged edition, *Selected Letters* (London: Oxford University Press, 1979), p. 194. In certain important respects, *De Profundis* is a conscious renunciation by Wilde of his transgressive aesthetic. This is a work which registers many things, not least Wilde's courage and his despair during imprisonment. It also shows how he endured the intolerable by investing suffering with meaning, and this within a confessional narrative whose aim is a deepened self-awareness. "I could not bear [my sufferings] to be without meaning. Now I find hidden somewhere away in my nature something that tells me that nothing in the whole world is meaningless . . . that something . . . is Humility." Such knowledge and such humility, for Wilde (and still, for us now), is bought at the cost of fundamentally—deeply—renouncing difference and transgression and the challenge they present. In effect, Wilde repositions himself as the authentic, sincere subject which before he had subverted: "The supreme vice is shallowness," he says in his work, and he says it more than once. And later: "The moment of repentance is the moment of initiation" (ibid., pp. 195, 154, 215). This may be seen as that suffering into truth, that redemptive knowledge which points beyond the social to the transcendent realization of self, so cherished within idealist culture; those who see *De Profundis* as Wilde's most mature work often interpret it thus. I see it differently—as tragic, certainly, but tragic in the materialist sense of the word: a kind of defeat of the marginal and the oppositional which only ideological domination can effect; a renunciation which is experienced as voluntary and self-confirming but which is in truth a self-defeat and a self-denial massively coerced through the imposition, by the dominant, of incarceration and suffering and their "natural" medium, confession. What Wilde says here of the law is true also of the dominant ideologies he transgressed: "I . . . found myself constrained to appeal to the very things against which I had always protested" (ibid., p. 221).

at least in this period, it was also becoming the medium for what Foucault calls a reverse or counter-discourse,[59] giving rise to what is being explored here in relation to Wilde—what might be called the politics of inversion/perversion (again crossing over and between the different senses of these words). Derrida has argued persuasively for binary inversion as a politically indispensable stage toward the eventual displacement of the binary itself.[60] The case of Wilde indicates, I think, that in actual historical instances of inversion—that is, inversion as a strategy of cultural struggle—it already constitutes a displacement, if not of the binary itself, then certainly of the moral and political norms which cluster dependently around its dominant pole.

We begin to see, then, why Wilde was hated with such an intensity, even though he rarely advocated in his published writings any explicitly immoral practice. What held those "wholesome, manly, simple ideals of English life" in place were traditional and conservative ideas of what constituted human nature and human subjectivity, and it was *these* that Wilde attacked: not so much conventional morality itself as the ideological anchor points for that morality; namely, notions of identity as subjective depth whose criteria appear in the Y column above. And so it might be said that here, generally, as he did with Gide more specifically, Wilde subverts the dominant categories of subjectivity which keep desire in subjection and subverts the essentialist categories of identity which keep morality in place. Even though there may now be a temptation to patronize and indeed dismiss both the Victorians' "wholesome, manly, simple ideals of English life" and Wilde's inversion of them, the fact remains that, in successively reconstituted forms, those ideals, *together with* the subject positions which instantiate them, come to form the moral and ethical base of English studies in our own century and, indeed, remain culturally central today.

I am thinking here not just of the organicist ideology so characteristic of an earlier phase of English studies, one that led, for example, to the celebration of Shakespeare's alleged "national culture, rooted in the soil and appealing to a multi-class audience," but more specifically and importantly of what Chris Baldick in his excellent study goes on to call its "subjective correlative"; namely, the *"maintenance of the doctrine of psychic wholeness in and through literature as an analogue for a projected harmony and order in society."*[61] For I. A. Richards, all human problems (continues Baldick) become problems of mental health, with art as the cure, and literary criticism becomes "a question of attaining the right state of mind to judge other minds, according to their degree of immaturity, inhibition, or perversion." As Richards himself puts it, sincerity "is the quality we most insistently require in poetry. It is also the quality we most need as critics."[62] As a conception

[59] Foucault, *History*, p. 101.
[60] Jacques Derrida, *Positions* (London, 1981), pp. 41–42.
[61] C. Baldick, *The Social Mission of English Criticism 1848–1932* (Oxford: Clarendon, 1983), pp. 213–18 (my italics).
[62] I. A. Richards, quoted in ibid., p. 215.

of both art and criticism, this is the reverse of Wilde's. Similarly with the Leavises, whose imperative concept was the related one of "maturity," one unhappy consequence of which was their promotion of the "fecund" D. H. Lawrence against the perverse W. H. Auden. As Baldick goes on to observe, "this line of critics is not only judicial in tone but positively inquisitorial, indulging in a kind of perversion-hunting" which is itself rooted in "a simple model of [pre- or anti-Freudian] normality and mental consistency."[63]

This tradition has, of course, been subjected to devastating critiques in recent years; in particular, its notions of subjective integration and psychic wholeness have been attacked by virtually all the major movements within contemporary critical theory, including Marxism, structuralism, poststructuralism, and psychoanalysis. Yet Wilde's subversion of these notions is still excluded from consideration, even though we now think we have passed beyond that heady and in many ways justified moment when it seemed that only Continental theory had the necessary force to displace the complacencies of our own tradition. The irony, of course, is that while looking to the Continent we failed to notice that Wilde has been and remains a very significant figure there. (And not only there: while the *Spectator* [February 1891] thought *The Soul of Man under Socialism* was a joke in bad taste, the essay soon became extremely successful in Russia, appearing in many successive editions across the next twenty years.) Perhaps, then, there exists or has existed a kind of "muscular theory," which shares with the critical movements it has displaced a significant blindness with regard to Wilde and what he represented. This almost certainly has something to do with the persistence of an earlier attempt to rid English studies of a perceived "feminized" identity.[64]

Recent critics of postmodernism, including Fredric Jameson, Ihab Hassan, Dan Latimer, and Terry Eagleton,[65] have written intriguingly on one of its defining criteria: the disappearance of the depth model. In a recent essay, Eagleton offers an important and provocative critique of postmodernism: "confidently postmetaphysical [it] has outlived all that fantasy of interiority, that pathological itch to scratch surfaces for concealed depths." With the postmodern there is no longer any subject to be alienated and nothing to be alienated from, "authenticity having been less rejected than merely forgotten." The subject of postmodernist culture is "a dispersed, decentred network of libidinal attachments, emptied of ethical sub-

[63]Ibid., p. 217.

[64]B. Doyle, "The Hidden History of English Studies," in Peter Widdowson, ed., *Re-Reading English* (London: Methuen, 1982); Terry Eagleton, *Literary Theory: An Introduction* (Oxford: Blackwell, 1983); Baldick, *Social Mission*. On Wilde in Germany, see Manfred Pfister, ed., Oscar Wilde, *The Picture of Dorian Gray* (Munich: Wihelm Fink, 1986).

[65]Fredric Jameson, "Postmodernism and Consumer Society," in H. Foster, ed., *The Anti-Aesthetic: Essays on Postmodern Culture* (Washington, D.C.: Bay Press, 1983); Fredric Jameson, "Postmodernism, or the Cultural Logic of Late Capitalism," *New Left Review* 146 (1984); Ihab Hassan, "Pluralism in Postmodern Perspective," *Critical Inquiry* 12, no. 3 (1986): 503–20; Dan Latimer, "Jameson and Postmodernism," *New Left Review* 148 (1984): 116–28; Terry Eagleton, "Capitalism, Modernism and Postmodernism," in *Against the Grain* (London: Verso, 1986), pp. 131–47.

stance and psychical interiority, the ephemeral function of this or that act of consumption, media experience, sexual relationship, trend or fashion." Modernism, by contrast, is (or was) still preoccupied with the experience of alienation, with metaphysical depth and/or the psychic fragmentation and social wretchedness consequent upon the realization that there is no metaphysical depth or (this being its spiritual instantiation) authentic unified subject. As such, modernism is "embarrassingly enmortgaged to the very bourgeois humanism it otherwise seeks to subvert"; it is "a deviation still enthralled to a norm, parasitic on what it sets out to deconstruct." But, concludes Eagleton, the subject of late capitalism is actually neither the "self-regulating synthetic agent posited by classical humanist ideology, nor merely a decentred network of desire [as posited by postmodernism], but a contradictory amalgam of the two." If in one respect the decentered, dispersed subject of postmodernism is suspiciously convenient to our own phase of late capitalism, it follows that those poststructuralist theorists who stake all on the assumption that the unified subject is still integral to contemporary bourgeois ideology, and that it is always a politically radical act to decenter and deconstruct that subject, need to think again.[66]

Eagleton's argument can be endorsed with yet further important distinctions. First, even though the unified subject was indeed an integral part of an earlier phase of bourgeois ideology, the instance of Gide and the tradition he represents must indicate that it was never even then exclusively in the service of dominant ideologies. Indeed, to the extent that Gide's essentialist legitimation of homosexual desire was primarily an affirmation of his own nature as pederast or paedophile, some critics might usefully rethink their own assumption that essentialism is fundamentally and always a conservative philosophy. In Gide we find essentialism in the service of a radical sexual nonconformity which was and remains incompatible with conventional and dominant sexual ideologies, bourgeois and otherwise. Even a glance at the complex and often contradictory histories of sexual liberation movements in our own time shows that they have, as does Eagleton's contradictory subject of late capitalism, sometimes and necessarily embraced a radical essentialism with regard to their own identity, while simultaneously offering an equally radical antiessentialist critique of the essentializing sexual ideologies responsible for their oppression.

This is important: the implication of Eagleton's argument is not just that we need to make our theories of subjectivity a little more sophisticated, but rather that we need to be more historical in our practice of theory. Only then can we see the dialectical complexities of social process and social struggle. We may see, for example, how the very centrality of an essentialist concept to the dominant ideology has made its appropriation by a subordinate culture seem indispensable in that culture's struggle for legitimacy; roughly speaking, this corresponds to Gide's position as I am representing it here. The kind of challenge represented by Gide—

---

[66]Eagleton, "Capitalism, Modernism and Postmodernism," pp. 143, 132, 145, 143–45.

liberation in the name of authenticity—has been more or less central to many progressive cultural struggles since, though it has not, of course, guaranteed their success.[67] Conversely, we may also see how other subordinate cultures and voices seek not to appropriate dominant concepts and values so much as to sabotage and displace them. This is something we can observe in Wilde.

Whether the decentered subject of contemporary poststructuralism and postmodernism is subversive of, alternative to, or actually produced by late capitalism, there is no doubt that Wilde's exploration of decentered desire and identity scandalized bourgeois culture in the 1890s and in a sense cost him his life. The case of Wilde might lead us to rethink the antecedents of postmodernism and, indeed, of modernism as they figure in the current debate which Eagleton addresses. Wilde prefigures elements of each, while remaining importantly different from—and not just obviously prior to—both. If his transgressive aesthetic anticipates postmodernism to the extent that it suggests a culture of the surface and of difference, it also anticipates modernism in being not just hostile to but intently concerned with its opposite, the culture of depth and exclusive integration. Yet Wilde's transgressive aesthetic differs from some versions of the postmodern in that it includes an acute political awareness and often an uncompromising political commitment; and his critique of the depth model differs from the modernist in that it is accompanied not by *Angst* but by something utterly different, something reminiscent of Barthes's *jouissance,* or what Borges has perceptively called Wilde's "negligent glee . . . the fundamental spirit of his work [being] joy."[68]

An antiessentialist theory of subjectivity can in no way guarantee, *a priori,* any effect, radical or otherwise; nor, more generally, can any transgressive practice carry such a guarantee. But there is much to be learned retrospectively both from the effects of antiessentialism and the practice of transgression, especially in the light of the currently felt need to develop new strategies and conceptions of resistance. Orthodox accounts of resistance have proved wanting, not least essentialist ideas of resistance in the name of the authentic self, and—in some ways the opposite—resistance in terms of and on behalf of mass movements working from outside and against the dominant powers. And so we have become acutely aware of the unavoidability of working from within the institutions that exist, adopting different strategies depending on where and who we are, or, in the case of the same individual, which subject positions he or she is occupying. But is this the new radicalism, or incorporation by another name?

It is in just these respects, and in relation to such pressing questions, that, far from finding them irrelevant—the one a *passé* wit and the other a *passé* moralist/essentialist—I remain intrigued with Wilde and Gide. In different ways their work explores what we are now beginning to attend to again: the complexities, the potential, and the dangers of what it is to transgress, invert, and displace *from*

[67]M. Berman, *The Politics of Authenticity: Radical Individualism and the Emergence of Modern Society* (London: Allen & Unwin, 1971).
[68]Ellmann, ed., *Oscar Wilde,* p. 174.

within,[69] the paradox of a marginality which is always interior to, or at least intimate with, the center.

I began with their encounter in Algiers in 1895. Gide, dispirited in the sense of being depressed and unsure of himself, sees the names of Wilde and Douglas and erases his own name as a result, preempting perhaps the threat to his own identity, social and psychic, posed by Wilde's determination to demystify the normative ideologies regulating subjectivity, desire, and the aesthetic. Nevertheless the meeting does occur, and Gide does indeed suffer an erasure of self, a decentering which is also the precondition for admitting transgressive desire, a depersonalization which is therefore also a liberation. Yet, for Gide, transgression is embraced with that same stubborn integrity which was to become the basis of his transgressive aesthetic, an aesthetic obviously indebted, yet also formed in reaction to, Wilde's own. Thus liberation from the self into desire is also to realize a new and deeper self, belief in which supports an oppositional stand not just on the question of deviant sexual desire, but on a whole range of other issues as well, cultural and political. Integrity here becomes an ethical sense inextricably bound up with and also binding up the (integral) unified self.[70] So the very categories of identity which, through transgression, Wilde subjects to inversion and displacement are reconstituted by Gide for a different transgressive aesthetic, or, as it might now more suitably be called in contradistinction to Wilde, a transgressive ethic: one which becomes central to the unorthodoxy which characterizes his life's work. In 1952, the year after his death, his entire works were entered in the Roman

---

[69]See Jacques Derrida, *Of Grammatology* (1967), trans. Gayatri Spivak (Baltimore, Md., and London: Johns Hopkins University Press, 1976), pp. lxxvi–lxxviii; Derrida, *Positions*, pp. 41–42; R. Terdiman, *Discourse/Counter Discourse: Theory and Practice of Symbolic Resistance in Nineteenth-Century France* (Ithaca, N.Y.: Cornell University Press, 1985), esp. Introduction. Some of the most informative work addressing inversion and transgression is historically grounded; I have in mind especially recent work on early modern England. See, for example, D. Kunzle, "World Turned Upside Down: The Iconography of a European Broadsheet Type," in Barbara Babcock, ed., *The Reversible World: Symbolic Inversion in Art and Society* (Ithaca, N.Y., and London: Cornell University Press, 1978); Christopher Hill, *The World Turned Upside Down: Radical Ideas during the English Revolution* (Harmondsworth: Penguin, 1975); P. Stallybrass and A. White, *The Politics and Poetics of Transgression* (London: Methuen, 1986); S. Clark, "Inversion, Misrule and the Meaning of Witchcraft," *Past and Present* 87 (1980): 98–127. Kunzle, discussing the iconography of the world turned upside-down broadsheets, offers a conclusion which registers the complex potential of inversion and is, quite incidentally, nicely suggestive for understanding Wilde: "Revolution appears disarmed by playfulness, the playful bears the seed of revolution. 'Pure' formal fantasy and subversive desire, far from being mutually exclusive, are two sides of the same coin" ("World Turned Upside-Down," p. 89). This is the appropriate point at which to note that the fuller study to which this article is a contribution necessarily addresses other considerations in relation to transgression in Wilde and Gide, most especially those of class race and colonialism. A crucial text for the latter is Gide's *Travels in the Congo* (1927–28), trans. D. Bussy (Harmondsworth: Penguin, 1986). But see also Jean-Paul Sartre, *What Is Literature?* (1948; London: Methuen, 1967), esp. pp. 52, 98–99, 133.

[70]It is instructive to see in Gide's writing how complex, vital, and unconventional the existential and humanist commitment to sincerity of self could be, especially when contrasted with its facile counterpart in English studies, or indeed (a counter-image) the reductive ways in which it is sometimes represented in literary theory. See especially the following entries in Gide's *Journals*: December 21 and detached/recovered pages for 1923; January 1925; October 7 and November 25, 1927; February 10 (especially) and December 8, 1929; August 5 and September 1931; June 27, 1937.

Catholic Index of Forbidden Books; six years earlier he had been awarded the Nobel Prize for Literature.

Wilde's fate was very different. Within weeks of returning from Algiers to London he was embroiled in the litigation against Queensberry which was to lead to his own imprisonment. He died in Paris in 1900, three years after his release. So, whereas Gide lived for fifty-seven years after that 1895 encounter, Wilde survived for only six. And yet it was also Wilde's fate to become a legend. Like many legendary figures, he needs to be rescued from most of his admirers and radically rethought by some, at least, of his critics.

Creating the Audience

Regenia Gagnier

But what completely fettered the artist was the pressure (and the accompanying drastic threats) always to fit into business life as an aesthetic expert. Formerly, like Kant and Hume, they signed their letters "Your most humble and obedient servant," and undermined the foundations of throne and altar. Today they address heads of government by their first names, yet in every artistic activity they are subject to illiterate masters. . . .

The blind and rapidly spreading repetition of words with special designations links advertising with the totalitarian watchword. . . . All the violence done to words is so vile that one can hardly bear to hear them any longer.

> —Max Horkheimer and Theodor Adorno,
> "The Culture Industry: Enlightenment as Mass
> Deception," in *Dialectic of Enlightenment*

One of the results of the extraordinary tyranny of authority is that words are absolutely distorted from their proper and simple meaning, and are used to express the obverse of their right signification.

> —"The Soul of Man Under Socialism"

In *The Trembling of the Veil,* Yeats says that Wilde had a genius for political life but that the corruption of the late-Victorian public was such that he could only indulge a contemptuous wit in set theatrical pieces. Yet Wilde's aesthetic and political theory, written before he turned to the stage, may be one of the last serious, if by no means solemn, attempts by an artist to construct a public not worthy of contempt. On the one hand, he exhibits the sadistic attitude toward a mass public that was characteristic of the great cultural critics since the Romantics. When he attacked an existing institution—the press, the academy, or the art world—he employed and subverted the very languages he criticized. When he considered the creation of an ideal audience, on the other, he changed his style. Perceiving a fallen art world and an unregenerate public, Wilde had two alternatives: to respond cynically or idealistically. He chose both alternatives and developed two distinct styles to represent them. He displays his cynicism in his technique of ironic reference, his idealism in imaginary dialogues of purple prose between two men. The first technique would lead to his theater and comedies; the second to a select audience of artful young men, romances, and prose poems. The first style was Wildean wit; the second, a prose jeweled and seductive. This doubleness constituted Wilde's response to the modern bourgeois artist's dilemma between private art and the need for a public.

Wilde composed his major theoretical works between 1885 and 1891, after he had toured the United States and during the period he was working as a journalist in London. The volume *Intentions* (1891), including four essays considerably revised from their first publication in periodicals, received predominantly favorable reviews in both London and the United States as a serious contribution to the contemporary debate over modern, or realist, art, although reviewers were quick to warn the public not to be put off by the "paradoxical," "bewildering" forms with which Wilde advanced his arguments for nonrepresentational art, or "lying."[1]

Two additional essays, "The Portrait of Mr. W. H." (1889) and "The Soul of Man Under Socialism" (1891), published only in article form, applied the principles introduced in *Intentions* to literary criticism and social theory.[2] Neither of these essays was formally reviewed, but both were to have resonance during Wilde's trials. His contemporary biographers Frank Harris and Robert Sherard wrote that "Mr. W. H." confirmed Wilde's homosexuality for many suspicious readers while it simultaneously affirmed the Cause for homosexual coteries. And Sherard wrote that although "The Soul of Man" was extremely popular in Central and Eastern Europe and among revolutionary groups in the United States, among the moneyed classes in England it produced a feeling of ill will against Wilde.[3] His plays would somewhat mollify the feeling, but the first reaction to the earlier essay would be remembered during the trials. Although Wilde's aesthetic and social theory has typically been treated as the popular manifesto of art for art's sake, by far the greatest part of these essays is devoted to the public and journalism—in fact, to the creation of a audience for art and life. I shall conclude the chapter, however, with a discussion of a poem rather than an essay, for "The Sphinx" illustrates in applied form what the essays theoretically propose with respect to the creation of an audience.

---

[1]"The Truth of Masks: A Note on Illusion" was first published in *Nineteenth Century*, May 1885, as "Shakespeare and Stage Costume"; "The Decay of Lying: An Observation" in *Nineteenth Century*, January 1889; "Pen, Pencil, and Poison: A Study in Green" in *Fortnightly Review*, January 1889; and "The Critic as Artist" as "The True Function and Value of Criticism" in *Nineteenth Century*, July and September 1890. Twentieth-century criticism of Wilde's literary theory can be divided between critics concerned with Wilde's themes and those concerned with his style. On Wilde and the form of Platonic dialogue, see Roditi, *Oscar Wilde*, ch. 5. On Wilde and Romantic and late-Victorian Hegelian dialectics, see Chamberlin, *Ripe Was the Drowsy Hour*, ch. 4. For Wilde's demonstration of Paterian flux in the forms of his essays, see Sussman, "Criticism as Art." For the themes, as opposed to the forms, of Wilde's critical writing, see Ericksen, *Oscar Wilde*, ch. 4; Shewan, *Wilde: Art and Egotism*, ch. 3; and San Juan, *Art of Wilde*, ch. 3.

[2]"The Portrait of Mr. W. H." was first published in *Blackwood's Magazine*, July 1889. After a long history of delays the expanded version was published in 1921. "The Soul of Man Under Socialism" was published in *Fortnightly Review*, February 1891.

[3]Sherard, *Life of Oscar Wilde*, pp. 129–32.

Playful and scintillating with wit, Wilde's essays also take up a sadistic attitude toward the public that attempted to influence artists and art. England ("the home of lost ideas"), he wrote in "The Critic as Artist," "has invented and established Public Opinion, which is an attempt to organize the ignorance of the community, and to elevate it to the dignity of physical force." And in "The Soul of Man Under Socialism":

> The public try to exercise over [art] an authority that is as immoral as it is ridiculous, and as corrupting as it is contemptible. . . . They are continually asking Art to be popular, to please their want of taste, to flatter their absurd vanity, to tell them what they have been told before, to show them what they ought to be tired of seeing, to amuse them when they feel heavy after eating too much, and to distract their thoughts when they are wearied of their own stupidity.

> With the decorative arts it is not different. The public clung with really pathetic tenacity to what I believe were the direct traditions of the Great Exhibition of international vulgarity, traditions that were so appalling that the houses in which people lived were only fit for blind people to live in.

By the public Wilde often means journalists, who produce a kind of anti-art that shares equally with art the focus of Wilde's theory. In "The Critic as Artist" he ironically concedes that

> there is much to be said in favour of modern journalism. By giving us the opinions of the uneducated, it keeps us in touch with the ignorance of the community. . . . [Journalists] give us the bald, sordid, disgusting facts of life. They chronicle, with degrading avidity, the sins of the second-rate, and with the conscientiousness of the illiterate give us accurate and prosaic details of the doings of people of absolutely no interest whatsoever.

The public and journalists impede art and menace the imagination, first because they are entirely utilitarian ("Don't degrade me into the position of giving you useful information," says the older Gilbert to the younger Ernest in the dialogue of "The Critic as Artist"; "nothing that is worth knowing can be taught"); second because they have gone over to specialization ("Each of the professions means a prejudice," continues Gilbert; "we live in the age of the overworked, and the undereducated, the age in which people are so industrious that they become absolutely stupid"); and third because specialization has forced them to value evidence and proof above all. In the face of extreme purposiveness, productivity, and proof, Wilde opts, as in "The Decay of Lying," for the undirected, unproductive, and immature.

> Many a young man starts in life with a natural gift for exaggeration which, if nurtured in congenial and sympathetic surroundings, or by the imitation of the best models, might grow into something really great and wonderful. But, as a rule, he comes to nothing. He falls into careless habits of accuracy . . . or takes to frequenting the society of the aged and the well-informed. . . . And in a short time he develops a morbid and unhealthy faculty of truth-telling, begins to verify all statements made in his presence, has no hesitation in contradicting people who are much younger than himself, and often ends by writing novels which are so like life that no one can possibly believe in their probability.

Debord has observed how the false choices presented in spectacular abundance in the mass media gave rise to competitive oppositions like commercialized youth and age, which are meant to stimulate loyalty to quantitative trivialities. Wilde's oppositions here were shown to be false insofar as he discovered in the trials that the adult was not master of his life nor was youth the property of the young: both were subject to the dynamic of the system. Yet from these exhibitions two things become clear. Wilde wants public recognition as a Professor of Aesthetics who is able to lead the public toward art, and he wants a private life in which young men may realize their personalities, as he would say in "The Portrait of Mr. W. H.," "on some imaginative plane out of reach of the trammeling accidents and limitations of real life." The first desire can perhaps be seen most clearly in "The Soul of Man Under Socialism" and the second in "The Portrait of Mr. W. H." and "The Sphinx."

Yet before seeing Wilde's relatively controlled and stylized reaction, it is worth seeing the reactions of his cultural predecessors to their growing publics. For Wilde's jovial contempt at the expense of the public—or at the very least the bourgeois author's awareness of the distance between writer and general readers ("the quarter-educated" as Gissing calls them in *New Grub Street*)—was especially pronounced in the 1890s, but it was a well-established tradition. Images of print as self-devouring but paradoxically infinitely reproducible had multiplied during the century, not as the potentially positive collapse of the Benjaminian "aura" but as voracious vacuities, cheap thrills, implements of crime, and finally a total environmental hazard, an ecological disaster.

In 1831, Carlyle had complained about critics and reviewers who were stealing the market from authors: "At the last Leipzig Fair, there was advertised a Review of Reviews. By and by it will be found that all Literature has become one boundless self-devouring Review."[4] By the time he wrote "Shooting Niagara" (*Macmillan's Magazine*, August 1867), Carlyle was prepared to instruct the public to "leave Literature to run through its rapid fermentations . . . and to fluff itself off into Nothing, in its own way—like a poor bottle of soda-water with the cork sprung." *Culture and Anarchy* (1869) may be read as a lament for the British reading public's promiscuity: the newspapers Arnold mocks flaunt slogans as flat as Carlyle's soda-water. In 1872, in his letters to workers called *Fors Clavigera*, Ruskin associated the new reading public with thieves in a scorchingly contemptuous description of two rich American girls reading novels on a train—"cheap pilfered literature" Ruskin calls the new railroad fiction, which read like a form of rapid transit.[5] Wilde, in "The Soul of Man," coupled journalism and vandalism in describing journalists who "use the words very vaguely, as an ordinary mob will use ready-made paving-stones."

---

[4]Cited in Gross, *Rise and Fall*, p. 1. I owe many of the following quotations to the attentiveness and energy of Deidre Lynch in my seminar on Victorian lives, Stanford University, autumn 1983.
[5]Ruskin, *Genius*, p. 394.

In "Fiction, Fair and Foul" (1880), Ruskin despaired over the vulgarity of fictional deathbed scenes—the drama most accessible to inhabitants of the city—tailored for the market, and he wished for audiences worthy of Scott rather than Dickens. The causes of the decline of health and dignity in literature were, of course, economic and social: "Nell, in *The Old Curiosity Shop*, was simply killed for the market, as a butcher kills a lamb," whereas Scott "never once . . . permitted the disgrace of wanton tears round the humiliation of strength, or the wreck of beauty."[6] One might recall Wilde's own bright response to the Dickensian public's sentimentality, that one would have to have a heart of stone not to laugh at the death of Little Nell, or Q. D. Leavis's correct observation that Bulwer Lytton's novels exploited each possible market: *Pelham*, novel of fashion, 1828; *Devereux*, historical romance, 1829; *Paul Clifford*, novel with a thesis, 1830; *Eugene Aram*, idealization of crime, 1832; *Godolphin*, philosophical-fashionable, 1833; *Last Days of Pompeii* and *Rienzi*, historical, 1834–35; *Ernest Maltravers*, realism and philosophy, 1837; *Zanoni*, supernatural, 1842.[7] Out of patience, Ruskin, Wilde's teacher at Oxford, simply condemns the urban public, railroads, readers, and writers and gathers "into one Caina of gelid putrescence the entire product of modern infidel imagination, amusing itself with destruction of the body, and busying itself with aberration of the mind."[8]

Print polluted the world. Literature had become litter, the very acme, as Deidre Lynch has said, of conspicuous consumption and built-in obsolescence. The narrator of *Our Mutual Friend* (1864) looks at London wondering: "That mysterious paper currency which circulates . . . when the wind blows . . . whence can it come, whither can it go? It hangs on every bush, flutters in every tree, is caught flying by the electric wires, haunts every enclosure, drinks at every pump, cowers at every grating, shudders upon every plot of grass, seeks rest in vain behind the regions of iron rails."[9] In Ruskin's close-up of the desecrated English landscape in "Fiction, Fair and Foul," the infamy is presided over by print, like flies over excrement:

> Mixed dust of every unclean thing that can crumble in draught, and mildew of every unclean thing that can rot or rust in damp; ashes and rags, beer-bottle and old shoes, battered pans, smashed crockery, shreds of nameless clothes, door-sweepings, floor-sweepings, kitchen garbage, back-garden sewage, old iron, rotten timber jagged with out-torn nails, cigar-ends, pipe-bowls, cinders, bones, and ordure, indescribable; and variously kneaded into, sticking to, or fluttering foully here and there over all these, remnants, broadcast of every manner of newspaper, advertisement or big-lettered bill, festering and flaunting out their last publicity in the pits of stinking dust and mortal slime.[10]

[6]Ibid., p. 443.
[7]Leavis, *Fiction*, p. 163.
[8]Ruskin, *Genius*, p. 444.
[9]Charles Dickens, *Our Mutual Friend*, ed. Stephen Gill (Middlesex, 1971), p. 191.
[10]Ruskin, *Genius*, p. 436.

Crowning it all is the image of the collapse of Mudie's circulating library in the 1890s because of the cost of storing thousands of ephemeral three-decker "latest novels" after their brief span of popularity.[11]

There were hundreds of cheap books and articles written on the problem of trashy literature. Literary dystopias from *Culture and Anarchy* to H. G. Wells's *Tono-Bungay: A Romance of Commerce* (1908) portrayed the proliferation of print for the quarter-educated with more energy and wit than had been expended on art in years. Gissing's *New Grub Street* (1891) is the most urgent treatment of a literary dystopia in all its appalling horror, and it presents the various components of the market in the 1890s. Gissing defined the quarter-educated and their subliterary wants:

> No article in the paper is to measure more than two inches in length, and every inch must be broken into at least two paragraphs. . . . I would have the paper address itself to the quarter-educated; that is to say, the great new generation that is being turned out by the Board schools, the young men and women who can just read, but are incapable of sustained attention. People of this kind want something to occupy them in trains and on 'buses and trams . . . bits of stories, bits of description, bits of scandal, bits of jokes, bits of statistics, bits of foolery. . . . Everything must be very short, two inches at the utmost; their attention can't sustain itself beyond two inches.[12]

The hack writer inhabits a feverish, suppressed environment and, like his market, he suffers from a sort of consumption:

> Mr. Quarmby laughed in a peculiar way, which was the result of long years of mirth-subdual in the Reading-room. . . . His suppressed laugh ended in a fit of coughing—the Reading-room cough.[13]

Another hack writer wonders whether she might not be replaced by a machine:

> A few days ago her startled eye had caught an advertisement in the newspaper, headed 'Literary Machine'; had it then been invented at last, some automaton to supply the place of such poor creatures as herself, to turn out books and articles?[14]

She fears the insanity of the Reading-room:

> Her eye discerned an official walking along the upper gallery, and . . . she likened him to a black, lost soul, doomed to wander in an eternity of vain research along endless shelves. . . . The readers who sat here at these radiating lines of desks, what were they but hapless flies caught in a huge web, its nucleus the great circle of the Catalogue? Darker, darker. From the towering wall of volumes seemed to emanate visible motes, intensifying the obscurity; in a moment the book-lined circumference of the room would be but a featureless prison-limit.[15]

---

[11]See Heyck, *Transformation*, p. 204.
[12]Gissing, *New Grub Street*, pp. 496–97.
[13]Ibid., p. 114.
[14]Ibid., p. 138.
[15]Ibid.

The successful hack, on the other hand, has no time for such macabre fears. He recounts his day:

> I got up at 7:30, and whilst I breakfasted I read through a volume I had to review. By 10:30 the review was written—three-quarters of a column of the *Evening Budget*. . . . At eleven I was ready to write my Saturday *causerie* for the *Will o' the Wisp*; it took me till close upon one o'clock. . . . By a quarter to two, [I had] sketched a paper for *The West End*. Pipe in mouth, I sat down to leisurely artistic work; by five, half the paper was done; the other half remains for to-morrow. From five to half-past I read four newspapers and two magazines, and from half-past to a quarter to six I jotted down several ideas that had come to me whilst reading. . . . Home once more at 6:45, and for two hours wrote steadily at a long affair I have in hand for *The Current*.[16]

This particular hack marries "the woman who has developed concurrently with journalistic enterprise":

> She read a good deal of that kind of literature which may be defined as specialism popularised; writing which addresses itself to educated, but not strictly studious, persons. . . . Thus, for instance, though she could not undertake the volumes of Herbert Spencer, she was intelligently acquainted with the tenor of their contents; and though she had never opened one of Darwin's books, her knowledge of his main theories and illustrations was respectable. She was becoming a typical woman of the new time, the woman who has developed concurrently with journalistic enterprise.[17]

As for the rest, those whom Gissing sees as artists, the stylist dies of starvation and exposure, deliriously apologizing for his relative lack of productivity to the wife who has abandoned him because of his poverty, and the realist commits suicide with the help of toxins researched in the British Museum. Moreover, in one of Gissing's better tragicomic ironies, the realist, who has devoted his life to the theory of the "essentially unheroic" embodied in a novel entitled *Mr. Bailey, Grocer*, at one point throws himself into a burning building to rescue the unpublished manuscript. Possibly the only more sinister treatment of late-Victorian letters is Arthur Machen's thriller *The Three Impostors* (1895), in which all information bears the duplicity of crime, all stories are deceptions, all professional writers are mystified, and any attempt at interpretation is fatal.

New Grub Street illustrates that we are not merely talking about one division—between artists and an inartistic public—but rather about many divisions among writers, publics, and writers and publics: the quarter-educated; the specialized popularized audience as defined above by Gissing; the new journalist; the old (amateur) man of letters; the specialists themselves, both readers and writers; and so on. Q. D. Leavis saw the eighteenth-century novelists as writing for the best—and only—reading public, at the very least the novelist's peers. In the nineteenth century, they wrote for the shopkeeper and worker as well. In some cases the writer and a public *were* peers: Leavis cites Dickens as one such

<hr/>

[16]Ibid., p. 213.
[17]Ibid., pp. 397–98.

case.[18] The Thackeray/Trollope/Eliot public may have had occasion to despise the Dickens/Reade/Collins public, but in any case what could conceivably be called incipient middlebrow and lowbrow tastes were represented side by side in the shilling magazines and twopenny weeklies.

Leavis was hesitant to claim more than the beginnings of a split between popular and cultivated taste in the mid-Victorian period, but most historians agree that one occurred in the 1880s, about the time of *Treasure Island* (1882). By this time the standardizing effects of the public schools (discussed in Chapter 2), the rise of the new journalism facilitated by the expansion of advertising, and academic specialization had divided the market and was effectively silencing the former man of letters. The biographer of the newspaper entrepreneur Northcliffe recited the differences between the old elite and the democratic new journalists:

> The props of the Old Journalism feel bewildered. Their task, they believe, is to enlighten such of the public as can profit by enlightenment on political questions, on foreign policy. Their duty, they maintain, is to guide opinion concerning matters which may affect national well-being, cause changes of Government, raise the issue of peace or war. They have nothing to do with increase of circulation. They call this "pandering to mob interest in trivialities," commercial, undignified. Their standard of importance is set by the chiefs of political parties, Foreign Office, and the Treasury; by the famous Clubs (Reform, Carlton, Athenaeum); by the great country houses, the country rectories; by the Universities, by Bench and Bar. Now the standard is to be set by the mass of the people; the New Journalism will put in the foreground whatever is of interest to them, whatever will make them "hand the paper about."[19]

The growth and splintering of the reading publics, the marketing changes of 1840–80 that resulted in the professionalization of authorship—for example, specialist readers at publishing houses, literary agents, author's royalties, the Society of Authors—and the high and low culture industries contributed to the hostility rampant in the press. Far from appreciating the new platforms for exposure and the more respectable status of authors, the traditional men of letters and great social critics more often than not felt drowned out by triviality and claptrap.[20] The new journalists, they felt, represented not democracy but demagoguery. By the 1880s, according to John Gross's *Rise and Fall of the Man of Letters,* Oxbridge produced as many journalists as philosophers, and the ambitious graduates plagued traditional men of letters like Gissing's Alfred Yule in *New Grub Street.* After a life of unappreciated scholarly toil—that is, he was never even offered an editorship—the embittered Yule goes mad and blind and must be supported until his death by a hack-writing daughter. Within the universities, research experts exposed inaccurate and insufficient information in amateur writing—of the sort that Lady Carbury produces in Trollope's *The Way We Live Now.* Sidney Colvin

---

[18]Leavis, *Fiction*, p. 157.
[19]Ibid., p. 191.
[20]See Gross, *Rise and Fall*, p. 26.

finally formulated the brutal choice: "There comes a time when you must choose between the dispersion and fragmentariness, which is the habit of journalism and life in a hurry, and the concentration and completeness which is the habit of serious literature."[21]

Reading all that trash, however, had an effect on its critics. Arnold studied it to mock it, and the result was a work of satiric genius richer and livelier than anything he had written before.[22] The texts that make up his *Culture and Anarchy: An Essay in Political and Social Criticism* provide excellent examples of the encroachment of anarchy on Culture, for they include more anarchy than Culture. With the skill of a caricaturist, Arnold labels an unpleasant audience and attempts to construct a pleasant one. He pilfers clichés out of newspapers and parodies them with his own clichés, absorbing them with the intention of subverting them. Like his labels Barbarians, Philistines, and Populace, even his central terms Hebraism and Hellenism smack to a classicist of tags or slogans soliciting a congeries of slightly evangelical attitudes toward education and reform.

With low cunning he quotes the classes on themselves: "the great broad-shouldered genial Englishman"; "the great middle class of this country, with its earnest common-sense penetrating through sophisms and ignoring commonplaces"; "the working man with his bright powers of sympathy and ready powers of action." He parodies religions "with their so many thousand souls and so many thousand rifles" and their "Dissidence of Dissent and Protestantism of the Protestant Religion." He parodies John Bright's "commendable interest in politics." He parodies himself as he is represented in the press, "a plain, unsystematic writer, without a philosophy." Against these he shoots his own slogans—phrases that sound like advertisements: "From Maine to Florida, and back again, all America Hebraises"; "Take care that your best light be not darkness" (pilfered from Bishop Thomas Wilson). One must cultivate, Arnold reiterates, one's Best Self, Right Reason, Sweetness, and Light. Here again we find the primitive form of the spectacular society's competitive oppositions, as if Arnold's readers could choose to be Barbarian, Philistine, or Populace.

Arnold probably deliberately permitted the forms of newsprint to dominate his style: he knew his market. By depoliticizing society and proposing the impossible conjunction of hypostatized qualities like Hebraism and Hellenism, Arnold thought to create something out of nothing, a solid State out of anarchy, an audience out of the public. He tried to sell Culture, and so, like most advertisers, he sloganized, reasoning by definition or tautology. Yet because his definitions generally took care to be idiosyncratic, nominal identities rather than empirical or functional consensus, he often succeeded in excluding from the definitions any ordinary (or practical) point of view. Therefore he produced rhetoric, but few sales.

<hr />

[21]Sydney Colvin, "Fellowships and National Culture," *Macmillan's* (June 1876), p. 141; cited in Heyck, *Transformation*, p. 229.

[22]Critics today are only beginning to appreciate this aspect of Arnold. See "Function of Matthew Arnold."

Thus he was able to say that culture is spiritual, therefore machinery (materialism) is not culture; or that criticism alone, "the free disinterested play of mind," rather than the practical point of view, can see the object as it really is ("The Function of Criticism at the Present Time"). The resultant slogan could be *Criticism alone sees the object as it really is.*

In a country where there is no "sovereign organ of opinion" or "recognised authority in matters of tone and taste"—that is, nothing like the French Academy—there may be poetry and genius, writes Arnold, but prose and intelligence will always bear "a note of provinciality" ("The Literary Influence of Academies"). This exemplifies reasoning by tautology, for the key roots are "centre" (the academy) and "province," which are by definition mutually exclusive. The resultant slogan could be *For tone and taste, try an Academy.*

Arnold could also write that "human nature" is the impulse to relate all knowledge to our sense of conduct and beauty, and so he could deduce that since science is only instrumental knowledge, which has nothing to do with conduct and beauty, the study of science alone can never satisfy human nature. Art, on the other hand, is one manifestation of the human relationship to beauty, and the great actions in great art refer to conduct, so literature by definition is sufficient ("Literature and Science"). The resultant slogan: *Only art can satisfy.* In *Seven Types of Ambiguity* (1947), William Empson felt that the "increasing vagueness, compactness, and lack of logical distinctions" in English journalism may "yet give back something of the Elizabethan energy to what is at present a rather exhausted language."[23] Although Empson was half-ironic here, in Arnold's case the exuberant, exploitative wordplay resulted in a sort of un-self-conscious poetry. One might even say that it resulted in his best poetry.

Of course, Arnold's word games were in the service of proclaiming that—again a slogan—"the men of Culture are the true apostles of equality," much as Wilde would claim that "the new Individualism is the New Hellenism" in the conclusion of "The Soul of Man Under Socialism." But without wit, slogans are no less than mental bondage. If *Culture and Anarchy* were not so exuberant in Arnold's destruction of his adversaries' speech, the reader who accepted Arnold's pious nomenclature would suffer a sort of textual bondage. Those who do not like his slogans find themselves alienated from the text or reduced to an epithet. Those who do not share his concept of Culture and its "disinterested study" are in bondage to the Ordinary—not Best—Self.

Wilde admired Arnold, but he discerned both this verbal bondage, duplicating the press's power over the public, and Arnold's tendency toward authoritarianism. As Gilbert shrewdly observed in "The Critic as Artist," the logical culmination of Arnold's disinterested study was in fact "to see the object as in itself it really was not." Art, for Wilde in "The Soul of Man Under Socialism," is no more autonomous than it is for Ruskin and Arnold: it is political.

[23]Empson, *Seven Types*, pp. 236–37.

Despite the seasoned debate among twentieth-century critics over whether Wilde was individualist, socialist, or anarchist,[24] "The Soul of Man" is in fact about the press and media control. Early in the essay Wilde establishes that the two problems of the modern world are pain and poverty; he predicts that inevitably the first will be solved by medical science and the second by socialism. Once the State, "a voluntary association that will organize labour, and be the manufacturer and distributor of necessary commodities," takes over the production of "useful things," it will be left to the individual "to make what is beautiful."

Here Wilde raises to an ideal level the socialist position, common not only to Kropotkin and Marx but also to local labor leaders like John Burns and Tom Mann, that technology would level the workers. But beyond leveling them, it would liberate them to be artists, or people who produce according to their own desires and natures, rather than people like journalists, who produce for the status quo. The best that a journalist can do, under the current regime, is to do what Wilde did in "The Soul of Man"—to use the techniques of satire, the revenge of beauty upon ugliness; and at this point Wilde launches into the kind of Juvenalian invective toward the public that was cited earlier. On the other hand, it is for the artist to try to revive a language mortified by the system. Just as the authority of the State will pass away, just as ecclesiastical and governmental authority had passed away from the pursuit of speculative thought in the universities, so too must the public authority over art through the form of journalism wither away.

In the remainder of the essay, Wilde instructs the public how to be receptive rather than authoritative toward art. Instead of calling books, like his own *Dorian Gray,* "immoral, unintelligible, exotic, and unhealthy"—typical journalistic favorites—the public should concede that "the work of art is to dominate the spectator." Having instructed the public, Wilde concludes the essay with the reinscription of art into life: "One of the results of the extraordinary tyranny of authority is that words are absolutely distorted from their proper and simple meanings, and are used to express the obverse of their right signification. What is true about Art is true about Life. . . . Under Individualism people will be quite natural and absolutely unselfish, and will know the meanings of the words, and realise them in their free, beautiful lives." In teaching the spectator how to be receptive to art, Wilde teaches the public the political message of how to be receptive to the lives of others not like oneself: "Selfishness [like censorship] is not living as one wishes to live, it is asking others to live as one wishes to live."

---

[24]For a discussion of Wilde's linking individualism and socialism, which were generally considered antithetical in the last decades of the nineteenth century, see Thomas, "The Soul of Man Under Socialism." Thomas also draws an explicit connection between the Fabians, especially Sydney Olivier, Shaw, Morris (see especially p. 93 n. 10) and Wilde; and he deals with sources cited by other Wilde critics but which he considers spurious, like Godwin, Kropotkin, and Chuang-tze. Masolino D'Amico, on the other hand, sees Kropotkin's anarchism as the major source of Wilde's formulation of individualism. D'Amico traces socialist references and sympathies in Wilde's major works and concludes that he was more anarchist than socialist. See D'Amico, "Between Socialism and Aestheticism."

There is no question but that Wilde's socialism includes elements of the strange miscellany characterizing the socialist and labor platforms of the last 25 years of the nineteenth century: the Marxists of the Socialist Democratic Federation; the Fellowship of the New Life, modeled on the American transcendentalists; William Morris's Socialist League; the Fabians; the Independent Labour Party; and the ethical idealists like Edward Carpenter.[25] The religious and ethical socialism of Ruskin's Guild of St. George had been increasingly exposed for what it was: a paternalistic return to harmonious master-servant relations, intended to solve the class conflict brought about by competition and the cash nexus.[26] Unlike Ruskin, Wilde and others were not content to make of the laborer a glorified beast of burden, although they were not always in agreement about the alternatives.

"The Soul of Man" combines elements from many of these representative versions of socialism, as well as remnants of Renan's primitive, revolutionary Christianity in *The Life of Jesus*, a book Wilde admired throughout his life. Wilde had learned their language and catch phrases as well as Blatchford would for *Merrie England* (1894). Nor is there any question but that Wilde was sympathetic to socialism.[27] Although he was not actively involved with the various socialist and labor programs, his sympathies with those who were extended considerably beyond his youthful admiration of, and later friendship with, Morris.

Yet beyond Wilde's socialism, his essay presents a more significant attack on the fin-de-siècle culture industry, and this is where he perfects Arnold's tactics against the press he despises. Shaw blasted Wilde's "snobbery" in declaiming against the vulgarity of the British journalist in a manner, he said, that displayed "the odious feeling that is itself the vilest vulgarity."[28] Yet Shaw was among the minority of progressive and radical thinkers in not attacking the press. In *News from Nowhere*, published just before "The Soul of Man" and undoubtedly influential on Wilde's work, Morris presented a fantasy of a perfect socialist community set in England in 2050 A.D. The time-traveller William "Guest" hears from an old man that the nineteenth-century press was almost entirely reactionary. Only through a general strike that prevented publication and the defection of one sole courageous editor to the side of the revolution did the revolutionaries gain control of the papers and institute the great "Change," or socialism. Given the British press, good news came from nowhere.

Part of this concern with the language of the media may be attributable to the free speech movement of the time, which linked radicals and socialists and had

[25]See Rowbotham and Weeks, *Socialism*, pt. I, secs. 2–5; and Hobsbawm, *Labour's Turning Point*.

[26]Although recent critics (e.g., Ellmann and Ericksen) frequently emphasize the effect of Ruskin's social thought on Wilde, the latter's contemporaries saw Wilde as much more radical than his alleged master. See Sherard, *Life of Oscar Wilde*, pp. 129–31.

[27]The debate over the "sincerity" of Wilde's socialism in "The Soul of Man" is aged and prolific. For an example of the opposing sides see George Woodcock, "The Social Rebel," in Ellmann, *Wilde: Critical Essays*, pp. 150–68, and Ericksen, *Oscar Wilde*, pp. 90–95. In "Irony of a Socialist Aesthete" (*Crazy Fabric*, pp. 138–50), A. E. Dyson considers Wilde's socialism as well as his oblique style.

[28]Pearson, *Wilde: Life and Wit*, p. 152.

organized demonstrations like what came to be called "Bloody Sunday" (13 November 1887) in Trafalgar Square. Part was due to cultural critics like Arnold, whose success in publicizing the press's corruption of language was considerable. As early as 1844 Engels had noticed that the English language was "permeated" by the ideology of the bourgeoisie.

> Even the English language is permeated by the one idea that dominates the waking hours of the bourgeoisie. People are "valued" in terms of hard cash. They say of a man: "He is worth £10,000," and by that they mean that he possesses that sum. Anyone who has money is "respectable." He belongs to "the better sort of people." He is said to be "influential," which means that what he says carried weight in the circles in which he moves. The spirit of petty bargaining permeates the whole language.[29]

Although in his 1892 preface to the English edition of *The Condition of the Working Class in England,* Engels disparaged Wilde's socialism, which "has not only become respectable, but has actually donned evening dress and lounges lazily on drawing-room *caseuses,*" even in 1844 he had begun to perceive the distortion of language or rigidification of bourgeois ideology in the press that Wilde considered a threat to art and liberty. In its use of middle-class newspapers, Engels's method, like Wilde's, had been to subvert the speech of his adversaries. "Charity," Engels raves, continuing the passage above on language, "—when he who gives is more degraded than he who receives. Charity—when the recipient is trodden even deeper into the mud than he was before. Charity—when those who dispense alms insist that those who receive them must first be cast out of society as pariahs and must be deprived of their last shred of self respect by being *forced to beg!*" "I enjoy," he writes, "making my opponents provide me with evidence."[30] "Charity," Wilde writes in "The Soul of Man," "creates a multitude of sins."

For this kind of language, which deconstructed bourgeois categories of thought, one might use the term "dialogical." In *Problems of Dostoevsky's Poetics,* Bakhtin cites Wilde—from Wilde's reviews of Dostoevsky—as one of the first readers to accurately understand Dostoevsky's most significant contribution to literary modernism, that is, what Bakhtin terms the "inner unfinalizability" of Dostoevsky's characters.[31] Bakhtin calls this quality "dialogicality" or "polyphonism," as opposed to the monologicality of traditional novels. Through his characters, Dostoevsky is multi-voiced, dialogic; all views are enunciated in dialogue between characters or in a character's dialogue with itself. In the case of a character's dialogue with itself, Bakhtin cites the phenomenon of "double-voiced words," in which an interior monologue consists of rephrasing and altering the words of an external adversary. The heroes in Dostoevsky *are* their ideas, but these ideas are constantly in flux, "unfinalizable." Bakhtin contends that previous readers have finalized (or "monologized") this openness by trying to identify the man

[29]Engels, *Condition of the Working Class,* pp. 312–13.
[30]Ibid., pp. 370, 313–14, 82.
[31]Bakhtin, *Dostoevsky's Poetics,* p. 234.

Dostoevsky (the man with social and religious beliefs) with certain of his characters, and then by "dialoging" with a particular character as if it represented the
views of Dostoevsky. This dialogicality of double-voiced words amounts formally
to what Debord calls the revolutionary and dialectical style of diversion, the style
connecting Hegel, Feuerbach, and Marx.

In creating his characters as generating subjects rather than finalized objects or
finished products, Dostoevsky's works posed significant alternatives to society as
he saw it as well as to previous literature. Like Bakhtin's "double-voiced" words,
Wilde's epigrams and paradoxes exploit the self-critical possibilities of Victorian
language and thought patterns. As Debord writes:

> Diversion leads to the subversion of past critical conclusions which were frozen into
> respectable truths, namely transformed into lies. . . . It is the obligation of *distance*
> toward what was falsified into official truth which determines the use of diversion. . . .
> Ideas improve. The meaning of words participates in the improvement. Plagiarism is
> necessary. Progress implies it. It embraces an author's phrase, makes use of his expres-
> sions, erases a false idea, and replaces it with the right idea. Diversion is the opposite of
> quotation . . . [which is] a fragment torn from its context, from its movement, and ulti-
> mately from the global framework of its epoch. . . . Diversion is the fluid language of
> anti-ideology.[32]

In addition, the larger forms of Wilde's essays are dialogical. "The Truth of
Masks" proposes and defends a theory of dramatic coherence and interpretation
only to conclude with Wilde's disavowal of the theory: "Not that I agree with
everything that I have said in this essay. There is much with which I entirely disagree. The essay simply represents an artistic standpoint, and in aesthetic criticism
attitude is everything. . . . It is only in art-criticism, and through it, that we can
realize Hegel's system of contraries." "The Portrait of Mr. W. H." presents a dialogical production of a theory through three separate advocates, and the narrator's
ambivalence at the end emphasizes its unfinalizability. And "Pen, Pencil, and
Poison" is an ironic, or double-voiced, treatment of the art/life dichotomy.

In "The Soul of Man Under Socialism" Wilde focuses directly on the press's
distortions of language—its "respectable truths"—and employs wit to subvert
their bourgeois meanings, using, as had Arnold, the language he is criticizing. The
first part of the tract argues against current notions of philanthropy, individualism,
and the Christian virtues. "Altruism" or otherness, it turns out, is a mere distortion
of language in a society based on competition rather than cooperation:

> With admirable though misdirected intentions, [altruists] very seriously and very senti-
> mentally set themselves to the task of remedying the evils that they see. But their reme-
> dies do not cure the disease: they merely prolong it. Indeed, their remedies are part of
> the disease.
>
>   They try to solve the problem of poverty, for instance, by keeping the poor alive or, in
> the case of a very advanced school, by amusing the poor.

[32]Debord, *Society of the Spectacle*, pp. 206–8.

> But this is not a solution: it is an aggravation of the difficulty. *The proper aim is to try and reconstruct society on such a basis that poverty will be impossible.* . . . Charity creates a multitude of sins. . . . It is immoral to use private property in order to alleviate the horrible evils that result from the institution of private property.

With such subversive phrases as "Charity creates a multitude of sins," "In the interest of the rich we must get rid of private property," "Disobedience is man's original virtue," and "Democracy is the bludgeoning of the people by the people for the people," Wilde cheerfully advocates agitators, demagogues, and violence for the temporary relief of the poor. In the long run, all authority must be abolished altogether.

But Wilde argues that the tyranny exercised by journalists over public opinion is the worst sort of tyranny, for "the pen is mightier than the paving-stone, and can be made as offensive as the brickbat." To return to words "their proper and simple meanings," their "right signification," he wields his tricks of paradox. One such use is his treatment of the word "unpractical," which the popular press frequently applied to utopian schemes such as his:

> It will of course be said that such a scheme as is set forth here is quite unpractical, and goes against human nature. This is perfectly true. It is unpractical, and it goes against human nature. This is why it is worth carrying out, and that is why one proposes it. For what is a practical scheme? *A practical scheme is either a scheme that is already in existence, or a scheme that could be carried out under existing conditions.* But it is exactly the existing conditions that one objects to; and any scheme that could accept these conditions is wrong and foolish. The conditions will be done away with, and human nature will change. . . . The systems that fail are those that rely on the permanency of human nature, and not on its growth and development.

In "Pen, Pencil, and Poison: A Study in Green," Wilde included in his attack the current art world as well as the press, again using the institutional style to criticize the institution. He ironically parodies a topical genre, aesthetic appreciations of bizarre, perverse, often criminal, historical figures, in order to indicate the art world's incriminating engagement with culture. In doing so, he confirms the impossibility of separating creation from criticism, doing from talking, and, ultimately, life from art.

By the 1870s, novelists and dramatists had exhausted the material in the *Newgate Calendar,* the last nineteenth-century edition of which was published in 1845. First published in 1773, the calendar offered memoirs of notorious malefactors and transcriptions of their last exclamations, generally from the scaffold. Bulwer Lytton and Harrison Ainsworth were only the most prominent of novelists who ransacked its pages for material on burglary, highway robbery, swindling, and murder, and they were imitated by hack novelists as well as dramatists, who plagued the censors with law-defying brigands like Jack Sheppard. The Newgate novel and drama, sensational permutations of the historical romance that were suspected by the authorities of making crime attractive to the young and ambitious, were eventually superseded by contemporary accounts of murder readily available in all gruesome detail in the press.[33] In "Pen, Pencil, and Poison," however, Wilde was not so concerned with popular forms of literature and drama as he was with their offspring, the critical appreciations of criminals, which claimed more objective status and more psychological subtlety. That is, the essay is directed against academic, as well as popular, representatives of the art world.

Critics have always interpreted "Pen, Pencil, and Poison," Wilde's aesthetic appreciation of the artist and murderer Thomas Griffiths Wainewright, as forwarding Wilde's alleged view that ethical judgments have no place in assessments of art works, that art works are autonomous objects of beauty independent of spectatorial exigencies. Recently Lance Morrow in *Time* magazine used the conclusion of Wilde's essay—"The fact of a man being a poisoner is nothing against his prose"— to represent Mailer's defense of Jack Abbott.[34] Yet this interpretation, imputing to Wilde a simplicity and transparency entirely uncharacteristic, is wrong; the key passages of the essay containing authorial comment are best understood as ironic.

First, Wilde suggests that the aesthetic, impressionist, or Paterian school of criticism mystified the past, that is, that critics primarily concerned with art and artists obfuscated certain unconscionable facts of history in order to justify their own sense of the primacy of art. Second, he says explicitly that although such an obfuscation of history may have been attractive, it was dangerous for the present. Third, he demystifies "gentlemen" of the present, exposing their own pose of "culture" as historically linked with "criminal" behavior. And finally, he undercuts art as a bearer of absolute value and takes artists to task for their lack of critical, that is, dialogical, perspective. It is increasingly clear that the essay is ironic if we also consider the view advanced in every other of Wilde's essays, that art should be normative, and if we also remember that Wilde, unlike some of his French and English contemporary "decadents," never once wrote a story or scenario without a "moral." (*The Importance of Being Earnest* is a possible exception. The obscurity of the moral here has, for some, redeemed Wilde as a modern writer.)

The essay begins benignly enough with the observation that artists and men of letters generally lack wholeness and completeness of nature. "This must necessarily be so," writes Wilde, "for that very concentration of vision and intensity of purpose which is the characteristic of the artistic temperament is in itself a mode of limitation." As the essay progresses, the emphasis will fall increasingly on the limitations. Here Wilde introduces apparent exceptions: Rubens serving as ambassador, Goethe as state councillor, Milton as Latin secretary to Cromwell, Sophocles in civic office, American artists as diplomatic representatives—and Wainewright, "being not merely a poet and a painter, an art-critic, an antiquarian, and a writer of prose, an amateur of beautiful things, and a dilettante of things delightful, but also a forger of no mean or ordinary capabilities, and as a subtle and secret poisoner almost without rival in this or any age." The conjunction of the

---

[33] For a discussion of the Newgate drama and its sources in popular fiction, see Stephens, *Censorship*.

[34] "The Poetic License to Kill," *Time*, 1 Feb. 1982, p. 82.

lawless Wainewright and accepted geniuses who were also civil servants anticipates the link between art, or "culture," and crime that will later surface as the
dominant view of the essay.

Throughout the biographical summary of Wainewright's occupations and avo-
cations, there are equally remarkable elisions between his art and criminality:
"Indeed, painting was the first art that fascinated him. It was not till much later
that he sought to find expression by pen or poison"; and "However, we must not
forget that the cultivated young man who penned these lines, and who was so susceptible to Wordsworthian influences, was also, as I said at the beginning of this
memoir, one of the most subtle and secret poisoners of this or any age." Wilde
deftly juxtaposes Wainewright's poisoning of his sister-in-law with the drawing he
made of his victim: "After the doctor's morning visit, Mr. and Mrs. Wainewright
brought her some poisoned jelly, and then went out for a walk. When they
returned Helen Abercrombie was dead. She was about twenty years of age, a tall
graceful girl with fair hair. A very charming red-chalk drawing of her by her
brother-in-law is still in existence, and shows how much his style as an artist was
influenced by Sir Thomas Lawrence. . . ." When Wainewright gratuitously poisons
a friend, Wilde mentions his immediate embarkation on a sketching tour: "His
friend died the next day in his presence, and he left Boulogne at once for a sketching tour through the most picturesque parts of Brittany." And art and crime are
again linked, with more general culpability, when "Dickens, Macready, and
Hablot Browne came across [Wainewright] by chance" in jail: "They had been
going over prisons of London, searching for artistic effects, and in Newgate they
suddenly caught sight of Wainewright. He met them with a defiant stare, Forster
tells us, but Macready was 'Horrified to recognize a man familiarly known to him
in former years, and at whose table he had dined.' "

Wilde's prolonged, controlled discussion of Wainewright's art, with its casual
but insistent repetition of its customary result in murder, produces in readers,
depending upon their mood, either a gleeful recognition of Wilde's masterly use of
irony, the master trope, or a mad, nightmarish sensation, rather like that produced
by Swift's "Modest Proposal." In neither case can one take the essay as a defense
of the autonomy of art, despite the fact that bourgeois art critics have done so for a
century. Like "A Modest Proposal," Wilde's essay builds a case, through irony,
against specialization (including a specialized "art world"), the division of labor,
scientific standards, and, in this case, journalism.

> If we set aside his achievements in the sphere of poison, what he has actually left to us
> hardly justifies his reputation. But then it is only the Philistine who seeks to estimate a
> personality by the vulgar test of production.

> The fact of a man being a poisoner is nothing against his prose. The domestic virtues are
> not the true bases of art, though they may serve as an excellent advertisement for sec-
> ond-rate artists.

> [Historical felons] have passed into the sphere of art and science, and neither art nor sci-
> ence knows anything of moral approval or disapproval.

The exotic aura with which Wilde surrounds Wainewright, his strange room and library, his fascination with cats and hermaphrodites, Wilde's repetition of "strange," "mysterious," "fascinating," also suggest a parody of the Paterian school of criticism. At the conclusion of the essay Wilde ironically remarks that had Wainewright lived during a more distant time, we might have been better able to assess his aesthetic work: "It is impossible not to feel a strong prejudice against a man who might have poisoned Lord Tennyson, or Mr. Gladstone, or the Master of Balliol. But had the man worn a costume and spoken a language different from our own, had he lived in imperial Rome, or at the time of the Italian Renaissance, or in Spain in the seventeenth century, or in any land or any century but this century and this land, we would be quite able to arrive at a perfectly unprejudiced estimate of his position and value."

Also ironically, Wilde goes on to disclaim any moral judgments applied to history or to history as represented through art, saying that we need not judge Tiberius or Cæsar Borgia because we no longer fear them. But the corollary of this is that we must judge what we fear. And since we fear Wainewright as one of our own contemporaries, he should not be the subject of "charming studies":

> At present I feel that he is just a little too modern to be treated in that fine spirit of disinterested curiosity to which we owe so many charming studies of the great criminals of the Italian Renaissance from the pens of Mr. John Addington Symonds, Miss A. Mary Robinson, Miss Vernon Lee, and other distinguished writers. However, Art has not forgotten him. He is the hero of Dickens's *Hunted Down*, the Varney of Bulwer's *Lucretia;* and it is gratifying to note that fiction has paid some homage to one who was so powerful with "pen, pencil, and poison." To be suggestive for fiction is to be of more importance than a fact.

That last sentence, a statement that critics have read solemnly, is ironic, as are Wilde's praises of "charming studies" of Renaissance criminals. The pen and pencil, he suggests, are poison.

Wilde himself is critical of his object, and he does not hesitate to demystify Wainewright's false status as an artist—while he simultaneously identifies him with the journalists who have brought his kind of "art" up to the present. He deftly exposes Wainewright's (and by extension others') artistic "sensitivity": "His delicately strung organization, however indifferent it might have been to inflicting pain on others, was itself most keenly sensitive to pain." He is suspicious of Wainewright's status as an artist: "His life-work falls naturally under the three heads suggested by Mr. Swinburne [pen, pencil, and poison], and it may be partly admitted that, if we set aside his achievements in the sphere of poison, what he has actually left to us hardly justified his reputation." He quotes at length from Wainewright's impressionistic art criticism and says of it that "there is much that is terrible, and very much that is quite horrible, but it is not without a certain crude form of power, or at any rate, a certain crude violence of words, a quality which this age should highly appreciate, as it is its chief defect."

In fact, the most that Wilde can say of Wainewright's "art" is that it is the Ur-form of modern sensational journalism; and far from presenting the object as it really was, Wainewright's gorgeous style, like that of Wilde's own contemporary impressionistic critics, concealed and mystified the object: "One side of his literary career deserves especial notice. Modern journalism may be said to owe almost as much to him as to any man of the early part of this century. He was the pioneer of Asiatic prose, and delighted in pictorial epithets and pompous exaggerations. To have a style so gorgeous that it conceals the subject is one of the highest achievements of an important and much admired school of Fleet Street leader-writers." Wilde adds that if we are to make a literary spectacle of Wainewright, it should be for his crime of journalism: "There is, however, something dramatic in the fact that this heavy punishment [for forgery] was inflicted on him for what, if we remember his fatal influence on the prose of modern journalism, was certainly not the worst of all his sins."

Wilde claims that the fascination of respectable critics and artists with criminals is indivisible from and implicated in their own personalities—a recurrent Wildean claim for the Unconscious against the progressive moral cant of the day—and that their own perverse personalities quite frequently falsify their subjects: "M. Zola, in one of his novels, tells us of a young man who, having committed a murder, takes to art, and paints greenish impressionist portraits of perfectly respectable people, all of which bear a curious resemblance to his victim." Similarly, Wainewright's "cultured," gentlemanly qualities, like those of many of Dickens's gentlemen, are merely a shiny veneer to cover his crimes. Wainewright reportedly told a visitor to his jail cell, which "was for some time a kind of fashionable lounge": "But, sir, I will tell you one thing in which I have succeeded to the last. I have been determined through life to hold the position of a gentleman. I have always done so. I do so still. It is the custom of this place that each of the inmates of a cell shall take his morning's turn of sweeping it out. I occupy a cell with a bricklayer and a sweep, but they never offer me the broom!"

Wilde stresses that in fact the only thing that makes Wainewright interesting to gentlemen is that he was a "cultured" man who sinned through leisure. In this way Wilde leaves the critics with the uncomfortable association of crime and their own class rather than with the lower class and its uninteresting criminality that resulted from poverty: "From Newgate he was brought to the hulks at Portsmouth, and sent from there in the *Susan* to Van Diemen's Land along with three hundred other convicts. The voyage seems to have been most distasteful to him, and in a letter written to a friend he spoke bitterly about the ignominy of 'the companion of poets and artists' being compelled to associate with 'country bumpkins.' The phrase that he applied to his companions need not surprise us. Crime in England is rarely the result of sin. It is nearly always the result of starvation."

Finally, in a notorious concluding statement, Wilde says that crime constitutes a large part of the aesthetic past and that present fascination with this past indicated the conservative function of the art world: "That [Wainewright] had a sincere love of art and nature seems to me quite certain. There is no essential incongruity between crime and culture." (Earlier in the decade Wilde had lectured in Boston on "that dreadful record of crime known as history," admonishing parents of undergraduates that "You give the criminal calendar of Europe to your children under the name of history."[35]) That is, men of "culture" had justified their own culture by mystifying the past, by taking Wainewright's gaudy career as the object of art rather than by seeing the larger movements of history (like the colonial deportation of 300 starving convicts) and offering a solution or alternative to these. That "there is no essential incongruity between crime and culture" is understatement: it accused culture, just as many critical "appreciations" valorized crime. The cultured man's "very concentration of vision and intensity of purpose" amounts to a limited conception of social life and a dangerously isolated egocentrism. The essay becomes a critique of what is commonly understood to be *l'art pour l'art*.

In a striking contrast, "The Portrait of Mr. W. H." presents a meaningful and engaged, indeed a seductive, art, an art not criminal, in a very dramatic form. At the same time the essay is a satire on standards of evidence and proof in a scientific, utilitarian age and a kind of parable of the loss of faith—for Wilde, imagination—in the nineteenth century. In the sensational conclusion to the essay, the skeptical narrator cries out, "To die for one's theological opinions is the worst use a man can make of his life; but to die for a literary theory! It seemed impossible." Yet "The Portrait of Mr. W. H." is a story of two characters who die for their belief in a literary theory that is never proven and of the narrator who finally thinks that there is "really a great deal to be said" for that theory.

Erskine, an older man, tells the young narrator the history of his friend Cyril Graham, a boy actor who invented a theory that the Mr. W. H. to whom Shakespeare's Sonnets were dedicated was a boy actor named Willie Hughes. Graham's theory was based on purely "internal evidence," that is, evidence within the Sonnets themselves—although for the reader the term "internal evidence" will have increasing relevance to the internality of the theorists. Despite Graham's extensive exegesis and intense desire that it persuade Erskine, his friend, a hard-headed rationalist, remained skeptical, insisting that the theory assumed the existence of the Willie Hughes that it had intended to prove; he demanded "independent evidence." Cyril Graham consequently had a portrait forged of W. H., by which he finally persuaded Erskine. By chance, however, Erskine detected the fraud, had words with Graham, and Graham, in a state of extreme abjection, killed himself as a final testimony to his belief in the theory.

The narrator is convinced by Graham's theory and goes off to lock himself up with the Sonnets to develop it further, despite Erskine's admonition that "a thing is not necessarily true because a man dies for it." He considerably expands the theory, and at this point Wilde's text is saturated with quotations from the Sonnets. Through Willie Hughes, the narrator comes to understand Shakespeare's theory of drama; he writes a history of English boy actors of the sixteenth and seven-

[35]Pearson, *Wilde: Life and Wit*, p. 58.

teenth centuries; he discovers the relationship of Shakespeare and Willie Hughes to the Dark Lady; and he finally comprehends the actual "drama" of the Sonnets.

He writes the expanded theory to Erskine, but in the process he loses his belief. That is, once he extracts himself from the absorbing drama to produce an argument, the unilateral form of rhetoric reduces the theory to one polemic among many. As such, it is exposed to the sorts of rational constraints that are expected of theories—for example, that they not assume the thing they are to prove. Erskine, however, is now persuaded and, agitated by the narrator's admission that he had assumed all of what he intended to prove, removes himself to Germany, where the narrator had speculated that Willie Hughes died. Failing to find proof in Germany, Erskine writes to the narrator that he intends to offer his own life as the second martyrdom to the theory. The narrator rushes off to prevent the suicide, but arrives after Erskine has died. He learns that Erskine had not killed himself at all, but had expected for some time to die of consumption. The narrator inherits the forged portrait, but skeptically echoes Erskine to Cyril Graham to the effect that the "pathetic fallacy" of martyrdom proves nothing, that it "is merely a tragic form of scepticism, an attempt to realise by fire what one had failed to do by faith." But sometimes, alone in his library with the forged portrait, the narrator thinks that "there really is a great deal to be said for the Willie Hughes theory of Shakespeare's Sonnets."

The argument here is not only in favor of other truths than the scientific, which Wilde had argued in "The Truth of Masks," but it also opposes Wilde's version of hermeneutics to the public and journalistic value of objectivity. "For in art," "The Truth of Masks" concludes, "there is no such thing as a universal truth. A Truth in art is that whose contradictory is also true. . . . It is only in art-criticism, and through it, that we can realize Hegel's system of contraries. The truths of metaphysics are the truths of masks."[36] It is precisely his belief in interpretation, or the practice of criticism, that prevents the divorce, despite his contempt for the public, between art and life. The hermeneutic was contained in "The Decay of Lying": "There may have been fogs for centuries in London. I dare say there were. But no one saw them, and so we do not know anything about them. They did not exist till Art had invented them. Now, it must be admitted, fogs are carried to excess. They have become the mere mannerism of a clique, and the exaggerated realism of their method gives dull people bronchitis. Where the cultured catch an effect, the uncultured catch cold."

"The Portrait of Mr. W. H." presents a theory that Wilde understood to be no more than a fanciful construction answerable to the private exigencies of his own personality. Not only did it confront bourgeois standards of truth, it also affronted professional standards of originality and honesty, for it is a plagiarism, having been

---

[36]Wilde's 1880s commonplace book of notes, now at the Clark Library, indicates his familiarity with Kant and Hegel, with the then current debates between metaphysics and positivism, and his own conclusion that studies in metaphysics should be revised as studies in method, that metaphysics should be limited to metacriticism.

first advanced in 1766 by a Shakespearean scholar named Thomas Tyrwhitt and then duly incorporated in Malone's 1780 edition of *The Poems of Shakespeare*. Moreover, in the *Woman's World* of September 1888, Wilde had edited an article by Amy Strachey entitled "The Child-Players of the Elizabethan Age," from which he had also borrowed significantly. As Debord says, a dialectical and historicizing plagiarism is necessary for progress, and Wilde is clearly using Tyrwhitt's theory in the service of his own freedom.

In the introduction to his anthology of Victorian texts dealing with homosexual subjects, Brian Reade places this as the first short story in English to dwell upon pederasty, although Sir Richard Burton had already called Shakespeare "that most debauched genius" in his "Terminal Essay," the history of pederasty, to his translation of *The Book of the Thousand Nights and a Night* (1885).[37] Significantly, Wilde's essay begins with Erskine and the narrator, a much younger man, discussing literary forgeries. The narrator claims that "all Art being to a certain degree a mode of acting, an attempt to realize one's own personality on some imaginative plane out of reach of the trammeling accidents and limitations of real life, to censure an artist for a forgery [is] to confuse an ethical with an aesthetic argument." In the story, the characters enact this notion that the experience of art, for spectator as well as artist, is a kind of forgery. After working out the "drama" of Shakespeare's Sonnets, the narrator will say, "I had lived it all." In "The Critic as Artist," Gilbert calls literary criticism "the highest form of autobiography": "give the artist a mask, and he will tell you the truth." And Wilde does tell the truth in the story, realized "on some imaginative plane."

Erskine, Cyril, and the narrator seek themselves and their own homoeroticism in Shakespeare's art. Erskine fails because he can only go as far as reason; he seeks external authority (facts) for artistic interpretation. Cyril recognizes and acknowledges his homoeroticism, he can trust "internal evidence," but he is too dependent upon Erskine's approbation; he seeks external authority in the other (the art world). The narrator believes and doubts at once, allowing himself a sort of conscious repression, unfinalizability, or, if you will, a willing suspension of disbelief. He does not act on what he learns of Shakespeare and his boy, but he contemplates the portrait alone in his library and sometimes thinks that "there really is a great deal to be said for the Willie Hughes theory of Shakespeare's Sonnets." He also shows the forged portrait to his friends as a test of either their gullibility or seducibility: "They have decided that it is not a Clouet, but an Ouvry."[38]

At this point one need hardly say that as he composed "The Portrait of Mr. W. H." in conversations with Robert Ross, Wilde was practically concerned with what the narrator calls "the ambiguity of the sexes." He was meeting with a number of young actors; and, if Croft-Cooke is right in his characterization of Wilde's emotional make-up, he was much like his own picture of Willie Hughes: "He could act love, but could not feel it, could mimic passion without realising it."

---

[37]Reade, *Sexual Heretics*, pp. 47, 160n. For the "Terminal Essay," see Burton, *Thousand Nights*, vol. 10, pp. 63–302.

[38]I have come to this analysis of homoeroticism in "The Portrait of Mr. W. H." with the help of Ira Livingston in my Decadents and Aesthetes Seminar, Stanford University, autumn 1984.

The narrator writes that the creative energy of art is "objective," whereas such scomingly "real," substantial attributes as sex are "mere accidents"; this is consistent with Wilde's characteristic devaluation of science. The narrator also surmises that Willie Hughes died in Germany, having brought "the Romantic Movement," equal to playacting or imaginative posing, into that land; and Vivian had heralded "the return of Romance" in "The Decay of Lying." The idea that Shakespeare had worked out his theory of the drama in his Sonnets is duplicated in Wilde's working out his theory of the drama in "The Portrait of Mr. W. H." The Sonnets become a drama of Shakespeare's life, and "Mr. W. H." is also a drama, in five acts, dramatizing Wilde's theories of art and love.

Two bizarre notes to the story indicate the extent to which Wilde's fiction affected the lives of real boys for a half-century and thus the extent to which Wilde succeeded in creating an audience, fit though few. John Moray Stuart-Young's long poem *Osrac, the Self-Sufficient* (1905) is prefaced by two forged photographs: one of Johnnie, signed "Yours sincerely J. M. Stuart-Young," holding a volume of Wilde's *Poems,* and one of Wilde, bearing the forged autograph "Oscar Wilde to Johnnie September 1894." The epigraph to the poem is *"Rien n'est vrai que le beau."*[39] The homosexual Johnnie apparently fabricated a relationship with his much-admired master, Wilde, as Wilde had fabricated a precedent relationship between Shakespeare and Willie Hughes. Moreover, Johnnie went on in *Osrac, the Self-Sufficient* to attribute Wilde's downfall to what the boy considered his own downfall to have been: masturbation, or "the witchery of the hand"—hence "self-sufficient." Johnnie's own eventual prison sentence even further enforced his identification with his idol.

Perhaps not surprisingly, it was Wilde's own dear boy who proved—at least to the satisfaction of many of his contemporaries, including Shaw—the theory of Shakespeare's boy that Wilde had taught him and that Erskine had taught the young narrator. In 1933 Alfred Douglas published the *True History of Shakespeare's Sonnets,* the research for which, he claimed, destroyed his eyesight. In Part I, as well as in his unpublished letters to Adrian Earle, Douglas explains that whereas Wilde did not acknowledge his predecessors Tyrwhitt and Malone, and whereas Samuel Butler, who "spent years of his life trying to find a Will Hewes," did not acknowledge Wilde, Douglas acknowledges them all and adds his own touches to the theory.

Although Douglas's book still relied on "internal" evidence, after it was published he acquired the evidence that everyone but Wilde had sought. In a letter to Earle of 18 August 1942, he wrote that reference to a William Hewes had been discovered in the archives in Canterbury: he had been a freeman by apprenticeship to John Marlowe (Christopher's father), shoemaker, in 1593. Hence Willie Hughes's connection to Marlowe's and Shakespeare's companies. A scholar had read Douglas's book, recalled something he had seen in Canterbury, and Douglas had forthwith made the fruitful inquiries. Douglas's later correspondence with

---

[39]For a brief biography of the strange but enchanting John Moray Stuart-Young, see Appendix A in Smith, *Love in Earnest,* pp. 202–19.

Earle indicates that the young Earle and other devotees of the now aged Douglas continued to refine the theory. While its literalism at their hands entirely missed the point of Wilde's essay, its power of influence was right in its spirit.[40] An artistic community, of a sort, had been created.

In tracing alternatives, like "Mr. W. H.," to the institutional languages that Wilde inverted as a form of critique, "The Sphinx" is the summa of Wilde's art-as-seduction. Rather than the measured substitutions and inversions of wit, here the language is excessive and unrestrained, indiscriminate, not deriding an existing audience, but teasing an ideal one. In the poem the boy of hardly "twenty summers" ultimately banishes (represses) his uninnocent desires, but not without an excess of eroticism.

> In a dim corner of my room for longer than my fancy thinks
> A beautiful and silent Sphinx has watched me through the shifting gloom.

Whether these opening lines refer to an objet d'art or are entirely a product of the student's imagination, in the course of the poem that imagination destroys any illusions of innocence in the human psyche. Trying to imagine the (Paterian) Sphinx's "thousand weary centuries" of experience, the student exhausts a vocabulary of rhymes from a schoolboy's classics, depletes the excesses of school sexuality: Hieroglyphs/Hippogriffs, obelisks/Basilisks, Cyprian Kiss/Heliopolis, catafalque/ Amenalk, odorous/Antinous, corridors/Mandragores, sarcophagus/Tragelaphos, cubits' span/Kurdistan, new-made wine/insapphirine, Corybants/elephants, Nubians/peacock fans, Bedouin/paladin, striped burnous/Titan thews, figured coins/barren loins, amorous jests/agate breasts, and so forth.

"Inviolate and immobile," the Sphinx, clandestinely come to inhabit the student's "cell," suffers him to interrogate her about her lovers:

> Did Gryphons with great metal flanks leap on you in your trampled couch?
>
> Did monstrous hippopotami come sidling toward you in the mist?

As his imagination grows bolder, the student's queries become assertions.

> White Ammon was your bedfellow! Your chamber was the steaming Nile!

After hundreds of lines of this, he energetically encourages her to

> Follow some roving lion's spoor across the copper-coloured plain,
> Reach out and hale him by the mane and bid him be your paramour!
>
> And take a tiger for your mate, whose amber sides are flecked with black,
> And ride upon his gilded back in triumph through the Theban gate.

Under the delusion that his Sphinx is not his own imagination, he sends her packing; and with a gesture toward the deconstruction of Roman Catholicism in

---

[40]Douglas's correspondence with Adrian Earle is at the Clark Library, as are Shaw's letters on the matter of William Hewes.

the nineteenth century, he repositions his meditation on another objet d'art, his crucifix,

> Whose pallid burden, sick with pain, watches the world with wearied eyes,
> And weeps for every soul that dies, and weeps for every soul in vain.

In exhibiting "The Sphinx" in standard accounts of the subject as the quintessentially decadent poem—in the sense of exhausted, erethistic, and esoteric—critics have overlooked the fact that it is a very funny and very sexy piece: it should be read among friends, like many of John Ashbery's new poems with equally clunky rhythms. Part of its charm lies in the generosity of the poet who pours into the ear of his beloved a ten-year treasure trove of research in improbable rhymes, a textbook-complete catalogue, as Ira Livingston has put it, of polymorphous perversity. The poem is a poem of excess in the sense that the object of desire is technically absent; the desire compulsively flows from the subject's brain. But the consummate mastery, the *style*, of having the shy beloved *seduce himself* must be admired.

"To Marcel Schwob in friendship and admiration" Wilde dedicated the poem. Although he began the poem at Oxford sometime in 1874–76, he did not finish it until he was in Paris in 1883 and did not publish it until 1894. Since he was 40 years old in 1894, hyperliteral critics ridiculed him for presenting himself as hardly having seen "some twenty summers." Yet Wilde was neither vain nor posing as an innocent. The student represents Schwob, a French symbolist writer, who was 16 when Wilde met him in Paris and 27 when the poem was published. In writing the poem, Wilde the seducer/Sphinx confronted the reticent student/Schwob with Schwob's own thinly repressed desires. That Schwob was at least theoretically seducible by this schoolboy chant is suggested by the fact that the most puerile of all insurrectional works of art, *Ubu Roi*, was also dedicated to him in 1896. Ada Leverson evidently penetrated the mystery as a Wildean strategy for seduction when she parodied the poem in *Punch* (21 July 1894) under the title "The Minx." More importantly for our thesis, Wilde himself drew the line between his public and private arts when he informed John Lane in 1892 that the poem could not be brought out in a popular or cheap edition.[41]

A private art-as-seduction or a public diversion-as-critique were Wilde's options as engaged bourgeois artist. He employed both styles: one to criticize an irresponsible mass audience and the other to create an audience of intimates. "The Critic as Artist," which, like "The Decay of Lying," is set in a private library intentionally far from the madding crowd, presents the play of two men, again an older and a younger. The older man wants to play for the younger "a fantasy by Dvorak. He writes passionate, curiously-coloured things," but Ernest (the younger) wants him to "Turn round and talk to me. . . . There is something in your voice that is wonderful." Undoubtedly, the heightened purpleness of the prose throughout the lengthy dialogue is intended as a seduction, especially since the man with the mag-

---

[41]Wilde, *Letters*, p. 319.

ical voice will not be "degraded into the position of giving you useful information.
. . . Nothing that is worth knowing can be taught."

On the other hand, the thesis of "The Critic as Artist" is a political one: if everyone were a literary critic, no one would make war. Cultural criticism would render
invidious nationalism obsolete:

> It is Criticism that makes us cosmopolitan. The Manchester school tried to make men
> realize the brotherhood of humanity, by pointing out the commercial advantages of
> peace. It sought to degrade the wonderful world into a common marketplace for the
> buyer and the seller. It addressed itself to the lowest instincts, and it failed. . . . Criticism
> will annihilate race-prejudices, by insisting upon the unity of the human mind in the
> variety of its forms. If we are tempted to make war upon another nation, we shall
> remember that we are seeking to destroy an element of our own culture, and possibly its
> most important element. . . . [People] will not say "We will not war against France
> because her prose is perfect," but because the prose of France is perfect, they will not
> hate the land. Intellectual criticism will bind Europe together in bonds far closer than
> those that can be forged by shopman or sentimentalist. It will give us the peace that
> comes from understanding.

Understanding the importance of the culture industry as a transnational political force, Wilde both satirized and exploited it. Since journalism ruled, he became
a critic, but he insisted that his criticism was creative: "The highest criticism really
is the record of one's own soul. . . . I am always amused by the silly vanity of those
writers and artists of our day who seem to imagine that the primary function of the
critic is to chatter about their second-rate work." Since criticism had become a
profession, he opted for talking over acting, and finally, in a parody of Gramsci's
"traditional" intellectual, doing nothing at all. "I said to you some time ago that it
was far more difficult to talk about a thing than to do it. Let me say to you now that
to do nothing at all is the most difficult thing in the world, the most difficult and
the most intellectual." The lines are Gilbert's in "The Critic as Artist," in which the
subtitles indicate the importance of "doing nothing" and "discussing everything."
This is the philosophy of a dandy who is satirizing the pose of a gentleman: for
what a gentleman *was,* as A. Smythe Palmer wrote in *The Ideal of a Gentleman,*
was infinitely more significant than what he *did.*[42] ("Do you smoke?" Lady
Bracknell asks Jack. "Well, yes, I must admit I smoke." "I am glad to hear it. A man
should always have an occupation of some kind.") Short of any serious social
change as envisioned in "The Soul of Man under Socialism"—that is, short of any
real alliance between Gramsci's traditional intellectuals and "organic" intellectuals
in a productive or creative economy—seduction was the alternative to the slogans
and inversions of slogans.[43]

---

[42]Cited in Letwin, *Gentleman in Trollope*, p. 272 n. 32.
[43]See "The Intellectuals" in Gramsci, *Prison Notebooks*, esp. p. 18.

Oscar Wilde, W. H., and the Unspoken Name of Love

Lawrence Danson

Time: April 3, 1895. Scene: The Old Bailey. Edward Carson, Q.C., M.P., Counsel for the Marquess of Queensberry, questioning Oscar Wilde:

> Carson: I believe you have written an article to show that Shakespeare's sonnets were suggestive of unnatural vice?
>
> Wilde: On the contrary, I have written an article to show that they were not. I objected to such a perversion being put upon Shakespeare.[1]

I

It was one of his most daring paradoxes, the idea of a love between men that is not "unnatural," not "a perversion"; in 1895 it was a contradiction almost beyond the reach of language. What would you call it? Words that made sense in the Old Bailey, "sodomy," "buggery," and their cognates, were words of legal condemnation, implying "disgust, disgrace, vituperation."[2] The prison house of language wasn't all you had to fear if your love used those words to speak its name. There were other possibilities. The word "homosexuality," for instance, had been coined by a Swiss doctor in 1869. But in England in the nineties, "homosexuality" belonged to the discourse of science; it named a medical problem, and its truth was not yours. "Urning," "inversion," even Whitman's term "adhesiveness" were neologisms, "suggestive of" something strange and new.[3] But the desire they tried to name was as familiar and old as the world. Was there any language that would not falsify your desire—and Shakespeare's and Michelangelo's and Plato's—in the process of speaking it?

From *ELH* 58:4 (Winter 1991). Reprinted with permission of the Johns Hopkins University Press.

[1] H. Montgomery Hyde, ed. *The Trials of Oscar Wilde* (London: William Hodge, 1948), 130; hereafter referred to parenthetically as *Trials*.

[2] John Addington Symonds, *A Problem in Greek Ethics* (1883), reprinted in *Male Love*, ed. John Lauritsen (New York: Pegasus, 1983), 80.

[3] Jeffrey Weeks, *Coming Out: Homosexual Politics in Britain, from the Nineteenth Century to the Present* (London: Quartet Books, 1977), 1, 3, 14, 47, 55.

The article in question at the Old Bailey was "The Portrait of Mr. W. H."; Wilde published it in *Blackwood's Edinburgh Magazine* in 1889, and a century later it is still necessary to ask what it is "suggestive of," what it's all about. Wilde's story or essay or hoax—one hardly knows what to name *it*—poses a question about the representation of homosexual desire that is only partly bound to the particular circumstances of Victorian reticence and fear. And to that question I will return. In the first place, however, it is necessary to ask what "The Portrait of Mr. W. H." is about because the obvious answer (it's about Shakespeare's love for Mr. W. H., "the onlie begetter" of his sonnets) is radically undercut by the very narration that proposes it.

Wilde creates a daisy chain of converts and skeptics to tell his story, and the resulting self-subverting narrative enlists a tale of scholarly detection in the service of the indeterminate. Wilde's narrator hears from his friend Erskine the story of Cyril Graham, the beautiful boy who as an undergraduate acted to perfection the part of Rosalind and who later solved the mystery of Shakespeare's Sonnets. According to Cyril Graham, the "Mr. W. H." of the Sonnets' dedication was Willie Hughes, a boy player in Shakespeare's company, and the sonnets tell the story of their love. Erskine, unconvinced by Graham's theory, wanted "some independent evidence about the existence of this young actor."[4] So Graham gave him ocular proof, the portrait of Mr. W. H. But Erskine quickly discovered that the portrait was a forgery. Erskine lost his belief, and Cyril Graham committed suicide, a martyr to his theory about Shakespeare's love. Now the narrator, having heard Erskine's story of faith and fraud, inherits Graham's belief in the theory, and despite Erskine's warning that "there is nothing in the idea of Willie Hughes" (21) he takes up the cause. After further research he writes a letter to Erskine in which he puts "all my enthusiasm . . . all my faith," with the result that immediately "it seemed to me that I had given away my capacity for belief in the Willie Hughes theory of the Sonnets, that something had gone out of me, as it were" (80–81). Erskine, however, is reconverted by the very letter that drains the narrator of conviction, and he writes to the narrator that he intends to commit suicide as a sign of his faith. The narrator rushes to stop this second martyrdom but is too late: Erskine is dead, but not, it turns out, by his own hand. He died of consumption, his last evidence of faith another fraud.

In form, then, "The Portrait of Mr. W. H." denies as much as it affirms the theory it creates. What it really says or means to say about Shakespeare's love always remains inaccessible. Or does it? Most of Wilde's readers, then and now, think they know exactly what it says: that Shakespeare, like Oscar Wilde, loved boys and acted on that love. Every narrative denial is converted to affirmation in a reading process that we can also see at work in the proceedings at Wilde's trial. More famously, of course, such a process was at work in the reception of *The Picture of Dorian Gray*, published in magazine form the year following "The Portrait of Mr.

[4]Oscar Wilde, *The Portrait of Mr. W. H.*, ed. Vyvyan Holland (London: Methuen, 1958), 16. This is the revised text, and is hereafter referred to parenthetically as the expanded version.

W. H." By refusing to affirm anything, the novel denies nothing; for instance, we are told that Basil Hallward's love for Dorian "had nothing in it that was not noble and intellectual. It was not that mere physical admiration of beauty that is born of the senses and that dies when the senses tire."[5] Such negatives of direct statement can be subverted into sexual affirmations by the innuendos that made the novel a *succès de scandale*. For many of Wilde's readers "this rationalization of homosexual desire as aesthetic experience" (in Elaine Showalter's apt phrase) was merely a verbal fig leaf bulging with a phallic reality.[6] At Oxford in 1893 an undergraduate paper called *The Ephemeral* ran a mock "missing-word competition" with this puzzle:

> To . . . .
> He often writes of things with brazen candour
> *Non inter Christianos nominanda.*[7]

No one had trouble filling in the blank with the name "Oscar Wilde" or supplying "sodomy" in place of the unspeakable Latin.[8] Where or what then was the truth in Wilde's speaking about a desire he called "noble and intellectual" and the law called criminal? Do Wilde's verbal gestures in "The Portrait of Mr. W. H." point to heart and soul or to penis and anus? Not that these are exclusive choices, except in linguistic situations like the one I've just created. But in "The Portrait of Mr. W. H." Wilde very elaborately creates just such a situation of mutually-exclusive categories, and adds this further twist: his language demands a choice, but it also

---

[5]*The Picture of Dorian Gray*, in *Oscar Wilde*, ed. Isobel Murray (Oxford: Oxford Univ. Press, 1989), 136; hereafter referred to parenthetically as *DG*. Note also Carson's attempt at the first trial to make *Dorian Gray* and "Mr. W. H." reciprocally reveal each other's sodomitical reality, and to make both of them dependent on Wilde's own sexual nature: Carson quotes from *Dorian Gray* the phrase, "I quite admit that I adored you madly," and asks Wilde, "Have you ever adored a young man madly?" Wilde replies, "No, not madly; I prefer love. . . ." Carson: "Then you have never had that feeling?" Wilde: "No. The whole idea was borrowed from Shakespeare, I regret to say—yes, from Shakespeare's sonnets," which provokes the exchange with which I begin this essay: "I believe you have written an article to show that Shakespeare's sonnets were suggestive of unnatural vice?" (*Trials*, 129).

[6]Elaine Showalter, *Sexual Anarchy: Gender and Culture at the Fin de Siècle* (New York: Viking, 1990), 176.

[7]Stuart Mason, *Art and Morality: A Record of the Discussion which Followed the Publication of "Dorian Gray,"* 2nd ed. (London: Frank Palmer, 1912), 22. How explicitly *Dorian Gray* was supposed, by some readers, to speak the legally unspeakable is made painstakingly clear in the "Plea of Justification Filed by the Defendant" in Wilde's first trial, his libel suit against Queensberry. Queensberry charges that "the said Oscar Fingal O'Flahertie Wills Wilde in the month of July in the year of our Lord One thousand eight hundred and ninety did write and publish and cause and procure to be printed and published with his name upon the title page thereof a certain immoral and obscene work in the form of a narrative entitled 'The Picture of Dorian Gray' which said work was designed and intended by the said Oscar Fingal O'Flahertie Wills Wilde and was understood by the readers thereof to describe the relations intimacies and passions of certain persons of sodomitical and unnatural habits tastes and practices" (*Trials*, 344).

[8]Ed Cohen, "Writing Gone Wilde: Homoerotic Desire in the Closet of Representation," *PMLA* 102 (1987): 801–13, writes that "the aftermath of Wilde's trials has left no doubt in the critical mind that the 'immorality' of Wilde's text paralleled that of his life. Yet this critical reflection has never directly addressed the question of how Wilde's 'obviously' homoerotic text signifies its 'deviant' concerns while never explicitly violating the dominant norms for heterosexuality" (805).

makes either choice seem inadequate or wrong.[9] If we decode Wilde's denials into affirmations, we deliver his text into the hands of Mr. Justice Wills; and even if we do not share that eminent jurist's "utmost sense of indignation at the horrible charges brought home" to Wilde, still we have agreed with judge and jury about the facts that Wilde's text is at pains to deny (*Trials*, 339). But if we accept Wilde's denials, we not only convict ourselves of naivete; ironically, we still condone the court's judgment, by agreeing in effect that a sexual reading must be a peccant one. Any attempt to stop the play of Wilde's narrative and to say what it is *really* about will either demonize or neuter it.[10]

In "The Portrait of Mr. W. H.," then, Wilde tried to speak about homosexual desire by denying the language of his own speaking—always deferring the revelation the language promises, because that revelation, being *in* language, would necessarily falsify the truth. But Wilde's representative reader was Mr. Edward Carson, Q.C., M.P., lawyer for the Marquis of Queensberry, and Carson was not much interested in narrative indeterminacy.

Queensberry had also published an ambiguous text. On the eighteenth of February, 1895, he entered Wilde's club, the Albemarle, and handed the hall porter a visiting card addressed to Wilde. On the card his lordship (whose handwriting was not the best) seems to have written: "Oscar Wilde posing Somdomite," or as Wilde's counsel, Sir Edward Clarke, interpreted it, "Oscar Wilde posing as a sodomite."[11] Clarke provided his own exegesis of the offensive text:

> The words of [Queensberry's] accusation are not directly an accusation of the gravest of all offences—the suggestion is that there was no guilt of the actual offence, but that in some way or other the person of whom those words were written did appear—nay, desired to appear—and pose to be a person guilty of or inclined to the commission of the gravest of all offences.
>
> (*Trials*, 108)

Queensberry had chosen his words, if not spelled them, as carefully as Wilde habitually chose his. Between the signifier (Wilde's pose) and the signified ("the abominable crime of buggery with mankind" [*Trials*, 107]) there was a loophole big enough to drive a libel through. What may seem surprising, then, is that Carson largely ignored the loophole. He chose not to let his client slip

[9]Several recent authors interestingly take up the challenge of reading "The Portrait of Mr. W. H.": see Gerhard Joseph, "Framing Wilde," *Victorian Newsletter* 72 (1987): 61–63; William A. Cohen, "Willie and Wilde: Reading *The Portrait of Mr. W. H.*," *South Atlantic Quarterly* 88 (1989): 219–245, reprinted in *Displacing Homophobia: Gay Male Perspectives in Literature and Culture*, ed. Ronald R. Butters et al. (Durham: Duke Univ. Press, 1989), 207–33; and Kevin Kopelson, "Wilde, Barthes, and the Orgasmics of Truth," *Genders* 7 (1990): 22–31; Claude J. Summers, *Gay Fictions: Wilde to Stonewall, Studies in a Male Homosexual Literary Tradition* (New York: Ungar, 1990), 29–42.

[10]Richard Ellmann thinks that Wilde read Queensberry's text as "To Oscar Wilde, ponce and Somdomite," but that Queensberry actually wrote "To Oscar Wilde posing Somdomite," which Queensberry read in court as " 'posing as a Somdomite,' an easier accusation to defend" (*Oscar Wilde* [New York: Knopf, 1987], 438).

[11]See Lee Edelman, "Homographesis," *Yale Journal of Criticism* 3 (1989): 189–207, on "the gay body as text" bearing legible signs of its difference.

through the gap between seeming and being, signifier and signified; instead he brought them violently together. Where Wilde's lawyer, Clarke, read Queensberry's accusation symbolically, or as a medieval exegete might say, *in bono*—Wilde *posed* in the sense of seeming to be something he was not—Carson read it literally, or *in malo*—Wilde *posed* in the sense of extravagantly displaying what in fact he was. In order to imprison Wilde, Carson chose first to imprison language itself; he would capture language—not only Queensberry's but Wilde's too—within the court's strict construction, stripping it of its subversive indeterminacy.

So Carson's questioning of Wilde became a contest of hermeneutic principles, a battle over the protocols of reading. Carson appealed to the "common sense" of the "ordinary individual" who knows that where there's smoke there's fire. Wilde countered with the radically antimimetic and subjectivist philosophy of "The Decay of Lying" and "The Critic as Artist," proposing that language is its user's personal creation, not a common denominator, and that it creates its truth, rather than mimicking a truth that precedes it. In Carson's forensic reading, the Wildean text is transparent: Wilde posed as a sodomite; only a pervert would pose as a sodomite; the pose told the truth; and the truth was available for all to read. And books? Carson wants to know whether "a perverted novel might be a good book?" But Wilde does "not know what you mean by a 'perverted' novel":

> Carson: Then I will suggest *Dorian Gray* as open to the interpretation of being such a novel?
> Wilde: That could only be to brutes and illiterates. The views of Philistines on art are incalculably stupid.
> Carson: An illiterate person reading *Dorian Gray* might consider it such a novel?
> Wilde: The views of illiterates on art are unaccountable.
>
> (*Trials*, 124)

From Carson's point of view, illiterates can read perversion as well as anyone else. The truth of Wilde's test is open to all, and it is identical to the truth of Wilde's life.

Carson asks if it isn't true that "the affection and love of the artist of *Dorian Gray* might lead an ordinary individual to believe that it might have a certain tendency?" (*Trials*, 124). The phrase "a certain tendency" may seem as ambiguous as the passages in *Dorian Gray* it is meant to explicate; but Carson has faith that "an ordinary individual" will know precisely what is meant. The author of *Dorian Gray*, however, says that he has "no knowledge of the views of ordinary individuals." Indeed Wilde repeatedly disclaims knowledge of the very language Carson is speaking: these words are not his. Did Wilde think that the story "The Priest and the Acolyte" was "blasphemous"?

> Wilde: I think it violated every artistic canon of beauty.
> Carson: That is not an answer.
> Wilde: It is the only one I can give.
>
> (*Trials*, 121)

Carson demands, repeatedly, that Wilde speak the court's language; and repeatedly Wilde refuses any language except his own:

Carson: I wish to know whether you thought the story blasphemous.
Wilde: The story filled me with disgust. The end was wrong.
Carson: Answer the question, Sir. Did you or did you not consider the story
             blasphemous?
Wilde: I thought it disgusting.

And once again: "Do you consider that blasphemous?" "I think it horrible. 'Blasphemous' is not a word of mine" (*Trials*, 121–22). "Blasphemy," like "sodomy," is a word that designates a criminal offense. Verbal fastidiousness isn't all that's at stake in Wilde's attempt not to be imprisoned in Carson's literalizing hermeneutics.

Why did Wilde charge Queensberry? Why, against the good advice of all his friends except Bosie Douglas, did he put himself in the legal arena where language is policed as the preliminary enforcement to all others? The answer is heavily overdetermined, but one element, I suggest, is Wilde's optimistic belief in the power of *his* language to name *his* desire, precisely in its evasions, its silences, its refusals of determinate meaning. What Wilde tried to get away with in court, telling his own truth in his own words, he had tried already in "The Portrait of Mr. W. H."

II

But not to his perfect satisfaction. By September 1893, he had revised and expanded the published story to more than twice its original length.[12] On February 28, 1895, on his way to the Albemarle Club where he would find the card left for him ten days earlier by the Marquis of Queensberry, Wilde visited C. H. Shannon and Charles Ricketts at their studio in Chelsea.[13] For over a year the manuscript of the expanded story had been in Shannon and Ricketts's possession: they were supposed to design a new edition, complete with a frontispiece that would purport to be the (forged) portrait of Mr. W. H. The designers' delay was not Wilde's only problem in getting the book into print. In late August through September 1894,

[12]I establish the date of the completed revision from Wilde's letters. He wrote to Elkin Mathews and John Lane in September 1894 that "the manuscript has been in Mr. Ricketts's hands for *more than a year*." In an earlier letter that month he wrote: "Eighteen months ago—at any rate considerably more than a year ago—Mr. Lane on behalf of the firm . . entered into an agreement with me to publish 'The Portrait of Mr. W. H.'" (*The Letters of Oscar Wilde*, ed. Rupert Hart-Davis [New York: Harcourt, Brace & World, 1962], 366, 367).

[13]This account of events is given by Ricketts in *Oscar Wilde: Recollections* (London: Nonesuch, 1932). Ricketts's book is in the form of a narrative by a fictitious Frenchman named Jean Paul Raymond and of fictitious letters to "Raymond" from Ricketts. H. Montgomery Hyde, in *Oscar Wilde: A Biography* (New York: Farrar, Straus and Giroux, 1975), accepts Ricketts's version as fact (196); Ellmann's biography is silent about it

his publishers, Elkin Mathews and John Lane, were dissolving their partnership, and in the process dividing up Wilde's work. "The Portrait of Mr. W. H." became a hot potato between them. Wilde proposed that Lane retain rights to the plays and that Mathews publish "Mr. W. H." Mathews refused: he would not publish "The Portrait of Mr. W. H.," he said, "at any price." But Mathews did want the plays; only Lane "pointed out that if he takes the plays he must also take 'Mr. W. H.'"—with the result that "he declines both." Lane finally agreed to publish the plays and "Mr. W. H.," but with a proviso: "I am sure that you as a man of the world would not expect me or any other publisher to issue a book he had never seen."[14] He hadn't seen the book because Ricketts and Shannon had the manuscript in Chelsea; but it sounds as though he hoped he'd never see it. After all, "as a man of the world," he'd seen enough in the earlier, unexpanded version. More of the same could only make things worse.[15]

In fact, Wilde's judgment in expanding the story is questionable on various grounds. The added freight of Shakespearean scholarship tips a sharp, ingenious parable in the direction of heavyweight exegesis. Wilde runs the danger of replicating Cyril Graham's fatal error, bringing a fine theory down to the level of forensic (if forged) evidence. But Lane's great fear—that the expansion will make the story's "tendency" more explicit—is only partly realized, for the expanded version simultaneously hides more than the original, by creating more spaces into which interpretation must pry. In both versions, the narrator asks, "Who was that young man of Shakespeare's day who, without being of noble birth or even of noble nature, was addressed by him in terms of such passionate adoration that we can but wonder at the strange worship, and are almost afraid to turn the key that unlocks the mystery of the poet's heart?" (expanded version, 12): the additions in the revised text oddly do nothing to remove the teasing vagueness ("*strange* worship") and hesitancy ("*almost afraid* to turn the key") of the sketchier original.[16] Wilde's apparent explicitness always leaves the impression of something more to be said; hence there is a regress of revelations, each one provoking the need for another.[17]

[14]Lane letter to Wilde, September 7, 1894, in *More Letters of Oscar Wilde*, ed. Rupert Hart-Davis (New York: Vanguard Press, 1985), 124–25.

[15]The manuscript of the expanded version (interleaved in a copy of the *Blackwood's* text) was thought to have disappeared from Wilde's Tite Street house on the day of his bankruptcy sale. In 1921 it was published in a limited edition in New York by Mitchell Kennerley, without any explanation of its provenance. The full history of the manuscript's reappearance is still in doubt, but the available facts are judiciously assessed by Horst Schroeder, *Oscar Wilde, The Portrait of Mr. W. H.: Its Composition, Publication and Reception* (Braunschweig: Technische Universität Carolo-Wilhelmina, 1984), 36–39. The manuscript was bought from Kennerley by A. S. W. Rosenbach and is now at the Rosenbach Museum and Library in Philadelphia.

[16]The original *Blackwood's* text is in *Lord Arthur Savile's Crime and Other Prose Pieces*, ed. Robert Ross, in *The First Collected Edition of the Works of Oscar Wilde* (1908; reprint, London: Dawson's of Pall Mall, 1969), 160.

[17]Linda Dowling, "Imposture and Absence in Wilde's 'The Portrait of Mr. W. H.,'" *Victorian Newsletter* 58 (1980): 26–29, writes, "Our real clue to the secret of Willie Hughes and to the 'secret' of the narrator's own text is the picture that is not inside the chest, an image of absence. Like the empty chest, the hollow text can only be filled by imposture (Lat. *imponere*, to put in), by putting presence in the place of absence" (27).

The deferral of ultimate revelation invites the reader to go beneath the surface into the suggestive spaces created by the story's absences; but as Wilde puts it in the Preface to *Dorian Gray*, "Those who go beneath the surface do so at their peril"—for "it is the spectator, and not life, that art really mirrors."[18] In the revised version Wilde added several passages about the circular creation of personality and personal truth from the art we create in order to create ourselves. With more sublimity than the wisecracking mode of "The Decay of Lying," he writes about the precedence of language: "It is never with impunity that one's lips say Love's Litany. Words have their mystical power over the soul, and form can create the feeling from which it should have sprung. Sincerity itself, the ardent, momentary sincerity of the artist, is often the unconscious result of style" (expanded version, 63; not in original). Carson's "ordinary individual" thinks that art is a window on reality; Wilde's narrator knows that "art, even the art of fullest scope and widest vision, can never really show us the external world. All that it shows us is our own soul, the one world of which we have any real cognizance" (expanded version, 76; not in original). But even that "cognizance" is partial, unstable, for the "one world" of the soul turns out to be multiple and shifting. The revelation of the self to itself in art also changes, creates, and recreates the self. The proof is in this very narrative of gained and lost belief.

In Cyril Graham's theory and in Shakespeare's Sonnets the narrator found his personal truth: "The soul, the secret soul, was the only reality. How curiously it had all been revealed to me! A book of Sonnets, published nearly three hundred years ago, written by a dead hand and in honour of a dead youth, had suddenly explained to me the whole story of my soul's romance" (expanded version, 79; not in original). But almost immediately with the revelation came the change: the narrator wonders why his passionate belief in Willie Hughes left him as soon as he expressed it:

> Had I touched upon some secret that my soul desired to conceal? Or was there no permanence in personality? Did things come and go through the brain, silently, swiftly, and without footprints, like shadows through a mirror? Were we at the mercy of such impressions as Art or Life chose to give us? (expanded version, 81; not in original)

The work of art—Shakespeare's Sonnets, Wilde's "The Portrait of Mr. W. H."—tells us what we are and in the process makes us something different. Its meaning is as elusive as personality, from which it derives, and which it creates, and in which it can never rest.

So how is the reader of Wilde's story to know what Wilde's story means? Or, perhaps, since "it is the spectator, and not life, that art really mirrors," *who* it means? When the narrator tells us that Shakespeare's Sonnets (in the Cyril Graham version) had "suddenly explained to [him] the whole story of [his] soul's romance," are we to understand that the Sonnets had revealed to him the homo-

[18]See, for example, Wilde's defense in the controversy over *The Picture of Dorian Gray*: "Each man sees his own sin in Dorian Gray. What Dorian Gray's sins are no one knows. He who finds them has brought them." (Letter to the editor of *The Scots Observer*, July 9, 1890, in Mason [note 7], 81.)

sexual nature of his genital desire? Or does the phrase "soul's romance" imply something more sublimated or sublime, to which genital sexuality is irrelevant? What in fact was the nature of Shakespeare's love for Willie Hughes? Did they sleep together? Who did what to whom? At Wilde's second trial, a chambermaid testified that the sheets in Wilde's room at the Savoy Hotel "were stained in a peculiar way" (*Trials*, 220): was this the stain of truth, at last, or an irrelevant accident of the body?[19] "The Portrait of Mr. W. H.," a fiction in the form of a theory denied in its making, invites the reader to "go beneath the surface" to explore an absence ("There is nothing in the idea of Willie Hughes"); what the reader finds is a reflection of his or her own interminable quest for meaning.

Wilde's additions to the published version tempt the reader deeper into its illusory depths. In the *Blackwood's* text, the narrator says, "I did not care to pry into the mystery of [Willie Hughes's] sin"—in a context that makes the "sin" seem to be Willie's desertion of Shakespeare for a rival playwright. The expanded version has: "I did not care to pry into the mystery of his sin *or of the sin, if such it was, of the great poet who had so dearly loved him*" (35, my italics)—where the effect is to make the reader ask *what* sin ("if such it was") Shakespeare may have been guilty of. The expansion is richer in reticence: still the narrator will not pry into the mystery he has created, but now he has nominated it a "sin" only to wonder if in fact it was a sin, and add the phrase "so dearly loved him" which may lead us to suppose either a sexual sin or a sin against art. Like Queensberry accusing Wilde not of being but of posing as a "Somdomite," Wilde's addition opens the text to interpretation. The "ordinary reader" will undoubtedly find "a certain tendency" in it, a tendency Carson will designate "unnatural" and "perverted." But Wilde will protest that the meanings of "brutes and illiterates" cannot be his.

In revision, Wilde added long passages about Hellenism, Platonism, and neo-Platonism. These are the passages that most precisely describe the nature of Shakespeare's attachment to Willie Hughes. Or seem to: in the narrative context they can only tell us the precise nature of the narrator's belief (now disavowed) about the nature of that attachment. But the indeterminacy of the added passages derives not only from the self-subverting narrative context. In the last decades of the nineteenth century, the invocation of Hellenism, Platonism, and neo-Platonism was richly ambiguous in ways Wilde knew well and brilliantly exploited.

In *The Victorians and Ancient Greece* Richard Jenkyns recounts in detail the pervasive influence of a renascent and reconstituted Hellenism in the period.[20] But Jenkyns has little patience for what he sees as the interpretive inaccuracies of Pater (the villain of his piece) and Wilde. Privileging his own professional scholarship over the artistic purposes of the Victorians, he repeatedly concludes that the

---

[19]Interestingly, even this forensic revelatio : only provokes the need for another: were the "peculiar stains" fecal or seminal? In either event the ourt found that they could have been produced by non-criminal behavior.

[20]Richard Jenkyns, *The Victorians and Ancient Greec* (Oxford: Basil Blackwell, 1980), hereafter ·ited parenthetically in the text

moderns are simply wrong when, like Pater, for instance, they transmute Plato's advocacy of "a temperance entirely freed from the tyranny of the senses . . . into an aesthetic cult of sensuous austerity" (257). According to Pater, Platonism "is not a formal theory or body of theories, but a tendency, a group of tendencies—a tendency to think or feel . . . in a particular way"; according to Jenkyns, "These words can scarcely be read without amazement and indignation" (259). Jenkyns's indignation arises partly from offended professionalism, but his repeated use of the anachronistic epithet "invert" to characterize the offending writers suggests yet another area of indignation. A century after the fact, that is, the Paterian or Wildean appropriation of the language of Hellenism could still seem a sexual as well as a scholarly affront.

In "The Portrait of Mr. W. H.," Wilde immediately Victorianizes his Platonic discourse by introducing it with a version of the Arnoldian distinction between Hebraism and Hellenism: " 'The fear of the Lord is the beginning of Wisdom,' said the stern Hebrew prophet: 'The beginning of Wisdom is Love,' was the gracious message of the Greek" (expanded version, 42; not in original). This is the gracious message the Renaissance ("which already touched Hellenism at so many points") learned to read, but by no ordinary process of reading; it was only by "catching the inner meaning of this phrase and divining its secret" that the Renaissance "sought to elevate friendship to the high dignity of the antique ideal" (42). Already, the suggestion of a hidden meaning or subcultural code, presumably unavailable to "brutes and illiterates" (in court, read "ordinary persons"), begins to press the Arnoldian distinction into the service of erotic, and specifically homosexual, libertinism.

Ficino's translation of the *Symposium* is for Wilde's narrator the nearly-magical link between ancient Greece and Renaissance England. The description of the translation itself and of its effects is marked by the numinous words—"strange," "curious," "subtle"; "colour," "influence," "passion"—that also describe the "poisonous" yellow book that Lord Henry Wotton gives Dorian Gray.[21] But it is not only the decadent keywords that give the passage its illicit spice:

> This wonderful dialogue, of all the Platonic dialogues perhaps the most perfect, as it is the most poetical, began to exercise a strange influence over men, to colour their words and thoughts, and manner of living. In its subtle suggestions of sex in soul, in the curious analogies it draws between intellectual enthusiasm and the physical passion of love, in its dream of the incarnation of the Idea in a beautiful and living form, and of a real spiritual conception with a travail and a bringing to birth, there was something that fascinated the poets and scholars of the sixteenth century. Shakespeare, certainly, was fascinated by it. (expanded version, 42; not in original)

---

[21]The yellow book is on a "pearl-coloured octagonal stand" that looked to Dorian like "the work of some strange Egyptian bees"; the book tells about a young Parisian who tried to realize "all the passions" of every century but his own; it was written in a "curious jewelled style"; its metaphors were "as subtle in colour" as orchids; and, "for years, Dorian could not free himself from the influence of this book" (*DG*, 141–42).

In another context, the "subtle suggestion of sex in soul" and the analogies "between intellectual enthusiasm and the physical passion of love" might, for all their apparent explicitness, pass as unexceptionable. But the fact that the dialogue "exercise[s] a strange influence over men," coloring "their words and thought, and manner of living," is almost a parody of what the homophobe most fears about the freemasonry of sexual perversion. Plato's book, like Oscar Wilde himself, seems to beckon from—here I quote Mr. Justice Wills's words to Wilde—"the centre of a circle of extensive corruption of the most hideous kind among young men" (*Trials*, 339). On this reading, Plato's "strange influence" passed to Ficino, who passed it to Shakespeare, who infected little Willie Hughes; the sonnets to Willie infect the already-effeminate Cyril Graham, who lures first Erskine and then the narrator into the secret circle; Erskine dies—nominally of consumption—but the book that records it all, "The Portrait of Mr. W. H.," carries the pernicious influence into the future.

According to Wilde's narrator, "It is only when we realise the influence of neo-Platonism on the Renaissance that we can understand the true meaning of the amatory phrases and words with which friends were wont, at this time, to address each other" (expanded version, 43; not in original). So to understand "the true meaning" of Shakespeare's language we must understand the true meaning of neo-Plantonic language; but to understand that we must understand the true meaning of Wilde's story, a story which purports to elucidate the languages, Platonic and Shakespearean, on which it in fact depends. On the question the forensic reader finds most urgent—is the sort of love designated by these discourses criminally culpable? is it in fact fully sexualized?—Wilde makes the mutual elucidations perfectly self-cancelling. "There was," he writes, "a kind of mystic transference of the expressions of the physical sphere to a sphere that was spiritual, that was removed from gross bodily appetite, and in which the soul was Lord" (expanded version, 43-44; not in original). Is this "transference of expressions" only a linguistic dodge, a code that directs us to go on understanding *body* where mystically it seems to put *soul?* Or would such a coded reading merely reproduce the error of those "who find ugly meanings in beautiful things" (Preface to *Dorian Gray*)? Wilde's next sentence is heavy with the language of mystic meaning: "Love had, indeed, entered the olive garden of the new Academe, but he wore the same flame-coloured raiment, and had the same words of passion on his lips" (44). This Love that looks and sounds like sex: what would it call itself if it dared to speak its name? Or would there be a name for it to speak?

III

If it is indeed the spectator that art really mirrors, it will be worth digressing here to ask what some of Wilde's readers were disposed to find in those hollows and hints created by his discourse of Platonism and neo-Platonism. We know what the prosecutorial reader, like Edward Carson, found there; and we know what the "brutes and illiterates" found. But what of the scholarly experts? Few readers could have known more about the key texts in the discourse of Hellenism than the Reverend J. P. Mahaffy (1839–1919), the man who had been Wilde's tutor in classics at Trinity College, Dublin, and in whose company Wilde traveled to Greece in 1877. When the first edition of Mahaffy's *Social Life in Greece from Homer to Menander* appeared in 1874, its preface acknowledged the help of "Mr. Oscar Wilde of Magdalen College." But a second edition, in 1875, no longer carried that acknowledgement.[22] And Wilde's name was not the only thing missing: "In one direction . . . this [second] edition is partially rewritten," Mahaffy explained:

> There were certain phases in Greek morals, which had hitherto not been fairly discussed and which had been consequently misunderstood, and upon those I wrote freely what I thought due to the Greeks and to their culture. I see no reason to retract one word I have written, and refer scholars interested in the byways of Greek society to my first edition which will thus retain for them an independent value. But there are things which ought to be said once, and which it is nevertheless inexpedient to repeat. I have therefore substituted for my discussions in Greek morals, new matter, which will, I hope, prove interesting, and which will be suited to all classes of readers; so that the book in its present form can be made of general use for school and family reading.[23]

In the section thus banished from "school and family reading," it's not hard to spot Wilde's "contribution" in a single sentence: "As to the epithet *unnatural*, the Greeks would answer probably, that all civilisation was unnatural" (first edition, 308).[24] The rest is pure Mahaffy.

Ten years after their trip to Greece, Wilde wrote a devastating (unsigned) review of a later Mahaffy book, taking his former teacher to task for his blatant imperialism, parochialism, and provincialism. Mahaffy not only wrote as a Unionist Irishman, but as if Greece *were* Ireland: "In his attempts to treat the Hellenic world as 'Tipperary writ large,' to use Alexander the Great as a means of whitewashing Mr. Smith, and to finish the battle of Chaeronea on the plains of Mitchelstown, Mr. Mahaffy shows an amount of political bias and literary blindness that is quite extraordinary."[25] Writing about Greek love in the first edition of *Social Life in Greece*, Mahaffy similarly provides evidence for Wilde's proposition that what we read in a text is inevitably ourselves. His comments tell us more about the anxieties of an Anglo-Irish heterosexual than they do about Greek homosexuality.

[22]Ellmann (note 10) notices the omission (29).

[23]J. P. Mahaffy, *Social Life in Greece from Homer to Menander*, 2nd ed. (London: Macmillan, 1875), x; citations from the first edition (London: Macmillan, 1874) are indicated as such parenthetically in the text.

[24]Ellmann (note 10) thus identifies the Wildean passage (29).

[25]*Pall Mall Gazette* 46 (November 9, 1887): 3; reprinted in *The Artist as Critic: Critical Writings of Oscar Wilde*, ed. Richard Ellmann (New York: Random House, 1969), 80.

Mahaffy's historical imagination extends only to seeing himself in fancy dress: "I can . . . easily imagine a modern Irishman transplanted to an old Greek sympo-sium, and there observing that in spite of the romantic feelings existing between the men present, nothing was done, or even hinted at, inconsistent with the strictest taste and propriety" (first edition, 396). Mahaffy gets around the embar-rassment of genital sexuality, whether Greek homo- or Irish hetero-, not exactly by denying its existence, but by relegating it to the aberrant. He admits that in homosexual Greek society there were exceptional "cases" where "sentiment . . . did ally itself with passion, and lead to strange and odious consequences," but Mahaffy asks us to remember "the modern parallel": "In the midst of all the romantic and chivalrous respect with which ladies are treated in society, there are also cases where sentiment allies itself with passion." Who are we to judge? After all, in heterosexual society the aberrant alliance of sentiment with passion "leads to consequences socially more serious, though less revolting (of course) to *our* tastes."

In its normative form, then, Greek love was as innocent of sexuality as the mod-ern love experienced by "every English gentleman, who has not gone in search of low philosophy to palliate bad morals." Such a gentleman knows "that though there is a distinct difference in his sentiment as regards friends of the opposite sex, yet to him, consciously at least, any physical cause is not only rare, but abhorrent":

> His sentiment takes the form of brighter conversation, or increased politeness, of volun-tary slavery, of keenness in argument or in teaching, and stops there in almost every case, giving him no trouble or thought when the hour passes, and is nowise related to that strong want with which the Darwinians identify it. (first edition, 307–8)

The ancient-modern parallel almost breaks down when Mahaffy bravely confronts the institution of heterosexual marriage; but that too is salvaged by being relegated to the aberrant and even then only grudgingly allowed any taint of sexuality: "Even in the exceptional case where this [modern] sentiment leads to the longing for a permanent union, it is held separate from the lower passion, so much so that a modern gentleman who married for the reasons admitted by S. Paul, would be justly stigmatised as a low and brutal creature, who was dishonouring the so-called object of his affections" (first edition, 308).

Thus Mahaffy can look at Greek homosexuality only by modeling it on hetero-sexuality, and he can look at heterosexuality only by seeing it as no sexuality at all. But the fact that Mahaffy suppressed even this sterilized account from his second edition proves that his prophylaxis was unsuccessful. The problem lay not in the ancient but the modern world, where it proved impossible to represent homosex-uality without the emphasis falling on the *sexuality*. The scandal of love between men is that it makes sexuality itself visible, thereby infecting even the love between men and women with the taint of a "strong want." The modern sexual invert—as opposed to the ancient asexual Greek lover of boys—must be "a low and brutal creature" (like the heterosexual who marries for sex) not because males are the object of his genital desire but simply because he desires.

The objects of Oscar Wilde's desire would be extensively examined and cross-examined at the trials; but the one thing no one doubted was that Oscar Wilde desired. His "pose" told them so, and his pose told the truth. Mahaffy's opinion of *The Picture of Dorian Gray* and "The Portrait of Mr. W. H." is not on record, but his efforts to clear himself of the taint of Wilde are. He expunged Wilde's name from *Social Life in Greece,* and in 1896 he refused to sign a petition for Wilde's release from prison, saying that Wilde was "the one blot on my tutorship."[26] Inevitably, when Mahaffy read the vagueness of *Dorian Gray* or the precision of "Mr. W. H.," the classical scholar, like Carson's "ordinary person," would find the allusions to Hellenism and Platonism "perverse" and "unnatural." He tried to read the author in the text in order to avoid reading himself, because for him sexuality itself was perverse and unnatural.

There was another classical scholar whose understanding of the transaction of desire between reader and text was closer to Wilde's, and who by both professional and sexual inclination was more prepared—eager, indeed—to find himself mirrored in the ancient texts. John Addington Symonds (1840–1893) was as learned in the classics as Mahaffy; but he was also a leading theorist, as well as indefatigable field worker, in the developing discourse of English homosexuality. In the expanded version of "The Portrait of Mr. W. H." Symonds actually makes an appearance: he is the narrator's authority for the opinion that "the Platonic conception of love [is] nothing if not spiritual" (44). In fact, however, Symonds's understanding of Platonic love, on the page and elsewhere, mixed spirit and flesh more complexly than that.

In his *Memoirs,* Symonds writes, "Our earliest memories of words, poems, works of art, have great value in the study of psychical development. They indicate decisive points in the growth of personality."[27] Two texts, one Shakespearean and one Platonic, stand as especially vivid indices of Symonds's personality. "Venus and Adonis" is the Shakespearean text. Symonds thinks he was less than ten years old when he read it: "It gave form, ideality, and beauty to my previous erotic visions" (63). Where his earlier fantasies had been of "adult males . . . shaggy and brawny sailors," he now found the "adolescent Adonis" a more complex and satisfying form for identification and projection:

> In some confused way I identified myself with Adonis; but at the same time I yearned after him as an adorable object of passionate love. Venus only served to intensify the situation. I did not pity her. I did not want her. I did not think that, had I been in the position of Adonis, I should have used his opportunities to better purpose. No: she only expressed my own relation to the desirable male. She brought into relief the overwhelming attraction of masculine adolescence and its proud inaccessibility. Her hot wooing taught me what it was to woo with sexual ardour. I dreamed of falling back like her upon the grass, and folding the quick-panting lad in my embrace. (63)

[26]Ellmann, *Oscar Wilde* (note 10), 29.
[27]*The Memoirs of John Addington Symonds,* ed. Phyllis Grosskurth (Chicago: Univ. of Chicago Press, 1984), 62.

It is a remarkable passage of introspection; its analysis of the narcissistic element in sexual desire and its acknowledgements of sexuality in childhood seem historically prescient until we remember how much of Freud's work was also being done while Victoria reigned in England. For the moment, however, I only want to emphasize the role that Symonds gives to *reading;* it was the Shakespearean work of art, seen by his unique personality, that made that personality know itself, and gave it form.

Thus taught by Shakespeare at ten, Symonds went on at thirteen to pursue his education at Harrow. It should have been the ideal place, but Symonds describes it as a sexual hell. Here in horrible abundance were parodies of the physical acts that might have gratified his sexual desires, mocking rather than fulfilling his personality:

> Every boy of good looks had a female name, and was recognized either as a public prostitute or as some bigger fellow's "bitch." Bitch was the word in common usage to indicate a boy who yielded his person to a lover. The talk in the dormitories and the studies was incredibly obscene. Here and there one could not avoid seeing acts of onanism, mutual masturbation, the sports of naked boys in bed together. There was no refinement, no sentiment, no passion; nothing but animal lust in these occurrences. They filled me with disgust and loathing. (94)

Amidst Harrow's pullulating adolescent sex, Symonds "remained free in fact and act from this contamination" (95).

It was a dangerous period for Symonds, not because of the easy availability of sex but because its avoidance tempted him to think that he "had transcended crude sensuality through the aesthetic idealization of erotic instincts" (96). Like the Reverend J. P. Mahaffy, the young Symonds "did not know how fallacious that method of expelling nature is" (96). But Symonds outgrew the belief that "crude sensuality" could be transcended. What saved him from the twin dangers of "aesthetic idealization" and "the animalisms of boyish lust" was "the gradual unfolding in [himself] of an ideal passion which corresponded with Platonic love" (96)—a Platonic love, it should already be clear, which does not exclude the flesh to gratify the spirit.

He was seventeen when he read the *Symposium.* Here was "the true *liber amoris* at last, the revelation I had been waiting for, the consecration of a long-cherished idealism. It was just as though the voice of my own soul spoke to me through Plato, as though in some antenatal experience I had lived the life of a philosophical Greek lover." In the *Symposium,* he "had obtained the sanction of the love which had been ruling [him] from childhood" (99). Symonds's revelatory reading of this *liber amoris* inevitably brings to mind Dorian Gray's reading of the "poisonous" yellow book: "Things that [Dorian] had dimly dreamed of were suddenly made real to him. Things of which he had never dreamed were gradually revealed" (*DG,* 141). Like Symonds, Dorian finds in the book a prescient portrait of the self he now knows he is destined to become: "The whole book seemed to [Dorian] to contain the story of his own life, written before he had lived it" (*DG,*

142).²⁸ In "The Portrait of Mr. W. H." too—where Wilde uses the trope of "the fatal book" even more centrally and ingeniously—the narrator, like Symonds, reads his way to self-revelation: "A book of Sonnets . . . had suddenly explained to me the whole story of my soul's romance" (79).

Symonds's discovery of himself in Plato's text seems to differ from the Wildean discoveries in one important respect: the Wildean texts bring death, the Platonic text points Symonds the way to life. In fact, however, Symonds's attitude toward the book that saved him is interestingly ambiguous. Following the passage which describes his reading of the *Symposium*, Symonds includes in his *Memoirs* the text of a letter he wrote in 1889 to Benjamin Jowett, warning the translator of Plato against the danger of "making Plato a textbook for readers in a nation which repudiates Greek love, while the baser forms of Greek love have grown to serious proportions in the seminaries of youth and in the centres of social life belonging to that nation" (101–2). Thus Symonds attempts to turn others away from the very book that ratified his own sexual identity. But while there is ambiguity, there is no necessary contradiction in Symonds's position. What's involved is precisely the interpretive issue I find in "The Portrait of Mr. W. H.": Symonds fears that "in a nation which repudiates Greek love" readers will interpret Plato as licensing not *his* desire but instead its parody, which the court designates by the words "buggery" or "sodomy." For Symonds, Greek or Platonic love is what Symonds feels and does, an entirely different thing (however much it may outwardly resemble it) from what the boys at Harrow do.

Symonds was perfectly aware how difficult it was to maintain the distinction between Harrovian animalism and his own version of platonized sexuality: scholarship as well as personal experience taught that difficulty, and here too the *Symposium* was a key text. Pausanius's speech on the "two loves"—the higher and the lower Aphrodite, different in essence yet so identical in appearance that any lover might be excused for mistaking the one for the other—is the dialogue's most confusing and turgid passage. What's lawful in one place, Pausanius says, is censured in another; distinctions here don't exist there. In Athens and Lacedaemon "the rules about love are perplexing," but in Elis and Boeotia, where there are men of few words, "they are very straightforward"; in Ionia "the custom is held to be dishonourable," but liberty-loving Athenians know the political value of strong friendships, except that nowadays those friendships are in ill repute because of "the evil condition of those who make them to be ill

---

²⁸See Linda Dowling's extensive treatment of "the fatal book" in *Language and Decadence in the Victorian Fin de Siècle* (Princeton: Princeton Univ. Press, 1986): "The full implications of Decadent linguistic anxiety converge most obviously in the fin de siècle notion of the 'fatal book,' something anticipated in 'The Portrait of Mr. W. H.,' where Wilde traces to Shakespeare's Sonnets the deaths of Cyril and Erskine, but finally something more complex and, properly understood, more terrible. The fatal book *is* fatal, that is to say, not because of its power to kill outright, but because of its power to change an individual life" (163–64). Dowling associates the "fatal book" with the "golden book" in Pater's *Marius the Epicurean*.

reputed"—and so on.[29] In a brief footnote in *A Problem of Greek Ethics* Symonds explains why Pausanius speech is so difficult. Noting that "Mr. Jowett censures this speech as sophistic and confused in view," Symonds agrees about the confusion but not about the censure: "It is precisely on this account that it is valuable. The confusion indicates the obscure conscience of the Athenians. The sophistry is the result of a half-acknowledged false position."[30]

Symonds may have been the best qualified person in late nineteenth century England—except perhaps Oscar Wilde—to understand the problem of naming homosexual desire. In the nineteenth century, wrote Symonds (in a phrase I have already alluded to), "The accomplished languages of Europe . . . supply no term for this persistent feature of human psychology, without importing some implication of disgust, disgrace, vituperation."[31] But in the *Laws*, Symonds writes elsewhere, Plato had explained why *no* single term could be adequate: "There are three distinct things, Plato argues, which, owing to the inadequacy of language to represent states of thought, have been confounded." Symonds continues with an analysis of Plato's distinctions between "friendship, desire, and a third, mixed species."[32] But the analysis is less important for my point than the phrase I have already quoted—"the inadequacy of language to represent states of thought": that phrase points us back to the evasive language of Wilde's "The Portrait of Mr. W. H."

IV

Under crossexamination at his second trial, Wilde was asked by the Counsel for the Crown, Charles Gill, about the meaning of Lord Alfred Douglas's poem "Two Loves":

Gill:　　There is no question as to what it means?
Wilde:　Most certainly not.
Gill:　　Is it not clear that the love described relates to natural love and unnatural love?
Wilde:　No.
Gill:　　What is the "Love that dare not speak its name?"

(*Trials*, 235–36)

Wilde's eloquent answer to this interpretive impasse threatens to reproduce the problem of "The Portrait of Mr. W. H." There is the definition by reference to texts which can go, as it were, in either direction: " 'The Love that dare not speak its name' in this century is such a great affection of an elder for a younger man as

[29]*The Symposium* 182b, in *The Dialogues of Plato*, trans. B[enjamin] Jowett, 4th ed. 5 vols. (Oxford: Clarendon Press, 1953), 1:513.
[30]*Male Love* (note 2), 31.
[31]*A Problem in Modern Ethics* (1891), in *Male Love* (note 2), 80.
[32]*A Problem in Greek Ethics*, in *Male Love* (note 2), 49.

there was between David and Jonathan, such as Plato made the very basis of his philosophy, and such as you find in the sonnets of Shakespeare and Michelangelo." Again there is the assertion of a spirituality that may rule out the sexuality it seems simultaneously to affirm: "It is that deep, spiritual affection that is as pure as it is perfect." But here Wilde confronts the problem of naming as such: "It is in this century misunderstood, so much misunderstood that it may be described as the 'Love that dare not speak its name,' and on account of it I am placed where I am now. It is beautiful, it is fine, it is the noblest form of affection. There is nothing unnatural about it" (*Trials*, 236).

The bold transvaluation of terms in Wilde's answer suggests that his tactic in "The Portrait of Mr. W. H." is neither a tease nor an evasion but an effort (in Blakean terms) not to be trapped in another man's system. The story's structure of self-subverting narratives and its deferral of determinate meaning are not on this account shirkings of authorial responsibility. In a century that could not name Wilde's love without making it "unnatural," the deferral of naming was a necessary act of resistance. But other accounts are possible. Six years after Wilde's death— six years out of the nineteenth century and into our own—James Joyce, writing to his brother Stanislas, said of *The Picture of Dorian Gray*,

> It is not very difficult to read between the lines. Wilde seems to have had some good intention in writing it—some wish to put himself before the world—but the book is rather crowded with lies and epigrams. If he had had the courage to develop the allusions in the book it might have been better.[33]

Wilde's expansion of the original version of "The Portrait of Mr. W. H." may show him hankering to speak the unspeakable with the kind of "courage" Joyce wishes for his countryman. But it also shows him cannily negotiating the danger (not only legal) of representing homosexual desire in Victorian England. In the neo-Platonic language of spirit and intellect, homosexual desire could both declare itself and efface itself. Through esthetic idealization the youthful male body could be represented as an object of desire and simultaneously denied as such. In the case of *Regina v. Wilde* the law tried to put a stop to such subversive doubleness of representation. For Wilde the result was fatal, but the case also marked a stage in the legitimization of indeterminacy as one stylistic choice among a wider range of styles, including even the unambiguous, available for the representation of homosexual desire.

[33]*Letters of James Joyce*, ed. Richard Ellmann, 3 vols. (New York: Viking, 1966), 2:105 (August 19, 1906), quoted by R. B. Kirschner, Jr., "Artist, Critic, Performer: Wilde and Joyce on Shakespeare," *TSLL* 20 (1978): 216–29.

Traversing the Feminine
in Oscar Wilde's *Salomé*

Richard Dellamora

In the opening chapter of *The Victorian Sage* (1953), John Holloway has argued that the Victorian sages attempt to communicate knowledge in ways that produce assent without relying on formal logic. Taking John Henry Newman's idea of "Real Assent" as a model of the sort of conviction that the sages aim for, Holloway refers to a "meaning which arises for the individual out of his own history, and exists for him in vivid particular images that bring his belief to life, and naturally lead him in the end to some active and practical step like joining a church."[1] In the following essay on Oscar Wilde, I propose a reading of sexual "history" that includes sexual relations with both intimates and casual acquaintances, with both men and women.

In *Salomé*, which Richard Ellmann has taken to signify a paradigmatic instance of Wilde's enrollment in an Oxonian tradition of sage discourse, I will argue that the "images" of special importance are those of the body, male and female, including fantasies of perverse sexual practices. Although men committed to sexual and emotional ties with other men did in fact gather in particular religious communities and parishes from the late 1860s until the end of the century, the "practical step" to which *Salomé* tends is not, as in the case of Newman, towards the church but towards Wilde's declaration of himself as a lover of men in all senses of the word.[2] The process central to sage writing that David DeLaura has described as "self-exploration and self-manifestation and the manipulation of one's own personal presence for highly personal ends" functions in a new way in *Salomé*.[3] In the play,

From *Victorian Sages and Cultural Discourse: Renegotiating Gender and Power*, Thais E. Morgan, ed., copyright © 1990 by Rutgers, the State University. Reprinted by permission of Rutgers University Press.

I would like to thank Gail Finney for providing me with an advance copy of a portion of the chapter on *Salomé* in her book, *Women in Modern Drama: Freud, Feminism, and European Theater at the Turn of the Century*.

[1] John Holloway, *The Victorian Sage: Studies in Argument* (New York: Norton, 1965), 7.

[2] For the connection between Anglo-Catholicism and emergent male homosexuality, see David Hilliard, "Unenglish and Unmanly: Anglo-Catholicism and Homosexuality," *Victorian Studies* 25 (1982): 181–210.

[3] David DeLaura, "The Allegory of Life: The Autobiographical Impulse in Victorian Prose," in *Approaches to Victorian Autobiography*, ed. George P. Landow (Athens: Ohio University Press, 1979), 333. The essay is the most significant further development of Holloway's argument in the opening pages of *The Victorian Sage*.

self-writing convokes and responds to diverse constituencies in a decade in which male homosexual existence became for the first time a significant feature of English middle-class culture. In these novel circumstances, possibilities of meaning occurred that simply had not existed earlier, even in the sexual polemics of Walter Pater, whom Ellmann names as one of the prime precursors of *Salomé*. The very specificity of the audiences for *Salomé*, however, also signals the end of Victorian sage discourse as an attempt to describe a new moral center for contemporary society.[4] *Salomé* takes relish in the eccentricity of its constituencies.

When English censors in 1892 decided to prohibit the staging of Wilde's play, they found it offensive not so much because it expresses desire between men as because Salomé asserts her desire as a woman. Hence, although within Paterian tradition Salomé is a male transvestite, within the field of struggle surrounding the figure of what was referred to at the time as the "New Woman," Salomé is a woman who challenges the ideology of the middle-class woman as an Angel in the House. In the decade in which Havelock Ellis produced case studies of female inversion and in which Wilde went to trial, Salomé also is a lesbian—although problematically so in a text in which lesbian connotation is evoked by a sexually nonconformist male writing for a predominantly male audience of diverse sexualities.[5] Salomé's double significance as a deviant male and a deviant female underscores how closely issues of sexual difference were related to those of gender roles in the 1890s.[6]

Salomé's desire could be used by members of a conservative male homosocial elite in prophylactic mockery of the anxieties that explicit female desire for a male provoked. The censor, Edward Pigott, wrote to a friend that Salomé's "love turns to fury because John will not let her kiss him *in the mouth*—and in the last scene, where she brings in his head—if you please—on a 'charger'—*she does* kiss his mouth, in a paroxysm of sexual despair." Besides defending himself against Salomé's excesses, Pigott's comments reinforce a sense of class superiority over "the average British public" that paradoxically justifies men like Pigott in reserving Wilde's text for themselves.[7] Nonetheless, *Salomé* could also be used by women to assert female power—a fact that Sarah Bernhardt, for instance, perceived immediately. Bernhardt, who intended to use the play as a vehicle with herself in the leading part, underwrote the expenses of the London production that Pigott subsequently canceled.[8] Moreover, as Sydney

---

[4]George P. Landow, *Elegant Jeremiahs: The Sage from Carlyle to Mailer* (Ithaca: Cornell University Press, 1986), Introduction.

[5]See Sheila Jeffreys, *The Spinster and Her Enemies: Feminism and Sexuality 1880–1930* (London: Pandora, 1985), ch. 6.

[6]For the distinction between gender inversion and homosexual desire, see George Chauncey, "From Sexual Inversion to Homosexuality: Medicine and the Changing Conceptualization of Female Deviance," *Salmagundi* 58–59 (Fall 1982–Winter 1983): 116.

[7]Quoted in Regina Gagnier, *Idylls of the Marketplace: Oscar Wilde and the Victorian Public* (Stanford: Stanford University Press, 1986), 171.

[8]Sara Bernhardt's actions contrast to the role that Dorian Gray projects for "his" actress, Sybil Vane. See Nina Auerbach's reflections on the powers that Victorian women found in acting in *Romantic Imprisonment: Women and Other Glorified Outcasts* (New York: Columbia University Press, 1985), Part 4.

Janet Kaplan has pointed out, to a generation of younger women writers like Katherine Mansfield, Wilde's assertions of desire were empowering—even if, in *Salomé*, that assertion invites women to a seeming endgame in which the pursuit of female desire is both repudiated (by John the Baptist) and punished (by Herod).[9] Accordingly, and despite the fact that Ellmann in his recent biography includes a semi-nude photograph of Wilde dressed as Salomé and reaching for the decapitated head of John, *Salomé* is a significant document in the history of a specifically female sexuality.

Among the works produced between 1885 and 1895, none is more outspoken, more outrageous, or more bodily than *Salomé* (1891), a play so sure to enrage English philistines that its conception needed to be translated into—perhaps even to be imagined in—French. Although Wilde developed the script of the play while in Paris, he nonetheless intended an immediate London production and began a vexed process of arranging its translation. Likewise, his efforts to bring out an edition in England situate the text in an artistic milieu that included innovative work by men who were beginning to be identifiable as "homosexual." Wilde fashions *Salomé* so as to develop a self-consciously homosexual outlook. By including a homosexual triangle in the play, he offers a dramatized representation of explicit male-male desire. He also, however, inscribes these representations of *l'amour de l'impossible* within relations of power: the page loves his social superior, the young Syrian captain of the guard, who in turn loves Salomé, the Tetrarch's niece. The Syrian has been brought to the Tetrarch's court after Herod drove his father, a king, from his throne. Later, when Herod enters, he jokes that the young man, who has just killed himself, has been "my guest, as it were" (16).[10] The members of the audience who share Herod's humor at this moment also share his contempt for a vanquished male—an apt object of aggressive laughter on the part of another male. Yet the identification of the Syrian as captive/captain/prince carries a subtle suggestion of another kingdom, in which princes would remain princes and desire between men would not drive one first to emotional isolation and then to suicide.

The fact that the first London production of *Salomé* was to be mounted for an audience that understood French indicates the elitism of the project. Moreover, the ability of the audience (and of Wilde) to participate emotionally in Herod's assertions of male power indicate the location of the play both inside and outside male homosocial culture. For Wilde, until the time of the 1895 trials, the position of both enjoying the benefits of male privilege and subverting the male gender roles in which these privileges were exercised appears to have been both welcome and necessary. Only when the 1895 trials brought this period to an end, did he fully emerge as homosexual; earlier, he continued to enjoy the benefits of a well-

---

[9]See Sydney Janet Kaplan, "Katherine Mansfield and the Problem of Oscar Wilde," ch. 2 of *Katherine Mansfield and the Origins of Modernist Fiction* (Ithaca: Cornell University Press, 1991).

[10]References to the English version of *Salomé* are to Oscar Wilde, *Salomé: A Tragedy in One Act*, with drawings by Aubrey Beardsley (Boston: Bruce Humphries, n. d.). Unless otherwise noted, references to *Salomé* are to this text.

placed man, head of household, husband, and father. Nonetheless, the drive towards undoing this complicit existence is evident in works like *The Picture of Dorian Gray* and even more so in *Salomé*. Both in dramatizing a rebellious woman and in portraying male-male desire, *Salomé* puts normal masculine representation under pressure.

Salomé turns on four spectacles: that of John's delayed entrance; that of Salomé's dance; that of her kissing John's severed head; and that of the final tableau of soldiers who, in the English translation, "rush forward and crush beneath their shields Salomé daughter of Herodias" (36). There is, however, another spectacle not seen in the course of the play but which is its central action: namely, the beheading of John the Baptist. Insofar as this act pertains to Herod, whom Ellmann regards as the protagonist of the play, the execution of John exemplifies the abuse of secular authority by a male agent.[11] The fourth spectacle, that of the execution of Salomé, perpetrates a like abuse. In ordering the execution both of the male as object of desire and of the female as subject of desire, Herod interdicts all sexuality except the conventional kind.[12] In the contemporary political context of the play, the murders resonate outwards to legislation like the Labouchère Amendment and to the office of the Lord Chamberlain, which prevented the performance of Wilde's play in England until 1931.[13]

By way of a number of essays published in the late 1960s, Ellmann has earned a significant place in the emergence of male homosexual desire as a topic of discussion in academic circles. In the Introduction to a collection of Wilde's critical essays (1969), Ellmann argues that Wilde's initiation by Robert Ross into homosexual activities in 1887 prompted the literary creativity of the next few years.[14] Although Ellmann may be mistaken to defer for so long the date of Wilde's entry into sexual activities with other men, his placement of male-male desire at the center of Wilde's work and his argument for the enabling power of that desire have been major contributions to the reconstitution of the sexual politics of the 1890s.[15] In "Overtures to *Salomé*" (1968), Ellmann inscribes Wilde anew within the tradition of Victorian sage discourse. Ellmann sees the play as dramatizing the pull between two diverse forces at Oxford in Wilde's undergraduate years: the

---

[11]Richard Ellmann, *Oscar Wilde* (New York: Viking, 1987), 326. Unless otherwise noted, references to Ellmann are to this text.

[12]I say all because Salomé also connotes lesbian desire. And in the instance of the crossdressed Wilde playing her, s/he denotes male homosexual desire.

[13]Gagnier, *Idylls*, 229–230n.

[14]The essay is reprinted in Richard Ellmann, *Golden Codgers: Biographical Speculations* (New York: Oxford University Press, 1973).

[15]Ellmann's reading leaves Wilde's engagement with male-male desire in suspension for years after Wilde was trading on sexual ambiguity in the successful pursuit of transatlantic celebrity. Other commentators such as Rupert Croft-Cooke, who dismisses the Ross story as a "myth," have set the date of Wilde's initiation earlier. Croft-Cooke contends that Wilde was active sexually with other men at least from his days at Oxford (*Feasting with Panthers: A New Consideration of Some Late Victorian Writers* [London: W. H. Allen, 1967], 172).

moralizing aestheticism of John Ruskin and the seductive, critical impressionism of Pater. Ellmann sees *Salomé* as an opportunity for some timely father-slaying on Wilde's part—of Ruskin's "weird chastity" in the figure of Iokanaan and of Pater's "diseased contemplation" in the figure of Salomé: "It is Salomé, and not Pater, who dances the dance of the seven veils, but her virginal yet perverse sensuality is related to Paterism."[16] Ellmann misses, however, the side of Ruskin that admires female power as well as the extent to which *Salomé* celebrates in dramatic form the male transvestism already present in Pater's 1869 essay on Leonardo da Vinci. Nevertheless, my main point here is that by identifying Wilde with Herod as protagonist of the play and by a factitious return to order at play's end, Ellmann synthesizes the antagonistic Ruskinian and Paterian elements into a conserving (male) order that recaptures Wilde for a moral tradition of high cultural discourse.

Ellmann contends that "at the play's end the emphasis shifts suddenly to Herod, who is seen to have yielded to Salomé's sensuality, and then to the moral revulsion of Iokanaan from that sensuality, and to have survived them both. In Herod Wilde was suggesting that *tertium quid* which he felt to be his own nature, susceptible to contrary impulses but not abandoned for long to either."[17] In view of the fact that immediately before her execution Salomé gives utterance to a long apologia in defense of "l'amour," Ellmann appears to misread the "emphasis" of the play at this moment.[18] Moreover, he takes this view despite the fact that, as Gagnier has pointed out, Wilde "consistently stressed that Salomé, rather than Herodias, Herod, or Iokanaan, was to be the focus for the audience."[19]

In effect, Ellmann imposes a Freudian model on *Salomé,* one implicit in the biographical reading of the play that he provides earlier, in which Herod performs the function of regulating ego in relation to the influence of Pater as libido and of Ruskin as superego. Ellmann's desire to conserve the normal structure of male psychology at the end of the play prompts him to identify aesthetic structure as a force that can sublimate the erotic revolts and disturbances of *Salomé* even if this solution means misrepresenting the play. In his reading of the ending, Ellmann fails to see that, as Elliot Gilbert has remarked, when Salomé kisses John's head, "what is, objectively—from the point of view of Herod, for example—the most repellent moment in the drama becomes, when seen from the point of view of Salomé, and with a proper sympathy, unaccountably touching."[20] Ellmann's comment overlooks both Salomé's lament and Herod's brutality in ordering the execution with which the play ends.

---

[16]Ellmann, "Overtures to *Salomé,*" in *Codgers,* 50, 57. Pater, however, does not commend virginity.
[17]Ellmann, *Codgers,* 58.
[18]References to the French text of *Salomé* are to Oscar Wilde, *Salomé,* vol. 4 of *The Plays* (Boston: John W. Luce and Co., 1920).
[19]Gagnier, *Idylls,* 165.
[20]Elliot Gilbert, " 'Tumult of Images': Wilde, Beardsley, and *Salomé,*" *Victorian Studies* 26 (1983): 144.

Ellmann's reading of the ending of *Salomé,* which may be described as the "consciousness-effect" of a conventionally masculine discourse, is motivated.[21] He defends Wilde (and himself, the tradition, and the male reader) against the "feminine" aspect of Pater, safely killed along with Salomé. This critical act murders the part of Pater that is responsive to female experience and, even more tellingly, Pater-as-homosexual, at least in the sense of the sexologists of the 1890s, including those who were themselves homosexual and who argued that the homosexual was a *tertium quid,* a female soul locked in a male body. As Christopher Craft has reminded us, both John Addington Symonds and Ellis share this view, formulated in the 1860s in Germany by Karl Ulrichs, an apologist for male-male desire. Ulrichs "regarded uranism, or homosexual love, as a congenital abnormality by which a female soul had become united with a male body—*anima muliebris in corpore virili inclusa.*"[22] Ellmann metaphorically does away with this corporeal oddity and metaphysical absurdity.

Although Elliot Gilbert also signs Freud's name to his critical reading both of *Salomé* and of Aubrey Beardsley's accompanying drawings, Gilbert's discussion begins a new stage in the consideration of the play, one that I refer to as the first-phase, feminist-identified male response to the emergence of the feminist critique of Victorian literature during the 1970s. Although Sandra M. Gilbert, Susan Gubar, Elaine Showalter, and Nina Auerbach are the best known among this group, their number is legion. Elliot Gilbert corrects Ellmann's reading by emphasizing Salomé's significance as a sign of female power in the face of a male literary culture that was defending itself against self-assertion by women writers, by feminists, and by New Women.[23] Although this response has advanced our understanding of the play, Gilbert's approach requires further revision in order adequately to take into account the interplay between the feminist-identified and the male homosexual politics of Wilde's text.[24] What Gilbert perceives as misogyny pertains less to the play than to his unreflexive use of yet another Freudian paradigm, namely that of the castration complex, which is both misogynistic and homophobic. Similarly, although the play, by remaining complicit to a degree with the male power that it satirizes, is itself also necessarily homophobic, Gilbert exaggerates

[21]I adapt the term "consciousness-effect" from Gayatri Chakravorty Spivak, "Can the Subaltern Speak?" in *Marxism and the Interpretation of Culture,* ed., Cary Nelson and Lawrence Grossberg (Urbana: University of Illinois Press, 1988), 287.

[22]This is Ulrichs's view as formulated by Havelock Ellis and quoted in Christopher Craft, " 'Kiss Me with Those Red Lips': Gender and Inversion in Bram Stoker's *Dracula," Representations* 8 (Fall 1984): 113.

[23]Cf. Elaine Showalter, A *Literature of Their Own: British Women Novelists from Brontë to Lessing* (Princeton: Princeton University Press, 1977), ch. 7; "Syphilis, Sexuality, and the Fiction of the Fin de Siècle," in *Sex, Politics, and Science in the Nineteenth-Century Novel,* Selected Papers from the English Institute, 1983–1984, New Series, n. 10, ed. Ruth Bernard Yeazell (Baltimore: Johns Hopkins University Press, 1986); *The Female Malady: Women, Madness, and English Culture: 1830–1980* (New York: Penguin, 1985), 104–106.

[24]For Wilde's Ibsenite feminism, see Jane Marcus, "Salomé: The Jewish Princess Was a New Woman," *Bulletin of the New York Public Library* 78 (Autumn 1974): 95–113. See also Gagnier, *Idylls,* 66.

Wilde's homophobia. Since 1983 when Gilbert wrote his essay, however, gay critics have pointed out the bias of Freud's position, as exemplified, for instance, in "Medusa's Head." In light of these discussions, second phase, feminist-identified male criticism bears a responsibility, both cognitive and moral, to avoid the deformations of conventional Freudian psychoanalysis.

Craig Owens has pointed out the culpable phrase in Freud's text: "Since the Greeks were in the main strongly homosexual, it was inevitable that we should find among them a representation of woman as a being who frightens and repels because she is castrated."[25] In one sentence, Freud manages to combine a masculinist description of woman (defined in terms of lacking a penis), homophobia (homosexuals are gynephobic), and racism. As for Gilbert's view of woman, he says: "As an artist and *male* homosexual . . . [Wilde] recoils from the full implications of an uncontrolled and murderous female energy. For no generous sharing of the subjectivity of his protagonist can in the end conceal from him the fact that it is *he* who is her proposed victim."[26] Gilbert identifies the Beardsley drawing in which Salomé, suspended in air with her own snaky locks, kisses John's severed, Medusan head as *tout court* a representation of the castration complex: "Medusa and her snakey [sic] locks—representing, as Freud suggests, 'the female genitals' and therefore male 'terror of castration/decapitation'—can kill at a glance, and it is this power Beardsley most dramatically portrays in Salomé's hungry peering at Iokanaan's severed head and in the head's blind, reciprocating gaze."[27] *Pace* Gilbert, however, "the head's" eyes are closed. What, moreover, does gender reversal mean in this drawing, in which the Medusa head is male and the subject of the gaze is female? The transposition of genders here suggests a more varied sense of sexuality in Wilde than Gilbert's identification of the drawing with the castration complex permits.

When not looking at Beardsley's drawings and Wilde's text through Freud's spectacles, Gilbert is much more aware of the complexities of *Salomé*. Beardsley was Wilde's most productive collaborator on *Salomé,* and his drawings are especially helpful in emphasizing a host of perverse sexual acts connoted in the script. "It is the *outré* art of Aubrey Beardsley, with its lurid representations of hermaphroditism, masturbation, genetic monstrosities, and full [male] nudity, that most accurately illustrates both the subject matter and the spirit of the play."[28] The drawing discussed above is a case in point.

The earlier version, entitled *J'ai baisé ta bouche Iokanaan,* was a free drawing that prompted John Lane to commission the illustrations of the 1894 English translation. Wilde, who also was enthusiastic, wrote on the copy that he gave Beardsley: "For Aubrey: for the only artist who, besides myself, knows what the

[25]Quoted by Craig Owens, "Outlaws: Gay Men in Feminism," in *Men in Feminism,* ed. Alice Jardine and Paul Smith (New York: Methuen, 1987), 229.
[26]Gilbert, "Tumult of Images," 154.
[27]Gilbert, "Tumult of Images," 159.
[28]Gilbert, "Tumult of Images," 138.

dance of the seven veils is, and can see that invisible dance."[29] The organ that Beardsley's inscription emphasizes is *la bouche,* the mouth. That it may signify both an orifice and an organ is suggested by metaphorical images of the vulva and the erect penis. There are the two upright peacock feathers with their "vulval . . . eyes"; as well, there are the flower and reeds at the bottom right of the drawing.[30] The calamuslike spike under John's head is suggestive of the head of the male member. In that case, a woman (or more likely a crossdressed male) is about to engage in fellatio. If, however, one stays with a Freudian typology in which decapitated head = female *pudenda,* or with a pun on *bouche/*"bush," then Salomé-as-woman may be engaging in lesbian cunnilingus. The proliferation of bodily signs suffused with implications of perverse sexual practices here indicates how Wilde and Beardsley can create representations of sexual difference while playing with a code that, in the register of an orthodox Freudian reading, connotes a masculinist fixation.

In the revision of the drawing for publication, Salomé's locks undergo a trimming and the title is changed to *The Climax,* a title denoting the forbidden subject of female sexual climax.[31] That Wilde and Beardsley intended this meaning is further borne out by the testimony of Alfred Douglas at the time of the Pemberton-Billing trials in 1918. When the dancer Maud Allan planned with J. T. Grein to mount a production of *Salomé* during World War I, she was attacked in *The Vigilante.* Allan sued, claiming, in an article entitled "The Cult of the Clitoris," that her portrayal of Salomé had been represented as "an inducement to lesbianism."[32] Douglas, testifying for the defense, answered the following questions put to him by the defendant acting as his own counsel:

> "Did Wilde intend that Salome should actually bite the lips of the Prophet?"
> "Yes, certainly."
> "Draw blood?"
> "Yes."
> "Suck them?"
> "Yes. That was the idea."
> "Was it intended by the writer that she should work herself up into a great state of sexual excitement?"
> "Yes."
> "Uncontrolled sexual excitement?"
> "Yes. A sort of orgasm. It is meant to be the culmination of sexual excitement."[33]

Beardsley's illustrations wittily combine gender confusion and reversal, sexual inversion, and parody. For instance, in the drawing originally entitled *The Man in*

---

[29]Quoted by Gilbert, "Tumult of Images," 135.
[30]Gilbert, "Tumult of Images," 153.
[31]Gilbert, "Tumult of Images," 158.
[32]Gagnier, *Idylls,* 199.
[33]Quoted in H. Montgomery Hyde, *Lord Alfred Douglas: A Biography* (London: Methuen, 1984), 225.

the Moon and subsequently retitled *The Woman in the Moon*, Beardsley caricatures Wilde as the face of the moon.[34] To the right, a nude John shields a similar figure of a fully dressed Salomé. This image draws on the literary tradition of the screen-woman, as in Dante's *La Vita Nuova* where the young poet pretends to address his poetry to one woman so as to screen the identity of another, who is the actual object of his ardor. In the Beardsley drawing, John screens Salomé from the lustful regard of Wilde/the Moon-figure. But John's frontal nudity reveals the actual object of Wilde's gaze, namely, the youthful male body. In this instance, the screen discloses a specifically male-male sexual desire.

Salomé carries the resistance of an earlier generation of polemicists out of sexual-aesthetic literary discourse and into the three-dimensional, collaborative world of the theatre. Wilde chose Charles Ricketts, the spousal companion of Charles Shannon, to design the London production. Likewise, the translation into English, to be written by Douglas, was intended to be a collaboration between the two men committed sexually and affectively to each other. Although Douglas was already polemicizing on behalf of men who loved other men, his linguistic incompetence, arrogance, and jealousy ruled out the possibility of success.[35] Wilde had to rewrite the translation—even though the English text is still headed by the rubric "Translated from the French of Oscar Wilde by Lord Alfred Douglas" in the edition of Wilde edited by his son, Vyvyan Holland.[36] Hence, to borrow a phrase from Jacques Derrida, the English *Salomé* may be regarded as a text "authorized but authorless," ambiguously floating on the waters of what was supposed to be mutual affection but what turned out, in fact, to be acrimony.[37] When the English version eventually appeared, Wilde's name stood on the title page; but the dedication was to Douglas as translator.[38]

Beardsley, who was drawn into the fracas, also unsuccessfully tried his hand at translating the play.[39] Although this sickly young man, only twenty-one in 1893, defined himself against Wilde's sexual deviance, he nonetheless proved to be his most intimate collaborator; the drawings effect a visual synesthesia that succeeds in evoking the somatic and specifically genital processes that Wilde intends his drama to bring vividly to mind. Moreover, while the illustrations evoke Beardsley's satiric view of the exploitative aspects of male-male sexuality, his repeated figurings of Wilde's presence in the play reveal Beardsley to have been one of Wilde's most discerning readers. Besides the figure of Wilde as the man/woman in the moon discussed above, Beardsley also images Wilde as Herod casting a voyeuristic glance at Salomé and, in another drawing, as the costumed master of revels who

[34]Gilbert, "Tumult of Images," 153.
[35]For Douglas's efforts to have sexual activities between men decriminalized, see Hyde, *Douglas,* ch. 2.
[36]Oscar Wilde, *Complete Works,* intro. Vyvyan Holland (London: Collins, 1967), 552.
[37]Jacques Derrida, "Women in the Beehive: A Seminar," in *Men in Feminism,* ed. Alice Jardine and Paul Smith (New York: Methuen, 1987), 189.
[38]Ellmann, *Wilde,* 380–381.
[39]Hyde, *Douglas,* 46.

presents the spectacle that stages his own obsessions.[40] In each of these equivocal images, Beardsley connotes within a sequence of putatively heterosexual representations a drive towards the unmasking of Wilde's fixation on the male body as an object of desire.

The gender of the actor who plays Salomé inflects the sexual politics of any particular production of the play. In *Salomé*, the body is not only an image but also a physical presence. When Stéphane Mallarmé, the hierophant of Symbolism, wrote to Wilde after the publication of *Salomé* in February 1893, Mallarmé located the body in the play between the ideal Symbolist state of consciousness, *le Songe*, and a term that in part signifies preterition, *l'indicible:* "I marvel that, while everything in your *Salome* is expressed in constant dazzling strokes, there also arises, on each page, the unutterable and the Dream."[41] Mallarmé then remarks: "So the innumerable and precise jewels can serve only as an accompaniment to the gown for the supernatural gesture of that young princess whom you definitively evoked."[42] Mallarmé poses *Salomé* between words that are a material, even painterly, veil and actions whose excess indicates a visionary perception. Between language and vision exists the body, the *geste surnaturel* of Salomé's dance and final, rapt kiss. Her body, adorned but withheld by textuality, on the one hand, and transformed into a symbol of the inexpressible, on the other, is dramatically perverse.

In the context of the sexual politics in the male press in England, Salomé's body is most definitely female, and her unleashed sexual appetite queasily conjures the current fears of that self-assertive type known as the New Woman. Linda Dowling has pointed out the connections that contemporary journalists observed between male decadence and the New Woman of the 1890s: "The New Woman . . . was perceived to have ranged herself perversely with the forces of cultural anarchism and decay precisely because she wanted to reinterpret the sexual relationship."[43] Wilde's Salomé, who exists for her own pleasure and not to grace, serve, or reproduce for the benefit of male interests, threatens the stability of normal gender relations. Beardsley accentuates the threat by drawing John as her double in *John and Salomé*. The fact that Wilde parodies while exploiting the veilings of Symbolist aesthetics should not obscure the existence, on another level, of his parody of the press's satiric representations of modern women, "the Militant Daughters, of Key and Club."[44]

---

[40]See the illustrations facing pp. 24 and 18.

[41]"J'admire que tout étant exprimé par de perpétuels traits eblouissants, en votre *Salomé*, il se dégage, aussi, à chaque page, de l'indicible et le Songe" (quoted in Ellmann, *Wilde*, 354).

[42]"Ainsi les gemmes innombrables et exactes ne peuvent servir que d'accompagnement sur sâ robe au geste surnaturel de cette jeune princesse, que définitivement vous évoquates" (quoted in Ellmann, *Wilde*, 354).

[43]Linda Dowling, "The Decadent and the New Woman in the 1890's," *Nineteenth-Century Fiction* 33 (1978): 440–441.

[44]Quoted from *Punch* (1894) in Dowling, "Decadent and New Woman," 440.

In the opening section, I mentioned the presence of four spectacles in the play. The first of these is the entry of John the Baptist onto the stage, an entry delayed so as to gain maximum advantage from the appearance of a semi-nude, slender male form. The language of Salomé's profane parody of the *Song of Songs* indicates that her attraction to this body is thoroughly phallicized: "Comme il est maigre aussi! Il ressemble à une mince image d'ivoire. On dirait une image d'argent. Je suis sûre qu'il est chaste, autant que la lune. Il ressemble à un rayon d'argent. Sa chair doit être très froide comme de l'ivoire" (14).[45] Likewise, her evocation of John's mouth is saturated by an obsession with male hegemonic power:

> Ta bouche est comme une branche de corail que des pêcheurs ont trouvée dans le crépuscule da [sic] la mer et qu'ils réservent pour les rois . . .! Elle est comme le vermillon que les Moabites trouvent dans les mines de Moab et que les rois leur prennent. Elle est comme l'arc du roi des Perses qui est peint avec du vermillon et qui a des cornes de corail. Il n'y a rien au monde d'aussi rouge que ta bouche. (17)[46]

Salomé projects herself as one of the kings who "take." Similarly, in the second spectacle in the play, or her dance, the bodily power that Herod wishes to take from his stepdaughter by staging her performance for the benefit of his visitors is reappropriated by Salomé, who dances for her own pleasure in a series of movements whose genital analogue is the practice of masturbation. The third, unseen spectacle in *Salomé* is the execution of John under the sign of the Tetrarch's authority, *"the ring of death"* (33). The fourth spectacle, a pratfall turned tragic, is the execution of Salomé herself.

The first three staged spectacles turn about the fourth. In terms of conventional sexuality, Salomé's dance represents a force of bodily attraction that is able to subvert the customary superiority of men; in terms that the Victorians would have regarded as perverse, the dance is also masturbatory. The final scene of *Salomé* represents the restoration of patriarchal authority at the price of negating Salomé and Herod as subjects of desire. The scene of the kissing of John's head implies not only a fixation on the cock—as Pigott surmised to his delight—but also a fixation on what a later reader might designate as the phallus.[47] When Salomé takes John's head, she is also taking Herod's power, even though, since she is still playing a game of which Herod is master, taking his power puts her in jeopardy. What makes Salomé's demand insufferable is neither her lust nor her vindictiveness, but the rupture that she forces in the tensions of patriarchal power. Herod attempts to balance the requirements of colonial administration against those of the religion of

---

[45]"How wasted he is! He is like a thin ivory statue. He is like an image of silver. I am sure he is chaste as the moon is. He is like a moonbeam, like a shaft of silver" (10). The final sentence in French is not translated.

[46]"Thy mouth is like a branch of coral that fishers have found in the twilight of the sea, the coral that they keep for the kings! . . . It is like the vermilion that the Moabites find in the mines of Moab, the vermilion that the kings take from them. It is like the bow of the King of the Persians, that is painted with vermilion, and is tipped with coral. There is nothing in the world so red as thy mouth" (12).

[47]According to Ellmann, Wilde, who did not practice anal copulation, favored the practices of "oral and intracrural intercourse" (*Wilde*, 433, 259).

Jehovah. In his mind, both powers have sway, so that the exercise of his function as King is neither simple nor univocal. By using his oath for herself and against him, Salomé undoes the Tetrarch's uneasy balance of conflicting anxieties. It is for this reason that Salomé must be destroyed—as if the destruction of her body, of her desire, could suture a wound torn in Herod by his desire for (power over) her.

Jonathan Dollimore has recently argued that in the critical apothegms of Oscar Wilde, one may ascertain that dissolution of the individual ego which is perceived as characteristic of our postmodern moment. If Dollimore is correct in suggesting that "for Wilde transgressive desire leads to a relinquishing of the essential self," then Wilde's writing provides one ground for understanding the end of sage tradition as it existed in Victorian England up through Arnold and Pater.[48] Although Wilde begins within this tradition, he produces work in which the body and its practices make their claims at the expense of psychological and social order. Yet if *Salomé* is material in the sense of being bodily, it is also material in the way in which it responds to and helps form new constituencies of readers: specifically, women and male homosexuals.[49] The deliberate construction of marginal discourses and their attendant readership occurs at the expense of the writing that characterizes the tradition as Holloway and DeLaura have described it.

By way of a conclusion, I will consider briefly how that tradition begins to be transformed as young women write from novel subject positions. While Virginia Woolf expresses her relation with Wilde by maintaining a complete silence about him in the first two volumes of her letters, other women have left responses that indicate their contradictory relation to the tradition that Wilde both inhabits and subverts.

As an undergraduate journalist, Willa Cather identified herself with Carlylean models of the writer as either "heroic warrior" or "divine creator."[50] Cather's anxiety that being a woman might disqualify her from becoming a serious writer helps explain why, writing late in 1894, she rejects the "driveling effeminacy" of Wilde and his transatlantic epigones.[51] Fear of the male with a female soul likewise signals Cather's concern that she might be accused of being a lesbian, that hybrid creature with the soul of a man in the body of a woman. Earlier in 1894, reviewing a production of *Lady Windermere's Fan,* she had been incensed at Wilde's characterization of Lady Windermere as lacking the natural feelings of a mother.[52] At

[48]Jonathan Dollimore, "Different Desires: Subjectivity and Transgression in Wilde and Gide," *Genders* 2 (July 1988): 31.

[49]Elaine Scarry has discussed the relation between the body and textuality in her Introduction to *Literature and the Body: Essays on Populations and Persons* (Baltimore: Johns Hopkins University Press, 1988), xx-xxi.

[50]Sharon O'Brien, *Willa Cather: The Emerging Voice* (New York: Oxford University Press, 1987), 147.

[51]Willa Cather, *The Kingdom of Art: Willa Cather's First Principles and Critical Statements 1893–1896* (Lincoln: University of Nebraska Press, 1966), 135. O'Brien, who cites the passage in *Willa Cather* (151), has an excellent discussion of the masculinist bias of Cather's aesthetic at the time (ch. 7).

[52]Cather, *Kingdom*, 389.

least in part, her aggressive assertion of the maternal character of female nature functions to ward off allegations that she herself might be unnatural.

This defensive posture is corroborated by the article on Wilde that Cather published in September 1895, after the trials.[53] In this essay, Cather recapitulates the elements of sage writing as characterized by Landow but translated into the terms of one of Wilde's constituencies.[54] After using Wilde's "insanity" as an example of contemporary decadence and remarking that "he has made even his name impossible," Cather nonetheless shows him the respect of specifying his deviance by quoting from an early poem, "Hélas!," where he writes:

> . . . lo! with a little rod
> I did but touch the honey of romance
> And must I lose a soul's inheritance?[55]

And, at the end of the essay, she turns his debacle to prophetic account by wondering aloud "whether Oscar Wilde, and all the rest of us for that matter, will not have another chance . . . where the soul can feel as here the senses do, where there will be a better means of knowing and of feeling than through these five avenues so often faithless, that alike save and lose us, that either starve us or debauch us."[56] This passage looks forward to an utopian time when what was sundered in Wilde will achieve integration. Moreover, by using the pronoun "us," she includes herself among homosexual men and women who face difficulties akin to his.

Cather was able to relinquish the example of Wilde no better than she was able to yield her desire for other women. In "The Novel Démeublé" (1922) she speaks both of love of women—and kinship with Wilde.[57] In this, her best known essay, Cather refers to the female friendship/love that animates her writing: "Whatever is felt upon the page without being specifically named there—that, one might say, is created. It is the inexplicable presence of the thing not named, of the overtone divined by the ear but not heard by it, the verbal mood, the emotional aura of the fact or the thing or the deed, that gives high quality to the novel or the drama, as well as to poetry itself."[58] Sharon O'Brien finds a clue to Cather's allusion to female

[53]Eve Kosofsky Sedgwick has commented on the homophobia of the essay in "Across Gender" (paper delivered at the Program Session "Men Reading Lesbian Literature and Women Reading Gay Literature," Modern Language Association Convention, San Francisco, 29 December 1987).

[54]"The Victorian sage adopts not only the general tone and stance of the Old Testament prophet but also the quadripartite pattern with which the prophet usually presents his message. . . . The prophets of the Old Testament first called attention to their audience's present grievous condition and often listed individual instances of suffering. Second, they pointed out that such suffering resulted directly from their listeners' neglecting . . . God's law. Third, they promised further, indeed deepened, miseries if their listeners failed to return to the fold; and fourth, they completed the prophetic pattern by offering visions of bliss that their listeners would realize if they returned to the ways of God" (Landow, *Elegant Jeremiahs*, 26).

[55]Cather, *Kingdom*, 389, 391.

[56]Cather, *Kingdom*, 393.

[57]O'Brien, *Cather*, 125–126.

[58]Willa Cather, *On Writing: Critical Studies on Writing as an Art* (New York: Knopf, 1949), 41–42. Next to this passage in the copy that I use from Robarts Library at the University of Toronto, are penciled glosses: "not named" and "grt. line."

intimacy in the phrase, "the thing not named," with its conscious echo of "the phrase used as evidence at Oscar Wilde's trial: the 'Love that dared not speak its name.' "[59] In this way, Cather identifies herself with the life of the man whom, in 1895, she had decried.

Katherine Mansfield was also an especially devoted reader of Wilde. After a young woman gave her a copy of *The Picture of Dorian Gray* in the unexpurgated version that had first appeared in *Lippincott's Magazine,* Mansfield copied numerous passages into her journal between 1906 and 1908. She divined a usable moral in Wilde's novel: "To love madly perhaps is not wise, yet should you love madly, it is far wiser than not to love at all."[60] When Mansfield became involved in love affairs with two young women in New Zealand in 1907, she did so directly under the influence of Wilde.[61] And when, two years later, she married George C. Bowden in a moment of panic, Wilde became a sign of all that she now put aside. In an extraordinary letter, written to an unnamed female friend, Mansfield says: "In New Zealand Wilde acted so strongly and terribly upon me that I was constantly subject to exactly the same fits of madness as those which caused his ruin and his mental decay. When I am miserable now—these recur. Sometimes I forget all about it— then with awful recurrence it bursts upon me again and I am quite powerless to prevent it—This is my secret from the world and from you."[62] In this letter, Wilde is portrayed as a sexual daemon whose unpredictable visitations presage disaster.

While Mansfield was less successful in dealing with lesbian desire and with the intimidating maleness of literary culture than Cather, Wilde remained a salient point of reference. Years later, shortly before her death, Mansfield wrote John Middleton Murry, her second husband, to say that she had had a dream about meeting Wilde after his imprisonment, in a café, and of deciding to take him home to her parents. Once there, Wilde tells her of a hallucination that combines fantasies of fellatio, cunnilingus, and possibly anilingus:

> "You know, Katherine, when I was *in that dreadful place* I was haunted by the memory of a *cake*. It used to float in the air before me—a little delicate thing *stuffed* with cream and with the cream there was something *scarlet*. It was made of pastry and I used to call it my little Arabian Nights cake. But I couldn't remember the name. Oh, Katherine, it was *torture*. It used to *hang* in the air and *smile* at me. And every time I resolved that next time *they let someone* come and see me I would ask them to tell me what it was but every time, Katherine, I was *ashamed.* Even now. . . ."

When Mansfield in the dream responds by providing the name, "Mille feuilles à la crème," she obliquely confesses both to the fantasies and to the carceral state that she shares with Wilde. They are fellow convicts.[63]

[59]O'Brien, *Cather,* 126–127.
[60]Quoted in Jeffrey Meyers, *Katherine Mansfield: A Biography* (London: Hamish Hamilton, 1978), 25.
[61]Antony Alpers, *The Life of Katherine Mansfield* (New York: Viking Press, 1980), 46.
[62]Quoted in Alpers, *Mansfield,* 91.
[63]Katherine Mansfield, *Letters to John Middleton Murry: 1913–1922,* ed. John Middleton Murry (London: Constable, 1951), 582–583; italics are Mansfield's.

Cather's and Mansfield's responses indicate how equivocal the legacy of Wilde's particular sort of self-expression was for brilliant, unconventional women. Nonetheless, for women too, Wilde moves forward novel forms of self-identification; despite the dangers that he signals, he helps women like Cather and Mansfield claim for themselves both a power of utterance and a power over their bodies and relationships. Wilde's engagement in sexual politics marks the contingent character of his writing, contingencies at odds with the centripetal tendency of earlier sage discourse. In this respect, he comes at the point of dispersion at the end of a tradition; or, rather, in a world in which marginalities become crucial, the voice of the sage, as even in Cather's essay of 1895, prophecies differently.

Wilde and the Evasion of Principle

Joseph Loewenstein

Oscar Wilde, to the actor-manager George Alexander, after the first performance of *The Importance of Being Earnest:* "Charming, quite charming. And, do you know, from time to time it reminded me of a play I once wrote called *The Importance of Being Earnest.*"

There is more than a little risk in this enterprise. Though Wilde was himself a famous, if not to say notorious, critic, he was also unkind enough to remark on the inevitable folly of public pronouncement. "How appalling," he writes, "is that ignorance which is the inevitable result of imparting opinions." I will not be the first critic to go on about *The Importance of Being Earnest,* while appearing steadily to descend the evolutionary chain in the course of doing so. The first person to feel this way was William Archer—one of the few drama critics whom Wilde seems to have respected. When Archer reviewed the play, he too began from the vantage of self-pity: "What can a poor critic do with a play which raises no principle, whether of art or morals . . . and is nothing but an absolutely wilful expression of an irrepressibly witty personality?" Shaw had taken just such a tack in a review of Wilde's previous play, a review written for the *Saturday Review* a few weeks before *Earnest* opened, in which he observed that Wilde had the peculiar "property of making his critics dull."

Whether or not one sympathizes with my predicament or with Shaw's, one should, I think, sympathize with Archer's. He was the champion of *serious* Victorian drama, which meant, for him, being a champion of Ibsen's plays and of those early plays by Shaw which *looked* like Ibsen's plays only without the snow. He liked Wilde's plays, though; he couldn't help liking them—this is no doubt why Wilde liked his reviews—but his own principles kept him from knowing what to say about them.

The temptation not to say anything about such a play as *Earnest* is strong; and the temptation not to say anything *serious* about such a play is exceptionally strong. Yet one resists the temptation on Wilde's own orders, for oddly enough his own lectures, plays, novels, and conversation are full of insistences that criticism shares the mission of art, that art must be critical and criticism creative. I could sum up what my own thinly creative contribution will be here, but that would be inartistic. Even to hint darkly that I think the play to have been very aptly named

From *South Atlantic Quarterly* 84:4 (Autumn 1985):392–400. Reprinted with permission of Duke University Press.

or to reveal that this essay ought properly be entitled "Wilde as Moralist" is to give too much of the game away. Wilde once wrote that the primary function of criticism was "to deepen a book's mystery." Mystery is more difficult to generate than many readers think, but in his own critical writing Wilde overcomes this particular difficulty by avoiding straightforward pronouncement: he characteristically argues a delicate point by telling a story. Let me follow his lead.

Picture Wilde on the 14th of February in 1895, backstage at the St. James Theatre in London. The habitual elegance of his appearance is considerably muted in the dim lights of the wings. Indeed, his appearance had sobered of late: at just about that time when his plays began to succeed he gave up the velvet knee breeches which had been his sartorial signature during early adulthood. (Ada Leverson speaks of his having been dressed that evening with "a sort of florid sobriety.") But more than darkness and a *slight* swerve towards more conservative tailoring restrain the air of carefree ease that makes him seem, in his photographs, like so much human drapery. I hope I shall not be betraying probability by making the irreverent suggestion that Wilde is *concentrating* backstage at the St. James. Franklin Dyall, who played Merriman in the first production, provides the evidence here. His role had rather few lines, but one of them won him the loudest and most sustained laugh of his career. The line was, "Mr. Ernest Worthing has just driven over from the station. He has brought his luggage with him," and it is Wilde's response to the laugh that proves how closely he was attending to the performance: Dyall reports, "As I came off Wilde said to me: 'I'm so glad you got that laugh. It shows they have followed the *plot*.'"

Let me explain why I think the anecdote is important. I shall try to obey Wilde's alter-ego, Algernon Montcrieff, who tells his friend Jack, "Now produce your explanation, and pray make it improbable." The plot. Let me tell you a plot. It begins, if you will excuse the formulation, years after it begins. What I mean to say is that the events of this play involve a complicated investigation of how things got into the state of confusion in which we find the characters at the beginning of the play itself. Years earlier an infant had been separated from its parents, an unfortunate fact of biography that has hardly inhibited the baby from growing up to be a hero and from getting a play named after him. Through a complex chain of events he discovers his true identity and is reunited with his family. It all leads up to a spectacular final scene, perhaps the most famous scene in the history of Western drama. Indeed it is probably the most famous play in the history of Western drama. It is called *Oedipus Rex*.

I trust that it will be granted that the comparison of Wilde's play to Sophocles' is sufficiently improbable. Certainly the plots are not *absolutely* identical. Wilde has taken considerable care about this. In the Greek story, for example, the hero has a terrifying encounter with a she-dragon famous for asking difficult questions and I want to insist that it would be entirely inappropriate to compare the sphinx to Lady Bracknell, who is, as Jack puts it, "a monster without being a myth." But there's no denying that Wilde flirts brilliantly with *Oedipus Rex*, elements of which drop casually and hilariously into *The Importance of Being Earnest*. Sophocles' story is essentially about mistaking one's relatives, of confusing mother and wife, and Wilde toys with such confusion in a wonderfully sidelong manner during the first act when he has Algernon muse, in mock perplexity, over "why an aunt, should call her own nephew her uncle." Certainly the central irony of Sophocles' play is that the bed of conception and birth should be transformed into a bier, a site of death. Ancient as this paradox is, it is news to the monstrous Lady Bracknell, who insists that "Until yesterday I had no idea that there were any families or persons whose origin was a Terminus."

Lady B is punning, of course, and that is just the point: Wilde is steadily converting the tragic into the comic, ironic paradox into shrewd witticism. That is an old strategy, of course: Roman New Comedy took just this sort of tragic or romance plot—of foundlings, confusions of identity, and scrambled erotic attachment—and made it its own, asserting equal rights to such confusions. If it weren't for its dalliance with the plot of *Oedipus Rex,* it might be enough to speak of Wilde's play simply as another New Comedy. Perhaps it would be truer to say that *The Importance of Being Earnest* recovers the originary moment of New Comedy, and renews it.

My improbable explanation has a number of implications which I want to tease out a bit. The first is that it might help to focus our attention on the play more appropriately. It has become the custom for inattentive directors to concentrate, in casting, on Algernon and Lady Bracknell, and then to let the rest of the roles get sorted out as best they can. But if *The Importance of Being Earnest* is indeed a comic imitation of *Oedipus Rex,* then it is clearly Jack, or Earnest, as he in fact discovers himself to be, who is at the dramatic center. It is he, after all, who turns out to possess the crucial name—you will notice that at the end of the play Wilde finesses the problem that Algernon *can't* take the name of Earnest, for his long-lost brother has title to that title, which leaves Algy stuck as Algy (and, as Cecily has said before, she might not be able to give a person so named her "undivided attention"). At any rate, it is more important to be Jack than Algernon, since Jack is Earnest, and thus is the elder brother, the true heir to the Montcrieff fortune, and above all, the possessor of the magic name. But he is important for other reasons as well.

It is often objected that Wilde's characters all talk more or less alike, that the characters are all more or less the same. But Jack Worthing does not talk like Algernon Montcrieff. He aspires to talk like Algernon, aspires to the masterful urbanity of an Algernon, but he is a dreadful failure at it. He loses his cigarette case, gets stuck with the bill for dinner, fails to get more than a muffin or two of his own to eat in the third act and a few portions of bread and butter in the first, while Algernon gorges on the cucumber sandwiches and gets almost all of the muffins. The fact is that Jack is too much in earnest. His deceptions are in service of the most formal and pedestrian courtship, whereas Algernon deceives in order to flirt wildly.

Before the trip to Jack's place in Hertfordshire, Algernon's deceptions had always been in service of nothing but deception itself. Both deception and flirtation have the same name for Algy; both are called "Bunburying." This is Important. For Algy, artifice and eros have the same name, whereas for Earnest, they are opposed. As with Buster Keaton, the elegance of Jack's facade is constantly being betrayed by the earnestness within. In Wilde, as in Keaton's best films, concentration is a kind of distraction. The huge difference between Algernon and Jack is nowhere more obvious than at their entrances in Act II. When Jack appears, he looks like an undertaker; when Algernon enters, he looks like an ad for Christian Dior.

And of course *that* is why the play's curtain line is so very good. When Jack says, "I've now realized for the first time in my life the vital Importance of Being Earnest" he is punning, like Lady Bracknell talking about origins and terminuses. What he means is that it's important to have the name, Earnest, and that that's the only "Earnest-ness" that's good for anything at all. Seriousness hasn't done him any good in the course of the play; worst of all, seriousness has sapped all of his deceptions of fluency, of artistry. The last line is a sign that Jack has finally learned his lesson, which is that he must stop caring so much about things, stop trying to keep up appearances for Cecily's sake. Appearances must be kept up, says Wilde, for their *own* sake, because appearances are so very nice to look at.

So that is the first implication of the link between this play and *Oedipus Rex:* both plays, like most good plays, dramatize the hero's coming-to-knowledge, in this case a coming-to-knowledge about the use and abuse of seriousness that frees the characters to get down to some genuine artificiality. The next implication has to do with the very fact that comparing the two plays seems so improbable. In Sophocles' play, plot is nearly everything, whereas in Wilde's play, the plot has a tendency to disappear under the wonderful surface of aphorism. I could again quote the play to illustrate my point about the value of plotting: take the little exchange between Algernon and Jack at the end of Act I, where Jack objects to Algernon's delightfully complicated techniques for pitching woo. "If you don't take care," he says, "your friend Bunbury will get you into a serious scrape one of these days," to which Algernon replies, "I love scrapes. They are the only things that are never serious." Scrapes is a handy term, since it trivializes those contortions of strategem and coincidence which are at the center of Sophoclean plotting. When Algernon says that such plotting, such scrapes, are never serious, he is speaking as Wilde the literary critic. And here a bit of dramatic history will be useful.

William Archer, the critic to whom I referred earlier, was not only a fan of Wilde's, he was the chief spokesman for a movement in English dramatic writing that was advocating a new attention to social issues and that would find an idiom which would lend philosophical and tragic dignity to matters of political and topical concern. What Archer was in fact reacting to was the pervasive influence of the dramatic techniques of the French playwright Eugène Scribe, the master of the so-called "Well-Made Play." The well-made play is characterized by precisely that calculation of scheme and coincidence, that trick of falling into place, which is the signal feature of *Oedipus Rex.* Now Wilde's attitude to both the old school of Scribe and the new school of Archer is subtle and hilarious. In effect he accepts Archer's position that the well-made play is a kind of dramatic Bunburying, nothing but a sequence of "scrapes," but then he fails to join Archer in a full-scale assault on such plotting. What Wilde is doing, if you will permit a slight anachronism, is to make the well-made play into a kind of "camp." No wonder Archer felt perplexed by Wilde. Wilde was lavishing a mock literary nostalgia on Scribe, but without identifying himself with the forces of what Archer regarded as "progressive" playwrighting. Archer is the theatrical spokesman for a particular kind of Victorian value, what Matthew Arnold called "high seriousness," compounded with a degree of reformist fervor; Wilde called it "earnestness" and punned it out of existence.

It's an extremely powerful effect. First of all, Wilde manages to absorb Scribe's techniques by imitating Scribe's great Sophoclean model, but—as I said before—he inundates this plot with a tide of wonderfully musical wit, so that you hardly notice the plot which provides the technical underpinnings of the drama. Scribe and Sophocles endure an homage that leaves them looking rather frail and silly. And when we get to that very stagey last line, which is right out of Scribe, and miles beneath the literary standards of Archer's favorite playwrights, we hardly notice that the line really is summing up the play, really is showing us how irrelevant Arnoldian or Archerian seriousness is to the world of Wilde's plays. All of Wilde's influences come out looking sheepish at best.

Archer against Scribe, Scribe against Archer. Nowhere does the trick of getting one's predecessors to beat each other into jelly show up so powerfully as it does during the final scene of the play. As we are discovering the secret of Jack's mysteriously terminal origins, a fine sequence of exchanges take place. Jack announces his identity to Miss Prism and Wilde signals the particularly conventional quality of the scene by telling us that the lines are delivered "in a pathetic voice." Here is the exchange:

Jack:	Miss Prism, more is restored to you than this handbag. I was the baby you placed in it.
Miss Prism:	[amazed.] You?
Jack:	[embracing her.] Yes . . . mother!

This out-Scribes Scribe. More is falling into place than actually needs to fall into place, for Miss Prism is *not* Jack's mother. But it takes several more lines in order to straighten the misunderstanding out. Miss Prism responds, "recoiling in indignant astonishment" according to the stage direction:

| [*Miss Prism:*] | Mr. Worthing! I am unmarried! |
| *Jack:* | Unmarried! I do not deny that is a serious blow. But after all, who has the right to cast a stone against one who has suffered? Why should there be one law for men, and another for women? Mother, I forgive you! |

Since the fate of the Fallen Woman is one of the great staples of late Victorian social drama in the Archer tradition, what we have here is a perfect example of out-Archering Archer. The breadth of spirit, the exquisite liberality of young Earnest Worthing is utterly unnecessary here, so that Scribe's plotting has disabled Archer's principles. It is a cunning scene, and a cunning piece of dramatic criticism.

Wilde's other plays are not really very good, but noticing the way in which they fail may help us to understand the peculiar character of Wilde's success in *Earnest*. Of all Wilde's other plays, the one that comes closest to working is his serious attempt to write an Archerian Fallen Woman play, *Lady Windermere's Fan*. (Archerian in conception, but *also* neatly Scribal: the crucial fan—like the handbag at Victoria Station—is an object invested with remarkable power over plot; such potent props were a staple of Scribe's Well-Made Play.) It fails because Wilde can't get his tone to settle down enough to accommodate the plot. Instead, the dialogue frequently rallies itself up to a sparkle that gets in the way of the slow workings of suspicion and self-defense that knit the play together. Wilde was shrewd enough to recognize finally that he didn't really like plots, so when he sat down to write *Earnest* he took a few bits of the most famous plot in existence, crumpled them up, and then smothered them with mannerism: in effect, he adapts form to content by papering over the content. That he chooses what must be called the master-plot of Western drama is both characteristically sophomoric and characteristically self-aware: if one is uncomfortable with plotting, why not sabotage the model of plotting, so that plotting itself will look like a game not worth playing?

The gesture is less cavalier than perhaps I have made it seem. If Wilde sacrifices plot to the surface sparkle of aphorism it's because he is one of the great English philosophers of the surface. It is also because he is, in his own way, a *moralist* of the surface.

The best way to explain what I mean by this is to change the subject. Consider a passage by another great poetic moralist, a passage from *The Marriage of Heaven and Hell* in which Blake gives his own very special definitions for the two partners, Heaven and Hell, whose marriage he is announcing:

> Without Contraries is no progression. Attraction and Repulsion, Reason and Energy, Love and Hate, are necessary to Human existence.
>
> From these contraries spring what the religious call Good & Evil. Good is the passive that obeys Reason. Evil is the active springing from Energy.

In what seems a moment of rhetorical condensation, Blake finishes his definitions thus:

> Good is Heaven. Evil is Hell.

Now this is very shrewd. The definitions stack up in such a way that one begins to suspect that Good is not so good, and that Evil, if it's allied to energy and activity, can't be all bad. So when we get to the final line it's hard to know how to take it. Yet it has the outward form of a perfectly comprehensible, perfectly orthodox assertion: Heaven is the good place, hell the bad place. Not only do we not know how to take it when Blake says this, not only do we not know what he means by Heaven, if it's good and good is passive and cut off from energy, but we also begin to doubt the very form of such pronouncements. What Blake manages to do is to take the form of the aphorism and make us wonder why we usually have such an unquestioning and docile attitude to ideas when they're cut up for us so neatly. The very simplicity of the proverb form is on display, and under attack.

Wilde may well owe as much to Blake as did his young friend Yeats. Certainly Wilde is no more devoted to witty iconoclasm than is Blake; certainly Wilde is no less devoted a practitioner of the anti-authoritarian proverb than is Blake. Blake's defense of the imaginary over the merely factual, as in the line, "What is now proved was once merely imagined," could be a snatch from Wilde's conversation, while Wilde's "Even things that are true can be proved" sounds just like Blake. (Only such an embittered remark as Wilde's "A thing isn't necessarily true because a man dies for it" reveals something—specifically a bitter hostility to romantic idealism—that could legitimately be claimed as beyond Blake's reach.) Both men are primarily interested in the Witticism as a form, because it manages to disguise the rebellious in the very garb of the prescriptive.

Consider the opening witticism from Wilde's famous "Phrases and Philosophies for the Young":

> The first duty in life is to be as artificial as possible. What the second duty is no one has as yet discovered.

Part of what makes this brilliant is that it seems to promise that you could make a list, in descending order of importance, of what a person ought to do. It then quite splendidly fails to deliver on the promise. At the same moment that it lays down a law, it makes a monkey of lawyers, who can't remember all the commandments but are sure that there are ten of them. The lawyers knew that they were being made monkeys of, though, for when Wilde was on trial for his relations with Douglas, the lawyers interrogated him very closely on "Phrases and Philosophies for the Young," recognizing that the form of the witty phrase itself was under attack, that the notion that morality can be summarized, that its complexities can be distilled into Rules was crumbling under Wilde's gloved hand.

Besides its crucial function of obscuring the plot, how does the form of witticism operate in *The Importance of Being Earnest*? Again, Wilde gives the characters something very telling to say on the matter. Here, again, is Algernon:

> | [Algernon]: | All women become like their mothers. That is their tragedy. No man does. That's his. |
> | Jack: | Is that clever? |
> | Algernon: | It is perfectly phrased! and quite as true as any observation in civilized life should be. |

Algernon is telling us exactly how to take the play. We are to approve the elegance of its phrasing, and to take its claims to truth with strictly measured amounts of salt. The Witticism does not pretend to truth with a capital T. What it pretends to is *accuracy,* by which I mean to say something like occasional appropriateness to the sweet and petty business of getting along in polite society, an observation pertinent, not to reality, but to civilized life.

It should be clear now why I intended to entitle this piece "Wilde as Moralist." Like Blake, Wilde hated Truths. They hated them because Truths put blinders on us, tell us what to do before we know who we are or where we are, in whose company, in what room. The primary function of Wilde's witticisms, so neatly packaged and so perfectly balanced, is to erode our confidence in neat packaging and perfect balance as a vehicle for inculcating ethical values. Wilde's description of a cigarette might as well be a description of the witticism as a form, or of *Earnest* as a piece of dramatic construction; "A cigarette," he says, "is the perfect type of a perfect pleasure. It is exquisite, and it leaves one unsatisfied." The witticism excites our delight in matters of moral concern and steadily denies us the satisfaction of easy or universally adequate reflections on those matters.

This, I take it, is a moral position. To bury plot under clever talk is to insist that what happens to people is never as important as what people make of what happens to them. Each time an event sinks beneath a wave of wit we are being shown how much more valuable sense is than sensation. And when a second witticism shoulders aside a first, and a third displaces the second, we are being shown that any act of making sense of sensation is merely provisional. Wilde shows us that there are no satisfactory rules to lay down about life save that no matter what happens, it is always pleasant to lay down a rule about it; or to translate this in such a way that it reveals the moral passion that animated so much of Wilde's work: There are no Moral Laws; there is only moral labor. Hence the justice of what Borges has to say about the man: "Like Gibbon, like Johnson, like Voltaire, he was an ingenious man who was also right."

"The Importance of Being Earnest"

Katharine Worth

First performed St James's Theatre, 14 February 1895. Published 1899 (in limited edition).

The Importance of Being Earnest is Wilde's funniest play and it is also the most poignant, if we have in mind—as how can we not?—the disaster that struck its author only a few weeks after its glittering first night when Queensberry instigated the process that led to Reading Gaol. It was just the terrible peripeteia he had imagined for Robert Chiltern: one moment the "splendid position," the next, public humiliation and the odious gloating of hypocrites. The fall was symbolically encapsulated in the fate of the posters advertising the new play and also *An Ideal Husband* which was still running at the Haymarket. A splendid position indeed, to have two plays enjoying huge success side by side in London's most fashionable theatres. Yet it was wiped out overnight, when Wilde's name was obliterated from the posters, by George Alexander at the St James's, and Lewis Waller at the Haymarket. It is something to set against the weakness of the two actors, who owed so much to Wilde, the courage of Charles Wyndham who refused to receive *An Ideal Husband* at his theatre, the Criterion (where it had been scheduled to move), unless Wilde's name were restored to the bills. And this was done.

In *The Importance of Being Earnest* the pleasure principle at last enjoys complete triumph. Some critics disapprove of this, notably Mary McCarthy who censures the dandies' determination to live a life of pleasure as "selfishness."[1] Perhaps it is, but we are not being required to examine their moral behaviour in humane Chekhovian terms. This is a philosophical farce, an existential farce, to use the modern term which modern criticism is beginning to see as appropriate for this witty exploration of identities. "Pleasure," a word which recurs much, is a shorthand for the idea Wilde expounded in "The Soul of Man under Socialism":

> Pleasure is Nature's test, her sign of approval. When man is happy, he is in harmony with himself and his environment. The new Individualism, for whose service Socialism, whether it wills it or not, is working, will be perfect harmony.[2]

Excerpted from Katharine Worth, *Oscar Wilde* (New York: Grove Press, 1983). Reprinted with permission of Macmillan Press Limited.

[1]M. McCarthy, "The Unimportance of Being Oscar" in R. Ellmann, ed., *Oscar Wilde: A Collection of Critical Essays*, pp. 107–10.

[2]For this and other quotations from the same source, see, "The Soul of Man under Socialism," *Works*, pp. 1018–43.

Only in Utopia can this harmony be achieved; in theatrical terms that meant farce, the form that refused the agonies of melodrama. Wilde had observed that farce and burlesque offered the artist in England more freedom than the "higher" forms of drama. He was following Nietzsche, who had said much the same thing a decade or so earlier. In this extravagant genre, which no one took seriously, the dionysiac spirit could be fully released, to overturn respectable reality, and through paradox, fantasy and contradiction establish a logic of its own, defying the censorious super-ego. As Wilde put it in an interview given before the first production, the philosophy of his piece is that "we should treat all the trivial things of life very seriously and all the serious things of life with sincere and studied triviality."[3] It is a play of mirror images in which ordinary, everyday life can still be glimpsed through the comic distortions imposed upon it. Everything is double, from the double life of Algernon and Jack to the sets of doubles at the end, when the girls form themselves into opposition to the male image which has so conspicuously failed to be "Ernest."

In this play more than in any of the others it is vital for the actors to seem unaware of the absurdity of what they do and say. In the first production Irene Vanbrugh, playing Gwendolen, was paralysed with terror at being unable to find the right style; someone advised her to "think" the lines before speaking them, and she felt she then became more natural. However, according to Shaw, the actors in the first production were insufferably affected: Cecily had too much conscious charm, the older ladies too much low comedy; even George Alexander, whose grave, refined manner as Jack made suitable contrast with Algernon's easy-going style, ruined the third act by bustling through at such a rate that he quite lost the "subdued earnestness" which Shaw felt should characterise the role.[4] (Wilde had doubted his suitability for the part.) A few years later (in the 1902 revival at the St. James) Max Beerbohm found the actors making the same mistakes. Only Lilian Braithwaite "in seeming to take her part quite seriously, showed that she had realised the full extent of its fun." George Alexander was still bustling—at breakneck speed—and the part of Chasuble was played "as though it were a minutely realistic character study of the typical country clergyman."[5]

"Everything matters in art except the subject," said Wilde. In *The Importance of Being Earnest* the subject certainly cannot be distinguished from the style, yet the fact that the play succeeded (as it did on both the occasions quoted) even when the actors were playing it wrongly shows what a steely construction it has. It must have given Wilde the craftsman much pleasure to take the familiar melodrama mechanism (mistaken identities, incriminating inscriptions, secrets of the past) and exploit its inherent absurdity instead of trying to restrain it. The closeness of farce to melodrama is one of his strong cards, in fact, allowing all kinds of oblique references to the oppressive moral laws which had malign consequences in the

[3] *St James's Gazette*, 18 January 1895. Mikhail, p. 250.
[4] G. B. Shaw, *Dramatic Opinions and Essays*, pp. 32–5.
[5] M. Beerbohm, *Around Theatres*, pp. 188–91.

earlier plays—and, as Wilde thought, in English society. As well as being an existential farce, *The Importance of Being Earnest* is his supreme demolition of late nineteenth-century social and moral attitudes, the triumphal conclusion to his career as revolutionary moralist.

Wilde has sometimes been seen as an over-tolerant, even careless craftsman, only too ready to accept textual alterations called for by his actor-managers. *The Importance of Being Earnest* has been cited as an illustration: it was originally in the more usual four-act form, but when Alexander asked him to shorten it (almost unbelievably, to make room for a curtain raiser) Wilde obliged him to the extent of dropping the third act. As Lady Bracknell might have said, to lose a scene or two might be regarded as a misfortune, to lose a whole act seems like carelessness. However, if we study the four-act draft, we can see how far from carelessly Wilde made his revisions and indeed how much the play is improved by rigorous cutting which gives it a more spare and modern look.[6] Farce should have the speed of a pistol shot, said Wilde, and speed is, indeed, a distinctive and curious feature of *The Importance of Being Earnest;* curious, because it co-exists with extreme slowness and stateliness in the dialogue. No one is ever so agitated that he cannot take time to round a sentence, find the right metaphor—or finish off the last muffin. Yet all the time sensational changes are occurring at the speed of light. Proposals of marriage are found to have been received even before they were uttered, relations lost and found before one can say "hand-bag." Time, like everything else, goes double and through the "gaps" Wilde insinuates the notion that the action is really all happening somewhere else, in the mental dimension where ruling fantasies are conceived, which is not to say of course that there is no connection with reality: "Life imitates Art far more than Art imitates life." The outlines of reality are easily discernible; Lane offering deadpan excuses for the absence of cucumber sandwiches, Dr Chasuble fitting in the absurd christening to his perfectly normal programme: "In fact I have two similar ceremonies to perform at that time. A case of twins that occurred recently in one of the outlying cottages on your own estate. Poor Jenkins the carter, a most hard-working man." What is wrong with this society, so the farce implies, is its fatal inability to distinguish between the trivial and the serious. Sense and nonsense, reason and fantasy, facts and truth, are juggled with, forcing new perspectives, offering release from the cramp of habit and logic:

Algernon:	Please don't touch the cucumber sandwiches. They are ordered specially for Aunt Augusta. *(Takes one and eats it.)*
Jack:	Well, you have been eating them all the time.
Algernon:	That is quite a different matter. She is my aunt.

How can one challenge the impeccable logic of this? Only by lapsing into earnestness, which the play is set up expressly to forbid. Shaw's complaint that the farce

---

[6]The fullest edition of the four-act version is S. A. Dickson, ed. 2 vols, New York Public Library, Arents Tobacco Collection Publication no. 6, 1956. An English edition was edited by V. Holland, 1957. The Gribsby episode is printed in the New Mermaids edition of the play.

was never lifted onto a higher plane was an extraordinary failure of judgment for him. How good-humoured of Wilde to say only "I am disappointed in you."

It is an urbane Utopia we see when the curtain goes up on the first act. Algernon's rooms in Half Moon Street (a more relaxed environment than the grand locales of earlier plays) are "luxuriously and artistically furnished"; music is heard from the off-stage piano (perhaps a dubious pleasure, as Algernon saves his science for life and relies on sentiment in his piano playing). The elegant sallies between Algernon and his "ideal butler," Lane, are another feature of Wilde's Utopia; servants are more than equal to masters. With the entrance of Jack, the "pleasure" motif rings out loud and clear:

Algernon:	How are you, my dear Ernest? What brings you up to town?
Jack:	Oh pleasure, pleasure! What else should bring one anywhere . . .

Tom Stoppard lifted this debonair entrance to serve as a "time stop" in *Travesties,* a sticking place in the mind to which the action obsessively returns. He assigns Jack's lines to Tristan Tzara, the Dadaist, making a connection between the pleasure philosophy, revolution and nihilism. Jack and Algernon are not exactly revolutionaries, but they do bring into the play from time to time a rather modern emphasis on the idea of nothingness, as when they discuss ways they might spend the evening:

Algernon:	What shall we do after dinner? Go to a theatre?
Jack:	Oh no! I loathe listening.
Algernon:	Well, let us go to the Club?
Jack:	Oh no! I hate talking.
Algernon:	Well, we might trot round to the Empire at ten?
Jack:	Oh no! I can't bear looking at things. It is so silly.
Algernon.	Well, what shall we do?
Jack:	Nothing!

The malaise is kept at bay most of the time by the complications of the double life. Wilde amusingly recalls the impassioned detective sequences of *An Ideal Husband* in the inquisition conducted by Algernon into Jack's secrets. A precious mislaid object, the inscribed cigarette case, provides a crucial clue (parallelling the bracelet/brooch of the other play); Algernon presses his questions as unremittingly as Lady Chiltern ("But why does she call you little Cecily, if she is your aunt and lives at Tunbridge Wells?") and like Robert Chiltern, Jack fights off discovery with inventive lies. "Earnest" was the word for the Chiltern double life and "Earnest" is the word for Jack's too, in the double sense perceived by Algernon the moment Jack reveals his "real" name:

Algernon:	. . . Besides, your name isn't Jack at all; it is Ernest.
Jack:	It isn't Ernest; it's Jack.
Algernon:	You have always told me it was Ernest. I have introduced you to everyone as Ernest. You answer to the name of Ernest. You look as if your name is Ernest. You are the most earnest-looking person I ever saw in my life.

The brilliant pun is the corner-stone of a structure dedicated to dualities of all kinds. Jack is "Ernest in town and Jack in the country": he becomes "Ernest" in fact when he wants to escape from being "earnest"; the pun perfectly encapsulates the split in the personality. Neatness, taken to the point of surrealist absurdity, makes the same sort of suggestion throughout. Algernon's situation is a mirror image of Jack's. When he sums up the situation, he falls into a rhythm which is the quintessential rhythm of the play; a balancing of opposites, the "masks," which as the play goes on are to be juggled with increasingly manic ingenuity:

> You have invented a very useful younger brother called Ernest in order that you may be able to come up to town as often as you like. I have invented an invaluable permanent invalid called Bunbury, in order that I may be able to go down into the country whenever I choose.

Critics in Wilde's time did not grasp the subtlety of the structure. Even Max Beerbohm, an admirer, thought the play triumphed despite its farcical "scheme" which he summarised as: "the story of a young man coming up to London 'on the spree,' and of another young man going down conversely to the country, and of the complications that ensue." This comes nowhere near expressing the mysterious sense of what "town" and "country" represent for Jack and Algernon. "On the spree" is a phrase for the French *boulevard* farce and its "naughty" behaviour, which English audiences could enjoy in suitably watered down adaptations, with a feeling of moral superiority. Wilde slyly draws attention to this characteristic hypocrisy when Algernon gives Jack some very French advice:

Algernon:	A man who marries without knowing Bunbury has a very tedious time of it.
Jack:	That is nonsense. If I marry a charming girl like Gwendolen, and she is the only girl I ever saw in my life that I would marry, I certainly won't want to know Bunbury.
Algernon:	Then your wife will. You don't seem to realise, that in married life three is company and two is none.
Jack:	*(sententiously)* That, my dear young friend, is the theory that the corrupt French Drama has been propounding for the last fifty years.
Algernon:	Yes; and that the happy English home has proved in half the time.

There is little sense in the play of orgiastic goings on. "Eating" is the chief symbol of sensual activity.[7] The dandies' will to eat is part of the larger will which drives them and the girls (and indeed everyone in the play). Shaw might have called it the Life Force. Wilde uses a favourite metaphor: health. As Jack explains to Algernon, he needs Ernest because as Uncle Jack he is expected to maintain a high moral tone, and a high moral tone can hardly be said to conduce to one's health or happiness. We might wonder why the insouciant Algernon needs an escape route. But we find out when Lady Bracknell appears on the scene, ringing the bell in "Wagnerian manner" and greeting her nephew in a most remarkable variant of

---

[7] See D. Parker, "Oscar Wilde's Great Farce: *The Importance of Being Earnest,*" *Modern Language Quarterly*, vol. 35, No 2, June 1974.

common usage: "I hope you are behaving very well?" He fights back with "I'm feeling very well, Aunt Augusta," only to be overridden with magisterial finality: "That is not quite the same thing. In fact the two rarely go together." Judi Dench's unusually youthful Lady Bracknell in the National Theatre's 1982 production clearly had a somewhat over-fond interest in her elegant nephew, an unexpected slant which increased the psychological interest (Peter Hall, directing, saw the play as being "about love and about reality").

Lady Bracknell herself is dedicated to health; a supreme irony. As she tells Algernon when he produces Bunbury's illness yet again, as an excuse for avoiding her dinner party:

> I think it is high time that Mr Bunbury made up his mind whether he was going to live or to die. This shilly-shallying with the question is absurd. Nor do I in any way approve of the modern sympathy with invalids. I consider it morbid. Illness of any kind is hardly a thing to be encouraged in others. Health is the primary duty of life . . .

We can well see why Lord Bracknell had to become an invalid: she has taken all the health for herself. It is a measure of Wilde's ability to stand back from his own passionately held beliefs that the most completely realised personality in the play should be such a monster; as Jack says, "a monster without being a myth, which is rather unfair."

There is no doubt in this play that "women rule society." Lady Bracknell has a more central position in the dramatic action than the dowagers of earlier plays. The marriages are in her control, and it is she who (unwittingly) holds the key to Jack's identity. She comes on with Gwendolen in tow, in the manner of the Duchess of Berwick and Lady Agatha, and though Gwendolen is no Agatha, she is just as much in thrall to her mother when husbands are in question. On one of its levels the farce is certainly conducting the old campaign against the tyrannies that afflict women. There is an extra layer of irony indeed; we see how the system will perpetuate itself as the victims prepare to become tyrants in their turn, for Gwendolen is clearly her mother's daughter. It is not just a joke when Jack anxiously enquires: "You don't think there is any chance of Gwendolen becoming like her mother in about a hundred and fifty years, do you, Algy?" The proposal scene certainly gives him warning, with its focus on Gwendolen's will and the intensity of the inner life which surfaces (in appropriately "absurd" form) in her curious obsession:

> My ideal has always been to love someone of the name of Ernest. There is something in that name that inspires absolute confidence. The moment Algernon first mentioned to me that he had a friend called Ernest, I knew I was destined to love you.

There is obviously a dig here at the troublesome idealists of earlier plays: the whole ideal-oriented ethos is reduced to absurdity. It is a philosophical as well as a social joke, however. Could she not love him if he had some other name? "Ah!" says Gwendolen, "that is clearly a metaphysical speculation, and like most metaphysical speculations has very little reference at all to the actual facts of real life as we know them." She says it "glibly"; that is Wilde's joke, for though Gwendolen may be intellectually shallow, her devotion to her "ideal" reflects concepts Wilde took very seriously. Gwendolen is making the sacred effort to "realise one's own personality on some imaginative plane out of reach of the trammelling accidents and limitations of real life." When Jack calls her "perfect" she resists the term: "It would leave no room for developments, and I intend to develop in many directions."

The "limitations of real life" are soon imposed on the idyll when Lady Bracknell sweeps in, to surprise Jack on his knees: "Rise, sir, from this semi-recumbent posture. It is most indecorous." Her marriage questionnaire carries, in its absurd way, the whole weight of the commercially-minded society she epitomises:

Lady Bracknell:	. . . What is your income?
Jack:	Between seven and eight thousand a year.
Lady Bracknell:	*(makes a note in her book)* In land, or in investments?
Jack:	In investments, chiefly.
Lady Bracknell:	That is satisfactory. What between the duties expected of one during one's lifetime, and the duties exacted from one after one's death, land has ceased to be either a profit or a pleasure. It gives one position, and prevents one from keeping it up. That's all that can be said about land.

Anyone who can talk as well as this is bound to charm—still she cannot be thought totally charming. Real life is hovering there in the background, making us feel just a little mean at laughing when she holds forth on the nature of society from the height of her conservative hauteur. Her power is political as well as social; Wilde's point is that the two are one. Liberal Unionists are acceptable, she concedes, when Jack admits to being one: "they count as Tories. They dine with us. Or come in the evenings, at any rate." The fine shades of her condescension are droll, but a telling reminder of a real-life Byzantine grading system which ensures that politics are controlled by the right people.

It does not really matter what Jack admits to in the way of taste: there is no way of kowtowing to Lady Bracknell, for, as Mary McCarthy says, she has the unpredictability of a thorough *grande dame*. Jack is no doubt taken aback, as we are, by the remarkable triviality of her first question—"Do you smoke?"—and no doubt equally surprised by her response to his admission that he does:

I am glad to hear it. A man should always have an occupation of some kind. There are far too many idle men in London as it is.

It makes him understandably wary when she declares that "a man who desires to get married should know either everything or nothing," and asks "which" he knows. It is only after some hesitation that he commits himself: "I know nothing, Lady Bracknell." A fitting remark for an existential hero. She, of course, takes it in a social sense, as she does everything, and approves; a rich irony, for Jack's devotion to "nothing" goes along with his mercurial changeability, something she would deeply disapprove of. "Knowing nothing" for her means "ignorance," a very desirable quality in the lower classes:

The whole theory of modern education is radically unsound. Fortunately in England, at any rate, education produces no effect whatsoever. If it did, it would prove a serious danger to the upper classes, and probably lead to acts of violence in Grosvenor Square.

Great fun, in the context, yet are we meant to quite shut out reverberations from history—the Nihilists, the Irish, all the social ferment which troubled Wilde's conscience and is reflected in his other plays? It seems not, for the revolution theme comes up again in an explicit historical reference when Jack reveals the peculiar circumstances of his birth. Even Lady Bracknell cannot assimilate that anarchical phenomenon:

> . . . I don't actually know who I am by birth. I was . . . well, I was found . . . In a hand-bag—a somewhat large, black, leather hand-bag, with handles to it . . .

All her worst nightmares crowd—majestically—into the scene:

> To be born, or at any rate bred, in a hand-bag, whether it had handles or not, seems to me to display a contempt for the ordinary decencies of family life that reminds one of the worst excesses of the French Revolution. And I presume you know what that unfortunate movement led to?

This is no casual reference. The French Revolution figures in "The Soul of Man under Socialism" as illustration of the inevitability of change: "The systems that fail are those that rely on the permanency of human nature, and not on its growth and development. The error of Louis XIV was that he thought that human nature would always be the same. The result of his error was the French Revolution. It was an admirable result." By analogy, Lady Bracknell is necessary to the process she is resisting; Wilde provides us with a moral justification for the fact that we cannot help liking the monster!

There is also a little germ of existential anxiety in the great joke: "being" in an empty hand-bag; being in a void. Like a Vladimir or a Winnie in Beckett's empty spaces, Jack has to construct himself from virtually nothing. That is more or less what Lady Bracknell advises him to do before she departs in high dudgeon at the idea of Gwendolen being asked to "marry into a cloak-room, and form an alliance with a parcel." "I would strongly advise you, Mr Worthing," she says, "to try and acquire some relations as soon as possible." Ridiculous, yet it has already happened. Younger brother Ernest is soon to acquire extraordinary reality. Jack's fertile imagination rises to these challenges. "Gwendolen, I must get christened at once," was his immediate reaction to the revelation that she could only love a man called Ernest.

At the fall of the curtain on the first act the metaphysical dimension is thickening. Jack is in a tortuous relationship with the mythic self which he needs both to destroy ("I am going to kill my brother") and at the same time possess more completely (by having himself christened, a comical psychic ordeal). And Algernon, with the address of "excessively pretty Cecily" surreptitiously registered on his shirt-cuff, is gleefully preparing to get into his Bunbury clothes and take over the adaptable "Ernest" identity for himself. The juggling with personae is becoming more and more "absurd" in the modern sense.

The second act opens in a garden, a utopian setting such as Wilde had never quite allowed himself in earlier plays where the furthest we got into nature was a lawn under a terrace (though one critic draws attention to garden imagery in the dialogue of *A Woman of No Importance*).[8] This is not very wild nature, of course: still, there is emphasis on luxuriance (an old-fashioned abundance of roses) and various hints that this is the scene where growth and change are to be achieved. The "blue glass" stage floor and cut-out garden accessories in Peter Hall's 1982 production struck the right note of artfully stylised simplicity. In the four-act version a gardener appeared, an unexpected addition to the usual cast of butlers and valets. Here Cecily (significantly seen at the back of the stage, deep in the garden) is doing the gardener's work, a fact Miss Prism observes with distaste:

> Miss Prism: (*calling*) Cecily, Cecily! Surely such a utilitarian occupation as the watering of flowers is rather Moulton's duty than yours? Especially at a moment when intellectual pleasures await you. Your German grammar is on the table. Pray open it at page fifteen. We will repeat yesterday's lesson.
>
> Cecily: (*coming over very slowly*) But I don't like German. It isn't at all a becoming language. I know perfectly well that I look quite plain after my German lesson.

The reference to German as the bone of contention is no accident. Like the "pessimist" joke at the close of act one (Algernon accuses Lane of being a pessimist and is told "I always endeavour to give satisfaction, sir"), it is one of those oblique allusions to German philosophy which slyly suggest that the characters are enacting a Schopenhauer style struggle to realise the "will" and engage with the concept of "nothing." Jack always lays particular stress on the importance of Cecily's German when he goes off to town (to become his alter ego). So Miss Prism observes, while Cecily notes the strain involved: "Dear Uncle Jack is so very serious! Sometimes he is so serious that I think he cannot be quite well." She draws attention to the existential confusion which surely overtakes the audience by now. Who really is Jack/Ernest? Is he acting when he is serious Uncle Jack and is Ernest his true identity (as Gwendolen asserts)? Or is he really Jack struggling to manage the wicked brother, Ernest? He is often half way between the two, as the fluctuations in his style indicate. The man who entered the play on so airy a note ("Oh, pleasure, pleasure!") can talk very sententiously, and look the part too, as Algernon had observed.

Cecily has no such complications. Yet she is also in her way an existentialist, using her diary as the young men use Ernest to act out her "will." Wilde strikes very modern notes in the discussion sparked off by the diary about the difficulty of distinguishing between memory and fiction, both seen here as part of the self-creating process:

[8]P. K. Cohen, *The Moral Vision of Oscar Wilde*, pp. 201–3.

Cecily:	I keep a diary in order to enter the wonderful secrets of my life. If I didn't write them down, I should probably forget all about them.
Miss Prism:	Memory, my dear Cecily, is the diary that we all carry about with us.
Cecily:	Yes, but it usually chronicles the things that have never happened, and couldn't possibly have happened. I believe that Memory is responsible for nearly all the three-volume novels that Mudie sends us.

Miss Prism's confession that she once wrote a three-volume novel (leading to her memorable definition: "The good ended happily, and the bad unhappily. That is what Fiction means") contributes to the Beckettian shades in the comedy. But she, like her other half, Canon Chasuble, is really essence of nineteenth century. Through their delicious absurdities we discern, like shadows, characteristics that had to be taken more grimly in earlier plays: pomposity, self-importance, cruelty even (Miss Prism is much given to pronouncing. "As a man sows, so also shall he reap"). But rigid morality loses its power when the absurdly serious pair represent it. They have a foot in the utopian world.

Miss Prism too pursues a dream: "You are too much alone, dear Dr Chasuble. You should get married. A misanthrope I can understand—a womanthrope, never!" His scholarly shudder at the "neologistic" phrase reminds us, like his reference to Egeria which Miss Prism fails to understand ("My name is Laetitia, Doctor"), that there is a social gulf between them. She is hardly a highly-educated governess; we learn later that she started life as a nursemaid. Wilde is extending the satire on Victorian moral attitudes to take in the middle to lower classes, an interesting development which makes one more than ever sad at what may have been lost when catastrophe brought his playwriting to an end.

Cecily soon clears the stage for her own freedom. In her manipulation of the wobbling celibates ("it would do her so much good to have a short stroll with you in the park, Dr Chasuble"), she displays the masterfulness which makes her, like Gwendolen, more than a match for the men. Like a modern girl, she cuts Algernon down to size when he makes his appearance as Ernest on a somewhat arch note:

| Algernon: | You are my little cousin, Cecily, I'm sure. |
| Cecily: | You are under some strange mistake. I am not little. In fact, I believe I am more than usually tall for my age. |

Algernon, says the stage direction, is "rather taken aback." Well he might be: it is the end of his Bunburying days when Cecily takes charge, leading him into the house to start the process of "reforming" him.

It is an exquisite stroke of comic timing that at the very moment when brother Ernest has materialised for the first time, Jack should enter, in mourning for his death in Paris of a chill. Pictures of George Alexander in the part show him the very spirit of lugubriousness, in funereal black, with the "crepe hatband and black glowes" which Dr. Chasuble calls his "garb of woe." It is a great visual joke, demonstrating, as C. E. Montague said, the scenic imagination which distinguishes playwrights from other writers: "To an audience, knowing what it knows, the mere first sight of those black clothes is convulsingly funny; it is a visible stroke of humour, a witticism not heard but seen."[9] Wilde did not make much of the stage directions for *The Importance of Being Earnest:* they are less detailed than in earlier plays. When preparing proofs for publication in 1899, he remarked to Robert Ross that he did not much like giving physical details "about the bodies whose souls, or minds, or passions, I deal with. I build up so much out of *words* that the colour of people's hair seems unimportant." Yet Montague was right to stress the value of the scenic element. We do not need to know the colour of the characters' hair—what colour would Ernest's be?—but, as in all the plays, a delicate visual symbolism operates in *The Importance of Being Earnest*, crystallising underlying meanings. The spectacle of the "man in black" making those absurd arrangements to be christened ("Ah, that reminds me, you mentioned christenings, I think, Dr. Chasuble?") is surely, for us now, an existential joke.

Of course none of this shows to the stage audience. Jack's rather disturbing fluidity of character is highlighted by the rigidity of Miss Prism and Canon Chasuble: they move on the narrowest of lines and appeal to our sense of humour by having none themselves. It is one of Wilde's most dionysiac moments of glee when Jack, acting solemnity, draws forth the real solemnity of the celibate pair:

Chasuble:	Was the cause of death mentioned?
Jack:	A severe chill, it seems.
Miss Prism:	As a man sows, so shall he reap.
Chasuble:	*(raising his hand)* Charity, dear Miss Prism, charity! None of us are perfect. I myself am peculiarly susceptible to draughts. Will the interment take place here?
Jack:	No. He seems to have expressed a desire to be buried in Paris.
Chasuble:	In Paris! *(shakes his head)* I fear that hardly points to any very serious state of mind at the last.

This is the sort of caricature which is more lifelike than life itself. The consistent pair are in their way an anchor to a solid world where we expect people to be much the same from one day to another. In the other dimension, where there seems no limit to the characters' ability to change themselves, the action is becoming manic:

My brother is in the dining-room? I don't know what it all means. I think it is perfectly absurd.

It is "absurd" in Pinteresque vein when Jack, in mourning for Ernest, is impudently advised to "change":

Why on earth don't you go up and change? It is perfectly childish to be in deep mourning for a man who is actually staying for a whole week with you in your house as a guest. I call it grotesque.

---

[9] C. E. Montague, *Dramatic Values*, p. 186.

The alter ego is out of hand. Even the imperturbable Algernon is taken aback, in his second scene with Cecily, to realise how firmly she has defined his role in her "girlish dream." It was "on the 14th of February last that worn out by your entire ignorance of my existence, I determined to end the matter one way or the other, and after a long struggle with myself I accepted you under this dear old tree here." A very determined piece of dreaming, this,—a comical version of Schopenhauer's "world as idea"—held together, like Gwendolen's scenario, by the "ideal" Ernest.

Repetition and increasingly heavy stylisation from now on build up the impression that some psychic process is being acted out—in the absurd form appropriate to events in the unconscious. Algernon and Cecily must go through the same performance as Jack and Gwendolen; he must react in the same way as Jack to the realisation that "Ernest" is no longer a voluntary role by rushing off to be christened. And Gwendolen must appear, for a quarrel scene with Cecily which is in a way closer to the norm of nineteenth century comedy (Gilbert's *Engaged* was mentioned by contemporary critics), but acquires strangeness from the dream-like gap Wilde contrives between the solid, decorous surface (Merriman totally absorbed in supervising the tea-table rites) and the increasingly uninhibited argument about someone who doesn't exist. As the lines become ever more crossed—"Oh, but it is not Mr Ernest Worthing who is my guardian. It is his brother—his elder brother"—the audience has almost certainly lost its own grip on who is who, a confusion Wilde surely intends.

He evidently intends also the exaggerated stylisation which begins to push the farce away from even minimal realism when Jack and Algernon are brought face to face with Gwendolen and Cecily. Like automata, the girls ask the same questions and use the same movements, each in turn demanding of "her" Ernest, "May I ask if you are engaged to be married to this young lady?", and on receiving the desired assurance, proceeding to prick the bubble of the other's dream with a mannered precision which has drawn from modern critics terms like "courtship dance" to describe the manoeuvrings of the quartet:

> The gentleman whose arm is at present round your waist is my guardian, Mr John Worthing.
>
> The gentleman who is now embracing you is my cousin, Mr Algernon Moncrieff.

The breaking up and re-forming of pairs, the neat oppositions, the stilted repetitions, the speaking for each other (Gwendolen takes over Cecily's unformed question, "Where is your brother Ernest?"); all create a curious impression, of personality flowing unstoppably between two poles. Everything surprises us by being its own opposite ("A truth in Art is that whose contradictory is also true"). Things taken with deadly seriousness in the "modern life" plays are stood on their head, as in Jack's parodic confession:

> Gwendolen—Cecily—it is very painful for me to be forced to speak the truth. It is the first time in my life I have ever been reduced to such a painful position, and I am really quite inexperienced in doing anything of the kind. However I will tell you quite frankly that I have no brother Ernest. . . .

A subtle joke; for by the end we know that his brilliant invention was the truth; it was the facts that were untrustworthy ("Life imitates art far more than art imitates life").

Before we arrive at that revelation, the doubles have to reorganise themselves. The female pair retire into the house "with scornful looks" and the male pair are left to pick up the pieces of the shattered personality. Time is going round in circles; we are almost back in the first act with the cucumber sandwiches when Algernon settles down to the muffins and Jack reproaches him: "How you can sit there calmly eating muffins when we are in this horrible trouble, I can't make out. You seem to me to be perfectly heartless." Never for him, it seems, the intellectual aplomb which allows Algernon to short-circuit "absurd" anxieties with absurd and unanswerable logic: "Well, I can't eat muffins in an agitated manner. The butter would probably get on my cuffs."

In the final act we move back into the house; the garden idyll (the "beautiful" act, Wilde called it) is over, the "truth" is out and time is flowing back towards daylight. Gwendolen and Cecily are seen looking out of the windows at the young men, as if no time at all has elapsed, or just enough for them to say, in the past tense, "they have been eating muffins." Stylisation reaches its peak when the young men join them and both pairs address each other in choral unison, Gwendolen beating time "with uplifted finger." In an early draft, this went on longer and lines were split between characters, as Russell Jackson says, accentuating the effect of a duet.[10] It is an altogether musical scene: the men come on whistling "some dreadful popular air from a British opera" (not identified, but could Wilde wickedly have intended *Patience*?). In earlier drafts the stylisation was even more extreme and balletic. Jack and Algernon were to "move together like Siamese twins in every movement" when they make their announcement that they are to be christened:

> First to front of sofa, then fold hands together, then raise eyes to ceiling, then sit on sofa, unfold hands, lean back, tilting up legs with both feet off the ground, then twitch trousers above knee à la dude . . .

It is almost surrealist farce now; Jarry's painted puppets are over the horizon, and Ionesco's automata chorusing "The future is in eggs." Directors, alas, seldom pick up Wilde's hints for a modern style; they tend to keep a uniform tone, ignoring the upsurge of stylisation that makes the characters speak in tune, whistle, chant in chorus until, symmetrical to the last, the pairs are reconciled and fall into each other's arms, exclaiming "Darling!"

Only if this fantastic, balletic/musical effect is achieved (Peter Hall's production went further in this direction than most), can there be the right contrast of tone when Lady Bracknell sweeps in to drag them back to the real world. Despite the fun, that is what is happening when she sets about demolishing one unsuitable

---

[10]See R. Jackson, ed., *The Importance of Being Earnest*, for references to the drafts.

engagement and investigating the other with the suspicion induced by the previous day's revelations. "Until yesterday I had no idea that there were any families or persons whose origin was a Terminus." The wit warms us to her but cannot quite disguise the glacial nature of the snub. The whole tone is harder in this scene, perhaps because she is ruder (she makes Jack "perfectly furious" and "very irritable"); perhaps because repetition slightly reduces the comicality of her routines, making their social unpleasantness more apparent. When she asks "as a matter of form" if Cecily has any fortune and on learning that she has a hundred and thirty thousand pounds in the Funds, finds her "a most attractive young lady," we laugh, of course, but remembering the similar business with Jack, probably feel the edge in the joke more. There is something increasingly alarming as well as droll about her unselfconsciousness: can she really be so unaware or impervious, we wonder, or is she amusing herself with conscious irony when she reflects on Cecily's "really solid qualities" and how they will "last and improve with time," and with supreme effrontery presents herself as the opponent of mercenary marriages:

> Dear child, of course you know that Algernon has nothing but his debts to depend on. But I do not approve of mercenary marriages. When I married Lord Bracknell I had no fortune of any kind. But I never dreamed for a moment of allowing that to stand in my way.

There is no way of penetrating that formidable façade, to find out what goes on behind it (Peter Hall saw the whole action as determined by the will to conceal very strong and real feelings). Wilde planted a time bomb in this character, seemingly set for our time, when there would be a better chance of audiences picking up the serious points the jokes are making—about the "woman question" and marriage. The revelation that Cecily remains a ward till she is thirty-five, for instance, yields much fun, culminating in Lady Bracknell's dry comment that her reluctance to wait till then to be married shows "a somewhat impatient nature." Yet there are sour realities at the back of it, which Wilde does not mean to go unnoticed: we are laughing at (laughing down?) the idea of women being always someone's property, always pawns in the marriage business. Lady Bracknell has made it grotesquely clear that "business" is the word, and she controls society. It is total impasse—the only way out in the other dimension, where Ernest has his equivocal being.

That unpredictable force makes its way back when Canon Chasuble appears, unctuously announcing that he is ready to perform the christenings. It is a wonderful clash of the two worlds. "Algernon, I forbid you to be baptised," booms Lady Bracknell. "Lord Bracknell would be highly displeased if he learned that that was the way in which you wasted your time and money." But the materialist money values, so comically invoked, must give way before the strange inner drive that dictated the christenings; now it brings on Miss Prism, in anxious pursuit of the Canon ("I was told you expected me in the vestry, dear Canon") to be confronted with Lady Bracknell's stony glare and the terrible question: "Prism! Where is that baby?" The absurd tale of the three-volume novel left in the perambulator and the baby left in the hand-bag closely parodies attitudes taken in Wilde's other plays. Miss

Prism "bows her head in shame," the young men "pretend" to protect the girls from hearing "the details of a terrible public scandal," Jack becomes ever more portentous, requiring Miss Prism to examine *his* hand-bag carefully to see if it is also hers: "The happiness of more than one life depends on your answer." The third act was "abominably clever," Wilde said. Nothing is cleverer than the way he uses the individualism of his characters to undermine the old attitudes, overturn them, indeed, by being irresistibly themselves. Miss Prism cannot keep her head down for long: one sight of the hand-bag, and she is away in her own world where other things, like damage to the lining, are far more important than a sense of shame:

> . . . here is the injury it received through the upsetting of a Gower Street omnibus in younger and happier days. Here is the stain on the lining caused by the explosion of a temperance beverage, an incident that occurred at Leamington. . . . The bag is undoubtedly mine. I am delighted to have it so unexpectedly restored to me. It has been a great inconvenience being without it all these years.

No melodrama morality could survive the absurdity of this. Wilde rolls the whole drama of the "woman with a past," the seduced victim, the illegitimate child (one critic would include the idea of incest), into the tiny hilarious episode when Jack tries to embrace Miss Prism, taking her for his mother. She recoils, exclaiming that she is unmarried, and he makes his sentimental declaration: "Unmarried! I do not deny that is a serious blow. But after all, who has the right to cast a stone against one who has suffered? Cannot repentance wipe out an act of folly? Why should there be one law for men and another for women? Mother, I forgive you."

Laughing at himself, as well as at the mores of his time, Wilde in this scene breaks quite free of his century and becomes the "modern" playwright he wished to be. It is a modern moment for an audience brought up on Pirandello and Beckett when Jack, turning from one character to another in search of the truth about himself, is directed by Miss Prism to Lady Bracknell—"There is the lady who can tell you who you really are"—and asks her the question that has been causing existential tremors throughout the play: ". . . Would you kindly inform me who I am?" The answer may be something we have seen coming but still it causes a shock and it is not purely comic; it is bound to be a little disturbing to find that his wild and seemingly casual invention was no more than the truth: he is the brother of Algernon and his name is Ernest.

The existential hero receives the news "quite calmly"—"I always said I had a brother! Cecily,—how could you have ever doubted that I had a brother?"; "I always told you, Gwendolen, my name was Ernest . . ." But it is surely the calm of one emerging from an experience that has been growing steadily more manic and disorientating. The crisis of identity is over. Each pair of the quartet fall into each other's arms with the usual symmetry, and Lady Bracknell and Jack share the curtain lines:

| *Lady Bracknell:* | My nephew, you seem to be displaying signs of triviality. |
| *Jack:* | On the contrary, Aunt Augusta, I've now realised for the first time in my life the vital Importance of Being Earnest. |

It is the recall to Lady Bracknell's world where "trivial" and "earnest" reverse the values the farce has been asserting. She has won, in a way: the nameless foundling whose very existence was subversive has been assimilated into the Establishment. His father a General, his aunt a Lady: the "decencies of family life" are safe from the revolutionary horrors conjured up by the notion of being "born, or at any rate, bred, in a hand-bag." Yet we cannot be sure. The pun retains its teasing irony to the end. Jack speaks as an actor, looking out to the audience, slyly (never openly) sharing with them the joke closed from Lady Bracknell, that if there is a moral it is only the title for a farce. And the title reminds us that the farce is about being an actor, playing a part, being Ernest by "realising" him, as actors and playwrights realise for their audiences the creations of their fantasy and everybody, in the long run, has to realise his own identity.

With *The Importance of Being Earnest* Wilde anticipated a major development in the twentieth century, the use of farce to make fundamentally serious (not earnest!) explorations into the realm of the irrational. The play has been immensely influential, serving as model for writers as diverse as T. S. Eliot, who gave a religious turn to the foundling motif in *The Confidential Clerk* (1953), and Charles Wood, in his bleakly funny play about the Second World War, *Dingo* (1969), which has British soldiers performing *The Importance of Being Earnest* in a German prison camp. Wilde's devotees, Joe Orton and Tom Stoppard, have paid especially full tribute to his genius. Orton, whose life had features in common with Wilde's (homosexuality, traumatic experience of prison), said that his aim was to write a play as good as *The Importance of Being Earnest*. He came very near to doing this in *What the Butler Saw* (1969), a more manic version, in the vulgar postcard, sexy style proclaimed by its title, of Wilde's farce of identity: characters split into two, commandeer each other's identities, discover that they really are what they thought they were only pretending to be, in a way which continually acknowledges the Wildean source. While by "borrowing" characters and whole episodes from *The Importance of Being Earnest* for his *Travesties*, Tom Stoppard demonstrates his belief that the play has entered the collective unconscious in the same way as the other masterpiece he uses in his own drama, *Hamlet*. Only if the play does indeed have that status, could the jokes of *Travesties* work to the full and the ruling ideas come over. *Travesties* is from first to last a piece of Wildean play on the relation between life and art in which everyone is juggling roles; Carr, who is never really in the play he thinks he is in, the Dadaist proclaiming "Pleasure, pleasure," the girls who enact the tea-party scene line for line as if they did not know they were playing it, the ideal butler who turns out to be a secret Leninist and James Joyce playing an Irish comedian version of the real James Joyce who played in *The Importance of Being Earnest* in Zurich in 1917.

Wilde would surely have been amused by all this tongue-in-the-cheek play with his play. Still less can one doubt that he would have approved W. H. Auden's comment that *The Importance of Being Earnest* was "the only pure verbal opera in

English."[11] In none of his plays, not even *Salomé*, is the musical treatment more pronounced. Verbal music is heightened by a host of musical devices and allusions; as in opera the curtain rises to the sound of music (Algernon's piano playing); Lady Bracknell contributes a Wagnerian peal and pays idiosyncratic tribute to the power of music by banning French songs from Algernon's concert programme; the spoken word moves irresistibly nearer the condition of music till the lovers are keeping the beat dictated by Gwendolen's uplifted forefinger, practically singing and dancing. Perhaps it is not surprising that actors have had difficulty in capturing this intricate stylisation. Modern actors may not make the same mistake as their Victorian predecessors:—at least they know to keep a straight face—and no doubt many modern productions have come nearer to Wilde's conception than the first ones did. But they may also have become more stereotyped. Some famous performances have come to be thought of as definitive: Edith Evans's magnificently sonorous "A hand-bag," Margaret Rutherford's piquantly obsessed Miss Prism, have established themselves rightly as high peaks in comic acting. These admired styles seem also to have fixed the pattern from which actors find it hard to move away. As Irving Wardle said of the 1982 National Theatre production, everyone was waiting to see how Judi Dench would handle the classic handbag line. Her low-key treatment (she concentrated on tearing up her notes on Jack's eligibility as a suitor) was in tune with a new conception of the role which preserved the veneer but allowed more of the human being to peep out from behind it.

In the post-Orton world we might hope for performances of *The Importance of Being Earnest* that would take yet another line and realise the "heartlessness" so troublesome to Shaw in bold, modern terms, bringing out the subversive and surreal elements. Such a production would have to end on a different note however, from the anarchic stupefaction of *What the Butler Saw*. Wilde does indeed, like Orton, show the world as tending to cruelty and heartlessness, life as an absurd performance, personality as a fluid thing, endlessly forming and reforming itself with the aid of masks (an emphasis on impermanence that alarmed even Yeats, the master of masks). But Wilde's optimistic, benevolent nature required a more harmonious ending for his farce than anything Orton, or perhaps any modern existentialist, would be likely to envisage. *The Importance of Being Earnest* ends with all the dissonances resolved and harmony achieved. It can only happen in Utopia, which means "nowhere"—but as Wilde said, "A map of the world that does not include Utopia is not worth even glancing at, for it leaves out the one country at which Humanity is always landing."

[11]W. H. Auden, "An Improbable Life: Review of *Letters of Oscar Wilde*," *New Yorker*, 9 March 1963. Ellmann, pp. 116–37.

The Significance of Literature:
The Importance of Being Earnest

Joel Fineman

Man, poor, awkward, reliable, necessary man belongs to a sex that has been rational for millions and millions of years. He can't help himself. It is in his race. The History of Women is very different. We have always been picturesque protests against the mere existence of common sense. We saw its dangers from the first.

—*A Woman of No Importance*

What I am outlining here summarizes portions of a longer essay I have been writing on Oscar Wilde's *The Importance of Being Earnest*. For the most part, I will forego discussion of the play and focus on the way in which Wilde's farce precisely figures the problem of "The Self in Writing."[1] You will perhaps recall that Jack-Ernest, the hero of the play, discovers the unity of his duplicity when he learns that as an infant he was quite literally exchanged for writing in the cloakroom of Victoria Station, his absent-minded governess having substituted for his person the manuscript of a three-volume novel which is described as being "of more than usually repulsive sentimentality." As a result, because Jack-Ernest is in this way so uniquely and definitively committed to literature, with literature thus registered as his alter-ego, he is one of those few selfs or subjects whose very existence, as it is given to us, is specifically literary, an ego-ideal of literature, as it were, whose form is so intimately immanent in his content as to collapse the distinction between a name and that which it bespeaks, and whose temporal destiny is so harmoniously organic a whole as to make it a matter of natural fact that his end be in his beginning—for Ernest is indeed, as Lady Bracknell puts it, paraphrasing traditional definitions of allegory, one whose origins are in a terminus.

Yet if Jack-Ernest is thus an ideal image of the relation of the self to writing, he is nevertheless himself a piece of literature, and therefore but a literary representation of the self's relation to literature, a fiction, therefore, if not necessarily a farce, and for this reason not to be trusted. This is the difficulty, I take it, that our

From *October* 15 (Winter 1980): 77–90. Reprinted with the permission of the estate of Joel Fineman and *October*.

[1]This paper was delivered at the 1979 convention of the Modern Language Association, at one of the several panels associated with the forum on "The Self in Writing." The essay on *The Importance of Being Earnest* has now grown into a chapter on Wilde which will take its place in a projected book on literary names. The notes have been added for this publication.

forum has been established to address, recognizing that while the self and writing are surely implicated each in the other, perhaps even reciprocally constitutive each *of* the other, they are so in a way that at the same time undermines the integrity and the stability of both. This we can see even in the delicate phrasing of our forum's title, where the vagueness of the preposition, the problematic and diffusive metaphoricity of its innocuous "in"—"The Self *in* Writing"—testifies to the fact that the Self *and* Writing, as literal categories with their own propriety, can only be linked together in a figural discourse, which, even as it is spoken, calls the specificity and the literality of its terms into question. Strictly speaking, of course, "The Self in Writing" is an impossible locution, for in writing we do not find the self but, at best, only its representation, and it is only because *in* literature, in a literary mode, we characteristically, if illegitimately, rush to collate a word both with its sense and with its referent that we are, even momentarily, tempted to forget or to suspend the originary and intrinsic difference between, on the one hand, the self who reads, and, on the other, the literary revision of that self who is read.

This is to insist upon the fact that the self's relation to literature is not itself a literary relation, and that only a sentimental and literary reading will obsessively identify a thing with its word, a signified with its signifier, or the self with its literary image. This is also to avoid simplistic dialectical accounts of the act of reading—either identificatory or implicative—whose mechanical symmetries programmatically reduce the self to its idealization: the so-called "ideal reader" of whom we hear a great deal of late. Instead, this is to recognize that if we are to speak of the relation of the self to the writing in which it finds itself written, or, stylizing this familiar topos, if we are to speak of the relation of the self to the language in which it finds itself bespoken, then we must do so in terms of a critical discourse that registers the disjunction and the discrepancy between being and meaning, thing and word, and which therefore locates the self who is committed to language in its experience of the slippage between its immediate presence to itself and its mediated representation of itself in a symbolic system. Moreover, since Being, to be thought, must be thought as Meaning, even this self-presence of the self to itself will emerge only in retrospect as less, with the self discovering itself in its own meaningful aftermath, just as Being can only be spoken in its own effacement, as Heidegger—not Derrida—has taught us.[2]

---

[2]See, for example, *The Question of Being*, or "The Temporality of Discourse" in *Being and Time* (IV,68,d). Derrida's project is effectively to apply Heidegger's critique of Western metaphysics to Heidegger himself (e.g., "Ousia and Grammè: A Note to a Footnote in *Being and Time*," in *Phenomenology in Perspective*, ed. F. J. Smith, The Hague, Martinus Nijhoff, 1970; also, "The Ends of Man," *Philosophy and Phenomenological Research*, 30, No. 1 (1969), also in *Marges de la philosophie*, Paris, Minuit, 1972, so as to show that even Heidegger repeats, rather than revises, traditional metaphysical assumptions. For this reason, Derrida argues, even Heidegger's being must be put under further erasure as part of an ongoing, ever-vigilant, vaguely messianic, deconstructive Puritanism. There is no doubt that Derrida makes this point persuasively; the question is whether this measures a blindness or an insight on Heidegger's part, for what is important to Heidegger is the specificity of his history of Western philosophical speculation. What for Derrida is the mark of Heidegger's failure is also a measure, or so Heidegger would no doubt respond, of *necessary* metaphysical limits, a determina-

As is well known, it is thanks to the patient, painstaking, and rigorous labors of the tradition of psychoanalysis—a tradition that begins with Freud and which probably concludes with Lacan that we possess a theoretical vocabulary sufficiently supple to capture this subject born in the split between self-presence and the representation of self. The insights of this tradition, however perfunctorily and schematically I refer to them here, are what enable us to situate the self of "The Self in Writing" in the metaphorical *in* whose very figurality is what allows us to articulate the problem in the first place, which is to say, in the same displacing place that Wilde—whose play will thematize this very problem of the place of the subject—places *Being,* midway between the import of *Importance* and a specifically literary pun on *Earnest*—the importance of *being Earnest*—as though the indeterminacy of meaning in turn determined *Being* as its own rueful double entendre.

What I should like to do here, however, recognizing, with some regret, that both the theory and the vocabulary of this psychoanalytic tradition are for many people both irritating and opaque, is translate its discourse into the more accessible and familiar terms of what today we will parochially call the Anglo-American speculative tradition. To that end, in an effort to sketch out the necessary contours of any psychoanalysis of what we can now identify as the "subject of literature," I would like to rehearse a rather well known paradox of logical reference, first formulated in 1908 by Kurt Grelling, but of interest to philosophy from Russell at least through Quine.

The paradox itself is relatively straightforward. Let us say, says the paradox, that there is a set of words that describe themselves, For example, *polysyllabic,* the word, is itself polysyllabic, *short* is itself short, and *English* is itself English, an English word. Let us call such self-descriptive words autological, because they speak about themselves. In addition, let us further say that there is another set of words that do not describe themselves. For example, *monosyllabic,* the word, is not itself monosyllabic, *long* is not itself long, *French* is not itself French. Let us now agree to call this second set of words heterological, because these are words that speak about things besides themselves—allegorical words, because they speak about the Other (*allos,* other; *agoreuein,* to speak), a *logos* of the *heteros,* or, in Lacan's phrase, a discourse of the Other. Having stipulated these two sets, the autological and the heterological, the question then emerges: is the word *heterological* itself autological or heterological? And here we discover the paradox, for simply asking the question forces upon us the odd conclusion that if *heterological,* the word, is itself heterological, then it is autological, whereas, in some kind of

---

tion of the way it is and is not, or, more modestly and historically, the way it has always been and seems still to be. I am here assuming, following Derrida himself, that it is one of Western metaphysics' special and perennial pleasures to have itself deconstructed, and that for this reason we must register Derrida's always already predetermined *différence* within the horizon of its always eventual determinate recuperation. This is not a static balance: it has a direction, from pre-beginning to end, and this directionality also has its obvious metaphysical—not to mention its more obvious psychological—consequences

contrast, if it is autological, then it is heterological. That is to say, given the definitions and a classical system of logic, the heterological can only be what it is on condition that it is what it is not, and it can only be what it is not on condition that it is
what it is.

Thus formulated, the paradox possesses both an elegance and a banality, and in
proportions that rather directly correspond to the brittle yet mandarin tenor and
texture we associate with Wilde's farce. So too, the paradox very neatly summarizes the plot of *The Importance of Being Earnest,* since Ernest will himself be
earnest only when he isn't, just as he will not be earnest only when he is. This paradoxical alternation and oscillation of the subject, a phenomenon to which the play
gives the general label Bunburyism, but which Lacan would call *auto-différence*, is
resolved at the end of the play when Ernest consults the book of the name of the
fathers and discovers that his name "naturally is Ernest," and that therefore to his
surprise, "all his life he has been speaking nothing but the truth."[3] Were there
time, we would want at this point to conduct both a phonological and a phenomenological analysis so as to explain why all the names of the fathers in the list that
Ernest reads begin with the name of the mother, "Ma"—Mallam, Maxbohm,
Magley, Markby, Migsby, Mobbs, Moncrieff—and we would want also to know
why this enumeration of nasal consonants not only spells an end to the labial
phonemics of *Bunbury,* but also marks the moment when denomination lapses
into description, when use turns into mention, and when Truth itself arrives after
the fact to validate what it succeeds.[4] Even putting these important questions to
the side, however, we can see that the intention of the farce is to resolve the paradox of autology and heterology by enacting it through to its absurd reduction, to
the point, that is, where Ernest becomes, literally becomes, his name.

Again, we might want to take this revival of the tradition of Paracelsian signa-
tures, this coordination of signifier and signified, as indicative of the literary *per se.*
But we can do so only if we recognize the specific twist or trope that literature
gives to this semiotics of correspondence. For Ernest only becomes earnest when
he recognizes in the heterology of words the paradoxical representationality of language, and thus discovers *in* the difference between a name and its thing the para-

---

[3]See "Le clivage du sujet et son identification," *Scilicet,* Nos. 2,3, Paris, Editions du Seuil, 1970, p.
127. Note that the fracture is imaginary, not symbolic.

[4]I have elsewhere argued that the first phonemes, labial /papa / or /baba/ and nasal /mama/, are
acquired in accordance with a structure that determines specific literary themes. See "The Structure
of Allegorical Desire," *October,* 12 (Spring 1980), 47–66. This "Pa/Ma" model phonologically instanti-
ates what Heidegger describes more generally in terms of the question whose asking renders metaphysics possible: "In the service of thought we are trying precisely to penetrate the source from which
the essence of thinking is determined, namely *alètheia* and *physis*, being as unconcealment, the very
thing that has been lost by 'logic' " (*An Introduction to Metaphysics,* trans. R. Manheim, New York,
Anchor Books, 1961, p. 102). In the same way that Heidegger's *alètheia* is forsworn by *logos*, the bab-
bling /papa/ through which speech is thought is irrevocably lost at the first moment of its meaningful
articulation. So too, as Heidegger predicts, the hidden unconcealment of truth always reemerges in literature as death, farcically so in *The Importance of Being Earnest:* "Bunbury is dead. . . . The doctors
found out that Bunbury could not live, that is what I mean—so Bunbury died." This has ramifications
for the metaphorics of literary sexuality, a point to which I refer briefly above.

doxical difference *between* himself and his name. Ernest therefore inherits his name only to the extent that its significance is restricted or promoted to its nominality, only to the extent, that is to say, that it becomes a signifier of itself *as* a signifier, not a signified. This is indeed a paradigm of literary language, of language that calls attention to itself as language, just as the pun on *Earnest* in the title possesses its literary effect precisely because it *doesn't* mean its double-meaning and thereby forces us to register the word as just a word, significant of just itself, with no meaning beyond its palpability as a signifier. This is also why Wilde's play or farce on names is itself so important, for we may say that the special propriety of a proper name with respect to common nouns corresponds precisely to the specialized charge of literature with respect to so-called ordinary language—"so-called" because there could no more be an ordinary language without its fictive complement than there could be a natural language bereft of its fantasy of the propriety of proper names.[5]

---

[5]I am assuming here Jakobson's "structuralist" definition of the literary function as that message which stresses itself as merely message, and I am assimilating this, for reasons discussed in the next footnote, to proper names, for these are nominal only because they stress their nominality. The opposition of meaningful words to meaningless proper nouns is therefore one instance of a more general system of opposition in *The Importance of Being Earnest* that manages consistently to juxtapose the serious against the trivial in such a way as to destabilize the integrity of meaningful binary antithesis. This is an obvious theme of *The Importance of Being Earnest*, which Wilde subtitled *A Trivial Comedy for Serious People* so as to make the very fact of farce a problem for whatever might be understood to be its opposite. In this way, by mentioning itself, Wilde's theme defends its own expression by referring the formal force of farce to an ongoing repetition internal to itself. This is, as it were, the asymptotic height of farce, which, because it is the genre that, as Marx suggested, imitates or repeats tragedy, is therefore the genre whose literary self-consciousness is formally most acute because thematically most empty.

The generic point is important because it shows us in what sense Wilde took his play seriously. For Aristotle, as for the serious literary tradition that succeeds him, tragedy is the imitation of a logically unified action, with the result that the hero of tragedy, his character subjected to his destiny, becomes a subjectivity as unified as the action he enacts. Hence Oedipus, whether Sophocles' or Aristotle's or Freud's, and the necessity historically attaching to the coherence of his person. It is this unity that makes tragedy, for Aristotle, the most important (and therefore the most "philosophical," see *Poetics*, chs. 9 and 26) of literary genres, just as this unity explains why, for Aristotle, Oedipus is both the perfect tragic object and the perfect tragic subject. In contrast, farce presents itself as the imitation of tragic imitation, as the action of imitation rather than an imitation of action, and the result of this double doubling is that the unifying logic of tragedy, which depends on imitation, is put into question by its own duplication. This sounds paradoxical, but it simply characterizes (1) the literary function as Jakobson describes it theoretically, i.e., the essential structural feature of literature, its recursive reflexivity, (2) the actual historical practice of a literary tradition that unfolds towards increasingly self-conscious forms and themes, i.e., the mocking mechanism, usually mimetic, by means of which literature regularly revives itself by calling attention to its conventions, for example, the way *The Importance of Being Earnest* (as do most of Wilde's plays) parodies what were in Wilde's theater established proprieties of stock and pointed melodrama (the crossed lovers, the bastard child, the discovery of origins that predetermine ends). On the one hand, this explains why farce is, again according to the tradition, of all poetic genres least important, for where tragedy is serious because it imitates something, farce is trivial because it imitates imitation (literature or literariness), which is nothing. (This is the case even if another principle of aesthetic meaning is substituted for imitation, for any notion of importance will be undone when it remarks itself.) But this is also why, on the other hand, because his play makes fun *of* tragedy, the farcically divided Jack-Ernest constitutes the most serious possible critique of Aristotle's tragically unified Oedipus, which explains why a critical tradition dominated by

Yet if this is a small-scale model, however general, of the literary, of language which stresses its literality, its letters, it is of course profoundly unlike the kind of ordinary language that philosophy, as opposed to literature, would instead prefer to speak—which is why where literature depends upon the paradox of heterology—philosophy instead prohibits it, with the notion of "metalanguage," which keeps the orders of reference in their hierarchical place. Logicians are of course entitled to introduce whatever constraints might be required to maintain the coherence of their artificial systems, but this remains a merely logical, not a psychological, necessity, which is why Lacan, recognizing the fact that a subject of discourse might at any moment stumble into heterology, says that there is no such thing as "metalanguage."[6] This is not the place to make the point in any detail, but I would want to argue that philosophy of language has always been autological, and that this can be precisely documented by tracing its attitude towards proper names, from *The Cratylus,* where a name will imitate its thing, through the epoch of representation, where a name will uncomplicatedly point to its thing, through Russell and Frege, where the immediate relation of a word to its referent is replaced by the equally immediate relation of a word to its sense, through to speech act theory, where a

---

Aristotle and by Oedipus finds nothing funny in the play's humor—Shaw, for example, who hated the play because he thought its wit was unimportant, or, more generally, the way the play is labeled marginal *because* the perfect farce.

As serious tragedy to trivial farce, so philosophy to literature, and for the same reasons. We know that this is historically the case if we recall that Plato condemns sophistic rhetoric for the way it mimes philosophy, or the way Plato objects to literature for being but an imitation of a more substantial truth. Again the same problem: if any given tragedy might be a perfect farce, how does philosophy defend itself from what would be its perfect imitation, for example Gorgias' parody of Parmenides, which "proves" through nominal negative existentials that "nothing exists." In this paper, therefore, I am not simply assuming that Wilde's farce reenacts, or represents within a literary mode, the traditional quarrel of literature with philosophy. More specifically, I am arguing, first, that Wilde's play on names, the play's thematic matter, is the objectification of its parodic manner; second, that it is by a commitment to the propriety of names that philosophy has historically defended itself against the possibility that it is its own dissimulation—a weak defense, given the historical failure, to this day, of the philosophy of proper names. Gorgias' onto-logical name-play is what makes rhetoric a *necessary* mockery of philosophy (as Gorgias describes it in one of the few surviving fragments)—"to destroy an opponent's seriousness by laughter and his laughter by seriousness"—just as it is the earnestness of "Earnest" that makes Wilde's "philosophy of the trivial" serious (as Wilde described it in an interview just prior to the play's premiere):

What sort of play are we to expect?
    It is exquisitely trivial, a delicate bubble of fancy and it has its philosophy.
    Its philosophy?
    That we should treat all the trivial things of life seriously, and all the serious things of life with sincere and studied triviality.

The relevant contemporary example is Derrida's parody, iteration, citation, quotation of Searle's defense of Austin (see "Limited Inc," *Glyph,* 2, Baltimore, Johns Hopkins University Press, 1977). Derrida not only makes fun of Searle's speech act theory and its notion of "copyrightable" proper names (for naively supposing some innocent principle of difference with which to distinguish a serious legitimate utterance from its nonserious illegitimate repetition); he also "proves" the point by making fun—a serious joke about corporeal anonymity—of "Searle-Sarl's" name itself.

    [6]See "D'une question préliminaire à tout traitement possible de la psychose," in *Écrits,* Paris, Editions du Seuil, 1966, p. 538. See also, Jacques-Alain Miller, "U ou 'Il n'y a pas de meta-langage,' " *Ornicar?,* 5 (1975–1976), pp. 67–72.

word uncomplicatedly reflects its speaker's intention. Of late, there are signs that this realism of nominalism has begun to lose its philosophical prestige, for example, Saul Kripke's devastating critique of Searle's theory of nominality, a critique whose account of reference constitutes the exact inverse of Derrida's equally devastating critique of Searle's hypothesis of expressable intention. On the assumption that the enemy of my enemy is my friend, it seems possible that continental and Anglo-American philosophy might eventually meet in the course of these complementary examinations of the propriety or impropriety of names. Leaving these relatively recent indications to the side, however, we may say that the perennial philosophical dream of true language, of language that always means what it says, stands in marked contrast to literary language which can never mean what it says because it never means anything except the fact that it is saying something that it does not mean.[7]

This traditional difference is worth developing, for it allows us to define the self of "The Self in Writing" as both the cause and the consequence of the paradox subtending the autological and the heterological. That is to say, the self becomes the difference between a discourse of things and a discourse of words, a subject

---

[7]Gwendolen and Cecily both give voice to this philosophical-philological, idealist dream of a true word: "My ideal has always been to love someone of the name of Ernest. There is something in that name that inspires absolute confidence." Or, "You must not laugh at me, darling, but it had always been a girlish dream of mine to love someone whose name was Ernest. There is something in that name that inspires absolute confidence." Here we can only briefly allude to the complications that make this confidence problematic. The traditional account of names—as formulated, for example, in Mill—is that a proper name has a denotation but not a connotation, in contrast to common nouns which have both. This is a muted version of Socrates' original philosophical desire for a language, whose words would necessarily metaphysically correspond with things, a language, as it were, where words literally *are* the things they speak, for example the way *R*, Socrates says in *The Cratylus*, is the letter of motion. The history of philosophy of names—from Aristotle's *Categories* on, through Stoic grammar, through medieval sign theory (via the incipient nominalism of Abelard, the modified realism of Aquinas, the straightforward nominalism of Ockham)—is a continual attempt somehow to nourish and to satisfy this initial philosophical desire for true language (for a truth *of* language, an *etymos* of *logos*) by lowering the ontological stakes to something merely nominal, for example, Mill's denotation theory where names merely indicate the things that formerly they were. The covert metaphysical assumptions embedded even in so modest a claim as Mill's were brought out by Frege and Russell in their well-known criticisms of denotation theory, first, with the instance of negative existentials, where there is no referent to which a name might point (Odysseus, golden mountains, etc.), second, with the instance of identity propositions, which give off information even though the names they contain share the same referent (e.g., "The Morning Star is the Evening Star," "Cicero is Tully"—these being the traditional examples, as though philosophy can only think the problem under the aegis of the queen of desire, Venus, and the king of rhetoric, Cicero). For these reasons, lest language call things into being simply by denominating them, Frege and Russell, in somewhat different ways, introduced between a name and its referent a third term which is its "sense," arguing that while a name must have a sense in order to refer, it need not have a referent in order to make sense. As a result, no longer the essence of things, names now will merely mean them; they are truncated definite descriptions, to use Russell's phrase, and so not really names at all, but abbreviated bundles of meaning which are only contingently related to a referent.

There are several difficulties with this account of names which understands them to refer by means of what and how they mean. (Neither does such an account eliminate metaphysics by transferring its claims to the register of meaning. Cf. Quine: "Meaning is what essence becomes when it is divorced from the object of reference and married to the word," in "Two Dogmas of Empiricism," in *From a Logical Point of View*, Cambridge, Mass., Harvard University Press, 1961, p. 21.) First of all, it must be decided which aspects of nominal sense will be essential in determining a name's referent, for two people might well have entirely different senses of "Aristotle" and yet surely refer to the same person when they use his name (my "Aristotle" may only have written the *Poetics* whereas yours may have only

situated midway between the subject of philosophy and the subject of literature, between ordinary and extraordinary language, in short, again, between *Importance* and *Earnest*. Where philosophy self-importantly commits itself to autology so as to make of language a transparent vehicle for the signifieds of which it speaks, literature, in contrast, "Earnestly" forswears signifieds altogether for the sake of the heterological materiality of its signifiers. The self between them constitutes the necessity of their difference, so that the ancient quarrel between philosophy and literature thus takes place over the body of the self in writing, with philosophy wanting to do with its signifieds what literature wants to do with its signifiers, and with the self in writing testifying to the fact that neither can do

---

tutored Alexander, and the real Aristotle might in fact have done neither). So too, there is an intuitive difficulty that comes of thinking names like *John* or *X* in fact possess a sense; this is to truncate description to a grotesque degree. These difficulties are not resolved even when the Russell-Frege account is "loosened up," as it is by Searle when, following Wittgenstein, he collates description and identification in a speech act theory of names. (See J. Searle, "Proper Names," *Mind*, 67 [1958]; see also the criticism of this in S. Kripke, "Naming and Necessity," in *Semantics of Natural Language*, eds., D. Davidson and G. Harman, Dordrecht, D. Reidel, 1972; also K. Donellan, "Speaking of Nothing," *The Philosophical Review*, 83 [1974]. Searle's essay should be read so as to notice the continuity subtending speculation about names in philosophy's *démarche* or retreat from ontology to psychology: first, names are the things to which they refer, then they imitate them, then they point to them, then they mean them, and then, in speech act theory, they "intend" them.) These difficulties, and others associated with them, have been much discussed in recent Anglo-American philosophy of language, by, amongst others, Donellan, Putnam, and, most influentially, Kripke. There is a good introduction to the topic, with bibliography, in *Naming, Necessity, and Natural Kinds*, ed. S. Schwartz, Ithaca, Cornell University Press, 1977. We cannot here discuss the technical issues involved, which begin, primarily with the way names rigidly designate the same thing in all possible worlds (e.g., "The author of the *Iliad* might not have been born and might not have been the author of the Iliad" makes sense, but, substituting a name for the description, as in "Homer might not have been born and might not have been Homer" does not), but the force of this recent theory is to oblige philosophy, for the most part, to give up a strong sense theory of nominal reference. Instead, as a possible alternative, Kripke proposes to explain nominal reference by appealing to history, relating every use of every name to a series of hypothetical causal chains which reach back to every name's original moment of ostensive baptism. The consequences of Kripke's novel account are subtle and far-reaching, and they remain important even though, still more recently, their argument has itself run into difficulties. Here we must be content simply to allude to the problem, and to mention these two points relevant to our discussion above.

First, though Kripke can demonstrate that a name cannot have a sense in a strong way such that it determines its referent, he must still account for the information we receive in identity propositions. Here, as N. Salmon suggests, the only sense a name conveys is of itself as a name. See Salmon's review of L. Linsky's *Names and Descriptions*, in *The Journal of Philosophy*, 76, No. 8 (1979). This is why I feel justified in assimilating proper names to Jakobson's account of literariness.

Second, Kripke has recently discovered a paradox built into his theory of causal chains, for he imagines a situation in which a single origin legitimately produces a divided name. See "A Puzzle about Belief," in *Meaning and Use*, ed. A. Margalit, Dordrecht, D. Reidel, 1979. Kripke confesses himself unable to resolve the paradox even though it calls his entire account of proper names into question (and, as Putnam points out, the paradox also infects a theory of natural kinds; see Putnam's "Comment" on Kripke's puzzle, also in *Meaning and Use*). Kripke's puzzle is an inversion of Derrida's differentiated, reiterated origin, which is why I suggest in this paper that the two philosophers, though neither speaks to or of the other, share a common criticism of Searle, and also why I say that Anglo-American philosophy of language and continental phenomenology are now drawing together in their discovery of the impropriety of proper names. This is also why they both share an interest in the ontological status of the fictive. This is a point to be developed elsewhere. The history of philosophy of names should, however, be of special interest to students of literature, for in many ways the progressive and increasingly dogmatic subordination by philosophy of nominal reference, first to extension, then to expression, then to intention, and finally to a historicity that postpones its temporality, in many

either. A signifier, says Lacan, is what represents a subject to another signifier. Literature and philosophy *are* thus the signifiers of each other, names, in this sense, whose "sense," or let us say significance, is what their readers are.

Situated thus, as both elision and bar between these two equally inhuman desires, the self in writing finds his own human desire strictly circumscribed, a desire that we might characterize as a lusting of the autological for the heterological, a desire that leaves something to be desired. "My ideal has always been to love someone of the name of Ernest," but "Bunbury is dead." In psychoanalytic terms this would correspond to the transition from narcissistic to anaclitic object choice, or to the difference between the self before and after what psychoanalysis thematizes as his accession to speech. If we recall, though, that desire too is an effect of the language, that Eros is the consequence of Logos, then our paradox will produce the appropriate Freudian paradigm without recourse to the Freudian lexicon. For now, remembering their etymology, we may rechristen the autological as the autosexual, or rather, the homosexual, and we may equally revalue the heterological as the heterosexual. This leaves us with the psychoanalytic conclusion that the fundamental desire of the reader of literature is the desire of the homosexual for the heterosexual, or rather, substituting the appropriate figurative embodiments of these abstractions, the desire of the man to be sodomized by the woman. This is a specifically obsessional desire, but it is one that Freud luridly locates at the center of his three major case histories: Ratman, Wolfman, Schreber. This would also explain why the only word that ends up being naturally motivated in *The Importance of Being Earnest* is not *Earnest* but *Bunbury* itself, which was not only British slang for a male brothel, but is also a collection of signifiers that straightforwardly express their desire to bury in the bun.[8]

---

ways parallels the development and eventual demise of an aesthetics of representation. That is to say, the perennial awkwardness philosophy discloses in the collation of word and thing is closely related to the uneasy relation our literary tradition regularly discovers when it connects literal to figurative literary meaning. So too, there is an obvious affinity between what are the topoi of a long philosophical meditation on names—e.g., the integrity of a clear-cut distinction between analytic and synthetic propositions, or the possibility of an overlap between *de dictu* intensional meanings and *de re* extensional truth values—and what are the corresponding chestnuts of hermeneutic concern—e.g., the relation of an autonomous text to its external context, or the imbrication of form with content, or medium with message. In this paper, however, I am more concerned with the difference, rather than the similarity, between philosophical and literary names, for this difference possesses a specificity of its own, and it can be identified, as I say above, with the significance (which is to be distinguished from the meaning) of literature. We assume (with De Man) that all literary texts share the same indeterminate meaning, but we further argue (with Lacan) that this indeterminacy of meaning in turn determines a specific literary significance.

[8]Again we cannot develop the point adequately, but we would begin our psychoanalytic account with Freud's essay on "The Uncanny" (which concludes, by the way, with a reference to Wilde), and we would conclude it with Lacan's discovery that there is no such thing as woman. See "Aristotle et Freud: L'autre satisfaction," also "Dieu et la jouissance de femme," in *Le Seminaire, Livre XX, Encore: 1972–1973*, Paris, Editions du Seuil, 1975. We thus assume, in traditional psychoanalytic fashion, that the subject of Western literature is male, that its object, which exists only as an effect which puts existence into question (in the same way that Wilde gives us *Being* flanked by punning), is female, and that its project is therefore the representation of desire. We deal here with the metaphorics of literary sexuality, with the way the male is historically a subject undone by its female sub-version. Hence our epigraph, or the way Wilde's farce repeats the erotic melodrama through which it is thought: "It is called

With this cryptographic reference to the death that we always find buried in the logos of desire we are very close to the impulse to death that Freud assimilated to the wanderings of Eros. There is no time to pursue this connection further, but I would like in conclusion at least to draw the moral. In our literature the heterological is the trope of the autological, just as the heterosexual is the trope of the homosexual, just as woman is the trope of man. This accounts, respectively, for the semiotics, the syntax, and the semantics of our literature. So too does it account for its ethics. Asked to summarize her novel, the novel whose loss is responsible for the subject of the play, Miss Prism, the governess, says, "The good ended happily, and the bad unhappily. That is what Fiction means." So it does, but this embedding of the moral in a necessarily fictive register equally measures the cost of what we must therefore call the fiction of meaning, at least for so long as both the Self and Writing are accorded an authority that even Wilde's farce thus fails to deconstruct.[9]

Lady Lancing on the cover: but the real title is *The Importance of Being Earnest*," letter to George Alexander, October 1894, printed in *The Letters of Oscar Wilde*, ed. R. Hart-Davis, New York, Harcourt, Brace, and World, 1962, pp. 375–376. For a summary of the proposed *Lady Lancing*, a cuckoldry plot which Wilde describes as "A sheer flame of love between a man and a woman," see the letter to Alexander, August 1894, *The Letters of Oscar Wilde*, pp. 360–362.

[9]Because the moral is imaginary it has that much more force. This speaks to an old psychoanalytic ambiguity, that the precursor of the super-ego is the ego-ideal. This raises a problem for Lacan's psychoanalytic topography, suggesting the possibility that Lacan's "Symbolic" is itself "Imaginary," the last lure of the "Imaginary." To discuss this problem properly we would necessarily consider a different literary genre: romance, which is not tragedy and is not farce, neither Oedipus nor his courtly derision.

Oscar Wilde in Japan: Aestheticism, Orientalism and the Derealization of the Homosexual

Jeff Nunokawa

The story is simply this . . . Two months ago I went to a [party] . . . after I had been in the room about ten minutes, talking to . . . tedious Academicians, I suddenly became conscious that someone was looking at me. I turned halfway round, and saw [him] for the first time. When our eyes met, I felt that I was growing pale. A curious sensation of terror came over me. I knew that I had come face to face with someone whose mere personality was so fascinating that, if I allowed it to do so, it would absorb my whole nature, my whole soul, my very art itself. I did not want any external influence in my life . . . I have always been my own master; had at least always been so, till I met [him] . . . Then—but I don't know how to explain it to you. Something seemed to tell me that I was on the verge of a terrible crisis in my life. I had a strange feeling that Fate had in store for me exquisite joys and exquisite sorrows.[1]

For all of its terror, the attraction confessed in this passage from *The Picture of Dorian Gray* is common to us; the coerciveness that characterizes desire in Wilde's telling of it, a coerciveness that, defeating initial efforts at containment (*"if I allowed it to do so*, it would absorb my whole nature, my whole soul, my very art itself*") eventually "master[s]" the subject it invades, makes his story difficult to distinguish from one closer to home. If this passage sounds like the confession of a modern homosexual, it's not because the man who admits his desire for another gains identity, but rather because he loses self-control. Whatever else separates the love featured in the contemporary coming out story, where desire is taken as the signature of its subject, from the one pictured in Wilde's text, where it disperses rather than defines him, they are united by the power to compel. Conceptions of desire as different from one another as the centrifugal from the centripetal, as an aesthetic of impersonality from a politics of identity, share a conviction that the shape of our passions, no less than the place of our birth, or the sources of our illnesses, is quite out of our hands. A fear of desire powerful enough in late nineteenth-century texts like *The Picture of Dorian Gray* and *Dr. Jekyll and Mr. Hyde* to become indistinguishable from desire itself, has its cause

Previously unpublished. Printed with permission of the author.

[1]Oscar Wilde, *The Picture of Dorian Gray*, Ed. Donald L. Lawler (New York: Norton, 1988), p. 11. Reprint of 1891 edition, London. All subsequent citations of Dorian Gray refer to this edition.

in its capacity to compromise the will of the subject confirmed or vaporized by it; a fear of desire no less hard at work in the late twentieth century than in the late nineteenth inhabits the common sense that what attracts coerces.

But however powerful the drive of desire may seem, the testimony of the merest whim will indicate that it's not pervasive. It is altogether absent for example in *The Importance of Being Earnest*, where the frightening passion Wilde calls the enthralling effects of Dorian Gray, and others before and after chart as the progress of primordial or viral forces, is faded into the daylight of a desire which, like the occasional cigarette, the weekend escapade, or the momentary reverie, are determined entirely by the subject who indulges them.

Such governance is administered by a variety of management styles in and beyond *The Importance of Being Earnest*, beginning with the familiar strategy of the double life, well outfitted here with false names and alibis. A tactic defined in the late nineteenth century by the difference between Dr. Jekyll and Mr. Hyde, between Dorian Gray and his portrait, and in the late twentieth by the difference between the wholesome heroine of the situation comedy and her dark cousin, leaves the pursuit of pleasure to the discretion of its subject:

> You have invented a very useful younger brother called Ernest, in order that you may be able to come up to town as often as you like. I have invented an invaluable permanent invalid called Bunbury, in order that I may be able to go down into the country whenever I choose.[2]

But the manipulation of desire in Wilde's comedy exceeds what is normally accommodated by the double life. The dandy that speaks in this passage is unusually modest in the account he furnishes of his *modus operandi:* the power he possesses over his wishes is more than the capacity to choose when he gives in to them; as half the labor performed by the term "Bunbury" indicates, a fiction which names both the "friend" who gives the pursuit of pleasure its excuse as well as the pleasure itself ("Bunburying"), Algernon determines not only the timing of his capitulation to his wishes, but also their very character.

Comprehending everything from cradle to grave in *The Importance of Being Earnest*, where characters are commended or condemned for the conditions of their birth, the circumstances of their death, and the state of their health, the spirit of voluntarism is never more striking than when it casts "an irresistible fascination" as an act of caprice: "For me you have always had an irresistible fascination . . . my ideal has always been to love some one of the name of Ernest" (229). This speech may put us in mind of the familiar testimony of the modern sexual subject, who might "respect" a member of the unpreferred gender, "might admire" his or her "character," but cannot offer "undivided attention" (259), but a gap as wide as the gulf between free will and fate divides Wilde's character from the one inducted by

---

[2]Oscar Wilde, *The Importance of Being Earnest*, Act I, in *Complete Plays* (London: Methuen, 1988), p. 224. *The Importance of Being Earnest* was first published in 1899. All subsequent citations of *Earnest* refer to this edition.

a more recent discourse of desire. For despite the claim that her preference for the name of Ernest is irresistible, it is readily abandoned. In the rush to the altar that concludes *The Importance of Being Earnest*, we may forget that Cecily is content with a man whose name she had earlier declared would disqualify him as the object of her "undivided attention"; we may forget that for fully fifty percent of the Ernestosexual community, being Ernest proves not so important after all. Freed from any responsibility to an anterior condition that can be ignored or concealed but hardly wished away, the subject of desire, like the masochist who knows the ropes better than the master who applies them, or a diarist whose record of events is a work of fantasy, paradoxically chooses what she cannot resist, and is thus just as free to choose to be released from it.

The light desire that governs *The Importance of Being Earnest* partakes of a late Victorian climate of manufactured and manipulable passion associated with Wilde in particular, and Aestheticism in general. When Cecily describes the diary of her fictional devotion to Ernest as "a very young girl's record of her own thoughts and impressions, and consequently meant for publication" (256), she embraces the exhibitionism that Gilbert and Sullivan, in their parody of the Aesthete's pretenses, arraign as Wilde's own most prominent feature. The character in *Patience* that everyone recognized as Aestheticism's self styled spokesman confesses that his "languid love for lilies," "Lank limbs and haggard cheeks," "dirty greens," and "all one sees/That's Japanese," is a sham affection, "born of a morbid love of admiration!"[3]

And if the passion championed by Wilde in *The Importance of Being Earnest*, the pre- or extra-marital proclivities contrived and controlled by the subject who entertains them, circulated more broadly in the culture of his day, other versions of it are rehearsed in our own. Wilde's brand of desire-lite will be both familiar and unfamiliar to those schooled in contemporary theories of dissident sexualities. Familiar because of its egregious artificiality: cutting itself off from Nature, where defenses of passions eccentric to the marriage plot from Whitman's to those of recent gay essentialists have found their grass roots support, asserting itself not as a fact of life, but as a work of art, such desire may put us in mind of the performances of gender and sexuality that recent theorists have celebrated.

Familiar because of the optimism of the will that defines it—Carole-Anne Tyler has argued that recent reviews of generic and sexual performance appeal to their actors' intentions to separate theaters of insurrection from rituals of conformity:

> [I]f all identities are alienated and fictional, then the distinction between parody, mimicry, or camp, and imitation, masquerade, or playing it straight is no longer self-evident. What makes the one credible and the other incredible when both are fictions? The answer, it seems, are the author's intentions: parody is legible in the drama of gender performance if someone meant to script it, intending it to be there.[4]

---

[3]Gilbert and Sullivan, *Patience*, in *Complete Plays* (New York: Norton, 1976), p. 168.

[4]Carole-Anne Tyler, "Boys Will Be Girls: The Politics of Gay Drag" in *Inside/Out: Lesbian Theories, Gay Theories*, ed. Diana Fuss (New York: Routledge, 1991), p. 54.

Wilde's light passion becomes unfamiliar though when we consider that this performance of desire works not to subvert heterosexual normativity, but rather to cooperate with it. Confined to the moment and to the materials of whimsy, the "irresistible attraction" for the name of Ernest is abandoned when it proves discordant to the wedding march; the desires embodied in Bunbury are made to disappear like so much smoke at the first sound of wedding bells.

Dwelling all in fun and easily put aside before the altar, the airy passion of *The Importance of Being Earnest* is thrown into relief by the escalating anxiety about certain extra-marital pleasures that defined Wilde's cultural situation, an escalating anxiety marked and arranged by the scandals and legislation that crowded the decades during which he wrote, an escalating anxiety which culminated in the show trial where he found himself cast as the star witness for a love that he had spent considerable wit to avoid having to name. An acquired passion, less like an infectious disease than a love of the dance, the desire that, for all its lightness, moves more than the plot of *The Importance of Being Earnest*, is no apology for dissident sexualities: it is rather an effort to prevent the need to make one.

To recognize that Wilde is never more a good citizen than when he flouts the conventions of referentiality is to notice again that social effects cannot be neatly collated with linguistic categories. But I want to suggest that the light passion that dwells on the surface of *The Importance of Being Earnest* does more to enhance our appreciation of the complexity of desire than encourage a by-now common apprehensiveness about certain post-structuralist efforts to align resistance to reference, with resistance to the Law. I want to suggest that desire-lite, the domesticated passion that we have sampled in *The Importance of Being Earnest*, sometimes has a surprisingly foreign source; I want to suggest that this house-brand of libido is often produced with foreign help.

Frantz Fanon describes an association of eros and exotic ethnicity more familiar than the one we will investigate here in his canonical account of the western sexual imagination; already active in the late nineteenth century, the association Fanon outlines has only intensified with the passing years: "One is no longer aware of the Negro, but only of a penis: the Negro is eclipsed. He is turned into a penis. He *is* a penis."[5] For all its raciness, the condensation the psychiatrist locates in the waking dreams of whites about blacks is as routine as a man in a polyester suit. Fanon's bold eye resolves the image of a cultural figure whose staying power has spanned several centuries, an image uncovered recently both by Robert Mapplethorpe's explicitness and by the often perfect integration of racial and sexual aversion that has attended it.

As its obtrusiveness in Mapplethorpe's photograph suggests, the threat of sexuality commonly embodied in the black man, as the black man, dwells in its undeniability; an undeniability rendered vivid by the failure to cover it. While the artful

[5]Frantz Fanon, *Black Skin, White Masks* (London: Paladin, 1970), p. 120.

passions featured in Wilde's comedy turn on a dime, or on a dictate of chapel and hearth, while "irresistible attractions" there disappear the instant they prove inconvenient to the regime of Church and State, the desire in and for what will not be contained by the polyester suit is itself too compelling to respect the white collar requirements of nine-to-five.

The field of color where appetites coercive enough to refuse the impressive demands of marriage plot or work place extends beyond the skin-tone recorded in the Mapplethorpe photograph. If the black man and black woman are typically cast as figures of a sexuality too compelling to be stopped by red lights, time clocks or the check points of apartheid, other races, such as those who attend the opium den which Dorian Gray frequents, are attached to other no less coercive strains of desire, cast either as their subject or object. Those addicted to what, in an irony of imperialism, was called a Chinese drug, "grotesque things that lay in . . . fantastic postures on the ragged mattresses" (224) are themselves "crouching Malays," whose nationality, like the "odour of opium," is absorbed by the den's clientele, generally: "A crooked smile, like a Malay crease, writhed across the face of one of the women" (225).

But if the dark compulsions clothed in the polyester suit of the black man or housed in the opium den are sometimes affiliated with exotic races, the desire that concerns us here sometimes takes its light from the land of the rising sun. In order to assess the labor done by the figure of Japan to promote safer passions, we need to recall that this malleable desire is first and foremost a work of art. Whatever it isn't, the work of art is the domain of the artist's will. If art, according to Wilde's famous meditations, evades the constraints of mimesis, it is all the more the servant of the artist; if Wilde frees art from its bondage to accuracy, he makes it the compliant medium of the artist's will.

Wilde's account of the work of art recalls the child's play recorded by Freud, in which the infant masters what elsewhere masters him. "I don't want to be at the mercy of my emotions," Dorian Gray declares in a fit of pique: "I want to use them, to enjoy them, and to dominate them." Such power is achieved only when emotions, and desire chief among them, are spirited away from the element of blind compulsion that Wilde, in the following passage, calls "action":

> There is no mode of action, no form of emotion, that we do not share with the lower animals. It is only by language that we rise above them, or above each other . . . [Action] is a blind thing dependent on external influences, and moved by an impulse of whose nature it is is unconscious.[6]

If Wilde's account of "action" resembles our own ideas about the vicissitudes of sexuality, this is not only because of its animal and unconscious elements, but also, and most importantly, because it is driven by "external influences" and "impulse[s]." As much as anything else, Wilde's aversion to the outdoors, his dis-

---

[6]"The Critic as Artist" (1891), in *The Artist as Critic: Critical Writings of Oscar Wilde*, ed. Richard Ellmann (Chicago: University of Chicago Press, 1968), p. 359.

taste for the natural, is a dislike for the coercions of desire that he finds there. Only when desire migrates to the house of art does it acquire the pliancy necessary to render it safe for Church law and family movie.

In the figure of Japan, the artfulness of desire-lite finds agreeable surroundings. When, in their litany of Aesthetic tastes, Gilbert and Sullivan mention the "longing for all one sees that's Japanese," they refer to a style as central to the 1880s as the color black was to the 1980s. A part of a long line of fashions given over to the celebration of the artificial, the rage for things Japanese was as much as anything else a longing for an exoticism removed from the realm of the real. In an early instance of Japanese exceptionalism, the land of the rising sun, in contrast to the various regions of the non-occidental world that imperial cartography mapped as a wildlife park, was apprehended by western eyes as a palace of art. Starting with its "opening" to the west in the middle of the nineteenth century, Japan had become a storehouse for English, American, and French artists and collectors—the Impressionists, for example, located Japan as the home of their signature styles.

"Now, do you really imagine that the Japanese people, as they are presented to us in art, have any existence? If you do, you have never understood Japanese art at all," Wilde declares in a famous oriental travelogue sandwiched into "The Decay of Lying"—less a travelogue, really, than an explanation of why no such thing is necessary: "The Japanese people are the deliberate self-conscious creation of certain individual artists."[7]

The deliberate self-conscious creation of certain individual artists such as Gilbert and Sullivan, whose cartoon rendering of Japan was never intended to fool anybody—Chesterton speaks the commonest sense in his review of *The Mikado* ("I doubt if there is a single joke in the whole play that fits the Japanese. But all the jokes in the play fit the English" [Baily, 83]). Its ostentatiously theatrical character relies upon and reproduces Japan's reputation as pure artifice—a reputation reflected by Rudyard Kipling in his musings on Japan:

> It would pay us to establish an international suzerainty over Japan: to take away any fear of invasion and annexation, and pay the country as much as ever it chose, on condition that it simply sat still and went on making beautiful things . . . It would pay us to put the whole Empire in a glass case and mark it *Hors Concours*, Exhibit A.[8]

Japan sets the stage for a story of love which, partaking of the general character of the light opera form that Gilbert and Sullivan stirred into the modern musical, is all show. When, in *The Mikado*, the two lovers enact as mere performance the intercourse denied to them in deed by a law that prohibits all flirting, the comedy derives from the impossibility of keeping the fiction of love separate from the fact of it in the world they inhabit.

---

[7]Wilde, "The Decay of Lying" (1891), in *The Artist as Critic*, p. 315.
[8]Rudyard Kipling, *From Sea to Sea* (London: 1900) v. 1, 335; p. 455.

Nanki-Po:	If it were not for the law, we should now be sitting side by side, like that (*sits by her*).
Yum-Yum:	Instead of being obliged to sit half a mile off, like that (*crosses and sits at other side of stage*).
Nanki-Po:	We should be gazing into each other's eyes, like that (*gazing at her sentimentally*).
Yum-Yum:	Breathing sighs of unutterable love—like that (*sighing and gazing lovingly at him*).
Nanki-Po:	With our arms round each other's waists, like that (*embracing her*).
Yum-Yum:	Yes, if it wasn't for the law.
Nanki-Po:	If it wasn't for the law.
Yum-Yum:	As it is, of course we couldn't do anything of the kind.
Nanki-Po:	Not for worlds![9]

The joke that Yum-Yum and Nanki-Po play here takes in more than the general ontology of the theater; it alludes to a whole nation cast as a work of art. Everything in *The Mikado*, most importantly the safe desire that propels its plot, is established by the chorus of Japanese Nobles who introduce it:

If you want to know who we are,
We are gentlemen of Japan;
On many a vase and jar—
On many a screen and fan,
We figure in lively paint . . .
Perhaps you suppose this throng
Can't keep it up all day long?
If that's your idea, you're wrong. (299)

The throng of artificial Japanese continue their song until the end of the play: all of its action is contained by it. Like the oriental objects that one "can touch and handle," the "lacquer-work" and "carved ivories" that Dorian Gray calls a means of inculcating "the artistic temperament," the floating world of *The Mikado* supplies local habitation and a name for passions light enough to carry on stage, and agreeable enough to be left at the church door. (For all its fun, the passion performed in *The Mikado*, like the pleasures of Bunburying and the passion of the Ernestosexual, cooperate utterly with the demands of the law, here resolved into a single edict forbidding "non-connubial affection." When love proves inconvenient for the successful resolution of the plot which enforces this edict by rendering it unnecessary, the lover simply drops the subject.)

And if the aesthetic character of Japan renders it a suitable theater for the production of desire lite, the process of its aestheticization supplies a paradigm and a catalyst for its production. In his guide to Japan, Wilde remarks not merely Japan's aesthetic character, but the process of its aestheticization:

---

[9]Gilbert and Sullivan, *The Mikado* in *Complete Plays*, p. 312. All subsequent citations refer to this edition.

If you set a picture by Hokusai, or Hokkei, or any of the great native painters, beside a real Japanese gentleman or lady, you will see that there is not the slightest resemblance between them. The actual people who live in Japan are not unlike the general run of English people; that is to say, they are extremely commonplace, and have nothing curious or extraordinary about them. In fact, the whole of Japan is a pure invention. There is no such country, there are no such people. One of our most charming painters went recently to the Land of the Chrysanthemum in the foolish hope of seeing the Japanese. All he saw, all he had the chance of painting, were a few lanterns and some fans. He was quite unable to discover the inhabitants . . . He did not know that the Japanese people are, as I have said, simply a mode of style, an exquisite fancy of art. And so, if you desire to see a Japanese effect, you will not behave like a tourist and go to Tokio. On the contrary, you will stay at home, and steep yourself in the work of certain Japanese artists, and then, when you have absorbed the spirit of their style, and caught their imaginative manner of vision, you will go some afternoon and sit in the Park or stroll down Piccadilly, and if you cannot see an absolutely Japanese effect there, you will not see it anywhere. . . .[10]

As he proceeds in this passage from the modest claim that Japan as it is depicted in art does not actually exist outside of it, to the bolder announcement that Japan only exists there, Wilde records the wholesale exodus of Japan into the region of *Japonisme*. If the misguided tourist who goes to Tokyo in the hope of discovering Japan finds the place abandoned, that is because the entire population has left town to take up residence in or on paintings, fans and tea cups, or in the style that is implied there.

As usual, Wilde's cheek is only the nerve and lucidity to pronounce an ideological operation that others don't think to say out loud. Like the belief that the Japanese are great technicians, a belief which expands metonymically into the sense that the Japanese are technology themselves, Wilde's account, which begins by noticing the skill of Japanese artists, and ends by celebrating all of Japan as a work of art, locates the land of the rising sun as a site, more generally, for the process of aestheticization.

We can catch the Japanese contribution to the aesthetization of desire on the first page of a text famously obsessed with the subject. Here is the opening of *The Picture of Dorian Gray*:

The studio was filled with the rich odour of roses, and when the light summer wind stirred amidst the trees of the garden, there came through the open door the heavy scent of the lilac, or the more delicate perfume of the pink-flowering thorn.

From the corner of the divan of Persian saddle-bags on which he was lying, smoking, as was his custom, innumerable cigarettes, Lord Henry Wotton could just catch the gleam of the honey-sweet and honey-coloured blossoms of a laburnum, whose tremulous branches seemed hardly able to bear the burden of a beauty so flame-like as theirs. (7)

The safety of the studio, filled with the luxuries of art and artifice, is compromised by its exposure to the outdoors—the heavy scent of the lilac intrudes through the

---

[10]Wilde, "The Decay of Lying," in *The Artist as Critic*, pp. 315–6.

open door, but more importantly, so does the sight of the laburnum, caught in a tremulous embrace of a flame like beauty, not unlike that of a young man destined by the dictates of nature to fade. ("Yes, there would be a day when his face would be wrinkled and wizen.") This arborial analogue to a passion for the novel's show-stopping hero is displaced, as the passage continues, by figures of art:

> Lord Henry Wotton could just catch the gleam of the honey-sweet and honey-coloured blossoms of a laburnum, whose tremulous branches seemed hardly able to bear the burden of a beauty so flame-like as theirs; and now and then the fantastic shadows of birds in flight flitted across the long tussore-silk curtains that were stretched in front of the huge window, producing a kind of momentary Japanese effect, and making him think of those pallid jade-faced painters of Tokio who, through the medium of an art that is necessarily immobile, seek to convey the sense of swiftness and motion. (7)

Retreating from the involuntary tremblings of a compelling passion, the first thing to be seen in the safety zone arranged by the pains of the aesthetic is a "Japanese effect," a wholly fantastic figure, as removed from "the burden of a [natural] beauty so flame-like" that it would burn anyone who seeks to play with it as a "medium of art that is necessarily immobile" from "the sense of swiftness and motion."

More than that though: put in mind of "those pallid jade-faced artists of Tokio" as he removes himself from the vicissitudes of the elements that his author placed outdoors, Lord Henry is put in the mind of a culture that renders the countenance of Japan as faces in jade. If the indoor landscape of the aesthetic features the familiar figures of the floating world, the journey there is guided and fueled by the impulse to artifice that defines more than Oscar Wilde's vision of Japan.

Writing Gone Wilde: Homoerotic Desire in the Closet of Representation

Ed Cohen

Oh! It is absurd to have a hard and fast rule about what one should read and what one shouldn't. More than half of modern culture depends on what one shouldn't read.

—Algy to Jack in *The Importance of Being Earnest*

. . . every reader of our columns, as he passed his eye over the report of Wilde's apology for his life at the Old Bailey, must have realized, with accumulating significance at each line, the terrible risk involved in certain artistic and literary phrases of the day. Art, we are told, has nothing to do with morality. But even if this doctrine were true it has long ago been perverted, under the treatment of the decadents, into a positive preference on the part of "Art" for the immoral, the morbid, and the maniacal. It is on this narrower issue that the proceedings of the last few days have thrown so lurid a light. . . . But this terrible case . . . may be the means of incalculable good if it burns in its lesson upon the literary and moral conscience of the present generation.

—The *Westminster Gazette* (6 Apr. 1895)
assessing the Marquis of Queensbury's
acquittal on charges of criminal libel

Prologue: A Trying (Con)text

During the late spring of 1895, the trials of Oscar Wilde erupted from the pages of every London newspaper. The sex scandal involving one of London's most renowned popular playwrights as well as one of the most eccentric members of the British aristocracy titillated popular opinion. And why not? For it had all the elements of a good drawing-room comedy—or, in Freudian terms, a good family romance. The characters were exact: the neurotic but righteously outraged father (the Marquis of Queensbury), the prodigal and effeminate young son (Alfred Douglas), and the degenerate older man who came between them (Wilde). Wilde was portrayed as the corrupting artist who dragged young Alfred Douglas away from the realm of paternal solicitude down into the London

Reprinted by permission of the Modern Language Association of America from *PMLA* 102 (1987):810–13.

underworld, where homosexuality, blackmail, and male prostitution sucked the lifeblood of morality from his tender body. How could such a story have failed to engage the public imagination?

Yet the widespread fascination with Wilde's trials should not be viewed solely as the result of a prurient public interest, nor should it be seen only as the product of a virulent popular desire to eradicate "unnatural" sexual practices. Rather, the public response must be considered in the light of the Victorian bourgeoisie's larger efforts to legitimate certain limits for the sexual deployment of the male body and, in Foucault's terms, to define a "class body." The middle-aged, middle-class men who judged Wilde—both in the court and in the press—saw themselves as attempting not merely to control a "degenerate" form of male sexuality but also to ensure standards for the health of their children and their country.[1] To this end, the court proceedings against Wilde provided a perfect opportunity to define publicly the authorized and legal limits within which a man could "naturally" enjoy the pleasures of his body with another man. The trials, then, can be thought of as a spectacle in which the state, through the law and the press, delimited legitimate male sexual practices (defining them as "healthy," "natural," or "true") by proscribing expressions of male experience that transgressed these limits.[2] The legal proceedings against Wilde were therefore not anomalous; rather, they crystallized a variety of shifting sexual ideologies and practices. For what was at issue was not just the prosecution of homosexual acts per se or the delegitimating of homosexual meanings. At issue was the discursive production of "the homosexual" as the antithesis of the "true" bourgeois male.

In Britain during the late nineteenth century, "the homosexual" was emerging as a category for organizing male experience alongside other newly recognizable "types" ("the adolescent," "the criminal," "the delinquent," "the prostitute," "the housewife," etc.).[3] Coined by the Swiss physician Aroly Benkert in 1869 and popu-

---

[1] Press reports of the trials note that court attendance was exclusively male. The defendant, the prosecution, all the court officials, as well as the audience and press, were also male; hence all that transpired and all that was reported occurred within an entirely male-defined social space for the benefit of a male public.

[2] For the theoretical underpinnings of this argument see Michel Foucault's *History of Sexuality*. Here Foucault counters the post-Freudian notion that Victorian practice repressed natural sexuality and, instead, considers the positive strategies that enveloped the body within particular historical discursive apparatuses. He suggests that the bourgeoisie's concern with regulating its own sexual practices stemmed not from an interdictive moral ideology but rather from an attempt to define its materiality—its body—as a class:

> The emphasis on the body should undoubtedly be linked to the process of growth and establishment of bourgeois hegemony: not, however, because of the market value assumed by labor capacity, but because of what the "cultivation" of its own body could represent politically, economically, and historically for the present and the future of the bourgeoisie. . . . (125–26)

[3] That "homosexuality" stood in a negative relation to "heterosexuality" is metaphorically indicated by the term *invert*, which historically preceded *homosexual* and often served as a synonym (see Chauncey for a more precise explanation of these two terms). Since this essay attempts to explore two particular textual negotiations of the emerging heterosexual-homosexual opposition, the use of both these terms here seems anachronistic. Thus, I use them advisedly and often quarantine them between

larized in the writings of the German sexologists, the word (along with its "normal" sibling, "the heterosexual") entered English usage when Krafft-Ebing's *Psychopathia Sexualis* was translated during the 1890s. The shift in the conception of male same-sex eroticism from certain proscribed *acts* (the earlier concepts "sodomite" and "bugger" were identified with specific legally punishable practices [see Trumbach; Gilbert]) to certain kinds of *actors* was part of an overall transformation in class and sex-gender ideologies (see Weeks, *Coming Out*, esp. chs. 1–3). If we think of the growth and consolidation of bourgeois hegemony in Victorian Britain as a process whereby diverse sets of material practices ("sex" and "class" among others) were organized into an effective unity (see Connell), then we can see that "the homosexual" crystallized as a distinct subset of male experience only in relation to prescribed embodiments of "manliness." This new conceptualization reproduced asymmetrical power relations by privileging the enactments of white middle-class, heterosexual men (see Cominos for the classic description of this privilege; see also Thomas).

In *Between Men: English Literature and Male Homosocial Desire*, Eve Kosofsky Sedgwick explores the range of "maleness" in English literature between the late eighteenth and early twentieth centuries and proposes that the normative structuring of relations between men established other male positionings within the larger sex-gender system.[4] Investigating the strategies whereby literary texts (primarily nineteenth-century novels) constructed a "continuum of homosocial desire," she illustrates that these texts articulate male sexuality in ways that also evoke asymmetrical power relations between men and women. Hence, she suggests that we must situate both the production and the consumption of literary representations depicting male interactions (whether overtly sexualized or not) within a larger social formation that circulates ideologies defining differences in power across sex and class.

This suggestion seems particularly applicable to Wilde's texts, which embody an especially contradictory nexus of class and sexual positionings. As the son of a noted Irish physician, Sir William Wilde, and a popular nationalist poet, Lady Jane Wilde (also called "Speranza"), Wilde was educated in a series of public schools and colleges before attending Oxford. After receiving a double "first" in 1879, Wilde "went down" to London, where, owing to his father's death and his family's insolvency, he was forced to earn his own income. From that time until his imprisonment in 1895, Wilde consciously constructed and marketed himself as a liminal

---

quotation marks to indicate that I am quoting from the larger cultural (con)text in which they have become commonplace. In a recent article Tim Calligan, Bob Connell, and John Lee note the enduring effects of this opposition (587). For details of the development of "the adolescent," see Ariès; Gillis, *Youth;* Gorham; and Donzelot. On "the criminal," see Lombroso's *Criminal Man* and *The Female Offender.* Judith Walkowitz details the emergence of "the prostitute." For "the delinquent" see Foucault, *Discipline,* and Gillis, "Evolution." On "the homosexual" see Weeks, *Coming Out;* Plummer; Faderman; Katz; and Chauncey.

 [4]The term belongs to Gayle Rubin, who initially defined it as "the set of arrangements by which a society transforms biological sexuality into products of human activity and in which these transformed sexual needs are satisfied" (159).

figure within British class relations, straddling the lines between nobility, aristocracy, middle class, and—in his sexual encounters—working class. The styles and attitudes that he affected in his writing and his life creatively packaged these multiple positionings; "I have put all my genius into my life," Wilde observed in his famous remark to André Gide; "I have only put my talents into my work." Typically, literary critics have explained this overdetermined positioning by situating Wilde among the nineteenth-century manifestations of decadence and dandyism, thereby emphasizing that his aesthetic paradoxically signified his dependence on the prevailing bourgeois culture and his detachment from it.[5] Yet his literary and personal practices also embodied a more contradictory relation to sexual and class ideologies.

As Regenia Gagnier demonstrates, these contradictions became evident in the contemporary reviews of *The Picture of Dorian Gray:*

> One is struck by the profusion of such terms [in the reviews of *Dorian Gray*] as "unclean," "effeminate," "studied insincerity," "theatrical," "Wardour Street aestheticism," "obtrusively cheap scholarship," "vulgarity," "unnatural," "false," and "perverted": an odd mixture of the rumors of Wilde's homosexuality and of more overt criticism of Wilde as a social poseur and self-advertiser. Although the suggestion was couched in terms applying to the text, the reviews seemed to say that Wilde did not know his place, or—amounting to the same thing—that he did know his place and it was not that of a middle-class gentleman. (59)

In Gagnier's analysis, the immediate critical response to *Dorian Gray* denounced the text's transgression of precisely those class and gender ideologies that sustained the "middle-class gentleman": the novel was seen as "decadent" both because of "its distance from and rejection of middle-class life" and because "it was not only dandiacal, it was 'feminine' " (65). Thus, the *Athenaeum* would refer to the book as "unmanly, sickening, vicious (although not exactly what is called 'improper'), and tedious and stupid" (Mason 200). And the *Scotts Observer* would remark:

> Mr. Wilde has again been writing stuff that were better unwritten and while 'The Picture of Dorian Gray,' which he contributes to *Lippincott's,* is ingenious, interesting, full of cleverness, and plainly the work of a man of letters, it is false art—for its interest is medico-legal; it is false to human nature—for its hero is a devil; it is false to morality— for it is not made sufficiently clear that the writer does not prefer a course of unnatural iniquity to a life of cleanliness, health and sanity. (Mason 75–76)

Emphasizing that Wilde's novel violated the standards of middle-class propriety, these characterizations illustrate the intersection of Victorian class and gender ideologies from which Wilde's status as the paradigmatic "homosexual" would emerge. For, in contrast to the "manly" middle-class male, Wilde would come to

---

[5]For a comprehensive survey of the critical appraisal of Wilde as "decadent" and "dandy," see Gagnier, especially ch. 2, "Dandies and Gentlemen."

represent—through his writing and his trials—the "unmanly" social climber who threatened to upset the certainty of bourgeois categories.

To situate Wilde's emergence as "a homosexual" in late nineteenth-century literary (con)texts and thereby explore the ways that sex-gender ideologies shape specific literary works, I focus first on *Teleny,* a novel widely attributed to Wilde and one of the earliest examples of male homoerotic pornography, whose encoding of sexual practices between men moves athwart those ideologies that sought to "naturalize" male heterosexuality. Then by analyzing the better-known and yet manifestly "straight" text *The Picture of Dorian Gray,* I illustrate that even in the absence of explicit homosexual terminology or activity, a text can subvert the normative standards of male same-sex behavior. In considering how these works challenge the hegemonic representations of male homoerotic experience in late Victorian Britain, I suggest how textual depictions of male same-sex experience both reproduce and resist the dominant heterosexual ideologies and practices.

Through the Revolving Door: The Pornographic Representation of the Homoerotic in Teleny

In *The Other Victorians,* Steven Marcus states:

> The view of human sexuality as it was represented in the [late Victorian] subculture of pornography and the view of sexuality held by the official culture were reversals, mirror images, negative analogies of each other. . . . In both the same set of anxieties are at work; in both the same obsessive ideas can be made out; and in both sexuality is conceived of at precisely the same degree of consciousness. (283–84)

While Marcus's analysis suggestively projects the "pornotopia" as the underside of bourgeois society, it fails to consider the ways that Victorian pornography not only reflected but refracted—or perhaps, more specifically, *interrupted*—the assumptions and practices of the dominant culture.[6] In other words, since Marcus relates the production of the pornographic only to institutionally legitimated forms of the sexual and the literary, he obscures the degree to which such an unsanctioned (and hence uncanonized) genre could provide positive articulations of marginalized sexual practices and desires.

One such textual affirmation can be found in *Teleny: Or, The Reverse of the Medal: A Physiological Romance.* Written in 1890 (the same year "The Picture of

---

[6]I take the concept "interruption" from David Silverman and Brian Torode, who define it as a practice that "seeks not to impose a language of its own but to enter critically into existing linguistic configurations, and to re-open the closed structures into which they have ossified" (6). This notion of interruption as a critical refiguring of ossified linguistic structures—itself a wonderful metaphor for ideological attempts to petrify historically constructed, hegemonically organized semiotic equivalences into timeless, natural usages—provides an excellent analytical tool for examining subcultural discourses that challenge a dominant culture's monovocalizing practices. I apply it to resistant or counterhegemonic textual strategies that reopen the polyvalence of linguistic practices—here specifically the homoerotic challenge to the conception of heterosexuality as natural.

Dorian Gray" appeared in *Lippincott's Monthly Magazine*), *Teleny* is reputed to be the serial work of several of Wilde's friends (who circulated the manuscript among themselves), with Wilde serving as general editor and coordinator.[7] Even if this genealogy proves apocryphal, the unevenness of its prose styles suggests that the novel was the collaboration of several authors and possibly a set of self-representations evolving out of the homosexual subculture in late Victorian London.

Chronicling the ill-fated love between two late nineteenth-century men, *Teleny* unfolds as a retrospective narrative told by the dying Camile Des Grieux to an unnamed interlocutor. Prompted by his questioner, Des Grieux unfolds a tale of seductions, sex (homo- and hetero-, oral and anal), orgies, incest, blackmail, rape, suicide, death, and love. Aroused by his passion for the beautiful—and well-endowed—young pianist René Teleny, Des Grieux opens himself to the varied possibilities of male sexual expression only to find himself drawn back again and again to a single object of desire: the male body of his beloved Teleny. Thus, Des Grieux's narrative represents an explicit set of strategies through which the male body is ensnared in the passions and excesses of homoerotic desire.

Introducing the image of its fatal conclusion, the novel's opening sentence directs us immediately to the body on which the narrative is inscribed: "A few days after my arrival in Nice, last winter, I encountered several times on the Promenade a young man, of dark complexion, thin, a little stooped, of pallid color, with eyes—beautiful blue eyes—ringed in black, of delicate features, but aged and emaciated by a profound ailment, which appeared to be both physical and moral" (21). The novel's conclusion can be initially "read off" from Des Grieux's degenerate condition only because his body serves as the "recording surface" for the story.[8] The narrator underscores this relation between body and narrative: "The account that follows is not, then, a novel. It is rather a true story: the dramatic adventures of two young and handsome human beings of refined temperament, high-strung, whose brief existence was cut short by death after flights of passion which will doubtless be misunderstood by the generality of men" (22). Here the generic "human beings" distinguishes the protoganists from the "generality of men" who will doubtlessly misunderstand them, introducing a fundamental opposition "fleshed out" in the text: by juxtaposing male same-sex passion with a cultural concept of "manliness" that seeks to exclude it, the novel deconstructs those definitions of human nature that deny the homoerotic as unnatural. Thus, even before its pornographic plot begins, the text attaches itself to

---

[7]This account is paraphrased from Winston Leyland's introduction to the Gay Sunshine reprint of *Teleny*. Leyland takes most of his information from H. M. Hyde's introduction to the 1966 British edition, which Hyde derives in part from the introduction of a 1934 French translation written by Leonard Hirsch, the London bookseller whose shop was supposedly the transfer point for the various authors.

[8]This terminology, which is implicit throughout my essay, derives from Gilles Deleuze and Félix Guattari. They develop the metaphors of "marking the body" and "recording surfaces of desire" to elaborate the mechanisms through which desire invests somatic experience as well as to consider the ways in which the socius "codes" the body. See especially their part 3, "Savages, Barbarians, Civilized Men."

the male body as the surface on which its markings will become legible and simultaneously undertakes to use this legibility to validate same-sex desire.

Within the novel's narrative logic, this validation derives from the irrationality of the attraction uniting Des Grieux and Teleny, in spite of their manifestly masculine (and hence ideologically rational) positioning. In the first chapter, positing their almost mystical affinity, Des Grieux recalls their "predestined" meeting at a London charity concert. On stage, Teleny, the pianist, senses the presence of a "sympathetic listener" who inspires him to incredible heights of virtuosity. In the audience, Des Grieux responds to Teleny's performance by visualizing a set of extravagant and exotic scenes—portraying classical European images of non-European sexualized otherness—which, we soon learn, are the same visions that Teleny conjures as he plays. Indeed, these images are so distinct that Des Grieux experiences them physically: "a heavy hand [that] seemed to be laid on my lap, something was hent and clasped and grasped, which made me faint with lust" (27). In the midst of this masturbatory incantation, Des Grieux succumbs to the novel's first stirrings of priapic ecstasy. Thus, when the young men meet and their first touch (a properly masculine handshake) "reawakens Priapus," Des Grieux feels that he has been "taken possession of" (29). The ensuing conversation leads the men to recognize their affinity and, at the same time, foregrounds the irrationality underlying their erotic connection. Describing the music that has brought them together as the product of a "madman," Teleny hints at "insanity" and "possession," enmeshing the two in a web of superstition and "unreason." By violating the dominant Victorian associations of masculinity with science and reason, the first encounter between the lovers casts their attraction as an implicit challenge to the normative ideologies for male behavior.

Following this initial highly charged meeting, the next four chapters elaborate the deferral of its sexual consummation, recounting Des Grieux's emotional turmoil as he comes to recognize, accept, and ultimately enjoy his physical desire for Teleny. The sexual content of this portion of the novel depicts primarily illicit—if not taboo—heterosexual practices. All these manifestly straight incidents, however, portray the heterosexual as a displacement of the true affection of one man for another; they juxtapose the universal acceptability and "naturalness" of heterosexual passion (even if accompanied by incest or violence) to the execration and "unnaturalness" of homoerotic desire.

As Des Grieux begins to make sense of his obsession with Teleny, he realizes that this natural-unnatural distinction is itself learned (i.e., cultural): ". . . I had been inculcated with all kinds of wrong ideas, so when I understood what my *natural* feelings for Teleny were I was staggered, horrified . . ." (63; my emphasis). This inverted use of the word *natural* deconstructs the mask of ideological neutrality and underscores the moral implications it attempts to conceal. Once he accepts that he "was born a sodomite," Des Grieux can remark that "I read all I could find about the love of one man for another, that loathsome crime against nature, taught to us not only by the very gods themselves, but by all of the greatest men of olden times. . . ." Thus the text mocks the culture's pretensions in defining as a "crime against nature" that which *his* nature demands and which the "very gods themselves" and the "greatest men of olden times" have practiced. By subverting the claims to "natural" (read "ideological") superiority by "honorable [heterosexual] men," the narrative's logic opens the possibility for a counterhegemonic representation of homoerotic desire

The first sexual encounter between Des Crieux and Teleny inaugurates this new representation of same-sex desire by reviving the "fatedness" of their relationship. As Des Grieux, convinced of the hopelessness of his passion for a man, stands on a bridge over the Thames and contemplates "the forgetfulness of those Stygian waters," he is grabbed from behind by the strong arms of his beloved Teleny, who is drawn to the spot by supernatural premonition (explained by Teleny's "gypsy blood"). This charmed meeting culminates in a scene of extravagant and abandoned lovemaking through which the two men form an inseparable bond that sustains them for many climaxes and an unforgettable orgy. The charm is broken, however, when Teleny—through a combination of boredom, irrepressible lust, and economic necessity—is led into an affair with Des Grieux's mother. The shock of discovering that his mother has usurped his place in Teleny's bed sends Des Grieux into a decline from which he never recovers, and the shock of being found out causes Teleny to take his own life.

This summary can only hint at the profusion of sexual representation the novel engenders. Despite its tragic ending, its depiction of male homoerotic desire and practice insists on not only the possibility but the naturalness of same-sex eroticism. Thus, in reflecting on the story of his first night with Teleny, Des Grieux offers one of the most articulate defenses of same-sex love to be found in late Victorian fiction. Responding to his interlocutor's question, "Still, I had thought, on the morrow—the intoxication passed—you would have shuddered at the thought of having a man for a lover?" Des Grieux asks:

> Why? Had I committed a crime against nature when my own nature found peace and happiness thereby? If I was thus, surely it was the fault of my blood, not myself. Who had planted nettles in my garden? Not I. They had grown there unawares from my very childhood. I began to feel their carnal sting long before I could understand what conclusion they imported. When I had tried to bridle my lust, was it my fault if the scale of reason was far too light to balance that of sensuality? Was I to blame if I could not argue down my raging motion? Fate, Iago-like, had clearly shewed me that if I would damn myself, I could do so in a more delicate way than drowning. I yielded to my destiny and encompassed my joy. (119)

By juxtaposing his homoerotic "nature" to a Victorian definition that criminalized it, Des Grieux's statement foregrounds the moral-ideological concerns implied in this naturalizing terminology. In so doing, he articulates a theory of "innate difference" similar to the third-sex theories first proposed by the late nineteenth-century apologists for same-sex desire (Edward Carpenter, J. A. Symonds, and Havelock Ellis).[9] Since these formulations assume the opposition between intellect and passion—or between male and female—found elsewhere in late Victorian discourse, they nec-

---

[9]For a discussion of these initial apologies for homoerotic behavior see Jeffrey Weeks, *Coming Out* and *Sexuality and Its Discontents*. On the body-mind dichotomy in nineteenth-century discourse, see Rosalind Coward.

essarily encode the implicit bias on which these dichotomies depend. Here, however, the polarities are resolved through an alternative outlet, physical and moral: joy. In affirming the naturalness of Des Grieux's homoerotic experience, this new joyous possibility undermines the monovocalizing strategies the bourgeois heterosexual culture used to ensure the reproduction of its dominance and thus opens up the possibility of representing a plurality of male sexualities.

Behind the Closet Door: The Representation of Homoerotic Desire in The Picture of Dorian Gray

What if someone wrote a novel about homosexuality and nobody came? To what extent is *The Picture of Dorian Gray* this book? And what does it mean to say that a text is "about" homosexuality anyway?

While *The Picture of Dorian Gray* has generated much speculation and innuendo concerning its author's sexual preferences, the aftermath of Wilde's trials has left no doubt in the critical mind that the "immorality" of Wilde's text paralleled that of his life. Yet this critical reflection has never directly addressed the question of how Wilde's "obviously" homoerotic text signifies its "deviant" concerns while never explicitly violating the dominant norms for heterosexuality. That Wilde's novel encodes traces of male homoerotic desire seems to be ubiquitously, though tacitly, affirmed. Why this general affirmation exists has never been addressed. To understand how "everyone knows" what lurks behind Wilde's manifestly straight language (i.e., without descending to a crude biographical explanation), we must examine the ways that Wilde's novel moves both with and athwart the late Victorian ideological practices that naturalized male heterosexuality.[10]

The Picture of Dorian Gray narrates the development of male identity within a milieu that actively subverts the traditional bourgeois representations of appropriate

---

[10]For a selection of articles showing how the contemporary press responded to *Dorian Gray*, along with Wilde's replies to these criticisms, see Stuart Mason. Later explanations of the relation between Wilde's personal and textual sexuality include G. Wilson Knight's "Christ and Wilde," which attributes Wilde's "perverse pleasures" (138, quoting Wilde's *De Profundis*) to his "mother fixation," to his mother's having "dressed him as a girl until he was nine," and to his "love of flowers and of male and female dress." Knight reads *Dorian Gray* as the "subtlest critique of the Platonic Eros ever penned" (143)—without stooping to textual exegesis—and then justifies Wilde's "homosexual engagements" as "a martyrdom, a crucifixion, a self-exhibition in agony and shame" deriving from both "the instinct . . . to plunge low when disparity between near-integrated self and the community becomes unbearable" and "a genuine liking for the lower orders of society" (144–45). Richard Ellmann informs us that Wilde changes the date of Dorian's murder of Basil Hallward from "the eve of his own thirty-second birthday" in the original Lippincott's version to "the eve of his own thirty-eighth birthday" in the bound edition to mask the reference to his first sexual experience with Robbie Ross, which—according to a mathematical extrapolation from Ross's memoirs—must have occurred during Wilde's thirty-second year (11). Other critical works that acknowledge Wilde's homosexuality without analyzing the "homotextual problematic" include those by Philip Cohen, Jeffrey Meyers, and Christopher Nassaar. Meyers is especially interesting, given his explicit project of examining the homosexual "in" literature, but unfortunately his eclectic methodology quickly descends into the biographical and associational strategies that characterize most criticism on *Dorian Gray*.

male behavior. While it portrays a sphere of art and leisure in which male friendships assume primary emotional importance and in which traditional male values (industry, earnestness, morality) are abjured in favor of the aesthetic, it makes no explicit disjunction between these two models of masculinity; rather, it formally opposes an aesthetic representation of the male body and the material, emotional, sexual male body itself. In other words, *The Picture of Dorian Gray* juxtaposes an aesthetic ideology that foregrounds representation with an eroticized milieu that inscribes the male body within circuits of male desire. To understand how this opposition operates, we must first consider the components of the male friendships in the novel.

The text of *Dorian Gray* develops around a constellation of three characters— Lord Henry Wotten, Basil Hallward, and Dorian Gray—who challenge the Victorian standards of "true male" identity. Freed from the activities and responsibilities that typically consumed the energies of middle-class men, they circulate freely within an aestheticized social space that they collectively define. As inhabitants of a subculture, however, they still use a public language that has no explicit forms to represent (either to themselves or to one another) their involvements; hence, they must produce new discursive strategies to express concerns unvoiced within the dominant culture. In producing these strategies, the novel posits its moral and aesthetic interests. By projecting the revelation, growth, and demise of Dorian's "personality" onto an aesthetic consideration of artistic creation, Wilde demonstrates how the psychosexual development of an individual gives rise to the "double consciousness" of a marginalized group.[11] Dorian Gray is to some extent born of the conjunction between Basil's visual embodiment of his erotic desire for Dorian and Lord Henry's verbal sublimation of such desire. From this nexus of competing representational modes, Dorian Gray constitutes his own representations of identity. But who then is Dorian Gray?

Within the narrative structure, Dorian is an image—a space for the constitution of male desire. From the time he enters the novel as the subject of Basil's portrait until the moment Wilde has him kill himself into art, Dorian Gray provides the surface on which the characters project their self-representations. His is the body on which Basil's and Lord Henry's desires are inscribed. Beginning with an interview between these two characters, the novel constructs Dorian as a template of desire by thematizing the relation between the inspiration derived from Dorian's "personality" and the resulting aesthetic products. For Basil, Dorian appears as an "ideal," as the motivation for "an entirely new manner in art, an entirely new mode

[11]My use of "double consciousness" derives largely from Jack Winkler's article relating the work of Sappho as a lesbian poet to the public discourse of the Greek polis. Winkler develops a concept reminiscent of W. E. B. Du Bois's notion of the "twoness" of the Afro-American experience (16–17) to refer to the overdetermined conditions of Sappho's representations. Because of her "double consciousness," Winkler suggests, the marginalized poet can speak and write in the dominant discourse but subvert its monolithic truth claims by recasting them in the light of personal, subcultural experience: "This amounts to a reinterpretation of the kinds of meaning previous claims had, rather than a mere contest of claimants for supremacy in a category whose meaning is agreed upon" (73). Applying this theory of "reinterpretation," I conclude that Wilde repeatedly deals with heterosexual morality to deconstruct its social force through wit and witticism.

of style." Dorian's mere "visible presence" enables Basil to represent emotions and feelings that he found inexpressible through traditional methods and themes: "1 see things differently now. I think of them differently. I can recreate life in a way that was hidden from me before" (150).

But what gives Basil's relation to Dorian this transformative power? In describing his friendship with Dorian to Lord Harry, Basil narrates the story of their meeting:

> I turned halfway round, and saw Dorian Gray for the first time. When our eyes met I felt I was growing pale. A curious sensation of terror came over me. I knew I had come face to face with someone whose mere personality was so fascinating, that if I allowed it to do so it would absorb my whole nature, my very art itself. . . . Something seemed to tell me that I was on the verge of a terrible crisis in my life. I had a strange feeling that fate had in store for me exquisite joys and exquisite sorrows. (146)

Dorian's "personality" enchants Basil and throws him back upon himself, evoking a physical response that is then translated into a psychic, verbally encoded interpretation. As an artist, Basil resolves this crisis by experientially and aesthetically transforming his representations of this experience. His fascination with Dorian leads him to foreground their erotic connection ("We were quite close, almost touching. Our eyes met again." [147]) and at the same time to legitimate it in the sublimated language of aesthetic ideals ("Dorian Gray is to me simply a motive in art." [151]).

This symbolic displacement of the erotic onto the aesthetic is reiterated by the absent presence of the "picture" within the novel. While homoerotic desire must be muted in a literary text that overtly conforms to dominant codes for writing— which have historically excluded same-sex desires as unrepresentable—it is nevertheless metonymically suggested by a verbally unrepresentable medium, the painting, whose linguistic incommensurability deconstructs the apparent self-sufficiency of these representational codes. Since the portrait stands outside the text and evokes an eroticized tableau transgressing the limits of verbal representation, it establishes a gap whereby unverbalized meaning can enter the text. In particular, its visual eroticism suffuses the dynamic between Dorian and Basil, thereby foregrounding the male body as the source of both aesthetic and erotic pleasure. The portrait provides the space within which, in contemporary psychoanalytic terminology, the phallic activity of "the gaze" encroaches on the dominant linguistic unrepresentability of male same-sex eroticism.[12] Thus, the picture's absent presence (which motivates the narrative development) interrupts the novel's overt representational limits by introducing a visual, extraverbal component of male same-sex desire.

Since Wilde defines painting as an active expression of personal meanings, Basil's "secret" infuses Dorian's picture with a vitality and passion that fundamen-

[12]On the connections between the construction of male sexual identity, visual eroticism, and desire see Jane Gallop's discussion of French feminist theory. Also see Toril Moi's suggestion, in her discussion of the readings of Freud in the texts of Luce Irigaray, that "the gaze [is] a phallic activity linked to anal desire for the sadistic mastery of the object" (134).

tally changes its "mode of style." Yet this secret does not lie in the work of art itself but rather grows out of Basil's emotional and erotic involvement with Dorian Gray, thereby establishing a new relation between the artist and his subject. As Basil eventually explains to Dorian:

> . . . from the moment I met you, your personality had the most extraordinary influence over me. I was dominated soul, brain, and power by you. You became to me the visible incarnation of that unseen ideal whose memory haunts us artists like an exquisite dream. I worshipped you. I grew jealous of everyone to whom you spoke. I wanted to have you all to myself. I was only happy when I was with you. When you were away from me you were still present in my art. . . . (267–68)

The emotional intensity with which Wilde describes Basil's passion for Dorian belies the Platonic invocation of "the visible incarnation of that unseen ideal," since this verbal interpretation merely echoes the available public forms of expression. That Wilde displaces Basil's physical domination onto a dream (albeit exquisite) indicates that there is no publicly validated visible reality to express male homoerotic desire. But because painting can only occur in the nonlinear, and hence extralinguistic, space where Basil synthesizes the visual elements of his emotional and aesthetic inspiration, this visual expression and its verbal analogue are necessarily disjunct. Thus, although Basil's painting is entirely exterior to the text, it provides the reference point for a mode of representation that admits the visible, erotic presence of the male body.

Nowhere is this disjunction made more obvious than in Wilde's distinction between Basil's visual and physical involvement with Dorian and Lord Henry's detached, ironic, and self-conscious verbal stance. In contrast to Basil, who has surrendered his "whole nature," his "whole soul," his "very heart itself," to the immediacy of Dorian Gray, Lord Henry first becomes interested in Dorian through the story of Basil's passion. As a consummate aesthete, Lord Henry derives his passions not from direct engagement with his object but through mediated representations. By separating "one's own soul" from the "passions of one's friends" (153), Wilde opposes Lord Henry's self-objectifying archness to Basil's passionate engagement with his inspiration's embodiment. To the extent that Basil, as a painter, seeks to create a spatialized frame that synthetically mirrors his emotional and erotic reality, Lord Henry, as a conversationalist, segments this aesthetic space into the paradoxes and conundrums that characterize his linguistic style. Basil himself exposes the logic behind this verbal analytics when he says to Lord Henry: "You are an extraordinary fellow. You never say a moral thing and you never do a wrong thing. Your cynicism is simply a pose" (144). It is precisely this cynical posture that distinguishes the two modes of representation the characters engender. For while Basil registers his passion in expressive forms, Lord Henry maintains an autonomous "pose" by detaching himself from his own passions. He never does a wrong thing because he distances himself from the material world of activity by representing reality, both to himself and to others, as an ongoing conversation in which he never says a moral thing. This discursive maneuver, which collapses the physical plenitude of bodily reality into abstract conceptualization, interrupts the visual inscription of Basil's picture and thereby opens the space from which "Dorian Gray" emerges.[13]

Chronologically, this emergence coincides with Basil and Lord Harry's rivalry for Dorian's attention. In recounting his story to Lord Harry, Basil initially hesitates to introduce Dorian's name for fear of violating his "secret." He pleads with Lord Henry not to "take away from me the one person who gives my art whatever charm it possesses," yet his plea merely confirms their competition for the same "wonderfully handsome young man." Though the motives behind this competition are left unspoken, it unfolds during Dorian's final sitting for his portrait. Here, in Basil's studio, the conflict plays itself out as a seduction: Lord Henry woos Dorian away from the adoring gaze of the painter to awaken him to a new, symbolic order of desire—an order at the very heart of the narrative.

Responding to Dorian's complaint that Basil never speaks while painting, Basil allows Lord Henry to stay and entertain Dorian. While Basil puts the finishing touches on the canvas, Lord Henry charms Dorian with a discussion of morality:

> The aim of life is self-development. To realize one's nature perfectly—that is what each of us is here for. People are afraid of themselves nowadays. They have forgotten the highest of all duties is the duty that one owes to oneself. Of course they are charitable. They feed the hungry and clothe the beggar. But their souls starve and are naked. Courage has gone out of our race. Perhaps we never really had it. The terror of society, which is the basis of morals, and the terror of God, which is the secret of religion—these are the two things that govern us. (158)

As Lord Henry's words provide Dorian with new vistas on the moral prejudices of their era, his "low musical voice" seduces the younger man, who becomes transfigured: ". . . a look came into the lad's face . . . never seen there before." Simultaneously, Basil inscribes this "look"—the object of both his artistic and erotic gaze—onto the canvas, thus doubly imbuing his aesthetic image with the representations of male homoerotic desire.

By dialectically transforming Lord Henry's verbal and Basil's visual representations, Dorian enters into the circuits of male desire through which these characters play out their sexual identities. He inspires both Basil and Lord Henry to new heights of expression, but only by internalizing and modifying images through which the older men would have themselves seen. Thus, the development of Dorian's "perfect nature" underscores the disjunction between male homoerotic experience and the historical means of expressing it, so that his strategic mediation between them enables desire to enter the novel explicitly. Lord Henry continues his moral panegyric, once again voicing the problem:

---

[13] Gallop connects "phallic suppression" and the evacuation of the body (67).

The body sins once and has done with sin, for action is a mode of purification. Nothing remains then but the recollection of a pleasure, or the luxury of a regret. The only way to get rid of a temptation is to yield to it. Resist it, and your soul grows sick with longing for those things it has forbidden to itself, with desire for what its monstrous laws have made monstrous and unlawful. (159)

Temptation resisted, Lord Harry suggests, gives rise to the image of a desired yet forbidden object. This overdetermined representation, in turn, mediates between the active body and the reflective mind by forbidding those desires that the soul's monstrous laws proscribe. Thus, these laws—the social representations of self-denial—separate the body as a source of pleasure from the interpretation of that pleasure as sin. By negating pleasure, the natural expression of the body, society (introjected here as "soul") inhibits the body's sensuous potential and circumscribes feeling within established moral codes.

Responding passionately to Lord Henry's critique of this interdictive morality, Dorian senses "entirely fresh influences . . . at work within him [that] really seemed to have come from himself." Since the older man's words counterpose the social to the personal, the desiring associated with self-development to the interdictions of culture, his influence on Dorian emphasizes the sensual as a strategy for resisting society's limitations. "Nothing can cure the soul but the senses, just as nothing can cure the senses but the soul." Although Lord Henry speaks only of the body's sensual possibilities, Dorian uses these words to formulate a new self-image: "The few words that Basil's friend had said to him—words spoken by chance, no doubt, and with willful paradox in them—had touched some secret chord that had never been touched before, but that he felt was now vibrating and throbbing to curious pulses" (160). By defining Dorian's formerly inchoate feelings and sensations, Lord Henry's language creates a new reality for Dorian (". . . mere words. Was there anything so real as words"), and Basil's canvas records Dorian's changing self-image—but only as expressed through Basil's desire. The rivalry between the two older friends for Dorian's affection vitalizes the surface of Basil's painting by attributing an erotic charge to Dorian's body itself. And as this body becomes the object of male attention and representation, the young man's concept of his own material being is transformed—he is "revealed to himself."

Looking on his completed portrait for the first time, Dorian encounters himself as reflected in the "magical mirror" of Basil's desire. This image organizes the disparate perceptions of his body into an apparently self-contained whole and reorients Dorian in relation both to his own identity and to his social context. He begins to conceive of his beauty as his own, failing to understand it as the product of the images that Basil and Lord Harry dialectically provide for him. Wilde describes this change as a physical response, thereby foregrounding the connection between psychic representation and somatic perception while indicating that this seemingly coherent internal representation synthesizes a complex nexus of social relationships. Hence, Dorian's identification with the painted image constitutes a misrecognition as much as a recognition, leading him to confuse an overdetermined set of representations with the "truth" of his experience.

Within these (mis)representations Dorian comes to view his body as distinct from his soul and misrecognizes the certainty of his aging and death. Splitting his self-image into two, Basil's visual representation and Lord Henry's verbal portrait, Dorian internalizes an identity that excites his body only to make it vulnerable to the passage of time. The transitiveness of this new self-recognition manifests itself as physical experience: "As he thought of it [his body's aging] a sharp pang of pain struck through him like a knife and made each delicate fibre of his nature quiver" (167). To avoid aging, Dorian inverts the imaginary and the real and thus conceptualizes the painful disjunction between the image of his body and his body itself as a form of jealousy:

> How sad it is! I shall grow old, and horrible, and dreadful. But this picture will always remain young. It will never be older than this particular day of June. . . . If it were only the other way! If it were I who was to be always young, and the picture that was to grow old! For that—for that—I would give everything. Yes there is nothing in the world I would not give! I would give my soul for that. (168)

In voicing this statement, Dorian executes a linguistic schism—dividing the "I" against itself—which repositions him within the narrative flow. As the "I" of the speaking character is projected against the visual image of the "I," his body is evacuated and thereby removed from the flow of time.

Dorian stakes his soul for the preservation of his physical beauty, of his body image, and Wilde makes the motive for this wager clear: Dorian fears that time will rob him of the youth that makes him the object of male desire: " 'Yes,' he continued [to Basil], 'I am less to you than your ivory Hermes or your silver faun. You will like them always. How long will you like me? Til I have my first wrinkle, I suppose. I know now, that when one loses one's good looks, whatever they may be, one loses everything. Your picture has taught me that' " (168–69). In portraying Dorian's self-perception as a function of Basil's erotic and aesthetic appreciation, Wilde fuses the artifacts of homoerotic desire and the representations that Dorian uses to constitute his identity. The classical images of male beauty and eroticism make Dorian jealous because he fails to understand that the body can have simultaneous aesthetic and erotic appeal. His focus on visual and sexual desirability emphasizes the importance that culturally produced representations have in the construction of male identity.

In describing Dorian's identity as a product of aesthetic and erotic images, Wilde locates "the problem" of male homoerotic desire on the terrain of representation itself. Since his characters encounter one another at the limits of heterosexual forms, they produce multiple positionings for articulating different desires, evoking possibilities for male same-sex eroticism without explicitly voicing them. Instead, Wilde posits many uncovered secrets (Basil's "secret," Dorian's "secrets," Lord Henry's continual revelation of the "secrets of life," even the absent portrait itself), thereby creating a logic of displacement that culminates in Dorian's prayer for eternal youth. Standing outside the text and yet initiating all further narrative development, the prayer is marked only by a caesura that transforms the relation between representation and desire. In a moment of textual silence, Dorian—misperceiving the true object of Basil's feeling—defends his idealized self-image by invoking the magical aspects of utterance. To maintain his identity as the object of another man's desire, he prays to exchange the temporality of his existence for the stasis of an erotically charged visual representation. Inasmuch as Basil's secret—his "worship with far more romance than a man usually gives a friend" (in the 1890 edition)—radiates from the canvas reflecting its subject's beauty, Dorian's profession, "I am in love with it, Basil. It is part of myself. I feel that," underscores the degree to which his male self-image reverberates with the passion of same-sex desire. And this passionate attachment inspires the supplication that makes his portrait perhaps the most well-known nonexistent painting in Western culture.

Not coincidentally, then, the famous reversal between the character and his portrait first appears to stem from the failure of the novel's only explicitly heterosexual element. By introducing the feminine into a world that systematically denies it, Dorian's attraction to the young actress Sibyl Vane (a vain portent?) seems to violate the male-identified world in which Basil and Lord Henry have "revealed [Dorian] to himself." Yet, Sibyl's presence can never actually disturb the novel's male logic, for her appearance merely shows how much an overtly heterosexual discourse depends on male-defined representations of female experience. For Dorian, Sibyl exists only in the drama. Offstage, he imbues her with an aesthetic excess, so that her reality never pierces his fantasy. His remarks to Lord Henry demonstrate that Dorian's passion is the passion of the voyeur, whose desiring gaze distances the viewer from the possibility (necessity?) of physical consummation:

"Tonight she is Imogen," [Dorian] answered, "and tomorrow she will be Juliet."
"When is she Sibyl Vane?"
"Never." (200)

When Dorian impassions Sibyl with a single kiss (the only physical [sexual?] expression that evades his aesthetic voyeurism), her own real passion renders her incapable of making a male-defined representation of female passion "real." Thus she fails to achieve the aesthetic standard he expects of her in the role of Juliet, and Dorian—unable to sustain his heterosexual fantasy—abandons her.[14]

This abandonment leads Sibyl to suicide and introduces the disjunction between Dorian and his portrait. Returning home after his final scene with her, Dorian finds the picture changed, marked by "lines of cruelty around his mouth as clearly as if he had been looking into a mirror after he had done some dreadful thing" (240). He senses anew that this representation "held the secret of his life,

---

[14]Many of Sibyl's roles involve her cross-dressing as a boy, which further complicates the problematic construction of heterosexual desire within the novel. For example, playing Rosalind dressed as a boy, she stirs the desire of Orlando, who is saved from the "horror" of this same-sex passion by the underlying premise that the boy is indeed a girl. (Of course, in Shakespearean theater, where boys played the female characters, the complexities were redoubled.) Dorian's remark on Sibyl's "perfection" in boy's clothes and *Portrait of Mr. W. H.*, which argues for the homoerotic inspiration of Shakespeare's sonnets, would both indicate that Wilde intended this resonance.

and told *his story*" (242; my emphasis). Where once the painting had been confined to the atemporality of the aesthetic moment, it now becomes the surface that records the narrative of his life, not only serving as a static reflection of the interiority of his soul but also telling his soul's story. A "magical mirror," it turns Dorian into a "spectator of [his] own life," thus creating a divided consciousness that initiates the remaining action in the novel.

As Dorian realizes the separation between self-representation and self-image, his behavior becomes ominous and degenerate. He enters into a world of self-abuse and destruction, through which he effects the downfall of many innocent men and women, and yet his body shows no sign of these activities. Only the picture—now locked away in an inaccessible room—reveals the depths to which he has descended. For, as the portrait tells his story, it graphically reveals the details of all he does. In time, the portrait's increasing grotesqueness begins to haunt Dorian. His awareness of the terrifying gap between the man whom others see and the representation that only he may view serves as the limit against which he conceives of his existence. He immerses himself in the life of the senses to test the absoluteness of this limit but finds that he cannot break through it. So long as he remains inscribed within the network of representations—both verbal and visual—that the painting constructs, he can only embody the agonizing dichotomy that it engenders.

Ultimately, seeking to free himself from the images that have ensnared and "destroyed" him Dorian kills the man who "authored" the "fatal portrait." This murder removes the one person to whom Dorian could impute responsibility for the portrait. The picture, which now also depicts the horror of Basil's death, remains only to remind Dorian of the monstrosity of his life. In the final pages of the novel, Dorian resolves to destroy the image. Standing before it, he faces both the material representation of his existence and the distance between that representation and himself. As he plunges the knife into the canvas that reveals his secret, he rends this disjunction, finally breaking free of its absolute limit. Yet, since the price of this freedom is the destruction of the complex configuration of images that motivate both the character and the narrative, the act that concludes the novel does so only by killing Dorian into art.

As his death brings the interplay between representation and the body full circle, the images that Dorian had reflected through his entry into the male-defined world presented by Basil Hallward and Lord Henry Wotten are once again inscribed on his body. And so, in the end, Dorian's corpse becomes the surface that records his narrative, liberating Dorian in death from the consciousness divided between experience and representation that had marked his life.

Coda: Out of the Theoretical Closet

To the extent that Wilde and contemporaries like him were beginning to articulate strategies to communicate—both to themselves and to others—the experience of homoerotic desire, their texts enact and virtually embody this desire. But since these men were also writing within a larger culture that not only denied but actively prosecuted such embodiments, they were forced to devise ways to mediate their expressions of passion. While in certain uncanonized genres, like pornography and to some extent poetry (e.g., the "Uranian" poets), relatively explicit statements of same-sex eroticism were possible, these statements were still posed in relation to the social norms that enjoined them. Thus, although *Teleny* explicitly represents sexual practices between men for an audience who either enjoyed or at least sympathized with such practices, it still reinscribes these representations within the (hetero)sexual symbolic order that it sought to interrupt. In a more canonized work, such as *The Picture of Dorian Gray*, the mediations are necessarily more complex. Wilde's text doubly displaces male homoerotic desire, thematizing it through the aesthetic production of a medium that the novel cannot represent. Basil's portrait of Dorian can embody his desire for the eponymous character, and yet male homoerotic passion remains, in the dominant representational codes of the period, *peccatum illude horribile non nominandum inter christanos*—or, in a bad paraphrase of Lord Alfred Douglas, a love whose name the text dare not speak. In *The Picture of Dorian Gray*, Wilde problematizes representation per se to move athwart the historical limitations that define male homosexuality as "unnameable," thereby creating one of the most lasting icons of male homoerotic desire.

By approaching *Teleny* and *The Picture of Dorian Gray* as complex cultural artifacts, we recognize them not just as texts but as contexts. For, as Raymond Williams says, "If art is a part of the society, there is no solid whole, outside it, to which by the form of our question, we concede priority" (45). Instead of seeing these literary works as ideological reflections of an already existing reality, we must consider them elements in the production of this reality. In analyzing the textual strategies through which these two novels put male desire for other men into discourse, we begin to understand some of the historical forms that such relations between men took and thereby begin to suggest others that they can take.[15]

Works Cited

Ariès, P. *Centuries of Childhood.* Trans. Robert Baldick. London: Cape, 1962.

Calligan, Tim, Bob Connell, and John Lee. "Towards a New Sociology of Masculinity." *Theory and Society* 14.5 (1985): 551–604.

Chauncey, George. "From Sexual Inversion to Homosexuality." *Salmagundi* 58–59 (1982–83): 114–46.

Cohen, Philip. *The Moral Vision of Oscar Wilde.* London: Fairleigh Dickinson UP, 1978.

---

[15]I wish to express my gratitude to all those who have commented on the numerous successive versions of this article. I especially wish to thank Regenia Gagnier, whose enthusiasm and support have encouraged me to persevere; Mary Pratt, who has taught me by her example that care and concern are the most essential elements of good scholarship; and Mark Frankel, at whose desk in Lytton basement this essay was first begun and to whom it is dedicated.

Cominos, P. "Late Victorian Sexual Respectability and the Social System." *International Review of Social History* 8 (1963): 18–48, 216–50.

Connell, R. W. "Class, Patriarchy and Sartre's Theory of Practice." *Theory and Society* 11 (1982): 305–20.

Coward, Rosalind. *Patriarchal Precedents.* London: Routledge, 1983.

Deleuze, Gilles, and Félix Guattari. *Anti-Oedipus: Capitalism and Schizophrenia.* Trans. Robert Hurley, Mark Seem, and Helen R. Lane. New York: Viking, 1977.

Donzelot, Jacques. *The Policing of Families.* Trans. Robert Hurley. New York: Pantheon, 1979.

Du Bois, W. E. B. *The Soul of Black Folks.* Greenwich: Fawcett, 1961.

Ellmann, Richard. "The Critic as Artist as Wilde." *Wilde and the Nineties.* Ed. Charles Ryskamp. Princeton: Princeton U Library, 1966. 1–20.

Faderman, Lillian. *Surpassing the Love of Men.* New York: Morrow, 1981.

Foucault, Michel. *Discipline and Punish.* Trans. Alan Sheridan. New York: Vintage, 1979.

———. *The History of Sexuality.* Vol. 1. New York: Vintage, 1980.

Gagnier, Regenia. *Idylls of the Marketplace: Oscar Wilde and the Victorian Public.* Stanford: Stanford UP, 1986.

Gallop, Jane. *The Daughter's Seduction: Feminism and Psychoanalysis.* Ithaca: Cornell UP, 1982.

Gilbert, Arthur. "Buggery and the British Navy, 1700–1861." *Journal of Social History* 10.1 (1976): 72–97.

Gillis, John. "The Evolution of Delinquency, 1890–1914." *Past and Present* 67 (1975): 96–126.

———. *Youth and History.* New York: Academic, 1974.

Gorham, Deborah. *The Victorian Girl and the Feminine Ideal.* Bloomington: Indiana UP, 1982.

Hyde, H. Montgomery. *The Trials of Oscar Wilde.* London: Hodge, 1948.

Katz, Jonathan. *Gay/Lesbian Almanac.* New York: Harper, 1983.

Knight, G. Wilson. "Christ and Wilde." *Oscar Wilde: A Collection of Critical Essays.* Ed. Richard Ellmann. Englewood Cliffs: Prentice Hall, 1969. 138–50.

Leyland, Winston. Introduction. Wilde, *Teleny* 5–19.

Lombroso, Caesar. *Criminal Man.* London, 1875.

———. *The Female Offender.* New York, 1897.

Marcus, Steven. *The Other Victorians.* New York: Basic, 1964.

Mason, Stuart. *Oscar Wilde: Art and Morality.* New York: Haskell, 1971.

Meyers, Jeffrey. *Homosexuality and Literature.* London: Athlone, 1977.

Moi, Toril. *Sexual/Textual Politics: Feminist Literary Theory.* New York: Methuen, 1985.

Nassaar, Christopher. *Into the Demon Universe.* New Haven: Yale UP, 1974.

Plummer, Kenneth, ed. *The Making of the Modern Homosexual.* London: Hutchinson, 1981.

Rubin, Gayle. "The Traffic in Women." *Towards an Anthropology of Women.* Ed. Rayna Reiter. New York: Monthly Review, 1975. 157–210.

Sedgwick, Eve Kosofsky. *Between Men: English Literature and Male Homosocial Desire.* New York: Columbia UP, 1985.

Silverman, David, and Brian Torode. *The Material World.* London: Routledge, 1980.

Thomas, Keith. "The Double Standard." *Journal of the History of Ideas* 20.2 (1959): 195–216.

Trumbach, Randolph. "London's Sodomites: Homosexual Behavior and Western Culture in the 18th Century." *Journal of Social History* 11.1 (1977): 1–33.

Walkowitz, Judith. *Prostitution and Victorian Society.* New York: Cambridge UP, 1980.

Weeks, Jeffrey. *Coming Out: Homosexual Politics in Britain from the Nineteenth Century to the Present.* New York: Quartet, 1977.

———. *Sexuality and Its Discontents.* London: Routledge, 1985.

Wilde, Oscar. "The Picture of Dorian Gray." *Lippincott's Monthly Magazine,* July 1890: 3–100.

———. *The Picture of Dorian Gray. The Portable Oscar Wilde.* Ed. R. Aldington and S. Weintraub. New York: Viking, 1974.

———. *Teleny.* San Francisco: Gay Sunshine, 1984.

Williams, Raymond. *The Long Revolution.* London: Chatto, 1961.

Winkler, Jack. "Garden of Nymphs: Public and Private in Sappho's Lyrics." *Women's Studies* 8 (1981): 65–91.

Promoting Dorian Gray

Rachel Bowlby

A cigarette is the perfect type of the perfect pleasure. It is exquisite, and it leaves one unsatisfied.[1]

These words, spoken by a character in Oscar Wilde's *The Picture of Dorian Gray* (1891), grant to a much-maligned weed a status possibly higher than any it has known before or since, and may well strike the late twentieth-century reader as rather strong. In representing the cigarette not only as a pleasure, but as the very quintessence of pleasure, they make the kind of exorbitant claim associated not so much with the refinement of aestheticism as with the advertisement's "unique selling point." It might seem natural to draw a distinction between aestheticism and advertising, identifying the latter with all the vulgarity rejected by the defenders of "art for art's sake." In this essay, I shall draw on Wilde's *Picture* as well as the cigarette to try to show the relative convergence of the two, both as practices and as philosophies. The aesthete, far from being different from the new consumer of the period, turns out to be none other than his or her "perfect type."[2]

The cigarette is itself a case in point. One of the most ubiquitous and widely advertised commodities of the late nineteenth century, it nonetheless occupies a prominent and honourable position in the work of an avowed critic of vulgarity. Apart from Lord Henry's epigrammatic eulogy, the utterances of the most tasteful characters in Wilde's novel are punctuated throughout by reference to their sophisticated modes of lighting up.[3]

The punchline of Wilde's aphorism could be taken as an analysis in miniature of the mechanism upon which advertising depends. The enjoyment of the "perfect pleasure" results not in satisfaction but in a lack of it, leaving open the demand for more, the search for the next (or the same) short-lived and necessar-

---

"Promoting Dorian Gray" by Rachel Bowlby, reprinted by permission from *The Oxford Literary Review* 9 (1987), pp. 147–62, © 1986 *Oxford Literary Review*.

[1] Oscar Wilde, The *Picture of Dorian Gray* (Harmondsworth: Penguin, 1949), p. 91. All further references will appear in the text.

[2] Other recent work exploring the parallels between aesthetes and consumers in literature includes Jean-Christophe Agnew's essay on "The Consuming Vision of Henry James," in *The Culture of Consumption*, edited by Richard Wightman Fox and T. J. Jackson Lears (New York: Pantheon, 1993); and Rosalind H. Williams's chapter on Huysmans's character Des Esseintes, in *Dream Worlds: Mass Consumption in Late Nineteenth-Century France* (Berkeley: University of California Press, 1992).

[3] And correspondingly, characters like the low tar James Vane (Sybil's sailor brother) are not represented as smokers.

ily incomplete pleasure. In its structure, the aphorism itself reproduces the process it describes. Short and quick, like the cigarette, it operates by means of an apparent non-sequitur: pleasure entails *non* satisfaction. The paradoxical disruption of common sense constitutes both its appeal, what makes it distinctive, and its tantalising refusal of the explanation which would also remove the source of that appeal.

Formally, then, the aphorism repeats the effects of pleasure and non-satisfaction attributed to its subject, securing a renewed quest for more satisfaction, be it of word or mouth. Lord Henry's view of the cigarette points, in fact, towards concerns engaging advertisers and aesthetes alike. "Pleasure" and the "exquisite" of beauty are two; a third is the question of representation. Wilde was violently opposed to the "vulgar realism" he caricatured in "the man who could call a spade a spade" (215). Overturning what he thereby mocked as Arnoldian literalism, he defined the purposes of art as "to see the object as in itself it really is not."[4] His concern, like that of the advertiser, was with making the object appear beautiful, presenting it as anything but the hypothetical "object in itself." The cigarette, as "the perfect pleasure," could in a sense have been anything else; alternatively, the list of its virtues might have been multiplied or varied *ad infinitum*.

Calling a cigarette a cigarette would be as dull, in this regard, as calling a spade a spade, and Wilde's novel demonstrates the untenability as well as the banality of any supposition of a fixed identity for things or people once they have been situated within any order of representation. The cigarette, again, is an apt illustration. It could connote the indolence of the beautiful life of the dandy but also, in another context, the sexually transgressive associations of the independent "New Woman" of the period. Rarely, if ever, is a cigarette only a cigarette: individuals, like objects, are open to any and every kind of verbal or visual portrayal without there being any original nature which the picture might be said to misrepresent. "It is simply expression which gives reality to things" (121), declares Lord Henry; "Words! Mere words! . . . Was there anything so real as words?" He refuses the mock title of Prince Paradox not on the grounds of inaccuracy but because "Names are everything" and because "From a label there is no escape" (215). The commercial-aesthetic *étiquette* of the label tickets human and other articles with tags that are quite arbitrary in their lack of relation to a prior essence.

The case of Sybil Vane, the actress with whom Dorian falls in love, shows the impossibility within the terms of the novel of anything like an "authentic" personality. Initially, Sybil appeals by appearing as anyone but Sybil Vane:

> Night after night I go to see her play. One evening she is Rosalind, and the next evening she is Imogen. I have seen her die in the gloom of an Italian tomb, sucking the poison from her lover's lips. I have watched her wandering through the forest of Arden, disguised as a pretty boy in hose and doublet and dainty cap. She has been mad, and has come into the presence of a guilty king, and given him rue to wear, and bitter herbs to

---

[4]"The Critic as Artist" (1890), in The *Portable Oscar Wilde*, edited by Richard Aldington and Stanley Weintraub (Harmondsworth: Penguin, 1981), p. 87.

taste of. She has been innocent, and the black hands of jealousy have crushed her reed-like throat. I have seen her in every age and in every costume. Ordinary women never appeal to one's imagination. They are limited to their century. No glamour ever transfigures them. One knows their minds as easily as one knows their bonnets. One can always find them. There is no mystery in any of them. They ride in the Park in the morning, and chatter at tea parties in the afternoon. They have their stereotyped smile, and their fashionable manner. They are quite obvious. But an actress! How different an actress is! (60)

Sybil's multiple, ever-changing identities are themselves already fictional, Shakespeare's female heroines figuring for Dorian in a spectacular history of "every age and every costume." An artistic identity may itself be a cover for another, as when Sybil plays Rosalind playing a boy, and the sexual ambiguity confirms the "mystery" attached to a Sybil known only as a discontinuous series of scripts and costumes, parts without a unifying whole. Against the lure of the mystery woman, or the woman as mystery, is set the "stereotyped" banality and predictability of "ordinary women," whose daytime transparency of repeated routines and identical clothes and manners bears no comparison to Sybil's shifting obscurities "night after night."

In Wilde's short story *The Sphinx Without a Secret*, the narrator's friend falls in love with a woman surrounded by an air of mystery, which he acknowledges to be a part of her attraction. The reason for this is never resolved. But at the end the question is no longer the nature of the secret, but whether there was one at all. The narrator concludes from his friend's story:

Lady Alroy was simply a woman with a mania for mystery. She took these rooms for the pleasure of going there with her veil down, and imagining she was a heroine. She had a passion for secrecy, but she herself was merely a Sphinx without a secret.[5]

As long as the Sphinx can maintain her illusion of posing a question and withholding an answer, of being other than she seems, she has the lover in her power: "I wonder?", he continues to ask at the end. The appeal is in the illusion of a concealed true identity, and nothing separates the illusion which is an illusion and the illusion which is only the illusion of an illusion.

Dorian's love for Sybil dies when she ceases to be able to act. Fascinated initially by the thought of "the wonderful soul that is hidden away in that little ivory body" (63), he is disillusioned by Sybil's own proclaimed acquiescence in this representation of herself as masking an identity off the stage:

Before I knew you, acting was the one reality of my life. It was only in the theatre that I lived. I thought that it was all true. I was Rosalind one night, and Portia the other . . . You came—oh, my beautiful love! and you freed my soul from prison. You taught me what reality really is. Tonight, for the first time in my life, I saw through the hollowness, the sham, the silliness of the empty pageant in which I had always played. Tonight, for the first time, I became conscious that the Romeo was hideous, and old, and painted, that

[5]Oscar Wilde, *Complete Shorter Fiction*, edited by Isobel Murray (Oxford: Oxford University Press, 1979), p. 58.

the moonlight in the orchard was false, that the scenery was vulgar, and that the words I had to speak were unreal, were not my words, were not what I wanted to say. You had brought me something higher, something of which all art is but a reflection. (98–99)

Sybil has discovered a language of authenticity, a real self and "what reality really is," against which the theatrical world is now perceived as false. The stage's former reality is now no more than ugly old men masquerading as lovers. But the reality she finds in Dorian is that of a "Prince Charming" who "has not yet revealed his real name. I think it is quite romantic of him" (74). It is by making a new fiction of the world outside that Sybil can come to see the "real" ugliness of her artistic world. But Sybil is now to Dorian what the ageing actors are to her. Having transferred her attachments from stage characters to himself, she performs "like a wooden doll" (97), as "stereotyped" as the contemptible "ordinary women" of the nineteenth century: "What are you now? A third-rate actress with a pretty face" (100). The logic of self-discovery compels her, as a Sybil speaking and acting in her own person, to suicide: her newfound real identity is ended by Prince Charming's abrupt rejection.

Sybil abandons the sexual, historical and imagistic mobility of her artistic persona for the deadly third-rateness of finding a true, consistent self. Dorian Gray, on the other hand, is introduced to an identity of his own which is at the same time that of an artistic image. The opening chapter of the novel brings together three men—the artist, Basil Hallward, the dandy philosopher, Lord Henry, and the subject himself—for a private view of the coming into the world of the picture of Dorian Gray. Before Dorian sees the finished portrait, in his state of "just conscious boyhood" (103), "unspotted from the world" (23), Lord Henry gives him a verbal glimpse of possibilities hitherto unimagined:

> You have a wonderfully *beautiful* face, Mr Gray . . . Ah! realize your *youth* while you have it . . . Be always searching for *new sensations*. Be afraid of nothing . . . A new Hedonism—that is what our century wants. You might be its visible symbol. With your *personality* there is nothing you could not do. The world belongs to you for a season. The moment I met you I saw that you were quite unconscious of what you really are, of what you really might be. There was so much in you that *charmed* me that I felt I must tell you something about yourself. (29–30; italics mine)

Beauty, youth, charm and the imperative to constant pleasures will now be the terms which frame Dorian's identification of his picture. Lord Henry's words supply a commentary which determines the way their subject sees a self of whose potential he was previously, according to this representation, "quite unconscious":

> His cheeks flushed for a moment with pleasure. A look of joy came into his eyes, as if he had recognized himself for the first time. . . . The sense of his own beauty came on him like a revelation. (32)

But the very recognition of the portrait as an image of perfection provokes a counter-movement from pleasure to fear. As a result of Lord Henry's "strange panegyric on youth" (33), Dorian comes to imagine that there would be a day when his face would be wrinkled and wizen, his eyes dim and colourless, the grace of his figure broken and deformed. . . . He would become dreadful, hideous and uncouth.

As he thought of it, a sharp pang of pain struck him through like a knife. (33)

The words prefigure the end of the novel, where Dorian strikes the portrait which has taken on the signs of his age and sins, and dies himself. It is the absolute perfection of his image and the pleasure of contemplating it which determine the supposition of a possibly flawed image and the slide into the opposite emotion. Beauty and youth are set from the start against the menace of their decline, and pleasure is marked as necessarily ephemeral: the world will belong to the perfect youth only "for a season." In seeing himself in an image of perfect beauty, Dorian also sees that image as potentially disfigured: the fulfilled idea suggests the risk of its failing. Similarly, the "pleasure" and "joy" of that rapturous recognition of a completed image of himself imply an inevitable disappointment, that looker and image will not always be the same.

At the very moment when Dorian Gray acquires an identity, then, that identity is seen as both vulnerable and ambiguously divided, between an image and a spectator of that image. But in the Faustian pact that follows—"If it were I who was to be always young, and the picture to grow old! . . . I would give my soul for that!" (33)—Dorian and the portrait change places. "Life imitates art," according to Wilde's critical dictum,[6] and Dorian can now parade in person as Lord Henry's "visible symbol" of the nineteenth century and Basil Hallward's artistic "masterpiece," categorically removed from the vulgar realistic constraints of physical deterioration or "wooden" conformity to an ordinary type. Unlike Sybil Vane, who fell from grace by assuming a personal identity outside art, Dorian Gray finds his unique self in the form of an idealised artistic representation.

The characteristics of Lord Henry's "visible symbol" of the modern age are not only those of the aesthetic philosopher's dream boy. A preoccupation with beauty, youthfulness, charm and the "grandiose illusions" of Lord Henry's "there is nothing you could not do" are also the terms in which Christopher Lasch censoriously defines the narcissistic personality type he associates with twentieth-century consumer society.[7] In one sense, then, *Dorian Gray* looks less like a late Victorian symbol than a prototype of something much more contemporary. Its hero is able to live out the fantasy of becoming as well as desiring an idealised image of himself in the form of a pleasure-seeking beauty. In his perfection, Dorian then comes to represent to others a fashionable model for emulation. He is invested with the originality of the ultimate *"arbiter elegantiarum"* (145):

His mode of dressing, and the particular styles that from time to time he affected, had their marked influence on the young exquisites of the Mayfair balls and Pall Mall club

[6]"The Decay of Lying" (1889), in *"De Profundis" and Other Writings* (Harmondsworth: Penguin, 1973), p. 74.
   [7]See Christopher Lasch, *The Culture of Narcissism: American Life in an Age of Diminishing Expectations* (New York: Norton, 1978).

windows, who copied him in everything that he did, and tried to reproduce the accidental charm of his graceful, though to him only half-serious, fopperies. (144-45)

While remaining himself only "half-serious" in his "affected" styles, Dorian's symbolic force is unassailable in his embodiment of "fashion, by which what is really
fantastic becomes for a moment universal, and Dandyism, which . . . is an attempt
to assert the absolute modernity of beauty" (144). He is both omnipotent and
invulnerable, even to the extent that he can appeal to his youthful appearance to
prove to her brother that he could not have been the "Prince Charming" who
caused the death of Sybil Vane eighteen years before. In his freedom from the
realistic necessities of physical decline, Dorian is like a walking advertisement, living proof that youth and beauty can, after all, be eternal.

This implicit convergence of the ideals of advertising and aesthetics can be further suggested by the growing habit during this period of commissioning famous
artists to design advertisements. The first and best-known of these, Millais'
Bubbles (1886), was an ad for Pears' soap showing a beautiful curly-haired boy
who might have been a prefiguring type for Dorian Gray himself.

A crucial aspect of Lord Henry's "new Hedonism" is the perpetual quest for
"new sensations." As in the fashion cycle, novelty is made a value in itself, and the
immediacy of sensation exceeds in worth the old-fashioned virtue of restraint.
"One could never pay too high a price for any sensation", says Lord Henry (67)
and the economic wording points both to the connection between experiences and
commodities as sources of gratification, and to a (new) focus on expenditure as
opposed to accumulation.

The prescription for Dorian's hedonistic lifestyle can be compared to a percep-
tible reorientation of economic theory at the end of the nineteenth century. Alfred
Marshall's *Principles of Economics*, published in 1890 when the first version of
Dorian Gray appeared, contains the following passage:

> The price which a person pays for a thing can never exceed, and seldom comes up to
> that which he would be willing to pay rather than go without it: so that the pleasure
> which he gets from its purchase generally exceeds that which he gives up in paying away
> its price; and he thus derives from the purchase a surplus of pleasure. The excess of the
> price which he would be willing to pay rather than go without the thing over that which
> he actually does pay, is the economic measure of this surplus pleasure, and may be
> called Consumers' Rent.[8]

The language implies a rational *homo economicus* soberly making his calculations
on the basis of a fully quantifiable set of variables concerning the purchase con-
templated. But Marshall nonetheless has recourse to a concept which seems by
comparison with price or surplus value remarkably vague. "Pleasure" is uneasily
expressed as a precise arithmetical unit: what the consumer would pay minus what
he does pay. The presupposition—that pleasure is conditional on the relative

---

[8]Vol. 1, p. 124 in Variorum edition (London: Macmillan, 1961).

avoidance of spending—is a nineteenth-century one, but the focus on pleasure is new and unsettles the rationalistic structure of the exposition.

Marshall is cited in the OED *Supplement* as one of the first instances of "consumer" used in its modern sense, and "consumption" also makes its appearance at about the same time. Palgrave's *Dictionary of Political Economy* (1894) states that *"Consumers' Goods* (or *Consumption Goods*) include all those desirable things which directly satisfy human needs and desires." The dominance of the repeated "desirable . . . desires" reflects, as in Marshall, the gradual departure from a framework assuming circumscribed, measurable "needs." Etymologically, the word "consumption" contains both these elements. In its basic sense of wastage or using up, the expenditure involved in consumption acquired all the dissolute connotations of Victorian "spending": the throwing away of a finite and precious substance on a solitary and debilitating pleasure. But the link with "consummation," more obvious in the French *"société de consommation,"* points to a more sublimely sexual meaning and to the possible fulfillment of Palgrave's unlimited "desires."

It is this modern, excessive and pleasurable aspect which finds expression in the aesthetes' predilection for the adjective "consummate." This is parodied in a song of the early 1880s, "My Aesthetic Love," which begins:

> She's utterly utter consummate too too!
> And feeds on the lily and old china blue,
> And with a sun flower she'll sit for an hour
> She's utterly utter consummate too too.[9]

The "consummate" spectacle of self-enclosed perfection here taken in by the aesthete is doubled in the figure of the girl herself, who "feeds on" or consumes the beautiful things caricatured as obvious indicators of the consciously aesthetic consumer lifestyle.

Lord Henry Wotton makes a similar contrast of economic principles by defining his own philosophy of pleasure against the concept of investment. The "aim" of the new Hedonism

> was to be experience itself, and not the fruits of experience, sweet or bitter as they might be. . . . It was to teach man to concentrate himself upon the moments of a life that is itself but a moment. (146)

This passage is close to one from Pater's "Conclusion" to *The Renaissance:*

> Not the fruit of experience, but experience itself, is the end. A counted number of pulses only is given to us in a variegated, dramatic life. . . . What we have to do is to be for ever curiously testing new opinions and courting new impressions.[10]

---

[9]T. S. Lonsdale, "My Aesthetic Love," verse reprinted on colour lithograph (1881) for sheet music edition, held by the Victoria and Albert Museum, London.

[10]Walter Pater, *The Renaissance: Studies in Art and Poetry* (1893), edited by Donald L. Hill (Berkeley: University of California Press, 1980), pp. 188–89. This is the fourth edition of a work originally published in 1873. Significantly, the "Conclusion" was omitted from the second edition because, says Pater in a footnote to the later edition in which it is restored, "I conceived it might possibly mis-

As in Wilde, the argument is against a puritanical deferral of gratification, the fruit rather than the experience, and celebrates in its place the "curiously testing" experiential-experimental openness to what is "new" in the form of "opinions" and "impressions." If life is only an "interval" before the inevitability of death,

> our one chance lies in expanding that interval, in getting as many pulsations as possible into the given time. Only be sure that it is passion, that it does yield you this fruit of a quickened, multiplied consciousness.[11]

Now experience is represented as a "fruit" or profit in itself: the goal of an individual's "interval" is the maximisation of this pulsating profit, exactly as the rational entrepreneur might calculate the relative gains from possible investments. But the overt emphasis is on the aesthete as a consumer or recipient of impressions, not a producer: like an alert shopper, he must select what is "choicer" in the forms or tones that surround him at any one moment.[12]

Lord Henry remakes Dorian as the advertiser markets his product. In representing his image to him as both the epitome of modern youth and beauty, "the finest portrait of modern times" (32) and "the real Dorian Gray" (35), he gives him an advertisement for himself, in relation to which Dorian is both the consumer and what he buys. He is taken over by words which impose on him an identity he will henceforth live as his own. But his very uniqueness is entirely derivative.

The portrait in which Dorian now claims to have "recognized himself for the first time" (32) is already Basil Hallward's creation and one into which the artist says he has put "too much of myself" (17). The "real" Dorian who emerges from the scene of initiation is thus composed of the image of the artist and the words of the philosopher. He assumes as his own this identity born of disparate parents: the visual and the verbal, the imagistic and the interpretative.

When image and slogans combined have sold Dorian the picture of himself as the modern idea, he can sell his outdated "soul" to the equally outdated devil, consigning the portrait of moral and physical decay to the attic. He exchanges a moral self for the unfettered freedom of the new hedonist, for whom "insincerity" is "merely a method by which we can multiply our personalities" (158):

> Eternal youth, infinite passion, pleasures subtle and secret, wild joy and wilder sins—he was to have all these things. (119)

---

lead some of those young men into whose hands it might fall" (p. 186). Wilde could be said to be one of the young men misled by this book; and *Dorian Gray* is all about the leading astray, or seduction, of an impressionable boy. Arguably, Wilde's overturning of Victorian bourgeois norms in the novel is all the more effective because of the double transgressiveness involved in the homosexual overtones and the "feminisation" of a boy into the pleasure-seeking pursuits typically associated with women.

[11]*Ibid.*, p. 190.

[12]*Ibid.*, p. 188: "Every moment some form grows perfect in hand or face; some tone on the hills or the sea is choicer than the rest."

There is no limit to what Dorian can have, to the number of "personalities" he can adopt, to the experiences he can sample. All poses, all personalities, are equal, circumscribed by neither moral nor numerical boundaries, and referrable to no state of authenticity from which they differ: "Being natural," too, "is simply a pose" (10).

After Lord Henry's words and his consequent identification with the portrait of himself as the perfection of youth, Dorian encounters a supplementary influence in the French novel lent him by the same friend. In it, he finds:

> a kind of prefiguring type of himself. And, indeed, the whole book seemed to him to contain the story of his own life, written before he had lived it. (142)

In his very appropriation of the book, making it his own and reading it as referring specifically to himself, Dorian thus relinquishes the uniqueness of a life which turns out to have been already written. The script is simply there for him to act out. "Life imitates art" once again: the authenticity of personal experience only appears as such in light of previously existing representations which also, necessarily, give the lie to the individuality they ostensibly uphold.

As a result of his reading, Dorian plunges into a renewed "search for sensations that would be at once new and delightful, and possess that element of strangeness that is so essential to romance" (147). Believing sometimes, like the hero of his novel, "that the whole of history was merely the record of his own life" (160), he becomes an intellectual narcissist, seeking and reading his story everywhere from Imperial Rome to Renaissance Italy. Losing even the relative singleness of an identity which imitates another or is "prefigured" in another, Dorian's grand aspirations, by identifying him with all the great men of history, reduce him to pure generality. Since he sees himself in everyone, his self can have no distinguishing features at all.

For all his advocacy in "The Soul of Man Under Socialism" and elsewhere of a "self-development" proper to each individual, Wilde could also maintain this contrary view, by which all that appears to mark off the unique "personality" is merely a matter of secondary surfaces:

> Where we differ from each other is purely in accidentals: in dress, manner, tone of voice, religious opinions, personal appearance, tricks of habit and the like. The more one analyses people, the more all reasons for analysis disappear. Sooner or later one comes to that dreadful universal thing called human nature.[13]

It is this underlying sameness, not the "secret" self, which is hidden beneath the surface of an individual personality. The scandal of the masquerade of individual poses or parts is that they hide nothing.

Lord Henry's objection to labels in the name of their potency is consistent with this structure. Since there is no individual before the mask or label which comes to identify him, the label, however arbitrary, is absolutely determining: there is no real self against which its truth or falsehood could be measured. It follows from

---

[13]"The Decay of Lying," *op. cit.*, p. 64.

this, according to "the philosophy of the superficial,"[14] that "it is only shallow people who do not judge by appearances" (29).

Dorian's literary tourism takes him not only into a history that mirrors himself, but along the paths of disparate intellectual interests—jewels, embroidery, Catholicism, music—without any connecting thread. Simply "that curiosity about life which Lord Henry had first stirred in him . . . seemed to increase with gratification. The more he knew, the more he desired to know" (144). His researches follow the pattern laid down in the influential book; as he followed it by putting on multiple identities in his reading of history, so he follows it in his passionate consumption, or taking in, of objects and facts pertaining to each new subject. And he lost—and made—himself in taking on other personae, so

> he would often adopt certain modes of thought that he knew to be really alien to his nature, abandon himself to their subtle influences, and then, having, as it were, caught their colour and satisfied his intellectual curiosity, leave them. (147)

Dorian remains a blank canvas, a *tabula rasa* for intellectual impressions ever susceptible and never retaining the imprint of what was previously marked upon it. Individual philosophies are treated like the rich or interesting objects Dorian accumulates, as temporary sources of pleasure to be given up, like cigarettes, when they have ceased to satisfy.

Nothing, then, marks a necessary terminus to Dorian's multiplication of pleasures and poses. He lives the dream life of the aesthetic consumer, culling momentary impressions and satisfactions from a world which withholds nothing and offers everything. His continual search for "new sensations" involves treating the world as a source of subjective gratifications to be enjoyed and used up, and the novel includes many descriptions of interior settings which sumptuously answer to this. The opening is a case in point:

> From the corner of the divan of Persian saddle-bags where he was lying, smoking, as was his custom, innumerable cigarettes, Lord Henry Wotton could just catch the gleam of the honey-sweet and honey-coloured blossoms of a laburnum, whose tremulous branches seemed hardly able to bear the burden of a beauty so flame-like as theirs. (7)

The passage poses Wilde's "art of lying" in a supinely synaesthetic atmosphere, with the aristocratic aesthete pleasurably and passively sucking in the manifold sensory stimulants that surround him. But the moment of Paterian perfection, of a "flame-like beauty" evanescently grasped, also resembles, in its luxurious fusion of "Persian" exoticism and a tastefully cultivated English garden, a lavish description from a catalogue of interior decoration.

The juxtaposition of aestheticism and domestic consumption merges concerns which Wilde himself considered inseparable. Like Ruskin and Morris, he was an

---

[14] *A Woman of No Importance* (1893), Third Act, in Oscar Wilde, *Plays* (Harmondsworth: Penguin, 1954), p. 115. In the same context, the same character remarks prophetically that "The future belongs to the dandy. It is the exquisites who are going to rule" (p. 115).

active and forthright campaigner for improvements in the artistic quality of home furnishings, regarding the education of taste in a public committed to the purchase of such goods as a worthy and attainable goal. In "The Soul of Man Under Socialism" (1891), he claims that there has been a shift from the "Great Exhibition of international vulgarity," so that "it is now almost impossible to enter any modern house without seeing some recognition of good taste, some recognition of the value of lovely surroundings, some sign of appreciation of beauty."[15] This "revolution" is owing, however, not to a grass-roots movement on the part of consumers, but

> to the fact that the craftsmen of things so appreciated the pleasure of making what was beautiful, and woke to such a vivid consciousness of the hideousness and vulgarity of what the public had previously wanted, that they simply starved the public out. . . . However they may object to it, people must nowadays have something charming in their surroundings. Fortunately for them, their assumption of authority in these art-matters came to entire grief.[16]

As well as taking for granted an absolute standard of beauty, Wilde assumes arbitrarily that the earlier taste for the mass-produced signs of "International Vulgarity" was the public's own, whereas the present more "civilised" taste was forcibly imposed by the lack of available alternatives. Ironically, in welcoming what he perceives as a return to authentic, artisanal forms of production, he valorises the workings of the large-scale marketing system he is implicitly opposing. In a lecture on "House Decoration" given in America in 1882, Wilde had said:

> We should see more of the workman than we do. We should not be content to have the salesman stand between us—the salesman who knows nothing of what he is selling save that he is charging a great deal too much for it.[17]

Here Wilde explicitly censures the middleman, and the infiltration of marketing into craftsmanship. But in the passage quoted above, he effectively congratulates the craftsmen for having succeeded in establishing a uniform monopoly, for imposing a certain kind of product on a public left with no other choice. It was upon just such a creation of previously non-existent demands and preferences that the new mass-marketing practices depended.

Wilde's partisanship and dogmatism here is quite unlike the philosophy articulated in *Dorian Gray* and elsewhere. Granting a supreme value to novelty and number, rather than to some innate quality, precludes there being any fixed criterion on which to base the evaluation of sensations, or to distinguish "artistic" from other sensations. But Wilde himself would regard the possibility of such a contradiction as irrelevant. He can write a soberly academic piece praising historical accuracy in productions of Shakespeare and then at the conclusion suddenly change tack:

---

[15]In *"De Profundis" and Other Writings, op. cit.*, pp. 45–46.
[16]*Ibid.*, p. 46.
[17]Wilde, *Essays and Lectures,* 3rd edition (London: Methuen, 1911), p. 169.

Not that I agree with everything that I have said in this essay. There is much with which I entirely disagree. The essay simply represents an artistic standpoint, and in aesthetic criticism attitude is everything. For in art there is no such thing as a universal truth. A Truth in art is that whose contradictory is also true.[18]

Different artistic standpoints can be differently valid, then, or differently invalid; and both sides of this must apply, paradoxically, to the one which claims the self-evidence of a single form of taste. Only in the realist world of "the man who could call a spade a spade" (215) does language claim to correspond to a truth it does not make, rather than to aim, like stage props, at "the illusion of truth." But perhaps Wilde is unwittingly, or wittily, consistent in his accidental endorsement in the lecture of the advertiser's philosophy of the value-free creation of new desires: it was also the philosophy of the aesthetes' New Hedonism.

It is in this mode of provocative non-commitment that the Preface to *Dorian Gray* deals summarily with the question of art and ethics:

> There is no such thing as a moral or an immoral book. Books are well written or badly written. That is all.
>
> No artist has ethical sympathies. An ethical sympathy in an artist is an unpardonable mannerism of style. (5)

Wilde teasingly raises only to repudiate the possibility of taking the novel as a morality tale. Given that it includes a paraphrase of the contents of a "poisonous book" (140), which is itself partly about the "strange manners of poisoning" known in the Renaissance (163), the novel's own critical condemnation as a "poisonous book" would seem to involve the kind of partial reading Wilde caricatured in another of the prefatory maxims: "It is the spectator, and not life, that art really mirrors" (6).[19] In any case, the fatal ending of the novel could equally well be taken to show its morally uplifting, admonitory effect. But as Roger B. Henkle has argued, the narrative of crime and punishment is a debunking, not a confirmation, of "the Puritan notion of moral consequence." Wilde is seeking to dispose of this paradigm by mockingly reconstructing it, and then throwing it by its own weight.[20]

[18]"The Truth of Masks" (1885), in *The Works of Oscar Wilde*, edited by G. F. Maine (London: Collins, 1928), p. 1016.

[19]The denunciation of the novel as a "poisonous book" occurred in an unsigned review of the first version in the *Daily Chronicle* for 30 June 1890. "It is a tale spawned from the leprous literature of the French *Décadents*—a poisonous book, the atmosphere of which is heavy with the mephitic odours of moral and spiritual putrefaction—a gloating study of the mental and physical corruption of a fresh, fair and golden youth, which might be horrible and fascinating but for its effeminate frivolity, its studied insincerity, its theatrical cynicism, its tawdry mysticism, its flippant philosophisings, and the contaminating trail of garish vulgarity which is all over Mr Wilde's elaborate Wardour Street aestheticism and obtrusively cheap scholarship," in *Oscar Wilde: The Critical Heritage*, edited by Karl Beckson (London: Routledge & Kegan Paul, 1970), p. 72. The linking of "effeminate frivolity," "garish vulgarity" and "cheap scholarship" as evidence of the "mephitic odours" that make the book stink suggests again how challenging it could seem to represent the casual pleasure-seeker as a man.

[20]Roger B. Henkle, *Comedy and Culture: England 1820–1900* (Princeton: Princeton University Press, 1980), p. 313.

Dorian Gray does not in fact fall straightforwardly into any generic category, and the narrative of a lost soul, sin and eventual repentance is only one of innumerable different forms and styles contained within it. It is partly a decadent psychological novel like J. K. Huysmans's *A Rebours* (1884), to which obvious allusion is made in the account of the "poisonous book"; partly, also, a novel about the *milieu* of art, like Zola's *L'Oeuvre* (1885). As Kerry Powell has documented, it utilises many features of a genre popular at the time which she summarises under the head of "magic picture realism."[21] In addition, there are scenes of drawing-room comedy anticipating the plays Wilde would write in subsequent years. Polite conversations and repartee, descriptions of high-class interior decor, scenes of vulgar dissipation, moments of Gothic horror, epigrammatic disquisitions on art and life, catalogues of *objets* and nuggets of information, farcical interludes like the "peppering beaters" incident: all these modes are there, alternating and overlapping in no particular order and with no obvious approach to the appearance of either a conventional linear narrative in the mode of realism, or a consistent symbolic line in the mode of allegory.

In that it incorporates and alludes to many disparate levels and styles and writing, the novel effectively sets them all at a distance. It becomes like a sample catalogue of literary forms which by arbitrary juxtaposition lose all connection with the notion of a unifying theme or action and its corresponding genre. Suggesting no privileged forms in terms of which to interpret the others, the novel reduces the morality plot to pastiche: "medieval emotions are out-of-date" (90). Even within this plot, Dorian dies not because of the unspecified sins he has committed but because, in slashing the image of his other self, subject to age and ethical laws, he has implicitly accepted its different order, looking upon it as a threat to be eliminated.

Far from being poisonous, or an antidote to poison, the morality plot functions more like a parody of the style of the "sensational" novels and tabloid newspapers of the period, with their regular presentation of the scandals of high life—murder, divorce, poison—for the public's ready consumption. When Lord Henry learns of Dorian's unusual parentage, involving a hushed-up aristocratic story of paternal jealousy and a husband's murder, he pronounces him, like a placard headline, "son of Love and Death" (45):

> Crudely as it had been told to him, (the story) had yet stirred him by its suggestion of a strong, almost modern romance. A beautiful woman risking everything for a mad passion. A few wild weeks of happiness cut short by a hideous, treacherous crime. Months of voiceless agony, and then a child born in pain. The mother snatched away by death, the boy left to solitude and the tyranny of an old and loveless man.

[21]Kerry Powell, "Tom, Dick and Dorian Gray: Magic-Picture Mania in Late Victorian Fiction," *Philological Quarterly* Vol. 62 No. 2 (Spring 1983), pp. 147–69.

The story is resumed in the language of popular journalism, with which Lord Henry shows himself to be aesthetically complicit. Far from detracting from Dorian's image,

> It was an interesting background. It posed the lad, made him more perfect as it were. Behind every exquisite thing that existed, there was something tragic. (44)

And right at the beginning, the novel takes its frame of reference from a tabloid scandal by introducing Basil Hallward as the artist "whose sudden disappearance some years ago caused, at the time, such public excitement, and gave rise to so many strange conjectures" (7).

"Sensations" in *Dorian Gray* are not confined to an isolated sphere of high art. As "the type which the age has been searching for," Dorian becomes something more than a pretty boy: he is sensational in the double sense of a newsworthy star and an aesthetic stimulus. In the same way, Dorian's experiencing of endlessly new sensations runs the gamut from the most "vulgar" to the most aesthetically refined.

Dorian Gray is a plug for aestheticism at the start of the decade that would see the movement reach the height of its public fashion. It is also, and by the same token, a catalogue of the forms of identification of the ideal consumer as dandy: a receptacle and bearer of sensations, poser and posed, with no consistent identity, no moral self. In the novel's terms, Sybil Vane's "tragedy" is not so much that Dorian deserts her, as that she casts off the role of actress in the belief that she has found a fixed identity beyond her various theatrical parts.

The narcissistic, pleasure-seeking dandy personifies a fantasy in which the ascetic bourgeois individual has ceased to be. "Pleasure," declares Lord Henry, "is the only thing worth having a theory about" (89), and his question, if not its uniqueness, was also implicit, as we have seen, in the economic language of the time. But the fullest interrogation of the nature of pleasure in its relation to the sexual and ethical determinations of the individual subject was to begin later in the decade with the extended researches of a certain Viennese neurologist. Lord Henry is himself not unlike an early version of the psychoanalyst, with his study of "the curious hard logic of passion" in which "he had begun by vivisecting himself, as he had ended by vivisecting others" (55); and Dorian Gray learns "to wonder at the shallow psychology of those who conceive of the Ego in man as a thing simple, permanent, reliable, and of one essence" (159).

The Picture posits a subject uncannily split, with the old-fashioned moral self there as a possible but not constitutive threat to what is otherwise an existence devoted purely to self-gratification. Freud's theory would bring that menace to the fore. As with Lord Henry's "new Hedonism," desires in Freud is endlessly unfulfilled, but its fulfillment is blocked off from the outset by the moral and sexual regime of identification which determines both the loss of imaginary satisfaction and the ceaselessly renewed quest for its recovery. In this light, the magical aspect of *Dorian Gray* becomes crucial: it is only because Dorian can suspend the conditions of reality which would otherwise limit his narcissistic pleasures that he can thrive in the perfect freedom of indulgence.

The fantasy of lawlessness thus operates as a powerful, if not sensational, source of pleasure, one which unites the interests of aesthete and consumer alike. In final support for such a connection, I can do no better than cite again from an authority which Wilde described as "that book which has had such strange influence over my life":[22]

> Art comes to you proposing frankly to give nothing but the highest quality to your moments as they pass, and simply for those moments' sake.[23]

Art's representative offers his product with all the pseudo-artlessness of the professional salesman, including a personal touch—"Art comes to you"—and "proposing frankly" its superior merits: "nothing but the highest quality." With his posture of one-to-one sincerity and his special recommendation, the author might have been writing a textbook example of advertising copy rather than an original aesthetic statement. But perhaps, after all, there is little to choose between Lord Henry's puff for cigarettes and Pater's endorsement of art. The final sentence of the "Conclusion" to *The Renaissance* is surely the last word in advertising technique. In its forceful promotion of the momentary personal pleasures promised by its object, it could be said to mark the beginning of modern consumer culture.

[22]*De Profundis* (1905), in *op. cit.*, p. 158.
[23]Pater, *The Renaissance, op. cit.*, p. 190.

Wilde, Nietzsche, and the Sentimental Relations of the Male Body

Eve Kosofsky Sedgwick

For readers fond of the male body, the year 1891 makes an epoch. Chapter 1 of *Billy Budd* opens . . . with a discussion of the Handsome Sailor—"a superb figure, tossed up as by the horns of Taurus against the thunderous sky" (1354). As Chapter 1 of *The Picture of Dorian Gray* opens, "in the centre of the room clamped to an upright easel, stood the full-length portrait of a young man of extraordinary personal beauty."[1] Like many Atget photographs, these two inaugural presentations of male beauty frame the human image high up in the field of vision, a singular apparition whose power to reorganize the visibility of more conventionally grounded figures is arresting and enigmatic.

For readers who hate the male body, the year 1891 is also an important one. At the end of *Dorian Gray* a dead, old, "loathsome" man lying on the floor is the moralizing gloss on the other thing the servants find in Dorian Gray's attic: "hanging upon the wall, a splendid portrait of their master as they had last seen him, in all the wonder of his exquisite youth and beauty" (248). The end of *Billy Budd* is similarly presided over by the undisfigured pendant: Billy noosed to the mainyard gallows "ascended, and, ascending, took the full rose of the dawn" (80). The exquisite portrait, the magnetic corpse swaying aloft: iconic as they are of a certain sexual visibility, their awful eminence also signalizes that the line between any male beauty that's articulated as such and any steaming offal strung up for purchase at the butcher's shop is, in the modern dispensation so much marked by this pair of texts, a brutally thin one.

In this chapter I am undertaking to consider some more of the modern relations over which this male body presides in formative texts of the late nineteenth century. Through a broader application of the same deconstructive procedure of isolating particular nodes in a web of interconnected binarisms, I move here from the last chapter's treatment of one 1891 text, *Billy Budd,* to treating a group of other texts dating from the 1880s and early 1890s, including the contemporaneous

Excerpted from Eve Kosofsky Sedgwick, *Epistemology of the Closet* (Berkeley: University of California Press, 1990). Copyright © 1990 The Regents of the University of California. Reprinted with permission of the University of California Press. Footnotes renumbered.

[1]Oscar Wilde, *The Picture of Dorian Gray* (Harmondsworth, Middlesex: Penguin, 1949), p. 7. Further citations are incorporated in parentheses in the text.

Picture of Dorian Gray. This chapter moves outward in two other principal ways, as well: from the sentimental/antisentimental relations around the displayed male figure toward, on the one hand, the modernist crisis of individual identity and figuration itself; toward, on the other, the intersections of sexual definition with relatively new problematics of kitsch, of camp, and of nationalist and imperialist definition.

The two, roughly contemporaneous figures whom I will treat as representing and overarching this process are Wilde and Nietzsche, perhaps an odd yoking of the most obvious with the least likely suspect. Wilde is the obvious one because he seems the very embodiment of, at the same time, (1) a new turn-of-the-century homosexual identity and fate, (2) a modernist antisentimentality, and (3) a late-Victorian sentimentality. Interestingly, the invocation of Nietzsche's name has become a minor commonplace in Wilde criticism, though certainly not vice versa. It has served as a way, essentially, of legitimating Wilde's seriousness as a philosopher of the modern—in the face of his philosophically embarrassing, because narratively so compelling, biographical entanglements with the most mangling as well as the most influential of the modern machineries of male sexual definition. Needless to say, however, the opposite project interests me as much here: the project of looking at Nietzsche through a Wildean optic. That, too, however, to the very degree that it does seem to promise access to the truths of twentieth-century culture, involves the built-in danger of a spurious sense of familiarity, given what the received figure "Nietzsche" has in common with certain received topoi of homosexuality and of sentimentality or kitsch: namely, that all three are famous for occasioning unresolved but highly popular and exciting "questions"—insinuations—about the underpinnings of twentieth-century fascism. To avoid the scapegoating momentum that appears to be built into the structure of sentimental attribution and of homosexual attribution in the culture of our century will require care.

This project involves, among other things, a binocular displacement of time and space between Germany of the 1880s (for my focus will be on Nietzsche's last several texts) and England of the 1890s. It also embodies the distance between a new, openly problematical German national identity and an "immemorial," very naturalized English one, though, as we shall see, one none the less under definitional stress for that. German unification under Prussian leadership, culminating with the proclamation of the Second Reich in 1871, led newly to the criminalization of homosexual offenses for the entire Reich—a process that coincided, as James Steakley points out, with "the escalating estimates of the actual number of homosexuals" in Germany, from .002 percent of the population in 1864, to 1.4 percent in 1869, to 2.2 percent in 1903. "These estimates," Steakley says, "appear astonishingly low in light of modern studies, but they nonetheless document the end of homosexual invisibility." The same period encompassed the first formation—in Germany—of organized homosexual emancipation movements.[2]

---

[2]Steakley, *The Homosexual Emancipation Movement in Germany*, pp. 14, 33.

It seems patent that many of Nietzsche's most effective intensities of both life and writing were directed toward other men and toward the male body; it's at least arguable, though not necessary for my present argument, that almost all of them were. Given that, and especially given all the thought recently devoted to the position of women in Nietzsche's writing, it is striking how difficult it seems to have been to focus on the often far more cathected position of men there. There are reasons for this even beyond the academic prudishness, homophobia, and heterosexist obtuseness that always seem to obtain: Nietzsche offers writing of an open, Whitmanlike seductiveness, some of the loveliest there is, about the joining of men with men, but he does so in the stubborn, perhaps even studied absence of any explicit generalizations, celebrations, analyses, reifications of these bonds as specifically same-sex ones. Accordingly, he has been important for a male-erotic-centered anarchist tradition, extending from Adolf Brand and Benedict Friedländer through Gilles Deleuze and Félix Guattari, that has a principled resistance to any minoritizing model of homosexual identity. (Friedländer, for instance, ridiculed those with an exclusively hetero- or homosexual orientation as *Kümmerlinge* [atrophied or puny beings].)[3] But the harder fact to deal with is that Nietzsche's writing is full and overfull of what were just in the process of becoming, for people like Wilde, for their enemies, and for the institutions that regulated and defined them, the most pointed and contested signifiers of precisely a minoritized, taxonomic male homosexual identity. At the same time it is also full and overfull of the signifiers that had long marked the nominally superseded but effectually unvacated prohibitions against sodomitic acts.

A phrase index to Nietzsche could easily be confused with a concordance to, shall we say, Proust's *Sodome et Gomorrhe,* featuring as it would "inversion," "contrary instincts," the *contra naturam,* the effeminate, the "hard," the sick, the hyper-virile, the *"décadent,"* the neuter, the "intermediate type"—and I won't even mention the "gay." Nietzsche's writing never makes these very differently valued, often contradictory signifiers coextensive with any totality of male-male desire; in many usages they seem to have nothing to do with it at all. This is because, to repeat, he never posits same-sex desire or sexuality as one subject. Instead, these signifiers—old markers for, among other things, same-sex acts and relations; incipient markers for, among other things, same-sex-loving identities—cut in Nietzsche's writing across and across particular instances or evocations of it. But they do it so repetitiously, so suggestively as to contribute, and precisely *in* their contradictoriness, to the weaving of a fatefully impacted definitional fabric already under way.

Just one example of the newly emerging problematics of male homosexuality across which Nietzsche's desire flung its stinging shuttle. The question of how same-sex desire could be interpreted in terms of *gender* was bitterly embattled almost from the beginnings of male homosexual taxonomy: already by 1902, the

---

[3]On Brand and Friedländer, see Steakley, *The Homosexual Emancipation Movement in Germany,* pp. 43-69; on *Kümmerlinge,* pp. 46–47.

new German gay rights movement, the first in the world, was to split over whether
a man who desired men should be considered feminized (as in the proto-modern
English "molly-house" culture and the emerging inversion model) or, to the contrary, virilized (as in the Greek pederastic or initiation model) by his choice of
object. The energy Nietzsche devotes to detecting and excoriating male effeminacy, and in terms that had been stereotypical for at least a century in antisodomitic usage, suggests that this issue is a crucial one for him; any reader of
Nietzsche who inherits, as most Euro-American readers must, the by now
endemic linkage of effeminacy with this path of desire will find their store of
homophobic energies refreshed and indeed electrified by reading him. But far
from explicitly making male same-sex desire coextensive with that effeminacy,
Nietzsche instead associates instance after instance of homoerotic desire, though
never named as such, with the precious virility of Dionysiac initiates or of ancient
warrior classes. Thus, his rhetoric charges with new spikes of power some of the
most conventional lines of prohibition, even while preserving another space of
careful de-definition in which certain objects of this prohibition may arbitrarily be
invited to shelter.

An even more elegant example is the insistence with which he bases his
defense of sexuality on its connection with "the actual road to life, procreation."[4] "Where is innocence? Where there is a will to procreate."[5] He execrates
antisexuality as a resistance to procreation, "*ressentiment against* life in its
foundations," which "threw *filth* on the beginning, on the prerequisite of our
life" (*Twilight*, 110). In the definitional stress he places on *this* defense of sexuality and in the venom he reserves for non-procreative acts and impulses, if anywhere, one might imagine oneself, according to discourses ranging from the
biblical to the nineteenth-century medical, to be close to the essence of an
almost transhistorical prohibition of a homosexuality itself thereby rendered
almost transhistorical. But, oddly, what Nietzsche, with the secret reserves of
elasticity that always characterized his relation to the biological metaphor,
framed most persistently within the halo of this imperative to procreate was
scenes of impregnation of men (including himself: "The term of eighteen
months might suggest, at least to Buddhists, that I am really a female ele-
phant")[6] or of abstractions that could be figured as male.[7] The space cleared by

---

[4]Friedrich Nietzsche, *Twilight of the Idols/The Anti-Christ*, trans. R. J. Hollingdale (New York:
Viking Penguin, 1968), p. 110. Further quotations from this edition will cite it as *Twilight* or *Anti* in
the text.
[5]Friedrich Nietzsche, *Thus Spoke Zarathustra*, trans. Walter Kaufmann (New York: Viking
Compass, 1966), p. 123. Further quotations from this edition will cite it as *Zarathustra* in the text.
[6]Friedrich Nietzsche, *Ecce Homo*, trans. R. J. Hollingdale (New York: Penguin, 1979), p. 99.
Further quotations from this edition will cite it as *Ecce* in the text.
[7]One example that may stand for many (Friedrich Nietzsche, *Beyond Good and Evil*, trans. R. J.
Hollingdale [New York: Viking Penguin, 1973], p. 161, sec. 248; further quotations from this edition
will cite it as *Beyond* in the text):

There are two kinds of genius: the kind which above all begets and wants to beget, and the kind
which likes to be fructified and to give birth. And likewise there are among peoples of genius those

this move for a sexy thematics of ripeness, fructification, mess, ecstatic rupture, penetration, between men was bought dearly, however, in the sense of being excruciatingly vulnerable to any increased definitional pressure from the angry impulsions that Nietzsche's own celebrations fed: the virulence, only a couple of decades later, of a D. H. Lawrence against a realm of desire that was by then *precisely* circumscribed as coextensive with "the homosexual," even with all the self-contradictions of that definition intact, borrowed wholesale from Nietzsche the rhetorical energies for anathematizing the desire that was Nietzsche's own, not to say Lawrence's own.

Greek/Christian

For Nietzsche as for Wilde, a conceptual and historical interface between Classical and Christian cultures became a surface suffused with meanings about the male body. In both German and English culture, the Romantic rediscovery of ancient Greece cleared out—as much as recreated—for the nineteenth century a prestigious, historically underfurnished imaginative space in which relations to and among human bodies might be newly a subject of utopian speculation. Synecdochically represented as it tended to be by statues of nude young men, the Victorian cult of Greece gently, unpointedly, and unexclusively positioned male flesh and muscle as the indicative instances of "the" body, of a body whose surfaces, features, and abilities might be the subject or object of unphobic enjoyment. The Christian tradition, by contrast, had tended both to condense "the flesh" (insofar as it represented or incorporated pleasure) as the *female* body and to surround its attractiveness with an aura of maximum anxiety and prohibition. Thus two significant differences from Christianity were conflated or conflatable in thought and rhetoric about "the Greeks": an imagined dissolving of the bar of prohibition against the enjoyed body, and its new gendering as indicatively male.

Dorian Gray, appearing in *The Picture of Dorian Gray* first as artist's model, seems to make the proffer of this liberatory vision—at least he evokes formulations

---

upon whom has fallen the woman's problem of pregnancy and the secret task of forming, maturing, perfecting—the Greeks, for example, were a people of this kind, and so were the French—; and others who have to fructify and become the cause of new orders of life—like the Jews, the Romans and, to ask it in all modesty, the Germans?—peoples tormented and enraptured by unknown fevers and irresistibly driven outside themselves, enamoured of and lusting after foreign races (after those which "want to be fructified") and at the same time hungry for dominion.

To ask who is *self* and who is *other* in these dramas of pregnancy is as vain as anywhere else in Nietzsche. The relation to Zarathustra may be taken as emblematic:

That I may one day be ready and ripe in the great noon: as ready and ripe as glowing bronze, clouds pregnant with lightning, and swelling milk udders—ready for myself and my most hidden will: a bow lusting for its arrow, an arrow lusting for its star—a star ready and ripe in its noon, glowing, pierced, enraptured by annihilating sun arrows—a sun itself and an inexorable solar will, ready to annihilate in victory! (*Zarathustra*, 214–15)

of its ideology from his two admirers. The artist Basil Hallward says of him, "Unconsciously he defines for me the lines of a fresh school, a school that is to have in it all the passion of the romantic spirit, all the perfection of the spirit that is Greek. The harmony of soul and body—how much that is! We in our madness have separated the two, and have invented a realism that is vulgar, an ideality that is void" (16–17). And Lord Henry Wotton addresses the immobilized sitter with a Paterian invocation:

> "The aim of life is self-development. To realize one's nature perfectly—that's what each of us is here for. People are afraid of themselves, nowadays.... And yet ... I believe that if one man were to live out his life fully and completely, were to give form to every feeling, expression to every thought, reality to every dream—I believe that the world would gain such a fresh impulse of joy that we would forget all the maladies of medievalism, and return to the Hellenic ideal—to something finer, richer, than the Hellenic ideal, it may be. But the bravest man among us is afraid of himself. The mutilation of the savage has a tragic survival in the self-denial that mars our lives. We are punished for our refusals." (25)

The context of each of these formulations, however, immediately makes clear that the conceptual divisions and ethical bars instituted by, or attributed to, Christianity are easier to condemn than to undo, or perhaps even wish to undo. The painter's manifesto for Dorian's ability to reinstitute a modern "harmony of soul and body," for instance, is part of his extorted confession—and confession is the appropriate word—to Lord Henry concerning "this curious artistic idolatry, of which, of course, I have never cared to speak to [Dorian]. He knows nothing about it. He shall never know anything about it. But the world might guess it; and I will not bare my soul to their shallow prying eyes" (17). To delineate and dramatize a space of *the secret* also emerges as the project of Lord Henry's manifesto, an address whose performative aim is after all less persuasion than seduction. Like Basil, Lord Henry constructs *the secret* in terms that depend on (unnameable) prohibitions attached specifically to the beautiful male body; and like Basil's, Lord Henry's manifesto for the Hellenic unity of soul and body derives its seductive rhetorical force from a culmination that depends on their irreparable divorce through shame and prohibition.

> "We are punished for our refusals.... The only way to get rid of a temptation is to yield to it. Resist it, and your soul grows sick with longing for the things it has forbidden to itself, with desire for what its monstrous laws have made monstrous and unlawful....
> You, Mr Gray, you yourself, with your rose-red youth and your rose-white boyhood, you have had passions that have made you afraid, thoughts that have filled you with terror, day-dreams and sleeping dreams whose mere memory might stain your cheek with shame—"
> "Stop!" faltered Dorian Gray, "stop! you bewilder me. I don't know what to say. There is some answer to you, but I cannot find it." (25–26)

The crystallization of desire as "temptation," of the young body as the always initiatory encroachment of rose-red on rose-white, gives the game of wholeness away in advance. Each of these enunciations shows that the "Hellenic ideal," insofar as its reintegrative power is supposed to involve a healing of the culturewide ruptures involved in male homosexual panic, necessarily has that panic so deeply at the heart of its occasions, frameworks, demands, and evocations that it becomes not only inextricable from but even a propellant of the cognitive and ethical compartmentalizations of homophobic prohibition. That it is *these* in turn that become exemplary propellants of homosexual desire seems an inevitable consequence.

In *The Victorians and Ancient Greece*, Richard Jenkyns points out that precisely a visible incipience or necessity of this phobic fall was read back into Greek selves and Greek culture *as* the charm of their wholeness, a charm defined by the eschatological narrative it appeared to defy or defer.[8] And this seems a good characterization of Nietzsche's classicism, as well, with its insistent pushing-backward of the always-already date of a fall into decadent moral prohibition defined as Christian, which, however deplored, makes the enabling condition for rhetorical force.

For example, consider, in the blush-stained light of Lord Henry's manifesto, the double scene of seduction staged in these sentences from the preface to *Beyond Good and Evil*:

> To be sure, to speak of spirit and the good as Plato did meant standing truth on her head and denying *perspective* itself, the basic condition of all life; indeed, one may ask as a physician: "how could such a malady attack this loveliest product of antiquity, Plato? did the wicked Socrates corrupt him after all? could Socrates have been a corrupter of youth after all? and have deserved his hemlock?"—But the struggle against Plato, or, to express it more plainly and for "the people," the struggle against the Christian-ecclesiastical pressure of millennia—for Christianity is Platonism for "the people"—has created in Europe a magnificent tension of the spirit such as has never existed on earth before: with so tense a bow one can now shoot for the most distant targets. (*Beyond*, 14)

With his characteristically Socratic flirtatiousness ("as a physician"!), Nietzsche frames the proto-Christian fall into metaphysics as an incident of classroom sexual harassment among the ancients. The seduction at which his own language aims, however, and which seems to mirror the first one at the same time as repudiate it by "worldly" trivialization, is the seduction of the reader. His tactics are those of the narrator of *Billy Budd*, mixing, under pressure of a very difficult style and argument, the threat of contempt for those who don't understand or *merely* understand ("the people") with a far more than Melvillean balm of flattery, hilarity, and futurity promised to those who can surrender themselves to his nameless projectile uses. Nietzsche makes almost explicit—what no character in *Dorian Gray* does more than demonstrate—that the philosophic and erotic potential lodged in this modern pedagogic-pederastic speech situation comes not from some untainted mine of "Hellenic" potency that could be directly tapped but,

---

[8]Richard Jenkyns, *The Victorians and Ancient Greece* (Cambridge: Harvard University Press, 1980), e.g., pp. 220–21.

rather, from the shocking magnetism exerted by such a fantasy across (i.e., because of) the not-to-be-undone bar of Christian prohibitive categorization. Modern homosexual panic represents, it seems, not a temporally imprisoning obstacle to philosophy and culture but, rather, the latent energy that can hurtle them far beyond their own present place of knowledge.

The assumption I have been making so far, that the main impact of Christianity on men's desire for the male body—and the main stimulus it offers to that desire—is prohibitive, is an influential assumption far beyond Wilde and Nietzsche. It is also an assumption that even (or especially) those who hold and wield it, including both Wilde (who was never far from the threshold of Rome) and Nietzsche (who, at the last, subscribed himself as "The Crucified"), know is not true. Christianity may be near-ubiquitous in modern European culture as a figure of phobic prohibition, but it makes a strange figure for that indeed. Catholicism in particular is famous for giving countless gay and proto-gay children the shock of the possibility of adults who don't marry, of men in dresses, of passionate theatre, of introspective investment, of lives filled with what could, ideally without diminution, be called the work of the fetish. Even for the many whose own achieved gay identity may at last include none of these features or may be defined as against them, the encounter with them is likely to have a more or other than prohibitive impact. And presiding over all are the images of Jesus. These have, indeed, a unique position in modern culture as images of the unclothed or unclothable male body, often in extremis and/or in ecstasy, prescriptively meant to be gazed at and adored. The scandal of such a figure within a homophobic economy of the male gaze doesn't seem to abate: efforts to disembody this body, for instance by attenuating, Europeanizing, or feminizing it, only entangle it the more compromisingly among various modern figurations of the homosexual.

The nominal terms of the Greek/Christian contrast, as if between permission and prohibition or unity and dichotomy, questionable as (we have seen) they may be in themselves, have even less purchase on this aspect of Christianity by which, nonetheless, they are inevitably inflected. Both in Nietzsche and in Wilde—and, partly through them, across twentieth-century culture—this image is, I believe, one of the places where the extremely difficult and important problematic of sentimentality is centered. Let me take a little time to explore why it is so difficult to get hold of analytically and so telling for the twentieth century, on the way back to a discussion of its pivotal place in the homo/heterosexual definitional struggles of Wilde and Nietzsche.

Sentimental/Antisentimental

One night in Ithaca in the mid-seventies, I happened to tune into a country music station in the middle of a song I had never heard before. An incredibly pretty male voice that I half recognized as Willie Nelson's was singing:

And he walks with me, and he talks with me,
And he tells me I am his own.
And the joy we share, as we tarry there,
None other has ever known.

He speaks; and the sound of his voice
Is so sweet the birds hush their singing.
And the melody that he gave to me
Within my heart is ringing.

And he walks with me, and he talks with me,
And he tells me I am his own.
And the joy we share, as we tarry there,
None other has ever known.

I'd stay in the garden with him
Though the night around me be falling,
But he bids me go through the voice of woe,
His voice to me is calling . . .

This blew me away. I had already listened to a lot of Willie Nelson's songs about Waylon Jennings, which I always interpreted as love songs, but I never thought I was meant to; and nothing had prepared me for a song in which the love and sensuality between two men could be expressed with such a pellucid candor, on AM shit-kicker radio or maybe anywhere.

A decade later, I noted an article by J. M. Cameron in the *New York Review* about religious kitsch, which, he says, "presents us with a serious theological problem and stands, far beyond the formal bounds of theology, for something amiss in our culture":[9]

Kitsch must include more than the golden-haired Madonnas, the epicene statues of Jesus, the twee pictures of the infant Jesus. . . . It must also include music, and the words of the liturgy, and hymns as well. . . . [An] example is:

I come to the garden alone,
While the dew is still on the roses.
And the voice I hear,
Falling on my ear,
The Son of God discloses.
And He walks with me and He talks with me,
And He tells me I am his own.
And the joys we share, as we tarry there,
None other has ever known.[10]

[9]J. M. Cameron, reply to a letter in response to the review quoted below, in *New York Review of Book*, 33 (May 29, 1986): 56–57.

[10]J. M. Cameron, "The Historical Jesus" (a review of Jaroslav Pelikan, *Jesus through the Centuries: His Place in the History of Culture*), *New York Review of Books*, 33 (February 13, 1986): 21.

Cameron considers it important not only to

> describe . . . this as sentimental . . . but . . . discuss it as what it surely is, a terrible degra-
> dation of religion not simply as a purveyor of the false and the unworthy but as a kind of
> nastily flavored religious jello, a fouling of the sources of religious feeling. It is as though
> the image of Jesus is caught in a cracked, discolored distorting mirror in a fun house.[11]

Let me remark on two possible sources for Cameron's ostentatious disgust
here, one topical, regarding the *subject* of sentimentality, and the other grammatical, regarding its *relations*. Topically, I have to wonder if a certain erotic foregrounding of the male body, what made the song so exciting to me, may not be
tied to the stigmatization of these verses as sentimental and kitsch. I have mentioned the difficult kind of cynosure that proliferating images of Jesus, what
Cameron refers to as the "epicene statues," create within a homophobic economy
of the male gaze. This scandal might account for the discomfort of a J. M.
Cameron with the hymn, but it does leave us with questions about the local speci-
fications of the sentimental, and in particular about its gender: if the sentimental,
as we have been taught, coincides topically with the feminine, with the place of
women, then why should the foregrounded *male* physique be in an indicative relation to it?

If indeed, however, as I want to hypothesize, the embodied male figure *is* a distinctive, thematic marker for the potent and devalued categories of kitsch and the
sentimental in this century, then it is only the equivocal use of the first person
("And he tells me I am his own")—the first person that could be your grandmother
but could be Willie Nelson, too, or even a distinguished professor of religion at the
University of Toronto—that lends such a nasty flavor to the gender-slippage of this
morsel of religious "jello" down the befouled and violated gullet of Mr. J. M.
Cameron. The gender-equivocal first person, or the impossible first person—such
as the first person of someone dead or in process of dying—are common and, at
least to me, peculiarly potent sentimental markers: my goose bumps, at any rate,
are always poised for erection at "She walks these hills in a long black veil,/ Visits
my grave when the night winds wail," and my waterworks are always primed for
"Rocky, I've never had to die before," or letters to Dear Abby purporting to be
from seventeen-year-olds who were too young to die in that after-school car crash.
Arguably, indeed, the locus classicus of this tonally and generically unsettling,
ingenuous-disingenuous first-person mode, other versions of which can be found
in any high school literary magazine, is the ballad that ends *Billy Budd:*

> No pipe to those halyards.—But aren't it all sham?
> A blur's in my eyes; it is dreaming that I am.
> A hatchet to my hawser? All adrift to go?
> The drum roll to grog, and Billy never know?
> But Donald he has promised to stand by the plank;

[11]Cameron, "The Historical Jesus," p. 22.

So I'll shake a friendly hand ere I sink.
But—no! It is dead then I'll be, come to think.
I remember Taff the Welshman when he sank.
And his cheek it was like the budding pink.
But me they'll lash in hammock, drop me deep.
Fathoms down, fathoms down, how I'll dream fast asleep.
I feel it stealing now. Sentry, are you there?
Just ease these darbies at the wrist,
And roll me over fair!
I am sleepy, and the oozy weeds about me twist.

These knowing activations of the ambiguities always latent in grammatical person as such, at any rate, point to the range of meanings of sentimentality that identify it, not as a thematic or a particular subject matter, but as a structure of relation, typically one involving the author- or audience-relations of spectacle; most often, where the epithet "sentimental" itself is brought onto the scene, a discreditable or devalued one—the sentimental as the *insincere*, the *manipulative*, the *vicarious*, the *morbid*, the *knowing*, the *kitschy*, the *arch*.

To begin with the question of thematic content. In recent feminist criticism, particularly that involving nineteenth-century American women's fiction, a conscious rehabilitation of the category of "the sentimental" has taken place, insofar as "the sentimental" is seen as a derogatory code name for female bodies and the female domestic and "reproductive" preoccupations of birth, socialization, illness, and death.[12] The devaluation of "the sentimental," it is argued, has been of a piece with the devaluation of many aspects of women's characteristic experience and culture: in this view "the sentimental," like the very lives of many women, is typically located in the private or domestic realm, has only a tacit or indirect connection with the economic facts of industrial marketplace production, is most visibly tied instead to the "reproductive" preoccupations of birth, socialization, illness, and death, and is intensively occupied with relational and emotional labor and expression. Since one influential project of recent popular feminist thought has been to reverse the negative valuation attached to these experiences, emphases, and skills by both high culture and marketplace ideology, an attempted reversal of the negative charge attached to "the sentimental" has been a natural corollary.

It would make sense to see a somewhat similar rehabilitation of "the sentimental" as an important gay male project as well—indeed, one that has been in progress for close to a century under different names, including that of "camp." This gay male rehabilitation of the sentimental obviously occurs on rather different grounds from the feminist one, springing as it does from different experiences. The kid in Ohio who recognizes in "Somewhere Over the Rainbow" the national anthem of a native country, his own, whose name he's never heard spoken is constructing a new family romance on new terms; and for the adult he

---

[12]For example, Jane P. Tompkins, *Sensational Designs: The Cultural Work of American Fiction, 1790–1860* (New York: Oxford University Press, 1985).

becomes, the sense of value attaching to a "private" realm, or indeed to expressive and relational skills, is likely to have to do with a specific history of secrecy, threat, and escape as well as with domesticity. A very specific association of gay male sexuality with tragic early death is recent, but the structure of its articulation is densely grounded in centuries of homoerotic and homophobic intertextuality;[13] the underpinnings here have long been in place for both a gay male sentimentality and, even more, a sentimental appropriation by the larger culture of male homosexuality as spectacle.

I have been arguing that constructions of modern Western gay male identity tend to be, not in the first place "essentially gay," but instead (or at least also) in a very intimately responsive and expressive, though always oblique, relation to incoherences implicit in modern male *hetero*sexuality. Much might be said, then, following this clue, about the production and deployment, especially in contemporary U.S. society, of an extraordinarily high level of self-pity in nongay men.[14] Its effects on our national politics, and international ideology and intervention, have been pervasive. (Snapshot, here, of the tear-welling eyes of Oliver North.) In more intimate manifestations this straight male self-pity is often currently referred to (though it appears to exceed) the cultural effects of feminism, and is associated with, or appealed to in justification of, acts of violence, especially against women. For instance, the astonishing proportion of male violence done on separated wives, ex-wives, and ex-girlfriends, women just at the threshold of establishing a separate personal space, seems sanctioned and guided as much as reflected by the flood of books and movies in which such violence seems an expression not of the macho personality but of the maudlin. (One reason women get nervous when straight men claim to have received from feminism the gift of "permission to cry.") Although compulsively illustrated for public consumption (see, on this, the *New York Times*'s "About Men," passim, or for that matter any newspaper's sports pages, or western novels, male country music, the dying-father-and-his-son stories in *The New Yorker,* or any other form of genre writing aimed at men), this vast national wash of masculine self-pity is essentially never named or discussed as a cultural and political fact; machismo and competitiveness, or a putative gentleness, take its place as subjects of nomination and analysis. Poised between shame and shamelessness, this regime of heterosexual male self-pity has the projective potency of an open secret. It would scarcely be surprising if gay men, like all women, were a main target of its scapegoating projections—viciously sentimental attributions of a vitiated sentimentality.

---

[13]One might look, for instance, to Achilles and Patroclos, to Virgilian shepherds, to David and Jonathan, to the iconography of St. Sebastian, to elegiac poetry by Milton, Tennyson, Whitman, and Housman, as well as to the Necrology of Vito Russo's *Celluloid Closet* . . .

[14]It was Neil Hertz, especially in some discussions of responses to his essay "Medusa's Head: Male Hysteria under Political Pressure" (now included in *The End of the Line: Essays on Psychoanalysis and the Sublime* [New York: Columbia University Press, 1985]), who alerted me to the importance of this phenomenon.

The sacred tears of the heterosexual man: rare and precious liquor whose properties, we are led to believe, are rivaled only by the *lacrimae Christi* whose secretion is such a specialty of religious kitsch. What charm, compared to this chrism of the gratuitous, can reside in the all too predictable tears of women, of gay men, of people with something to cry about? Nietzsche asks scornfully: "Of what account is the pity of those who suffer!" But, he explains, "a man who can do something, carry out a decision, remain true to an idea, hold on to a woman, punish and put down insolence . . . in short a man who is by nature a *master*—when such a man has pity, well! *That* pity has value!" (*Beyond*, 198). Both the mass and the high culture of our century ratify this judgment, by no means stopping short at such a man's pity for himself. Cry-y-yin'—lonely teardrops, teardrops cryin' in the rain, blue velvet through the tracks of my tears, the tears of a clown, maybe Cathy's clown, the Red Skelton clown by whose tears every show of lowbrow art must be baptized, the Norman Mailer or Harold Bloom buffoon by whose tears . . .

If these modern images borrow some of their lasting power from the mid-nineteenth-century association of sentimentality with the place of women, what their persistence and proliferation dramatize is something new: a change of gears, occupying the period from the 1880s through the First World War, by which the exemplary instance of the sentimental ceases to be a woman per se, but instead becomes the body of a man who, like Captain Vere, physically dramatizes, *embodies* for an audience that both desires and cathartically identifies with him, a struggle of masculine identity with emotions or physical stigmata stereotyped as feminine. Nietzsche says, "With hard men, intimacy is a thing of shame—and" (by implication: therefore) "something precious" (*Beyond*, 87). This male body is not itself named as the place or topos of sentimentality, the way the home, the female body, and female reproductive labor had been in the mid-nineteenth century. Rather, the relations of figuration and perception that circulate around it, including antisentimentality, might instead be said to enact sentimentality as a trope.

How, then, through the issue of sentimentality can we bring to Nietzsche questions that Wilde and the reading of Wilde may teach us to ask? Gore Vidal begins a recent essay on Wilde: "Must one have a heart of stone to read *The Ballad of Reading Gaol* without laughing?"[15] The opening points in only too many directions. Between it and the same remark made by Wilde himself, a century earlier, about the death of Little Nell, where to look for the wit-enabling relation? One story to tell is the historical/thematic one just sketched: that whereas in the nineteenth century it was images of women in relation to domestic suffering and death that occupied the most potent, symptomatic, and, perhaps, friable or volatile place in the sentimental *imaginaire* of middle-class culture, for the succeeding century—the century inaugurated by Wilde among others—it has been images of agonistic male self-constitution. Thus the careful composition of *The Ballad of Reading Gaol*, where Wilde frames his own image between, or even as, those of a woman-murder-

[15]Gore Vidal, "A Good Man and a Perfect Play" (review of Richard Ellmann, *Oscar Wilde*), *Times Literary Supplement* (October 2–8, 1987): 1063.

ing man and the Crucified, sets in motion every conceivable mechanism by which most readers know how to enter into the circuit of the sentimental:

> Alas! it is a fearful thing
>> To feel another's guilt!
> For, right, within, the Sword of Sin
>> Pierced to its poisoned hilt,
> And as molten lead were the tears we shed
>> For the blood we had not spilt.
>
> . . . .
>
> And as one sees most fearful things
>> In the crystal of a dream,
> We saw the greasy hempen rope
>> Hooked to the blackened beam,
> And heard the prayer the hangman's snare
>> Strangled into a scream.
>
> And all the woe that moved him so
>> That he gave that bitter cry,
> And the wild regrets, and the bloody sweats,
>> None knew so well as I:
> For he who lives more lives than one
>> More deaths than one must die.[16]

Think of the cognate, ravishing lines of Cowper—

> We perished, each alone,
> But I beneath a rougher sea
> And whelmed in deeper gulfs than he[17]

—and the cognate sentimental markers (the vicariousness, the uncanny shifting first person of after death, the heroic self-pity) that give them their awful appropriateness, their appropriability, to the narrow, imperious, incessant self-reconstitution of, say, Virginia Woolf's paterfamilias Mr. Ramsay. Yet the author of *Reading Gaol* is also the creator of "Ernest in town and Jack in the country" and of Mr. Bunbury, of men whose penchant for living more lives than one, and even dying more deaths, not to speak of having more christenings, seems on the contrary to give them a fine insouciance about such identity issues as the name of the father— which his sons, who have forgotten it, have to look up in the Army Lists. "Lady Bracknell, I hate to seem inquisitive, but would you kindly inform me who I am?" (*Earnest,* in *Complete,* 181). At the same time, the precise grammatical matrix of even the most anarchic Wildean wit still tends toward the male first-person singular in the mode of descriptive self-definition. "None of us are perfect. I myself am

---

[16]*The Complete Works of Oscar Wilde* (Twickenham, Middlesex: Hamlyn, 1963), pp. 732, 735. Further quotations from this edition will cite it as *Complete* in the text.

[17]William Cowper, "The Castaway," lines 64–66, in the *Complete Poetical Works of William Cowper,* ed. H. S. Milford (Oxford: Humphrey Milford, 1913), p. 652.

peculiarly susceptible to draughts." "I can resist anything except temptation." "I have nothing to declare except my genius." The project of constructing the male figure is not made any the less central by being rendered as nonsense; in fact, one might say that it's the candor with which Wilde is often capable of centering this male project in the field of vision that enables him to operate so explosively on it.

The squeam-inducing power of texts like *De Profundis* and *Reading Gaol*—and I don't mean to suggest that they are a bit the less powerful for often making the flesh crawl—may be said to coincide with a thematic choice made in each of them: that the framing and display of the male body be placed in the explicit context of the displayed body of Jesus. One way of reading *The Picture of Dorian Gray* would tell the same story, since the fall of that novel from sublime free play into sentimental potency comes with the framing and hanging of the beautiful male body as a visual index of vicarious expiation.

That the circumference of sentimental danger in Wilde's writing should have at its center the image of a crucified man would have been no surprise to Nietzsche. Nietzsche oriented, after all, his own narrative of the world-historical vitiation of the species around the fulcrum point of the same displayed male body; appropriately his meditations concerned, not the inherent meaning of the crucifixion or the qualities of the man crucified, but instead the seemingly irreversible relations of pity, desire, vicariousness, and mendacity instituted in the mass response to that image.

Evidently Nietzsche's ability to describe the relations around the cross from a new perspective depends on an Odyssean trick: blindfolding himself against a visual fixation on the focal figure aloft, deaf to the aural penetration of his distant appeal, Nietzsche (like the jello-phobic J. M. Cameron) gives himself over, in his discussions of Christianity, to the other three senses—taste, touch, smell, those that least accommodate distance, the ones that French designates by the verb *sentir*—and in the first place to the nose. "I was the first to sense—*smell*—the lie as a lie. . . . My genius is in my nostrils" (*Ecce*, 126). Possessing "a perfectly uncanny sensitivity of the instinct for cleanliness, so that I perceive physiologically—*smell*—the proximity or—what am I saying?—the innermost parts, the 'entrails,' of every soul" (*Ecce*, 48–49), Nietzsche is alive to "the complete lack of psychological cleanliness in the priest" (*Anti*, 169), is able "to *smell* what dirty fellows had [with Christianity] come out on top" (*Anti*, 183). He gags most on the proximity into which this spectacle of suffering draws the men who respond to it: "pity instantly smells of mob" (*Ecce*, 44). And in this phenomenon he finds the origin of virtually every feature of the world he inhabits. "One who smells not only with his nose but also with his eyes and ears will notice everywhere these days an air as of a lunatic asylum or sanatorium . . . so paltry, so stealthy, so dishonest, so sickly-sweet! Here . . . the air stinks of secretiveness and pent-up emotion."[18]

---

[18]"What noble eloquence flows from the lips of these ill-begotten creatures! What sugary, slimy, humble submissiveness swims in their eyes!" Friedrich Nietzsche, *The Birth of Tragedy and The Genealogy of Morals*, trans. Francis Golffing (New York: Doubleday Anchor, 1956), pp. 258–59. Further citations are given in the text as *Birth* or *Genealogy*.

Nietzsche, then, is the psychologist who put the scent back into sentimentality. And he did it by the same gesture with which he put the rank and the rancid back into rancor. The most durably productive of Nietzsche's psychological judgments was to place the invidious, mendacious mechanism rather mysteriously called *ressentiment*—re-sniffing, one might say as much as "resentment," or re-tonguing, re-palpating—at the center of his account of such ordinary anno Domini virtues as love, goodwill, justice, fellow-feeling, egalitarianism, modesty, compassion. *Ressentiment* was for Nietzsche the essence of Christianity and hence of all modern psychology ("there never was but one psychology, that of the priest");[19] and the genius of his nostrils repeatedly reveals these apparently simple and transparent impulses as complex, unstable laminates of self-aggrandizement and delectation with self-contempt and abnegation, fermented to a sort of compost under the pressure of time, of internal contradiction, and of deconstructive work like Nietzsche's own. The *re-* prefix of *ressentiment* marks a space of degeneration and vicariousness: the nonsingularity of these laminates as *re*doublings of one's own motives, and their nonoriginality as *re*flexes of the impulses of others. Thus the sentimental misnaming, in the aftermath of the crucifixion, of its observers' sensuality and will-to-power as *pity* becomes the model for the whole class of emotions and bonds of which Nietzsche was the privileged analyst:

> At first sight, this problem of pity and the ethics of pity (I am strongly opposed to our modern sentimentality in these matters) may seem very special, a marginal issue. But whoever sticks with it and learns how to ask questions will have the same experience that I had: a vast new panorama will open up before him; strange and vertiginous possibilities will invade him; every variety of suspicion, distrust, fear will come to the surface; his belief in ethics of any kind will begin to be shaken. (*Genealogy,* 154)

Sentimentality, insofar as it overlaps with *ressentiment* in a structure we would not be the first to call ressentimentality, represents modern emotion itself in Nietzsche's thought: modern emotion as vicariousness and misrepresentation, but also as sensation brought to the quick with an insulting closeness.

Direct/Vicarious; Art/Kitsch

It would be hard to overestimate the importance of vicariousness in defining the sentimental. The strange career of "sentimentality," from the later eighteenth century when it was a term of high ethical and aesthetic praise, to the twentieth when it can be used to connote, beyond pathetic weakness, an actual principle of evil—and from its origins when it circulated freely between genders, through the feminocentric Victorian version, to the twentieth-century one with its complex and distinctive relation to the male body—is a career that displays few easily articula-

---

[19]Paraphrased in Gilles Deleuze and Félix Guattari, *Anti-Oedipus: Capitalism and Schizophrenia,* trans. Robert Hurley, Mark Seem, and Helen R. Lane (New York: Viking, 1977), p. 110.

ble consistencies; and those few are not, as we have seen, consistencies of subject matter. Rather, they seem to inhere in the nature of the investment by a viewer *in a subject matter*. The sacralizing contagion of tears was the much reenacted primal scene of the sentimental in the eighteenth century. If its early celebrants found it relatively (only relatively) easy to take for granted the disinterestedness and beneficence of the process by which a viewer "sympathized" with the sufferings of a person viewed, however, every psychological and philosophic project of the same period gave new facilities for questioning or even discrediting that increasingly unsimple-looking bond.[20] Most obviously, the position of sentimental spectatorship seemed to offer coverture for differences in material wealth (the bourgeois weeping over the spectacle of poverty) or sexual entitlement (the man swooning over the spectacle of female virtue under siege)—material or sexual exploitations that might even be perpetuated or accelerated by the nonaccountable viewer satisfactions that made the point of their rehearsal. The tacitness and consequent nonaccountability of the identification between sufferer and sentimental spectator, at any rate, seems to be the fulcrum point between the most honorific and the most damning senses of "sentimental." For a spectator to misrepresent the quality or locus of her or his implicit participation in a scene—to misrepresent, for example, desire as pity, *Schadenfreude* as sympathy, envy as disapproval—would be to enact defining instances of the worst meaning of the epithet; the defining instances, increasingly, of the epithet itself. The prurient; the morbid; the wishful; the snobbish;[21] the knowing; the arch: these denote subcategories of the sentimental, to the extent that each involves a covert reason for, or extent or direction of, identification through a spectatorial route. As Nietzsche says of Renan (with whom he has so much in common), "I can think of nothing as nauseating as such an 'objective' armchair, such a perfumed epicure of history, half priest, half satyr. . . . [S]uch 'spectators' embitter me against the spectacle more than the spectacle itself" (*Genealogy*, 294).

It follows from this that the description of scenes, or even texts, as intrinsically "sentimental" (or prurient, morbid, etc.) is extremely problematical, not least because such descriptions tend to carry an unappealable authority: the epithet "sentimental" is *always* stamped in indelible ink. "Sentimental" with its quiverful of subcategories: don't they work less as static grids of analysis against which texts can be flatly mapped than as projectiles whose bearing depends utterly on the angle and impetus of their discharge? In the last chapter, we discussed "worldli-

---

[20]On this, see David Marshall, *The Surprising Effects of Sympathy: Marivaux, Diderot, Rousseau, and Mary Shelley* (Chicago: University of Chicago Press, 1989); and Jay Caplan, *Framed Narratives: Diderot's Genealogy of the Beholder* (Minneapolis: University of Minnesota Press, 1986).

[21]I mean "snobbish," of course, not in the sense of a mere preference for social altitude, but in the fuller sense explicated by Girard, the one whose foundational principle is Groucho Marx's "I wouldn't belong to any club that would have me as a member": it is the tacit evacuation of the position of self that makes snob relations such a useful model for understanding sentimental relations. See René Girard, *Deceit, Desire, and the Novel: Self and Other in Literary Structure*, trans. Yvonne Freccero (Baltimore: Johns Hopkins University Press, 1965), esp. pp. 53–82, 216–28.

ness" as an attribution whose force depended, not on its being attached firmly to a particular person or text, but on its ability to delineate a chain of attributive angles of increasing privilege and tacitness; a "worldly" person, for instance, is one whose cognitive privilege over a world is being attested, but the person who can attest it implicitly claims an even broader angle of cognitive privilege out of which the "worldly" angle can be carved, while a silent proffer to the reader or auditor of a broader angle yet can form, as we discussed, the basis for powerful interpellations. "The sentimental" and its damning subcategories work in an analogous way. Themselves descriptions of relations of vicariousness, the attributive career of each of these adjectives is again a vicariating one. For instance, it is well known that in Proust the snobbish characters are easy to recognize because they are the only ones who are able to recognize snobbism in others—hence, the only ones who really disapprove of it. Snobbism, as René Girard points out, can be discussed and attributed only by snobs, who are always right about it except in their own disclaimers of it.[22] The same is true of the phenomenon of "the sentimental" as a whole and of its other manifestations such as prurience and morbidity. *Honi soit qui mal y pense* is both the watchword and the structural principle of sentimentality-attribution. What chain of attribution is being extended, under pretense of being cut short, when Nietzsche exclaims, "O you sentimental hypocrites, you lechers! You lack innocence in your desire and therefore you slander all desire" (*Zarathustra*, 122–23)? What tacit relations of prurient complicity are compounded under the prurience-attribution of Nietzsche's discussion of the *Law-Book of Manu:*

> One sees immediately that it has a real philosophy behind it, *in* it . . . —it gives even the most fastidious psychologist something to bite on. . . . All the things upon which Christianity vents its abysmal vulgarity, procreation for example, women, marriage, are here treated seriously, with reverence, with love and trust. How can one actually put into the hands of women and children a book containing the low-minded saying: "To avoid fornication let every man have his own wife, and let every woman have her own husband . . . for it is better to marry than burn"? And is it *allowable* to be a Christian as long as the origin of man is Christianized, that is to say *dirtied,* with the concept of the *immaculata conceptio*? . . . I know of no book in which so many tender and kind remarks are addressed to woman as in the Law-Book of Manu; these old graybeards and saints have a way of being polite to women which has perhaps never been surpassed. "A woman's mouth"—it says in one place—"a girl's breast, a child's prayer, the smoke of a sacrifice are always pure." Another passage: "There is nothing purer than the light of the sun, the shadow of a cow, air, water, fire and a girl's breath." A final passage—perhaps also a holy lie—: "All the openings of the body above the navel are pure, all below impure. Only in the case of a girl is the whole body pure." (*Anti,* 176)

Vidal's score off Wilde, "Must one have a heart of stone . . . ?", seems to depend on the same structure. If the joke were that the Wilde who took advantage of the enormous rhetorical charge to be gained from hurling at Dickens the aspersion of

---

[22]Girard, *Deceit, Desire, and the Novel,* pp. 72–73.

sentimentality also at another time, perhaps later in his life when the hideous engines of state punishment had done their work of destroying the truth and gaiety of his sensibility, developed a proneness to the same awful failing, that would be one thing. Perhaps, though, the point is that there isn't a differentiation to be *made* between sentimentality and its denunciation. But then we are dealing with a joke that can only be on Gore Vidal himself, whose hypervigilance for lapses in the tough-mindedness of others can then only suggest that he in turn must be, as they say, insecure about his own. It may be only those who are themselves prone to these vicariating impulses who are equipped to detect them in the writing or being of others; but it is also they who for several reasons tend therefore to be perturbed in their presence.

By "they" here I definitionally mean "we." In order to dispense with the further abysmal structuring of this bit of argument through an infinity of insinuating readings of "other" writers, let me try to break with the tradition of personal disclaimer and touch ground myself with a rapid but none the less genuine guilty plea to possessing the attributes, in a high degree, of at the very least sentimentality, prurience, and morbidity. (On the infinitesimally small chance that any skepticism could greet this confession, I can offer as evidence of liability—or, one might say, of expert qualification—the pathos injected into the paraphrase of *Esther,* in Chapter 1, which I loved composing but which is rendered both creepy and, perhaps, rhetorically efficacious by a certain obliquity in my own trail of identifications. As a friend who disliked those paragraphs put it acidly, it's not me risking the coming out, but it's all too visibly me having the salvational fantasies.)

Clearly, this understanding of "sentimentality" makes problems for a project, whether feminist- or gay-centered, of rehabilitating the sentimental. The problem is not just that the range of discrediting names available for these forms of attention and expression is too subtle, searching, descriptively useful, and rhetorically powerful to be simply jettisoned, though that is true enough. A worse problem is that since antisentimentality itself becomes, in this structure, the very engine and expression of modern sentimental relations, to enter into the discourse of sentimentality at any point or with any purpose is almost inevitably to be caught up in a momentum of essentially scapegoating attribution.

The attempt to construct versions of the present argument has offered, I might as well say, startlingly clear evidence of the force of this momentum. Given a desire to raise the questions I'm raising here, it's all too easy to visualize the path of least resistance of such an argument. The ballistic force of the attribution of "sentimentality" is so intense today that I've found it amazingly difficult to think about any analytic or revaluative project involving it that wouldn't culminate its rehabilitative readings with some yet more damning unmasking of the "true," and far more dangerous, sentimentality of an author not previously associated with the term. This would be congruent with a certain difficult-to-avoid trajectory of universalizing understandings of homo/heterosexual definition—Irigaray's writing about the "hom(m)osexual" is the locus classicus of this trajectory, although feminist thought has no monopoly on it—according to which authoritarian regimes or homophobic masculinist culture may be damned on the grounds of being *even more homosexual* than gay male culture.[23] And each of these trajectories of argument leads straight to terrible commonplaces about fascism. In the case of Nietzsche and Wilde, the most readily available—the almost irresistibly available—path of argument would have been to use the manifestly gay Wilde as a figure for the necessity and truth of a "good" version of sentimentality, then to prove that the ostensibly heterosexual and antisentimental Nietzsche was, like Wilde, maybe even more actively than Wilde because unacknowledgedly, and in ways that could be shown to have implications for his writing and thought, "really" homosexual, and at the same time "really" sentimental.

Why should it be so hard to think about these issues without following an argumentative path that must lead to the exposure of a supposed fascist precursor as the *true* homosexual, or especially as the *true* sentimentalist? I have tried to avoid that path of exposure, for four reasons. First, of course, Nietzsche, like Whitman, is a cunning and elusive writer on whose self-ignorance one never does well to bet the mortgage money. Second, though, such a trajectory of argument presupposes that one has somewhere in reserve a stable and intelligible definition for both what is "really homosexual" and what is "really sentimental," while our historical argument is exactly the opposite: that those definitions are neither historically stable in this period nor internally coherent. Third, obviously, that argument necessarily depends for its rhetorical if not its analytic force on the extreme modern cultural devaluations of both categories, the homosexual and the sentimental—a dependence that had better provoke discomfort, however much Nietzsche's own writing may sometimes be complicit in those fatal devaluations. And finally, the most productive questions we can ask about these definitional issues must be, I think, not "What is the true meaning, the accurate assignment of these labels?" but, rather, "What are the relations instituted by the giving of these labels?" In that case, any enabling analytic distance we might have would be vitiated to the degree that our argument was so aimed as to climax with this act of naming.

The categories "kitsch" and "camp" suggest, perhaps, something about how the formation of modern gay identities has intervened to reimagine these potent audience relations. Kitsch is a classification that redoubles the aggressive power of the epithet "sentimental" by, on the one hand, claiming to exempt the speaker of the epithet from the contagion of the kitsch object, and, on the other, positing the existence of a true *kitsch consumer* or, in Hermann Broch's influential phrase, "kitsch-man."[24] Kitsch-man is never the person who uses the word "kitsch"; kitsch-man's ability to be manipulated by the kitsch object and the kitsch

[23]Craig Owens discusses this argument in "Outlaws: Gay Men in Feminism," in Alice Jardine and Paul Smith, eds., *Men in Feminism* (New York: Methuen, 1987), pp. 219–32.

[24]Hermann Broch, *Einer Bemerkungen zum Problem des Kitsches*, in *Dichten und Erkennen*, vol. 1 (Zurich: Rhein-Verlag, 1955), p. 295; popularized by, among others, Gillo Dorfles, in *Kitsch: The World of Bad Taste* (New York: Universe Books, 1969).

creator is imagined to be seamless and completely uncritical. Kitsch-man is seen either as the exact double of the equally unenlightened producer of kitsch or as the unresistant dupe of his cynical manipulation: that is to say, the imagined kitsch-producer is *either* at the abjectly low consciousness level of kitsch-man *or* at the transcendent, and potentially abusive, high consciousness level of the man who can recognize kitsch when he sees it. In the highly contestative world of kitsch and kitsch-recognition there is no mediating level of consciousness; so it is necessarily true that the structure of contagion whereby *it takes one to know one,* and whereby *any* object about which the question "Is it kitsch?" can be asked immediately *becomes* kitsch, remains, under the system of kitsch-attribution, a major scandal, one that can induce self-exemption or cynicism but nothing much more interesting than that.

Camp, on the other hand, seems to involve a gayer and more spacious angle of view. I think it may be true that, as Robert Dawidoff suggests, the typifying gesture of camp is really something amazingly simple: the moment at which a consumer of culture makes the wild surmise, "What if whoever made this was gay too?"[25] Unlike kitsch-attribution, then, camp-recognition doesn't ask, "What kind of debased creature could possibly be the right audience for this spectacle?" Instead, it says *what if:* What if the right audience for this were exactly *me?* What if, for instance, the resistant, oblique, tangential investments of attention and attraction that I am able to bring to this spectacle are actually uncannily responsive to the resistant, oblique, tangential investments of the person, or of some of the people, who created it? And what if, furthermore, others whom I don't know or recognize can see it from the same "perverse" angle? Unlike kitsch-*attribution,* the sensibility of camp-*recognition* always sees that it is dealing in reader relations and in projective fantasy (projective though not infrequently true) about the spaces and practices of cultural production. Generous because it acknowledges (unlike kitsch) that its perceptions are necessarily also creations,[26] it's little wonder that camp can encompass effects of great delicacy and power in our highly sentimental-attributive culture.

Neither rehabilitation nor rubbishing, wholesale, is a possible thing to do, then, with these representational meanings of "sentimental," "antisentimental," or even "ressentimental"; they stand for rhetorical—that is to say, for relational—figures, figures of concealment, obliquity, vicariousness, and renaming, and their ethical bearings can thus be discussed only in the multiple contexts of their writing and reading. Though each could be called a form of bad faith, each can also be seen as a figure of irrepressible desire and creativity—if only the sheer, never to be acknowledged zest of finding a way to frame and reproduce the pain or the plea-

---

[25]Personal communication, 1986. Of course, discussions of camp have proliferated since Susan Sontag's "Notes on 'Camp,' " in *Against Interpretation and Other Essays* (New York: Farrar, Straus & Giroux, 1966). One of the discussions that resonates most with this book's emphasis on the open secret is Philip Core, *Camp: The Lie That Tells the Truth* (New York: Delilah Books, 1984).

[26]"CAMP depends on where you pitch it. . . . CAMP is in the eyes of the beholder, especially if the beholder is camp." Core, "CAMP RULES," *Camp,* p. 7.

sure of another. "Good," Nietzsche remarks, but his affect here may be rather enigmatic, "is no longer good when your neighbour takes it into his mouth" (*Beyond,* 53).

Same/Different; Homo/Hetero

If sentimentality, antisentimentality, and ressentimentality are figures of vicariated desire, however, how is one to know whose desire it is that is thus figured? By whom can it be so figured? More: if we hypothesize that a central misrepresentation of Christian-era ressentimentality is the back-and-forth misrepresentation that incessantly occurs between the concepts "same" and "different," do we risk generalizing our topic out of existence? Of course we do; nothing, in Western thought, isn't categorizable and deconstructible under "same" and "different." Suppose we move to the Greek translation, then, and make the same hypothesis about ressentimentality as the mutual misrepresentation between *homo* and *hetero:* haven't we then already overspecified our topic fatally? Yet this is the overlapping field of double-binding binarisms into which we are indeed plunged by, not the scandalous, sentimental vicariety of Christian psychology itself, nor the desire in itself of many men for other men, but the late-nineteenth-century juxtaposition of these two things in the concepts homo- and heterosexuality.

Since Foucault, it has been common to distinguish a modern concept of "homosexuality"—delineating a continuous *identity*—from a supposedly premodern (though persistent) concept of "sodomy," which delineated discrete *acts.* More recent research has, however, been demonstrating that even within the minoritizing, taxonomic identity-discourses instituted in the late nineteenth century, there was an incalculably consequential divergence between terms Foucault had treated as virtually interchangeable: homosexuality and sexual inversion. As George Chauncey argues, "Sexual inversion, the term used most commonly in the nineteenth century, did not denote the same conceptual phenomenon as homosexuality. 'Sexual inversion' referred to an inversion in a broad range of deviant gender behavior"—the phenomenon of female "masculinity" or male "femininity," condensed in formulations such as Karl Heinrich Ulrichs' famous self-description as *anima muliebris virili corpore inclusa,* a woman's soul trapped in a man's body—"while 'homosexuality' focused on the narrower issue of sexual object choice."[27] According to David Halperin, "That sexual object-choice might be wholly independent of such 'secondary' characteristics as masculinity or femininity never seems to have entered anyone's head until Havelock Ellis waged a campaign to isolate object-choice from role-playing and Freud . . . clearly distinguished in the case of the libido between the sexual 'object' and the sexual 'aim.' "[28]

[27]Chauncey, "From Sexual Inversion to Homosexuality," p. 124.
[28]Halperin, *One Hundred Years of Homosexuality,* p. 16.

Halperin describes some consequences of this shift:

The conceptual isolation of sexuality *per se* from questions of masculinity and femininity made possible a new taxonomy of sexual behaviors and psychologies based entirely on the anatomical sex of the persons engaged in a sexual act (same sex vs. different sex); it thereby obliterated a number of distinctions that had traditionally operated within earlier discourses pertaining to same-sex sexual contacts and that had radically differentiated active from passive sexual partners, normal from abnormal (or conventional from unconventional) sexual roles, masculine from feminine styles, and paederasty from lesbianism: all such behaviors were now to be classed alike and placed under the same heading. Sexual identity was thus polarized around a central opposition rigidly defined by the binary play of sameness and difference in the sexes of the sexual partners; people belonged henceforward to one or the other of two exclusive categories. . . . Founded on positive, ascertainable, and objective behavioral phenomena—on the facts of who had sex with whom—the new sexual taxonomy could lay claim to a descriptive, trans-historical validity. And so it crossed the "threshold of scientificity" and was enshrined as a working concept in the social and physical sciences.[29]

It is startling to realize that the aspect of "homosexuality" that now seems in many ways most immutably to fix it—its dependence on a defining *sameness* between partners—is of so recent crystallization.[30] That process is also, one might add, still radically incomplete.[31] The potential for defamiliarization implicit in this historical perception is only beginning to be apparent.

The *homo-* in the emerging concept of the homosexual seems to have the potential to perform a definitive de-differentiation—setting up a permanent avenue of potential slippage—between two sets of relations that had previously been seen as relatively distinct: identification and desire.[32] It is with *homo*-style homosexuality, and *not* with inversion, pederasty, or sodomy (least of all, of course, with cross-gender sexuality) that an erotic language, an erotic discourse comes into existence that makes available a continuing possibility for symbolizing slippages between identification and desire. It concomitantly makes available new possibilities for the camouflage and concealment, or the very selective or pointed display, of proscribed or resisted erotic relation and avowal through chains of vicariation—through the mechanisms that, I argue, cluster under the stigmatizing name "sentimentality."

---

[29]Halperin, *One Hundred Years of Homosexuality*, p. 16.

[30]Indeed, though the two etymological roots of the coinage "*homo-sexuality*" may originally have been meant to refer to relations (of an unspecified kind) between persons of the *same sex*, I believe the word is now almost universally heard as referring to relations of *sexuality* between persons who are, because of their sex, more flatly and globally categorized as *the same*.

[31]For instance, many Mediterranean and Latin American cultures distinguish sharply between insertive and receptive sexual roles, in assessing the masculinity/femininity of men involved in male-male sex; the concept of homosexual identity per se tends not to make sense readily in these cultural contexts, or tends to make sense to self-identified *jotos* or *pasivos* but not *machos* or *activos*. And these are, along with the Anglo-European and others, among the cultures that are also U.S. cultures. See, for instance, Ana Maria Alonso and Maria Teresa Koreck, "Silences: 'Hispanics,' AIDS, and Sexual Practices," *Differences* 1 (Winter 1989): 101–24.

[32]On this, see Chapter 1 of *Between Men*.

Let me make it clear what I am and am not saying here. I do not, myself, believe same-sex relationships are much more likely to be based on similarity than are cross-sex relationships. That is, I do not believe that identification and desire are necessarily more closely linked in same-sex than in cross-sex relationships, or in gay than in nongay persons. I assume them to be closely linked in many or most relationships and persons, in fact. I certainly do not believe that any given man must be assumed to have more in common with any other given man than he can possibly have in common with any given woman. Yet these *are* the assumptions that underlie, and are in turn underwritten by, the definitional invention of "homosexuality."[33]

How does a man's love of *other* men become a love of the *same?* The process is graphic in *Dorian Gray,* in the way the plot of the novel facilitates the translation back and forth between "men's desire for men" and something that looks a lot like what a tradition will soon call "narcissism." The novel takes a plot that is distinctively one of male-male desire, the competition between Basil Hallward and Lord Henry Wotten for Dorian Gray's love, and condenses it into the plot of the mysterious bond of figural likeness and figural expiation between Dorian Gray and his own portrait. The suppression of the original defining *differences between* Dorian and his male admirers—differences of age and initiatedness, in the first place—in favor of the problematic of Dorian's *similarity to* the painted male image that is and isn't himself does several things. To begin with, the similarity trope does not, I believe, constitute itself strongly here as against an "inversion" model, in which Wilde seldom seemed particularly interested and whose rhetoric is virtually absent from *Dorian Gray.* Rather, this plot of the novel seems to replicate the discursive eclipse in this period of the Classically based, *pederastic* assumption that male-male bonds of any duration must be structured around some diacritical difference—old/young, for example, or active/passive—whose binarizing cultural power would be at least comparable to that of gender. Initiating, along with the stigma of narcissism, the utopic modern vision of a strictly egalitarian bond guaranteed by the exclusion of any consequential difference, the new calculus of homo/hetero, embodied in the portrait plot, owes its sleekly utilitarian feel to the linguistically unappealable classification of anyone who shares one's gender as being "the same" as oneself, and anyone who does not share one's gender as being one's Other.

---

[33]At the same time, the fact that "homosexuality," being—unlike its predecessor terms—posited on definitional similarity, was the first modern piece of sexual definition that simply took as nugatory the distinction between relations of identification and relations of desire, meant that it posed a radical question to cross-gender relations and, in turn, to gender definition itself. For the first time since at least the Renaissance, there existed the potential for a discourse in which a man's desire for a woman could not guarantee his difference from her—in which it might even, rather, suggest his likeness to her. That such a possibility is a clear contradiction of the *homo/hetero* gender definitions of which it is nonetheless also the clear consequence made a conceptual knot whose undoing may be said to have been the determinative project, continuously frustrated but continuously productive, of psychoanalytic theory from Freud to the present.

It served, however, an additional purpose. For Wilde, in 1891 a young man with a very great deal to lose who was trying to embody his own talents and desires in a self-contradictory male-homosocial terrain where too much was not enough but, at the same time, anything at all might always be too much, the collapse of homo/hetero with self/other must also have been attractive for the protective/expressive camouflage it offered to distinctively gay content. Not everyone has a lover of their own sex, but everyone, after all, has a self of their own sex.[34] (This camouflage, by the way, continues to be effective in institutions that connive with it: in a class I taught at Amherst College, fully half the students said they had studied *Dorian Gray* in previous classes, but not one had ever discussed the book in terms of any homosexual content: all of them knew it could be explained in terms of either the Theme of the Double—"The Divided Self"—or else the Problem of Mimesis—"Life and Art.")

For Wilde, the progression from *homo* to same to self resulted at least briefly, as we shall see, in a newly articulated modernist "self"-reflexiveness and antifigurality, antirepresentationism, iconophobia that struggles in the antisentimental entanglements of *Dorian Gray* and collapses in the sentimental mobilizations of *Reading Gaol.*[35] Nietzsche's use of the nascent accommodations of the new concept are oddly simpler, for all that you would have to describe him as the man who tried to put the hetero back into *Ecce Homo*. Freud in his discussion of Dr. Schreber gives the following list of the possible eroto-grammatical transformations that can be generated in contradiction of the sentence, unspeakable under a homophobic regime of utterance, "*I* (a man) *love him* (a man)." First, "I do not *love* him—I *hate* him"; second, "I do not love *him,* I love *her*"; third, "*I* do not love him; *she* loves him"; and finally, "I do not love him; I do not love any one."[36] None of these translations is exactly foreign to Nietzsche; in fact, one could imagine a Nietzsche life-and-works whose table of contents simply rotated the four sentences in continual reprise. But his own most characteristic and invested grammar for this prohibited sentence is a different one, one that underlies Freud's project so intimately that it does not occur to Freud to make it explicit, and far closer to

---

[34] If, at any rate, under this new definitional possibility, that which I *am* and that which I *desire* may no longer be assumed to be distinct, then each one of those terms can be subjected to the operations of slippage. We have seen how both Wilde and Nietzsche camouflage what seem to be the male objects of male desire as, "ultimately," mere reflections of a divided "self." But it can work in the other direction: the *homo*- construction also makes a language in which a man who desires may claim to take on some of the lovable attributes of the man desired. In Nietzsche, for example, the unimaginable distance between the valetudinarian philosopher who desires, and the bounding "masters of the earth" whom he desires, is dissolved so resolutely by the force of his rhetoric that it is startling to be reminded that "Homer would not have created Achilles, nor Goethe Faust, if Homer had been an Achilles, or Goethe a Faust" (*Genealogy*, 235). And, as we shall see, Wilde presents a similar double profile.

[35] For Nietzsche, whose literary impulses aren't in that sense modernist, the desired male figure never ceases to be visible as a male figure, except, as we've noted, in those instances where the sense of sight is willfully suppressed.

[36] "Psycho-analytic Notes upon an Autobiographical Account of a Case of Paranoia (Dementia Paranoides)," in *Three Case Histories*, ed. Philip Rieff (New York: Macmillan/Collier, 1963), pp. 165–68.

the bone of the emergent "homo-" reading of what it means for man to desire man: "I do not *love* him, I *am* him."

I do not desire, let us say, Wagner; I *am* Wagner. In the loving panegyric of *Wagner in Bayreuth,* "I am the only person referred to—one may ruthlessly insert my name . . . wherever the text gives the word Wagner" (*Ecce,* 82). (Or: "Supposing I had baptized my Zarathustra with another name, for example with the name of Richard Wagner, the perspicuity of two millennia would not have sufficed to divine that the author of 'Human, All Too Human' is the visionary of Zarathustra" [*Ecce,* 59].) It was not "one of my friends, the excellent Dr. Paul Ree, whom [in *Human, All Too Human*] I bathed in world-historic glory"; that was merely how, "with my instinctive cunning, I here too avoided the little word 'I' " (*Ecce,* 94). I do not desire Zarathustra, though "we celebrate the feast of feasts; friend *Zarathustra* has come, the guest of guests! Now the world is laughing, the dread curtain is rent, the wedding day has come for light and darkness" (*Beyond,* 204)—rather, at the moments of definitional stress, I *am* Zarathustra. I do not desire Dionysus, for all the gorgeous eroticism surrounding

> that great hidden one, the tempter god . . . whose voice knows how to descend into the underworld of every soul, who says no word and gives no glance in which there lies no touch of enticement . . . the genius of the heart . . . who divines the hidden and forgotten treasure, the drop of goodness and sweet spirituality under thick and opaque ice, and is a divining-rod for every grain of gold . . . the genius of the heart from whose touch everyone goes away . . . newer to himself than before, broken open, blown upon and sounded out by a thawing wind, more uncertain perhaps, more delicate, more fragile, more broken, but full of hopes that as yet have no names, full of new will and current, full of new ill will and counter-current. . . . Dionysus, that great ambiguous and tempter god. (*Beyond,* 199–200)

—no, in the last analysis, I *am* Dionysus. (The dedicatory phrases, for instance, that begin the "Dionysus" section of *The Will to Power,* "To him that has turned out well,* who does my heart good, carved from wood that is hard, gentle, and fragrant—in whom even the nose takes pleasure," turn up almost verbatim in the "Why I am so Wise" section of *Ecce Homo,* with the notation, "I have just described *myself.*")[37] Indeed, "What is disagreeable and offends my modesty is that at bottom I am every name in history."[38] And, as with Dr. Schreber, the whole elaborated syntax of the contraries of *these* propositions emerges in turn: Nietzsche as the *contra* Wagner ("we are antipodes");[39] *"Dionysus against the Crucified"* (the last words of *Ecce Homo*); Nietzsche, in perhaps the most central turn, as the Anti-Christ.

---

[37]*The Will to Power,* trans. Walter Kaufmann (New York: Vintage, 1968), p. 520 (hereafter cited in the text as *Will*); *Ecce,* 40–41.

[38]From his letter to Jacob Burckhardt, dated January 6, 1889; *The Portable Nietzsche,* ed. and trans. Walter Kaufmann (New York: Viking Penguin, 1976), p. 686.

[39]*Nietzsche Contra Wagner,* in *The Portable Nietzsche,* p. 662 (further citations are given as *Contra* in the text). "What respect can I have for the Germans when even my friends cannot discriminate between me and a liar like Richard Wagner?" (cancelled paragraphs for *Ecce,* in *Basic Writings of Nietzsche,* trans. Walter Kaufmann [New York: Modern Library, 1968], p. 798).

Abstraction/Figuration

To point to the paranoid structure of these male investments is not, in the framework I hope I have created, to pathologize or marginalize them but, rather, to redeploy their admitted centrality. "Madness is something rare in individuals— but in groups, parties, peoples, ages it is the rule" *(Beyond,* 85). To the degree that Nietzsche is here engaged in a projective heroics of embodiment already charac- teristic of post-Romantic projects, he provides an exemplar for the Gothic-marked view of the nineteenth century as the Age of Frankenstein, an age philosophically and tropologically marked by the wildly dichotomous play around solipsism and intersubjectivity of a male paranoid plot—one that always ends in the tableau of two men chasing one another across a landscape evacuated of alternative life or interest, toward a climax that tends to condense the amorous with the murderous in a representation of male rape.[40] What is anomalous about Nietzsche in this con- text is scarcely the hold this plot has on him, but indeed the flexuous sweetness with which sometimes he uniquely invests it:

> You who with your spear of fire
> Melt the river of my soul,
> So that, freed from ice, it rushes
> Toward the ocean of its goal:
> Brighter still and still more healthy,
> Free in most desired constraint—
> Thus your miracle it praises,
> January, lovely saint![41]

The overtly Gothic *Dorian Gray,* insofar as its plot devolves, as we've seen, from a worldly one of complex intersubjective rivalries to a hermetic one of the Double *tout court,* drinks as deeply and much more conventionally of this nine- teenth-century current by which the energies of a male-male desire by now com- plexly prohibited but still rather inchoately defined could be at once circulated, channeled, extended, and occluded. . . . What makes *Dorian Gray* so distinctively modern(ist) a book, however, is not the degree to which it partakes of the para- noid-associated homophobic alibi "I do not *love* him; I *am* him." It is a different though intimately related alibi that the *modernism* of *Dorian Gray* performs: the alibi of abstraction.

Across the turn of the century, as we know, through a process that became most visible in, but antedated and extended far beyond, the trials of Oscar Wilde, the discourse related to male homosexuality itself became for the first time extremely public and highly ramified through medical, psychiatric, penal, literary, and other social institutions. With a new public discourse concerning male homosexuality

---

[40]On this, see *Between Men,* Chapters 5, 6, 9, and 10.
[41]The translation is Hollingdale's *(Ecce,* 98). The poem appears as the epigraph to Book Four of *The Gay Science* and is translated by Walter Kaufmann in his edition of that book (New York: Random House/Vintage, 1974), p. 221.

that was at the same time increasingly discriminant, increasingly punitive, and increasingly trivializing or marginalizing, the recuperative rhetoric that emerged had an oddly oblique shape. I would describe it as the occluded intersection between a minority rhetoric of the "open secret" or glass closet and a subsumptive public rhetoric of the "empty secret."

The term "open secret" designates here a very particular secret, a homosexual secret. . . . I use it as a condensed way of describing the phenomenon of the "glass closet," the swirls of totalizing knowledge-power that circulate so violently around any but the most openly acknowledged gay male identity. The lavender button I bought the other day at the Oscar Wilde Memorial Bookstore, that laconically says, "I KNOW YOU KNOW," represents a playful and seductive version of the Glass Closet. Hitchcock's recently re-released Gothic film *Rope* is a good example of the murderous version. It opens with two men, clearly lovers, strangling a third man in a darkened penthouse; then pulling back the curtains from the skylight with orgasmic relief—"Pity we couldn't have done it with the curtains open, in bright sunlight. Well, we can't have everything, can we? We did do it in daytime"—they put their friend's dead body in a large box which they place in the middle of the living room and use as the buffet table and centerpiece for a party, the guests to which include the fiancée, the father, the aunt, the best friend, and the prep-school ex-housemaster of the murdered man. Needless to say, the two lovers manage to make sure that the existence of A Secret, and the location of that secret in the big box in the middle of the room, does not remain A Secret for long.

The public rhetoric of the "empty secret," on the other hand, the cluster of aperçus and intuitions that seems distinctively to signify "modernism" (at least, male high modernism), delineates a space bounded by hollowness, a self-reference that refers back to—though it differs from—nineteenth-century paranoid solipsism, and a split between content or thematics on the one hand and structure on the other that is stressed in favor of structure and at the expense of thematics. I will argue in the next chapter that this rhetoric of male modernism serves a purpose of universalizing, naturalizing, and thus substantively voiding—depriving of content—elements of a specifically and historically male homosexual rhetoric. But just as the gay male rhetoric is itself already marked and structured and indeed necessitated and propelled by the historical shapes of homophobia, for instance by the contingencies and geographies of the highly permeable closet, so it is also true that homophobic male modernism bears the structuring fossil-marks of and in fact spreads and reproduces the specificity of desire that it exists to deny.

The Picture of Dorian Gray occupies an especially symptomatic place in this process. Published four years before Wilde's "exposure" as a sodomite, it is in a sense a perfect rhetorical distillation of the open secret, the glass closet, shaped by the conjunction of an extravagance of deniability and an extravagance of flamboyant display. It perfectly represents the glass closet, too, because it is in so many ways *out* of the purposeful control of its author. Reading *Dorian Gray* from our twentieth-century vantage point where the name Oscar Wilde virtually *means* "homosexual," it is worth reemphasizing how thoroughly the elements of even this

novel can be read doubly or equivocally, can be read either as having a thematically empty "modernist" meaning or as having a thematically full "homosexual"
meaning. And from the empty "modernist" point of view, this full meaning—*any*
full meaning, but, in some exemplary representative relation to that, *this* very particular full meaning—*this* insistence on narrative content, which means the insistence on *this* narrative content, comes to look like kitsch.

Basil Hallward perfectly captures the immobilizing panic that underlies this
imperfect transformation of the open secret into the empty secret. He had been
able, in decent comfort, to treat artistically of his infatuation with Dorian so long as
he had framed it anachronistically, Classically—even while knowing that "in such
mad worships there is peril" (128)—but

> Then came a new development. I had drawn you as Paris in dainty armour, and as
> Adonis with huntsman's cloak and polished boatspear. . . . And it had all been what art
> should be—unconscious, ideal, and remote. One day, a fatal day I sometimes think, I
> determined to paint a wonderful portrait of you as you actually are, not in the costume of
> dead ages, but in your own dress and your own time. Whether it was the Realism of the
> method, or the mere wonder of your own personality, thus directly presented to me
> without mist or veil, I cannot tell. But I know that as I worked at it, every flake and film
> of colour seemed to me to reveal my secret. I grew afraid that others would know of my
> idolatry. I felt, Dorian, that I had told too much, that I had put too much of myself into
> it. . . . Well, after a few days the thing left my studio, and as soon as I had got rid of the
> intolerable fascination of its presence it seemed to me that I had been foolish in imagin-
> ing that I had seen anything in it, more than that you were extremely good-looking, and
> that I could paint. Even now I cannot help feeling that it is a mistake to think that the
> passion one feels in creation is ever really shown in the work one creates. Art is always
> more abstract than we fancy. Form and colour tell us of form and colour—that is all.
> (128–29)

Or, as Basil has put it earlier, interrupting his own confession of love and desire for
Dorian: "He is never more present in my work than when no image of him is
there. He is a suggestion, as I have said, of a new manner. I find him in the curves
of certain lines, in the loveliness and subtleties of certain colours. That is all" (17).

Passages like these, as well as some of the important antinarrative projects that
seem to shape the early parts of *Dorian Gray*, suggest the prefiguring manifesto of
a modernist aesthetic according to which sentimentality inheres less in the object
figured than in a prurient vulgarity associated with figuration itself. Postmodernism, in this view, the strenuous rematch between the reigning champ, modernist abstraction, and the deposed challenger, figuration, would thus *necessarily*
have kitsch and sentimentality as its main spaces of contestation. But insofar as
there is a case to be made that the modernist impulse toward abstraction in the
first place owes an incalculable part of its energy precisely to turn-of-the-century
male homo/heterosexual definitional panic—and such a case is certainly there for
the making, in at any rate literary history from Wilde to Hopkins to James to
Proust to Conrad to Eliot to Pound to Joyce to Hemingway to Faulkner to
Stevens—to that extent the "figuration" that had to be abjected from modernist

self-reflexive abstraction was not the figuration of just *any* body, the figuration of figurality itself, but, rather, that represented in a very particular body, the desired male body. So as kitsch or sentimentality came to mean representation itself, what represented "representation itself" came at the same time signally to be a very particular, masculine object and subject of erotic desire.

Invention/Recognition; Wholeness/Decadence

An antifiguralist modernism per se never seems to have formed any part of Nietzsche's program. It seems, however, that after the revulsion against his love for Wagner, opera functioned for Nietzsche rather as figuration itself did for Wilde; it stood, that is, for a fascinating, near-irresistible impulse barely transcended if transcended at all, but against which a scouring polemic might none the less productively and revealingly be mounted. Thematically and rhetorically, as well, Nietzsche's treatment of opera is similar to Wilde's treatment of mimesis—writing in 1886 about his major Wagnerian work of fifteen years before:

> To say it once more: today I find [*The Birth of Tragedy*] an impossible book: I consider it badly written, ponderous, embarrassing, image-mad and image-confused, sentimental, in places saccharine to the point of effeminacy, uneven in tempo, without the will to logical cleanliness . . . a book for initiates, "music" for those dedicated to music, those who are closely related to begin with on the basis of common and rare aesthetic experiences, "music" meant as a sign of recognition for close relatives *in artibus*. . . . Still, the effect of the book proved and proves that it had a knack for seeking out fellow-rhapsodizers and for luring them on to new secret paths and dancing places. What found expression here was anyway—this was admitted with as much curiosity as antipathy—a *strange* voice, the disciple of a still "unknown God." . . . Here was a spirit with strange, still nameless needs.[42]

Nietzsche calls the "image-mad" relations around Wagner "sentimental" in the specific sense that they involved his "confounding of myself with what I was not" (*Ecce*, 93); as for "the Wagnerian" more generally, "I have 'experienced' three generations of them, from the late Brendel, who confused Wagner with Hegel, to the 'idealists' of the Bayreuther Blätter, who confuse Wagner with themselves" (*Ecce*, 90). The promiscuously vicariating impulse triggered by Wagner, while entailing all the "uncleanliness" attributed to its Christian original ("I put on gloves when I read the score of *Tristan*" [*Will*, 555]), also performs, however, another function that Nietzsche finds more difficult to repudiate: a function of community-building through the mechanism of mutual recognition enabled by this slippage, among "initiates," between desire and identification. The very stress on the "secret,"

---

[42]From "Attempt at Self-Criticism," 1886 introduction to a reissue of *The Birth of Tragedy*, in *Basic*, pp. 19–20.

"curious," "strange," "unknown," and "nameless," terms that flamboyantly condense the open secret with the empty one, dares such recognitions.

One of the most Wildean functions that the opera serves in Nietzsche is to anchor a rhetoric of decadence. Wagner was a perfect foil for Nietzsche's erotic grammars here: himself certifiable as heterosexually active, if not hyperactive, he nonetheless, like Nietzsche, crystallized a hypersaturated solution of what were and were about to become homosexual signifiers. Set up under the notorious aegis of Ludwig II, the Wagnerian opera represented a cultural lodestar for what Max Nordau, in *Degeneration*, refers to as "the abnormals"; the tireless taxonomist Krafft-Ebing quotes a homosexual patient who is "an enthusiastic partisan of Richard Wagner, for whom I have remarked a predilection in most of us [sufferers from "contrary-sexual-feeling"]; I find that this music accords so very much with our nature."[43] Thus when Nietzsche refers to Wagner's "incredibly pathological sexuality" (*Will*, 555), he can characteristically tap into and refresh the energies of emergent tropes for homosexuality without ever taking a reified homosexuality itself as a subject. From the late twentieth-century retrospect there is, as we have mentioned, almost only one out of the panoply of nineteenth-century sexualities that represents *the* pathological (just as the phrase "sexual orientation" now refers quite exclusively to gender of object-choice); the reading of Nietzsche through these tendentiously filtered lenses certainly represents a violence to his meaning, but a violence in which he is anything but unimplicated.

The thematics as well as argumentation of decadence in Nietzsche are close to those of ressentimentality: loosening of the laminated integument, as in the "over-ripe, manifold and much-indulged conscience" of Christianity (*Beyond*, 57), a palpable gaping, crawling, or fermentation where firmness ought to be, like the Overture to *Meistersinger*, which has "the loose yellow skin of fruits which ripen too late" (*Beyond*, 151). Although the negative valuation attached to *ressentiment* per se—*ressentiment* under its own name—is one of the most consistent of Nietzsche's ethical judgments, it's nonetheless clear that his acuity as a psychologist of ressentimentality requires that he as well undergo subjection to its processes. It is an easy task for anyone instructed by Nietzsche to demonstrate the infusion of his most powerful thought with *ressentiment*, given both the absence in Nietzsche of any comparably psychologized alternative account of human emotion, and the implication in the very terminology of *ressentiment* that the supposed activity of emotion and the supposed passivity of perception are indistinguishable from one another, the degradation of *re-* already implicit in every sense of *sentiment*. But Nietzsche makes explicit about *décadence* what he leaves to be inferred about *ressentiment*—how absolutely its recognition, whether to celebrate or deprecate it, is implicated in the interminable logic of, among other things, homosexual attribution whereby *it takes one to know one:*

[43]Nordau, *Degeneration*, trans. from the 2d ed. of the German work, 6th ed. (New York: D. Appleton, 1895), p. 452; Krafft-Ebing, quoted by Nordau, p. 452*n*, from Richard von Krafft-Ebing, *Neue Forschungen auf dem Gebiet der Psychopathia sexualis* (Stuttgart: F. Enke, 1891), p. 128.

If one is to be fair to [*The Wagner Case*] one has to suffer from the destiny of music as from an open wound.—*What* is it I suffer from when I suffer from the destiny of music? From this . . . that it is *décadence* music and no longer the flute of Dionysos. . . . Supposing, however, that one in this way feels the cause of music to be *one's own* cause, to be the history of *one's own* suffering, one will find this writing full of consideration and mild beyond measure. . . . —I have loved Wagner.—Ultimately this is an attack on a subtle "unknown" who could not easily be detected by another, in the sense and direction of my task. (*Ecce*, 119)

His aptitude for perceiving decadence is traced directly to his affinity with it; correspondingly, the ability of others to suspect it in him is traced to their own.

I have a subtler sense for signs of ascent and decline than any man has ever had, I am the teacher *par excellence* in this matter—I know both, I am both.—My father died at the age of 36: he was delicate, lovable and morbid. . . . A doctor who treated me for some time as a nervous case said at last: "No! there is nothing wrong with your nerves, it is only I who am nervous." . . . —Convalescence means with me a long, all too long succession of years—it also unfortunately means relapse, deterioration, periods of *décadence*. Do I need to say that in questions of *décadence* I am *experienced*? I have spelled it out forwards and backwards. (*Ecce*, 38–39)

What is strangest is this: after [the ordeal of a long sickness] one has a different taste—a *second* taste. Out of such abysses, also out of the abyss of great suspicion, one returns newborn, having shed one's skin, more ticklish and sarcastic, with a more delicate taste for joy, with a more tender tongue for all good things . . . more childlike and yet a hundred times more subtle than one has ever been before. (*Contra*, 681)

The relatively relaxed openness with which this epistemological structure is acknowledged means that decadence, unlike the *ressentiment* to which it otherwise seems so closely to correspond, can often be discussed in Nietzsche without mobilizing the fierce, accusatory machinery of projective denial:

We Europeans of the day after tomorrow, we first-born of the twentieth century—with all our dangerous curiosity, our multiplicity and art of disguise, our mellow and as it were sugared cruelty in spirit and senses—*if* we are to have virtues we shall presumably have only such virtues as have learned to get along with our most secret and heartfelt inclinations, with our most fervent needs: very well, let us look for them within our labyrinths! (*Beyond*, 128)

Perhaps, indeed, the most exquisite erotic meditation of the nineteenth century lies spread out in this subcutaneous fermentation of the *décadent,* the "multitude of subtle shudders and trickles down to one's toes" (*Ecce*, 102–3) radiating around the point of a penetration whose object is both oneself and not. Where, for instance, to locate the boundary between self and other in Nietzsche's encounter with his own book *Daybreak*?

Even now, when I chance to light on this book every sentence becomes for me a spike with which I again draw something incomparable out of the depths: its entire skin trembles with tender shudders of recollection. (*Ecce*, 95)

As Nietzsche says of his own ideal, "It is impossible for the Dionysian man not to understand any suggestion of whatever kind, he ignores no signal from the emotions. . . . He enters into every skin" (*Twilight*, 73).

Voluntarity/Addiction; Cosmopolitan/National

Richard Gilman's important book *Decadence* suggests that a lot of the powerful illusion of meaning that clings to the notion of "decadence"—a notion whose absolute conceptual inanition he demonstrates—seems to have to do with something more thematic, a useful and frightening suppleness in its relation to the visualized outline of the individual organism. "As an adjective," Gilman writes, for example,

> ["decadent"] functions now like a coating, a sleek enameled skin applied to the "unhealthy" but not fully sinful; as a noun it exists as a disturbing substance with shifting, blobby outlines, like some animated and threatening gel from a science-fiction horror film.[44]

In fact, although Gilman's book is not interested in pursuing such an inquiry it shows that "decadence" is a centrally symptomatic laboratory-word for any exploration of the consequences of the irreducible immanence of the anthropomorphic within theory itself. Certainly this would be true in Nietzsche. And although, as we have seen, Nietzsche's tropism toward a thematics of the organ of the skin—its fit, its integrity, its concealments, its breachableness, the surface it offers or doesn't offer for vicarious relations—although that doesn't by any means *necessarily* entail a stance of paranoid defensive exclusion, the all but built-in potential in such a metaphorics for such a stance will inevitably ramify into the political career of these metaphorics, as well.

Some of the most important headings under which the work of decadence-attribution fatefully entangled, in Nietzsche's thought as in the ambient culture, other definitional nexuses themselves under stress include the relations of natural to artificial, of health to illness, of voluntarity to addiction, of Jew to anti-Semite, of nationality to cosmopolitanism. Nietzsche's habitual association of Wagner's sentimentality with drugs and addiction, for instance, of Wagner's "narcotic art" (*Ecce*, 92) with the "poison" (*Ecce*, 61) of a "hashish world" of "strange, heavy, enveloping vapors" (*Will*, 555), comes out of the late nineteenth-century reclassification of opiate-related ingestion behaviors that had previously been at worst considered bad habits, under the new medicalizing aegis of *addictions* and the corresponding new social entity of drug subcultures—developments that both paralleled and entangled the new developments in homo/heterosexual definition.[45] So Nietzsche says of the "total aberration of the instinct" that can attract young German men to Wagner's

---

[44]Richard Gilman, *Decadence: The Strange Life of an Epithet* (New York: Farrar, Straus & Giroux, 1979), p. 175.

[45]On this see Virginia Berridge and Griffith Edwards, *Opium and the People: Opiate Use in Nineteenth-Century England* (New Haven: Yale University Press, 1987). e.g., pp. 229–69.

art, "one piece of anti-nature downright *compels* a second" (*Ecce*, 91–92). In *The Picture of Dorian Gray* as in, for instance, *Dr. Jekyll and Mr. Hyde*, drug addiction is both a camouflage and an expression for the dynamics of same-sex desire and its prohibition: both books begin by looking like stories of erotic tensions between men, and end up as cautionary tales of solitary substance abusers. The two new taxonomies of the addict and the homosexual condense many of the same issues for late nineteenth-century culture: the old antisodomitic opposition between something called nature and that which is *contra naturam* blends with a treacherous apparent seamlessness into a new opposition between substances that are *natural* (e.g., "food") and those that are *artificial* (e.g., "drugs"); and hence into the characteristic twentieth-century way of problematizing almost every issue of will, dividing desires themselves between the natural, called "needs," and the artificial, called "addictions." It seems as though the reifying classification of certain particular, palpable substances as unnatural in their (artificially stimulating) relation to "natural" desire must necessarily throw into question the naturalness of any desire (Wilde: "Anything becomes a pleasure if one does it too often"),[46] so that Nietzsche's hypostatization of Will "itself," for example, would necessarily be part of the same historical process as the nineteenth-century isolation of addiction "itself."[47] Inexorably, from this grid of overlapping classifications—a purported taxonomic system that in fact does no more than chisel a historically specific point of stress into the unresolved issue of voluntarity—almost no individual practice in our culture by now remains exempt. The development of recent thought related to food is a good example: the concept of addiction to food led necessarily to that of addiction to dieting and in turn to that of addiction to exercise: each assertion of *will* made voluntarity itself appear problematical in a new area, with the consequence that that assertion of will itself came to appear addictive. (In fact, there has recently been a spate of journalism asserting that antiaddiction programs such as Alcoholics Anonymous and others modeled on it are addictive.) Some of the current self-help literature is explicit by now in saying that every extant form of behavior, desire, relationship, and consumption in our culture can accurately be described as addictive. Such a formulation does not, however, seem to lead these analysts to the perception that "addiction" names a counter-structure always internal to the ethicizing hypostatization of "voluntarity"; instead, it drives ever more blindly their compulsion to isolate some new space of the purely voluntary.

The "decadence" of drug addiction, in these late nineteenth-century texts, intersects with two kinds of bodily definition, each itself suffused with the homo/heterosexual problematic. The first of these is the national economic body; the second is the medical body. From the Opium Wars of the mid-nineteenth century up to the current details of U.S. relations with Turkey, Colombia, Panama, Peru, and the

---

[46]*Dorian Gray*, p. 236.

[47]This discussion of will and addiction, and what follows on opium as a figure for imperialist relations, builds on the discussion in Chapter 10 of *Between Men*, "Up the Postern Stair: *Edwin Drood* and the Homophobia of Empire," pp. 180–200.

Nicaraguan Contras, the drama of "foreign substances" and the drama of the new imperialisms and the new nationalisms have been quite inextricable. The integrity of (new and contested) national borders, the reifications of national will and vitality, were readily organized around these narratives of introjection. From as far back as Mandeville, moreover, the opium product—the highly condensed, portable, expensive, commerce-intensive substance seen as having a unique ability to pry the trajectory of demand conclusively and increasingly apart from the homeostasis of biological need—was spectacularly available to serve as a representation for emerging intuitions about commodity fetishism. The commodity-based orientalism of *Dorian Gray*, for instance, radiates outward from "a green paste, waxy in lustre, the odour curiously heavy and persistent" that represents an ultimate recourse for Dorian—outward through its repository, "a small Chinese box of black and gold-dust lacquer, elaborately wrought, the sides patterned with curved waves, and the silken cords hung with round crystals and tasselled inplaited metal threads"—outward through the "Florentine cabinet, made out of ebony, and inlaid with ivory and blue lapis," from whose triangular secret drawer his fingers move "instinctively" to extract the box (201–2). Like Wagnerian opera, *Dorian Gray* accomplished for its period the performative work of enabling a European community of gay mutual recognition and self-constitution at least partly by popularizing a consumerism that already derived an economic model from the traffic in drugs.

Take an example from the prodigally extravagant guide to lifestyle, interior decoration, and textiles offered in *Dorian Gray*'s aptly titled Chapter 11. A whole set of epistemological compactions around desire, identification, and the responsive, all but paranoid mutuality attributed to gay recognition are condensed in the almost compulsive evocation there, even more than elsewhere in the novel, of the drug-tinged adjectives "curious" and "subtle," two of the Paterian epithets that trace in *Dorian Gray* the homosexual-homophobic path of simultaneous epistemological heightening and ontological evacuation. Unlike the cognate labels attached so nearly inalienably to Claggart in *Billy Budd*, these adjectives float freely through the text: "some curious dream" (8), "this curious artistic idolatry" (17), "throbbing to curious pulses" (26), "a subtle magic" (26), "his subtle smile" (27), "a curious charm" (28), "a subtle fluid or a strange perfume" (44), "so curious a chance" (44), "women . . . are curious" (55), "a mad curiosity" (57), "a curious influence" (61), "some curious romance" (63), "a subtle sense of pleasure" (64), "poisons so subtle" (66), "the curious hard logic of passion" (66), "some curious race-instinct" (77), "curious Renaissance tapestries" (102), "pleasures subtle and secret" (119), "the curious secret of his life" (136), "curious unpictured sins whose very mystery lent them their subtlety and their charm" (137), "metaphors as monstrous as orchids, and as subtle in colour" (140), "subtle symphonic arrangements of exotic flowers" (144), "that curious indifference that is not incompatible with a real ardour of temperament" (147), "their subtle fascination" (148), "a curious pleasure" (148), "a curious delight" (150), and so on apparently endlessly. Besides being almost violently piquant and uninformative, "curious" shares with "subtle" a built-in epistemological indecision or doubling. Each of them can describe, as the OED puts it, "an object of interest": among the OED meanings for this sense of "curious" are "made with care or art, delicate, recherché, elaborate, unduly minute, abstruse, subtle, exquisite, exciting curiosity . . . queer. (The ordinary current objective sense)." At the same time, however, each adjective also describes, and in almost the same terms, the quality of the perception brought by the attentive subject to such an object: for "curious" "as a subjective quality of persons," the OED lists, e.g., "careful, attentive, anxious, cautious, inquisitive, prying, subtle." The thing known is a reflection of the impulse toward knowing it, then, and each describable only as the excess, "wrought" intensiveness of that knowledge-situation.

In their usage in the fetish-wrought Chapter 11, the epithets record, on the one hand, the hungrily inventive raptness of the curious or subtle perceiving eye or brain; and, on the other, the more than answering intricacy of the curious or subtle objects perceived—imported or plundered artifacts, in these typifying cases, whose astonishing density of jewels and "wrought" work such as embroidery testify, more than to taste, to the overt atrocities they sometimes depict, and most of all to the "monstrous," "strange," "terrible" (I use the Wildean terms) exactions of booty in precious minerals, tedious labor, and sheer wastage of (typically female) eyesight, levied on the Orient by the nations of Europe. "Yet, after some time, he wearied of them, and would sit in his box at the Opera, either alone or with Lord Henry, listening in rapt pleasure to 'Tannhauser' " (150).

Still, it would be reductive to confine the national question embodied in the sexuality of Dorian Gray to an exercise in orientalism. Indeed, the very patency of Wilde's gay-affirming and gay-occluding orientalism renders it difficult to turn back and see the outlines of the sexual body and the national body sketched by his occidentalism. With orientalism so ready-to-hand a rubric for the relation to the Other, it is difficult (Wilde seems to want to make it difficult) to resist seeing the desired English body as simply the domestic Same. Yet the sameness of this Same—or put another way, the homo- nature of this sexuality—is no less open to question than the self-identicalness of the national borders of the domestic. After all, the question of the national in Wilde's own life only secondarily—though profoundly—involved the question of overseas empire in relation to European patria. To the contrary: Wilde, as an ambitious Irish man, and the son, intimate, and protégé of a celebrated Irish nationalist poet, can only have had as a fundamental element of his own sense of self an exquisitely exacerbated sensitivity to how by turns porous, brittle, elastic, chafing, embracing, exclusive, murderous, in every way contestable and contested were the membranes of "domestic" national definition signified by the ductile and elusive terms England, Britain, Ireland. Indeed, the consciousness of foundational and/or incipient national difference already internal to national definition must have been part of what Wilde literally embodied, in the expressive, specularized, and symptomatic relation in which he avowedly stood to his age. As a magus in the worship of the "slim rose-gilt soul"—the individual or generic figure of the "slim thing, gold-haired like an angel" that stood at the same time for a sexuality, a sensibility, a class, and a narrowly English national type—Wilde, whose own physical make was of an opposite sort and (in that context) an infinitely less appetizing, desirable, and placeable one, showed his usual uncanny courage ("his usual uncanny courage," *anglice* chutzpah) in foregrounding his own body so insistently as an index to such erotic and political meanings. Wilde's alienizing physical heritage of unboundable bulk from his Irish nationalist mother, of a louche swarthiness from his Celticizing father, underlined with every self-foregrounding gesture of his person and *persona* the fragility, unlikelihood, and strangeness—at the same time, the transformative reperceptualizing power—of the new "*homo-*" homosexual imagining of male-male desire. By the same pressure, it dramatized the uncouth nonequivalence of an English national body with a British with an Irish, as domestic grounds from which to launch a stable understanding of national/imperial relations.

For Nietzsche, more explicitly antinationalist than Wilde, virulently anti-German, and by the later 1880s virulently anti–anti-Semitic (which is hardly to say he was not anti-Semitic), the conjunction of the drug topic with the national also evokes a dangerous rhetoric of the double-edged. He writes retrospectively, for instance:

> If one wants to get free from an unendurable pressure one needs hashish. Very well, I needed Wagner. Wagner is the counter-poison to everything German *par excellence*— still poison, I do not dispute it. . . . To become healthier—that is *retrogression* in the case of a nature such as Wagner. . . . The world is poor for him who has never been sick enough for this "voluptuousness of hell." . . . I think I know better than anyone what tremendous things Wagner was capable of, the fifty worlds of strange delights to which no one but he had wings, and as I am strong enough to turn even the most questionable and perilous things to my own advantage and thus to become stronger, I call Wagner the great benefactor of my life. (*Ecce*, 61)[48]

A characteristic gesture in Nietzsche is to summon up the spectre of an addiction, but at the same time to make an assertion of transcendent or instrumental will that might be paraphrased as "but as for me, I can take it or leave it." The ability to *use* a potentially addictive stimulus without surrendering to it is attributed to a laudable strength. Thus, for instance, "Grand passion uses and uses up convictions, it does not submit to them—it knows itself sovereign" (*Anti*, 172). *Zarathustra* says that sex is "only for the wilted, a sweet poison; for the lion-willed, however, the great invigoration of the heart and the reverently reserved wine of wines" (*Zarathustra*, 188).[49] The equivocal way Nietzsche describes the relation of Judaism to decadence has the same structure as the way he describes his own relation to the potentially addictive:

---

[48] Or of the English, "To finer nostrils even this English Christianity possesses a true English by-scent of the spleen and alcoholic excess against which it is with good reason employed as an antidote—the subtler poison against the coarser: and indeed a subtle poisoning is in the case of coarse peoples already a certain progress" (*Beyond*, 165).

[49] More: a section of *The Genealogy of Morals* juxtaposes, without confronting, the "drugged tranquillity" of the "impotent and oppressed" with the healthy "power of oblivion" of "strong, rich temperaments" (*Genealogy*, 172–73).

Considered psychologically, the Jewish nation is a nation of the toughest vital energy which, placed in impossible circumstances, voluntarily, from the profoundest shrewdness in self-preservation, took the side of all *décadence* instincts—*not* as being dominated by them but because it divined in them a power by means of which one can prevail *against* "the world." The Jews are the counterparts of *décadents*: they have been compelled to *act* as *décadents* to the point of illusion. . . . For the kind of man who desires to attain power through Judaism and Christianity, the *priestly* kind, *décadence* is only a *means*. (*Anti*, 135)

And any danger posed by nineteenth-century Jews to nineteenth-century Europe occurs because "that which is called a 'nation' in Europe today and is actually more of a *res facta* than *nata* (indeed sometimes positively resembles a *res ficta et picta*—) is in any case something growing, young, easily disruptable, not yet a race, let alone such an *aere perennius* as the Jewish" (*Beyond*, 163).

As always in Nietzsche, his implacable resistance to giving stable figuration to even the possibility of a minoritizing homosexual identity makes one hesitate to read into these passages what one might look for in, say, Proust. But nor is the figuration so very stable in Proust. For Proust, whose plots of Dreyfusism and of gay recognition are the organizing principles for one another as they are for the volumes through which they ramify, the numinous identification of male homosexuality with a *pre*-national, premodern dynastic cosmopolitanism, through the figure of Charlus as much as through the Jews, is no more than haunted by the spectre of a sort of gay Zionism or pan-Germanism, a normalizing politics on the nominally ethnic model that would bring homosexual identity itself under the sway of what Nietzsche called "that *névrose nationale* with which Europe is sick" (*Ecce*, 121). Each of these writers, at any rate, seems to use an erotics of decadence to denaturalize the body of the national per se. But, as Nietzsche's pseudo-psychiatric diagnostic stance in this memorable formulation may already suggest, the standpoint from which that denaturalization proceeds may itself present new problems.

Health/Illness

The most fateful aspect of Nietzsche's understanding of decadence is his philosophical reliance on a medical model of the human body. As we have seen, the thematics of decadence does not, of itself, entail for him any *necessarily* phobic ethical valuation—and this is true even as that thematics is crossed and recrossed by what had been and what were becoming the main signifiers of male-male-loving acts and identities. Indeed, Nietzsche's writing is rich in what amount to—in some cases, what explicitly present themselves as—avowals of identification with and desire for the signifieds of decadence. Such avowals barely loosen, however, the horrifyingly potent knot of accusatory decadence-attribution, so long as authority over that process is vested, as the anthropomorphizing logic of the metaphor historically required that it be, in an embattled and expansive expert science of health and hygiene.

It can be argued, after all, that Nietzsche made only one disastrously mistaken wager with his culture: the wager that the progress he had painfully made in wrestling the explicit bases of his thought inch by inch away from the gravely magnetic axis of good/evil could be most durably guaranteed by battening them to the apparently alternative, scientifically guaranteed axis of health/illness or vitality/morbidity. ("Whoever does not agree with me on this point I consider *infected*" [*Ecce*, 97].) The genocidal potential in his thought seems to have been retroactivated only through a cultural development that, however predictable it might have seemed to others, completely blindsided him. That is the indefatigably sinister hide-and-seek that ethicizing impulses have played in this century behind the mask of the human and life sciences. The hide-and-seek has depended, in turn, on the invisible elasticity by which, in the developments toward eugenic thought around and after the turn of the century, reifications such as "the strong," "the weak," "the nation," "civilization," particular classes, "the race," and even "life" itself have assumed the vitalized anthropomorphic outlines of the individual male body and object of medical expertise. For instance:

> To refrain from mutual injury, mutual violence, mutual exploitation, to equate one's own will with that of another: this may in a certain rough sense become good manners between individuals if the conditions for it are present (namely if their strength and value standards are in fact similar and they both belong to *one* body). As soon as there is a desire to take this principle further, however, and if possible even as the *fundamental principle of society*, it at once reveals itself for what it is: as the will to the *denial* of life, as the principle of dissolution and decay. One has to think this matter thoroughly through to the bottom and resist all sentimental weakness: life itself is *essentially* appropriation, injury, overpowering of the strange and weaker, suppression, severity, imposition of one's own forms, incorporation and, at the least and mildest, exploitation—but why should one always have to employ precisely those words which have from of old been stamped with a slanderous intention? Even that body within which, as was previously assumed, individuals treat one another as equals—this happens in every healthy aristocracy—must, if it is a living and not a decaying body, itself do all that to other bodies which the individuals within it refrain from doing to one another: it will have to be the will to power incarnate, it will want to grow, expand, draw to itself, gain ascendancy—not out of any morality or immorality, but because it *lives*, and because life *is* will to power. On no point, however, is the common European consciousness more reluctant to learn than it is here; everywhere one enthuses, even under scientific disguises, about coming states of society in which there will be "no more exploitation"—that sounds to my ears like promising a life in which there will be no organic functions. "Exploitation" does not pertain to a corrupt or imperfect or primitive society: it pertains to the *essence* of the living thing as a fundamental organic function, it is a consequence of the intrinsic will to power which is precisely the will of life. (*Beyond*, 174–75)

From the body of the "individual" to the body of the "healthy aristocracy" to "the will of life" itself: these invocations are no unproblematical metonymies, but anthropomorphic pseudo-equivalencies whose slippery scientism conceals the very violence it purports to celebrate.

Thus when Nietzsche comes, in a late book, to offer a description of the actual body of Christ, the terms he chooses are both tellingly congruent with his own decadent self-descriptions and at the same time tellingly distanced through the figuration and narrative implicit in the medical model in its most dangerously elastic incarnations.

> To make a *hero* of Jesus!—And what a worse misunderstanding is the word "genius"! To speak with the precision of the physiologist a quite different word would rather be in place here: the word idiot. We recognize a condition of morbid susceptibility of the *sense of touch* which makes it shrink back in horror from every contact, every grasping of a firm object. Translate such a physiological *habitus* into its ultimate logic—an instinctive hatred of *every* reality. . . .
>
> I call it a sublime further evolution of hedonism on a thoroughly morbid basis. (*Anti,* 141–42)

The word "idiot" here points in the direction of the blank male cynosure of erotic flux and surplus: "One has to regret that no Dostoyevsky lived in the neighbourhood of this most interesting *décadent*; I mean someone who could feel the thrilling fascination of such a combination of the sublime, the sick and the childish" (*Anti,* 143). Nothing in Nietzsche has licensed one to read this as merely a sneer; indeed, nothing has quite licensed one to read it as not about Nietzsche himself. The word "idiot" points as well, however, by the same gesture toward the taxonomic and ultimately eugenic sciences of the "morbid"—the sciences that move imperceptibly back and forth from delineating the outlines and describing the prognosis of the individual body to enforcing an ethics of collective hygiene, on an infinitely elastic scale, in response to a chimera of demographic degeneration and a fatally tacit swarm of phylogenetic fantasies. It points to the genocidal space of slippage, in a single page of *Beyond Good and Evil,* among the individual man, the "corruption of *the European race,*" and "the will to make of *man* a sublime *abortion*" (*Beyond,* 70–71; emphasis added).

It may be, then, that much of the heritage that today sets "sentimentality" and its ever more elusive, indeed, ever more impossible Other at the defining center of so many judgments, political as well as aesthetic, impinging so today on every issue of national identity, postcolonial populism, religious fundamentalism, high versus mass culture, relations among races, to children, to other species, and to the earth, as well as most obviously between and within genders and sexualities—it may be that the structuring of so much cultural work and apperception around this impossible criterion represents a kind of residue or remainder of erotic relations to the male body, relations excluded from but sucked into supplementarity to the tacitly ethicized medical anthropomorphizations that have wielded so much power over our century.

That antisentimentality can never be an adequate Other for "the sentimental," but only a propellant for its contagious scissions and figurations, means that the sources of courage or comfort for our homophobically galvanized century will remain peculiarly vulnerable to the impossibility of the male first person, the unexpected bathos of the anthropomorphic—for those who wish, in the words W. H. Auden wrote in 1933,

> That later we, though parted then,
> May still recall these evenings when
>   Fear gave his watch no look;
> The lion griefs loped from the shade
> And on our knees their muzzles laid
>   And death put down his book.[50]

[50]From "Out on the lawn I lie in bed" (1933), pp. 29–32, *W. H. Auden: Selected Poems,* ed. Edward Mendelson (New York: Random House/Vintage. 1979); lines quoted are from p. 30. I encountered these lines, not reading Auden, but in the obituary listings in the *New York Times,* July 23, 1988, where someone had purchased space to reproduce them as an unsigned memorial to a man, who had died the previous day, named Nick Knowlden.

Wilde's Hard Labor and the Birth of Gay Reading

Wayne Koestenbaum

Gay reading as a critical term may seem indefensible. Potentially oppressive, it is attractive only if considered part of a reverse discourse, elective and not imposed. Since recent histories of sexuality have shown that gay identity evolved from classifying, medical, and legal impulses, I threaten to gild the lily of homosexuality's roots in punishment by invoking, in this essay, an interpretive community founded on desire for the same gender.[1] Embracing without thought of consequence the dominant culture's assumption that sexualities are, like social security numbers, valid nodes of power and control, I risk submitting to a dangerously comfortable essentialism—as if gayness transcended gender, class, race, nationality, or epoch.

Although the notion of a "gay reader" may be fraught, I want to construct such a reader. The interpretive position I describe may be occupied by a woman, but it is most historically precise to speak of it as a gay man's. By referring only to men, I oversimplify. And yet this urge to warp evidence to fit the perimeters of wish is itself part of my subject: I acquiesce to "camp," to the grand urge to make irresponsible claims in the name of a self that, dreading erasure, writes itself in too bold a hand. Exaggerated masquerade helps the drag queen invent "identity"; he broadcasts an imagined and essential self through luridness, paint, and posing. My description of a limited point of view—mine—as if it were universal, shares with the drag queen a taste for absolute gesture, a desire to wear socially constructed identities (showgirl, secretary, prostitute, diva) as if they were god-given and natural.

Male feminist criticism means to articulate maleness as strange, outcast, and impermissible; gayness *is* outcast, and so I may discuss my reading of Oscar Wilde without apologizing for its partiality. Hedging bets—"what I describe here applies only to a small group of privileged gay men"—capitulates to homophobia.

[1]See the several volumes of Michel Foucault's *History of Sexuality*, particularly *Volume I: An Introduction*, trans. Robert Hurley (New York: Random House, 1980). See also John D'Emilio, *Sexual Politics, Sexual Communities: The Making of a Homosexual Minority in the United States, 1940–1970* (Chicago: University of Chicago Press, 1983), and Jeffrey Weeks, *Sexuality and Its Discontents: Meanings, Myths, and Modern Sexualities* (London: Routledge & Kegan Paul, 1985).

Assuming the prerogatives of *écriture feminine*, I will map gay reading as if it were a continent, though it may be only a peninsula.

The (male twentieth-century first world) gay reader, like the female spectator, knows the rewards of looking from the outside in. He reads resistantly for inscriptions of his condition, for texts that will confirm a social and private identity founded on a desire for other men—an urge strong enough that it seems a vocation and defines him and his kind as a separate world. Reading becomes a hunt for histories that deliberately foreknow or unwittingly trace a desire felt not by author but by reader, who is most acute when searching for signs of himself.

Two critics have begun to describe such a reader. Roland Barthes, under the guise of methodology-as-eros (S/Z), asks what other gay critics have been shy to answer: are there undermining and refiguring styles of reading that have either an imagined or actual connection to gay desires?[2] And D. A. Miller, in *The Novel and the Police*, closes with an essay on *David Copperfield* that playfully gestures toward David Miller reading Dickens: the importance of being David.[3]

On the one hand, I am invoking something as pedestrian as gay male reader-response criticism. (How do specific gay men read? What difference does it make if we postulate a gay male reader?) On the other, more provocative hand, I am hypothesizing that there are connections between gay identity and prison (both are enclosures established by social codes) and that a certain kind of involved, implicated reader is a gay man in the prison of his identity: the way we read now, our hunger to place ourselves in texts, began, in part, with Oscar Wilde in Reading Caol, sentenced in 1895 to two years of "hard labour" for "gross indecency" with men. In the letter he wrote from prison to his lover, Lord Alfred Douglas (Bosie), "In Carcere et Vinculis" (posthumously titled *De Profundis*), and in the poem he wrote after release, "The Ballad of Reading Gaol," Wilde gestured toward such a gay male reader and suggested that "gay identity" is constructed through reading, although once it has been located on the page, it glows like an essence that already existed *before* a reader's glance brought it to life.

It is strange that Oscar Wilde, hardly addicted to eternal verities, invented an essentialist gay reader. Recent studies of Wilde by Ed Cohen, Jonathan Dollimore, and Regenia Gagnier, among others, have shown Wilde's detachment from the intrinsic paradisaical "nature" that thrilled André Gide; a gay Satan, radically reversing the dominant logos, Wilde was precursor to such postmodernists as Andy Warhol.[4] Wilde, like Warhol, understood publicity to be modern art's pre-

[2]Roland Barthes, *S/Z: An Essay*, trans. Richard Miller (New York: Farrar, Straus and Giroux, 1988).

[3]D. A. Miller, *The Novel and the Police* (Berkeley: University of California Press, 1988).

[4]See Ed Cohen, "Writing Gone Wilde: Homoerotic Desire in the Closet of Representation," *PMLA* 102, 5 (October 1987):801–13; Jonathan Dollimore, "Different Desires: Subjectivity and Transgression in Wilde and Gide," *Genders* 2 (July 1988):24–41; Regenia Gagnier, *Idylls of the Marketplace: Oscar Wilde and the Victorian Public* (Stanford: Stanford University Press, 1986). I have had the privilege of reading important unpublished work on Wilde and on gay theory by Christopher Craft, Bruce Hainley, Patrick Horrigan, Michael Lucey, and Eve Kosofsky Sedgwick; I am grateful, as well, to the students in my 1988 undergraduate seminar at Yale on gay and lesbian literature.

eminent genre and saw himself as part of a literary and cultural marketplace; he recognized that mechanical reproduction was the empowering, if sometimes disenfranchising, fact of his age. When art can be copied, writes Walter Benjamin, the "aura" of an original is lost. Wilde, however, reclaimed aura for gay purposes by redefining mechanical reproduction *as* aura and insisting that the copy bears the original's transcendence.[5] Dollimore argues that Wilde, in his prison writings, retreated from anti-essentialism into the quietism of earnestness; on the contrary, I claim that, in *De Profundis* and "The Ballad of Reading Gaol," Wilde posits an essential "gay identity" in order to develop gay writing and gay reading as reverse discourses.

Obsessed with copying, cannily undermining essences, Wilde entertained the glittering, seductive, and centerless play of surfaces and refused to take essences earnestly. Though he celebrated the aura's degradation, Wilde, in fact, did not pledge strict allegiance to the copy; his texts acknowledge their status as reproductions, but they also feign, or contain, an aura. And the aura that Wilde's prison writings hide, beneath the sparkle of the secondhand, the derivative, and the stereotyped, is a "gay" essence. Because his imprisonment created, in a suffering instant, modern gayness—enough so that homosexuals became, in E. M. Forster's memorable phrase, "unspeakables of the Oscar Wilde sort"[6]—Wilde in jail could hardly avoid the knowledge that his name had become, like an instantly memorable advertising logo for a new product, the aura of gayness.

Although the "gayness" in a text may be merely an illusion of essence, a trope, a reflection, not a tangibility, the reader's hunger for textual gayness *as if it were real* is no different than the longing of any reader in a world saturated with copies for the original. Wilde took seriously this longing and satisfied it. He invented a reader who finds palpable gayness by unearthing Wilde's spirit—his figure—from the text's letter. Though essentialist, this postulated "gay reader" never abandons historical knowledge, never forgets that an actual man, Oscar Wilde, did two years of hard labor in prison; this reader (whether holding a work of Wilde's or a later gay text) is always searching for "Oscar Wilde" as the origin of an imprisoned indecency that contemporary gay men must recognize as their own. Wilde justified his incarceration by imagining a new kind of elucidator/disciple, in love with him enough to accord his "nature"—his sexuality—the status of an essence. Wilde's imprisonment taught a century the costs of being gay; the letter he wrote in prison preaches the rewards of using gayness to form a reverse discourse based on reading, a *vita nuova* founded, ironically, on the very name of his jail.

[5]See Walter Benjamin, "The Work of Art in the Age of Mechanical Reproduction," in *Illuminations* (New York: Schocken Books, 1969), 217–52.
[6]E. M. Forster, *Maurice* (New York: W. W. Norton, 1987), 156.

De Profundis: *The Gaol of Reading*

De Profundis, like many novels, warns that tragedies come from misreading, miswriting, or mishandling letters; but Wilde's letter is unique among self-conscious epistles because its writer and its implied reader are gay. This document asks: what difference does one new term—*gay*—make in reading a letter?

The "you" supplicated and denounced in *De Profundis* is Bosie (Wilde's lover) and the reader of the posthumously published letter. Bosie was a specific recalcitrant gay reader. Wilde, addressing him, made him emblematic. The fact that gay identity was born from Wilde's trial forces us to take this scene of reading between Bosie and Wilde seriously and to generalize from Bosie's position to the stance of post-Wilde gay readers. According to *De Profundis*, the reader is a young, attractive, indolent boy implored to perform something—to address the writer. The reader is a traitor, a boy who has been intimate with a famous man and has abused that privilege.[7] Not every reader of *De Profundis* is a lazy, indifferent ephebe. But Bosie's silence seems representative: the gay reader as imagined by Wilde is a querulous wordless presence, a renegade disciple, a disloyal fan, whose lack of fealty and whose silence make the writer write.

Bosie's silence forces Wilde to compose:

> Dear Bosie,—After long and fruitless waiting I have determined to write to you myself, as much for your sake as for mine, as I would not like to think that I had passed through two long years of imprisonment without ever having received a single line from you, or any news or message even, except such as gave me pain.[8]

Wilde's entire miraculous *De Profundis* is an answer to an unwritten letter, to a desired text's absence—as if he were indirectly bemoaning the absence of a tradition of gay belle letters to which he can respond. Wilde sends his epistle into the void that precedes the invention of gay writing.

If Bosie's silence infuriates Wilde, the youth's greater sin is that he has *tried* to write: Bosie, whom Wilde calls "the true author of the hideous tragedy" (130), has dared to publish the elder man's private love letters in the *Mercure de France* and to dedicate a volume of verse to him. The gay reader projected by *De Profundis* hubristically overreaches and claims a writer's prerogatives. Overinterpreting, throwing himself, like the hysteric, too fully into what he reads, he crosses, without the writer's permission, the boundary between private and public; throughout the letter, Wilde anxiously repairs those veils of privacy that he spent his career methodically rending. He denounces Bosie's use of the "open postcard"—as if in response to the indignity of having letters read in court and seeing them treated

---

[7]This reader resembles Proust's Albertine. Wilde, like Marcel, turned fear of infidelity into a prose-engendering germ.

[8]Oscar Wilde, "De Profundis," in *De Profundis and Other Writings*, ed. Hesketh Pearson (Harmondsworth: Penguin, 1986), 97. Further references appear in my text.

not as mediated representations but as damning realities. Ronald Firbank composed his novels on postcards—an emblematic space for openly gay writing; unlike the closet of sealed envelopes, postcards preclude privacy. Wilde, jailed, regretted the exposed page that seemed to unincarcerated Firbank a source of play. *De Profundis* is unhappy to resemble a postcard, open to the censoring eyes of prison officials, and inscribed with the message "Wish you were here."

In prison, Wilde was permitted to read before he was permitted to write.[9] The book lists that he gave the gaol officials do more than document his longing for imaginative liberty. They confirm that reading, as an act of will and pleasure, may take writing's place and that certain styles of reading, performed under strict, punitive circumstances (whether the prison or the closet), *are* writing and counteract servitude. Wilde's prison reading stands for elucidations that take place inside the closet. It is fair to treat Reading Gaol as figurative as well as literal, for Wilde himself turned it into trope: "on the day of my release, I shall be merely passing from one prison into another."[10] Thus the paradigmatic gay reader sketched by *De Profundis* is not simply Bosie, but the imprisoned writer, reduced by jailkeepers to mere reading and learning to find in the reader's position the seeds of a finer disobedience. "Better than Wordsworth himself I know what Wordsworth meant" (152), says Wilde, and "if I may not write beautiful books, I may at least read beautiful books" (153). The fear that *De Profundis* will never reach its intended reader or that language itself is fated by its elusive differential nature never to span the distance between speaker and listener empowers one to read beautiful books but not write them and to read beauty into them—to read even an ugly book as if it were beautiful.

De Profundis separates into two tonalities. The first is manic and particular: Wilde recites Bosie's sins, and compiles a minute, exacting history of various letters—their transmission, receipt, and consequence. He spends much of *De Profundis* recounting "revolting and loathsome letters" (103), "no less loathsome letters" (105), "one of your most offensive letters" (107), "one of the violent letters you wrote to me on the point" (107), "some equally unpleasant telegrams" (108), "passionate telegrams" (111), "a most pathetic and charming letter" (119), "a letter of fantastic literary conceits" (121), "dreadful letters, abusive telegrams, and insulting postcards" (124). Wilde claims, in fact, that he was imprisoned as a result of writing Bosie a "charming letter" (120). These letters evoke the world of mechanical reproduction—of repetitions so painful and numbing that Wilde in prison faces a shadow "that wakes me up at night to tell me the same story over and over till its wearisome iteration makes all sleep abandon me till dawn: at dawn it begins again" (125). This reiterative Wilde is a prisoner who has stumbled, newly stereotyped as gay, into literature's bloody arena, uncertain what to say, uncertain who is listening—acknowledging, by his confusion, that being, or becoming, gay changes everything textual and makes letter-writing a different act.

[9]See Richard Ellmann, *Oscar Wilde* (New York: Knopf, 1988), 508–9.
[10]Quoted in Robert Ross, "Preface," in Oscar Wilde, *De Profundis* (London: Methuen, 1905), vii.

The second tonality is the blurred realm of the aura. Wilde compares himself to Christ and forgives Bosie. The two lovers hardly require letters because nothing separates them—as if Wilde's fanciful dictum "There was no difference at all between the lives of others and one's own life" (170) had come true. When the gap between writer and reader vanishes, so does the gap between word and meaning; Wilde seeks signs thoroughly drenched with their referents—like a divinity's words untranslated, "the actual terms, the *ipsissima verba*, used by Christ" (174). Wilde wants a reader, like an enamored fan, to winnow *De Profundis* for traces of the writer's original mark. His ideal gay reader is like Bette Davis' vulture/protégé, Eve Harrington, who, loving the star, ruins her. The Wildean gay reader is a fan who longs to sleep with the beloved writer and who reads in order to wear, figuratively, the author's outfits.

Towards the end of *De Profundis*, Wilde describes his own page as a body. Indeed, *De Profundis* is a scarified body, whose every bleeding wound the reader should suck for the ichor of the writer's aura. If the woman has been compared to the blank page,[11] then the Wildean gay male may be called a wounded, stabbed page—a St. Sebastian marked by arrows, redeemed by gaping gashes. (Affairs between United States congressmen and their adolescent male pages is a more recent instance of the word "page" bearing homoerotic freight.) Wilde, describing *De Profundis*, invites the reader-as-Bosie to enjoy the gashed male textual body:

> I cannot reconstruct my letter or rewrite it. You must take it as it stands, blotted in many places with tears, in some with the signs of passion or pain, and make it out as best you can, blots, corrections, and all. As for the corrections and errata, I have made them in order that my words should be an absolute expression of my thoughts, and err neither through surplusage nor through being inadequate. . . . As it stands, at any rate, my letter has its definite meaning behind every phrase. There is in it nothing of rhetoric. Whenever there is erasion or substitution, however slight, however elaborate, it is because I am seeking to render my real impression, to find for my mood its exact equivalent. Whatever is first in feeling comes away last in form. (197–98)

Wilde, describing the flawed, tear-smudged letter, asks for the reader's forgiveness, but knows that erasures and emendations attest to originality. No mere copy, the letter is an authentic prison document. Its blots are signs of aura that the reader should treasure as stigmata. Thus Wilde succumbs to or invents Pound's modernist poetics of absolute rhythm—where every phrase faithfully represents, in a one-to-one correspondence, some essential emotion.

But is the page the writer's body or the reader's? The letter's rheumy accuracy portrays not its writer, but Bosie, its reader: "if you have read this letter carefully as you should have done you have met yourself face to face" (197). The reader is invited to study *De Profundis* in order to see himself—his moral ugliness—more

---

[11]Susan Gubar, " 'The Blank Page' and the Issues of Female Creativity," in Elizabeth Abel, ed., *Writing and Sexual Difference* (Chicago: University of Chicago Press, 1982), 73–94.

clearly. The text as mirror is a portrait of the reader as a young man, and its true subject is the reader's body experiencing Wilde's white-hot mark:

> you will let the reading of this terrible letter—for such I know it is—prove to you as important a crisis and turning-point of your life as the writing of it is to me. Your pale face used to flush easily with wine or pleasure. If, as you read what is here written, it from time to time becomes scorched as though by a furnace blast, with shame, it will be all the better for you. (130)

The lacerated page is Bosie's body, licked by the flames of Wilde's faithful portraiture.

In sum, *De Profundis* is a liminal, revolutionary document, a primary invocation to a historically constituted gay reader; it is the first text that Wilde wrote after he had been publicly branded as gay and one of the first texts ever written with the knowledge that it would be seen as the work of an "exposed" gay man. *De Profundis*, though composed in a prison cell, is uncloseted. Handing over its no longer secret preference, it coins a new gesture: it asks to be read as a document of a gay man's position and supposes that its canniest reader will be gay. Written as a private letter destined to be published posthumously, the epistle's central, burning problematic is the obsolescent distinction between public and private, the regrettable death of the division between commercial and domestic, open postcard and sealed missive.

Privacy lost, Wilde is reduced to the anonymous status of a letter:

> I myself, at that time, had no name at all. In the great prison where I was then incarcerated, I was merely the figure and *letter* of a little cell in a long gallery; one of a thousand lifeless numbers, as of a thousand lifeless lives. (136; emphasis added)

A letter is a private communication between writer and reader. But it is also a piece of alphabet—an *A*, for example, as in *The Scarlet Letter,* where *letter* implied, as it did for Wilde, a stigma, a fixed, blazoned identity, legible to strangers. Every reader of Wilde necessarily accuses him, remarks his sin. But the gay reader, himself scarlet, sees that the scarlet *A* means something other than its proscribed, punitive denotation.

When placed beside *figure, letter* refers to literality—the letter of the law. The question of letter in *De Profundis* is, finally, how literally we should take Bosie: Wilde's angry invocation to his lover is the document's loudest rhetorical gesture, and yet is the letter solely directed at the real, historical boyfriend? Isn't Bosie simply the disobedient lacuna where the post-Wilde gay reader finds himself—a reader who exists, in the first place, *because* a typology of homosexuality arose from Wilde's trial? *Letter* also denotes a bit of typeface, used to print. *De Profundis* balances the two meanings of *letter*—a communication between writer and reader, and a puncturing, imprinting fragment of typeface that can replicate itself, that generates unoriginal and inauthentic copies, but that has the power to wound the reader's conscience by reminding him of his own essential nature.

The Reproduction of Wilde's Prison Writings

Wilde gave fetishistic attention to the typing, printing, and publication of "The Ballad of Reading Gaol" and *De Profundis*. His fastidious, mannered interest in surface as opposed to depth seems to contradict my claim that certain texts possess gay "essences" that a reader can intuit and interpret. However, I would argue that Wilde's self-conscious commodification of his prison experience deepens, rather than flattens, the figure of his suffering. Attention to type, to publication, to the mechanics of a letter's spread, to language as a series of differences drifting away from a phantasmal source, needn't drain "life" from the image or negate an essential "gay identity." By commodifying his prison experience, Wilde tried to perpetuate, through the mechanics of modern publicity and publication, "imprisoned homosexuality" as an essential identity. "Gay reading" can live inside the copy as if it were the original because it has the knack of finding nature or essence within the copy reproduced unnaturally, by cloning.

Clone, a disparaging term for muscled gay men who dress and groom themselves stereotypically, signifies a mechanically reproduced masculinity inhabited as if it were real. One can acquire reality only by faking it. Men can acquire masculinity only by mimicking it. Because the word *clone* evokes laboratories, it also subtly derides a gay male's nonprocreative sexuality; it defines homosexuality as replication of the same. Gay men may father children, but homosexuality has often seemed equal to mechanical, not sexual, reproduction. Against this assumption that gay men are, at best, Petri dishes, gay criticism needs to develop a theory of typing or copying that wipes the tarnish off clones. Mechanical reproduction is *not* second-rate: there is nothing wrong with becoming a clone, wanting to be famous for fifteen minutes, striving to be sexy through mimicry, or commodifying one's life, body, and work. To consider replication degrading is, literally, homophobic: *afraid of the same*. If the patriarchal male pen is, figuratively, a fertilizing penis, let us enjoy the fact that the gay male instrument of textual dissemination may well be a xerox machine—or, in Wilde's time, a typewriter.

Indeed, *type* refers both to typeface and, in French, to a guy, a chap, a fellow. How do guys resemble typeface? When a man looks like a man, he possesses a reproducible, imitable essence of "maleness." Wilde, aware of masculinity and language as replicable properties, was obsessed with the word *type*. In his dialogue "The Decay of Lying," he wrote that "a great artist invents a type, and Life tries to copy it, to reproduce it in a popular form, like an enterprising publisher."[12] In *De Profundis*, Wilde describes Christ as having "the essentials of the supreme romantic type" (176) and condemns Lord Alfred Douglas as "a very complete specimen of a very modern type" (198); further, he admonishes Bosie, "you had better quote from it. It is set up in type" (209). Of course, Wilde was "stereo*typed*" (105) as a homosexual, and even described himself as "a specially typical example" of degen-

---

[12]Oscar Wilde, "The Decay of Lying," in Wilde, *De Profundis*, 74.

eration's "fatal law."[13] Wilde was content to be a type of the homosexual not because he enjoyed being stigmatized, but because he wished to puncture the future, to influence.[14]

To print successfully, moveable type must be, like Wilde's sexuality, inverted: the *Chicago Manual of Style* defines *type* as "individual bits of metal with the images of letters cast in reverse on their ends."[15] Letters, like *De Profundis*, have most hope of influencing when they come from reversal (of fortune, of sexual preference). Type makes impressions on a page: it is striking that Wilde should have titled several poems "Impressions" and that, after his death, Robert Ross should have remarked that "Wilde left curiously different impressions on professing judges."[16] Wilde's concern with "type" conceals a skewed query into the etiology of homosexuality (is it imprinted or chosen?) and the radical claim that one typesets, as it were, the page of one's own psyche.

With "The Ballad of Reading Gaol," Wilde monitored exactness and density of type and complained particularly about the weak impression made by his pseudonym, "C.3.3." Leonard Smithers, the publisher, wrote to Wilde:

> It has been a somewhat awkward title page to set with satisfaction, and even now, owing to the lightness of the impression of the "C.3.3." it does not look perfectly satisfactory. But this will be set quite right when the sheet is properly made ready for the press, which is a matter which takes several hours careful coaxing of the type to accomplish properly.[17]

Wilde was equally fastidious about the copying and typing of *De Profundis*. Exclaiming that Ross "must read it carefully and *copy it out carefully every word* for me," he longed to see the work typed.[18] Giving Ross the manuscript, Wilde was particular about the typewriter as the crucible through which this text must pass: "the only thing to do is to be thoroughly modern and have it typewritten."[19] Wilde mockingly described the typewriter as feminine: "I assure you that the typewriting machine, when played with expression, is not more annoying than the piano when played by a sister or near relation. Indeed many among those most devoted to domesticity prefer it."[20] It is significant that Wilde should call for a woman—and a modern contraption associated with female labor—to commit to print his messianic message. Homosexuality, in its earlier incarnation as sodomy, implied an

---

[13]Oscar Wilde's petition, written in Reading Gaol, to the Secretary of State for the Home Department; quoted in H. Montgomery Hyde, *Oscar Wilde: The Aftermath* (London: Methuen, 1963), 71.

[14]Typing—defined as the ability to make a fatal impression on a lover or on the next generation—resembles the poetics of infection that dominates homophobic constructions of AIDS: sexual magnetism as a contagion.

[15]*The Chicago Manual of Style*, 13th ed. (Chicago: University of Chicago Press, 1982), 587.

[16]Robert Ross, "Preface," ix.

[17]Quoted in Hyde, *Oscar Wilde*, 173.

[18]Ibid., 89.

[19]Quoted in ibid., 90.

[20]Quoted in ibid., 90.

alienation from procreative sex; and yet Wilde was a father, although he lost title to his children and to his literary estate while in prison. Oddly, his son, Vyvyan Holland, whom we might call an original and not a mechanically reproduced impression, became the custodian of what he terms "the original (if I may so call it) carbon copy" of *De Profundis*.[21] Wilde's son, Vyvyan, continues his father's struggle, through *De Profundis*, to redefine the meaning of reproduction. Even Wilde's punishment—called "hard labour" by the law—conceals a verdict on the relationship between homosexuality and reproduction. Parliament effected a pun: Wilde's labor gave birth to nothing. His punishment, which was literally oakum-picking, seems a metaphor for capitalism's alienated labor, for modern publication (mechanical reproduction), and for the "barrenness" of gay sex.

De Profundis invents a gay reader berated by the text into equivalence with the writer; appropriately, Wilde's contemporaries considered it a durance to read his prison works. Editions of "The Ballad of Reading Gaol" depicted the book as a jail. The leather cover of a 1937 limited edition reproduced a prison wall, down to the grilled window; a 1907 American edition, on its cover, invited the public to "Read the Greatest Tragical Poem in Literature," as if of first importance were not the poem itself but the reader's entrance into its imprisoning magnitude. This cover's mysterious insignia—a spirit lamp—implied that reading the poem might magically bring Wilde back.[22] When in 1907 Doubleday advertised its "Patrons' Edition De Luxe of Oscar Wilde," it lured the reader into an even more punitive proximity to the text: "Your name will be beautifully engrossed on the title page of the first volume of the set you own . . . To be identified with one's books has always been the truest mark of the book-lover. . . . It associates one more closely with the Masters one loves."[23] Reading a beloved author's books, one is pressed, like Bosie, into typeface, name sadistically "engrossed" on the book's cover—as in Kafka's story "In the Penal Colony," where letters are written on the prisoner's flesh. Wilde, angry that Bosie dedicated a book to him, understood that being tattooed on another man's page could be torment. Doubleday's 1907 edition pursues suggestions made by *De Profundis* itself—that the reader is no ordinary passive spectator, but a disciple whose body must sympathetically take on the writer's pains.

When parts of *De Profundis* were published after Wilde's death, readers fell under the spell of a man who seemed legibly alive. His readers obeyed the logic of "type," of cloning: they felt compelled to read Wilde twice. Laurence Housman wrote of *De Profundis*, "I read it once with great and almost entire admiration, and am now reading it again."[24] This repetition was exactly what Wilde, in the letter, demanded of Bosie: "you must read this letter right through,"

[21]Vyvyan Holland, "Introduction," in Wilde, *De Profundis and Other Writings*, 91.

[22]Abraham Horodisch, *Oscar Wilde's "Ballad of Reading Gaol": A Bibliographic Study* (New York: Aldus, 1954), 84, 59.

[23]"The Story of Oscar Wilde," Advertising brochure for the Patrons' Edition De Luxe of Oscar Wilde (New York: Doubleday, Page).

[24]Karl Beckson, ed., *Oscar Wilde: The Critical Heritage* (London: Routledge & Kegan Paul, 1970), 243.

must "read the letter over and over again till it kills your vanity" (97–98). A reviewer in the *Times Literary Supplement* commented that "everything which Wilde says of Christ in this little book is worth reading and considering and reading again."[25] By reading Wilde twice, readers engineered his resurrection: according to one reviewer, Wilde was a "revisiting shade of immortal Glamour" that fell "athwart every part of the poem."[26] Wilde's shade appeared to the automatic writer and medium Hester Travers Smith, who recorded Wilde's after-death pronouncements in her book, *Oscar Wilde from Purgatory*, and even André Gide was visited by the dead master in seances.[27] A homophobic reviewer of *De Profundis*, who commented "I refuse to forget that [Wilde] is most fearfully alive,"[28] inadvertently revealed that modern gayness may be defined as Wilde's posthumous persistence, and that the gay reader is constituted by the prison of *imitatio Oscar*—by the compulsion to fill Wilde's shoes. Leonard Smithers, first publisher of the "Ballad," continued until 1907 (seven years after Wilde's death) to use the date 1899 for new printings of the poem[29]—evading a new copyright and century, maintaining Wilde's perpetual presence, and feigning that every copy, further removed from Wilde's living, tear-stained page, retained some intrinsic connection to the original. But Wilde understood that cloning—mechanical reproduction—was useful to gay identity. When a difficult, new, rarefied, illegal pleasure repeatedly appears, it grows familiar; it enters the dictionary. Reading a copy of "The Ballad of Reading Gaol" is like caressing a saint's bone and feeling it to be the calcified origin of one's own seemingly immutable "gay identity"—rock-hard, contingent, textual.

"The Ballad of Reading Gaol": The Interpreted Cock

The gay reader is not merely a responder to printed matter. He is a commiserator. In Wilde's "The Ballad of Reading Gaol," the last thing he wrote for publication, there are two criminals. One is Wilde, in prison. He speaks of himself infrequently: "And I trembled as I groped my way/Into my numbered tomb."[30] He usually reverts to the plural ("We sewed the sacks, we broke the stones,/We turned the dusty drill" [238]), a "we" of prisoners united by the oppression of repetitive tasks and by a shared discursive position: they are each remonstrated to feel empathy with a greater, more emblematic criminal in their midst—a Christlike "He," whose execution they mourn. (This "He" is a man Wilde saw executed in Reading Gaol—Charles Thomas Wooldridge, who had murdered his wife, slitting her

[25]Ibid., 247.

[26]Ibid., 222.

[27]Hester Travers Smith, *Oscar Wilde From Purgatory* (New York: Henry Holt, no date), 97.

[28]*Oscar Wilde: The Critical Heritage*, 322.

[29]See Horodisch, *Oscar Wilde's "Ballad of Reading Gaol,"* 14.

[30]"The Ballad of Reading Gaol," in Wilde, *De Profundis and Other Writings*, 239. Page numbers will appear in my text.

throat three times.[31] Does a pact between gay male writer and reader depend on erasing the slain wife and justifying her death? Women are missing from my paradigm of gay male reading. Has something actual and feminine been figuratively slain to make room for this bucolic practice of gay male interpretation? Or is this parenthetical shudder homophobic?) If Wilde is the first criminal, the second is C. T. W., to whom the Ballad is dedicated. As Wilde mourns C. T. W., we, reading the poem, mourn Wilde, our greatest "He." Thus the poem does for gay community what a mass does for Christendom: it enacts, in little, the spectacle that started the "church." "God's son died for all" (247): Wilde died for the sins of us outcast men. Gay community begins around the vicarious experience of a Passion: the reader becomes gay—joins a community of outcast men—by reading Wilde, as Wilde became gay by commiserating with C. T. W. Cloned, the reader is remade in the image of the convict's type; cloning is not a lonely experience, because confessing outcast status enfolds one in a nation of others who are also like Wilde.

Reading the poem, we cross the space between ourselves and Wilde, as Wilde, commiserating, closed the gap between himself and C. T. W. The poem's subject is the distance between two outcast men, Wilde and the reader, who collide by crossing: "Like two doomed ships that pass in storm/We had crossed each other's way" (236). Wilde and the reader, after all, are alike: "A prison wall was round us both,/Two outcast men we were" (236). Both reader and writer are potentially criminals: "Yet each man kills the thing he loves,/By each let this be heard" (232). The words on Wilde's grave at Père-Lachaisse come from the "Ballad":

> And alien tears will fill for him
> > Pity's long-broken urn,
> For his mourners will be outcast men,
> > And outcasts always mourn. (248)

These lines predict the constituency of mourners who will arrive there and read the memorial as a mirror; this inscription projects gay identity forming around Wilde's emblematic imprisonment. The chiasmus in the lines "For his *mourners* will be *outcast* men,/And *outcasts* always *mourn*"—the way that the two words, *mourners* and *outcasts*, change relative places from one line to the next—further reflects gay identity's formation. The outcast identity grows to be independent of and prior to the act of mourning that originally constituted it: reading Wilde's grave creates a gay subjectivity empowered to read the grave. This chiasmus is the *cross* on which Wilde expired, a Calvary. Post-Wilde gay readers discover they are gay as if it were a fact already there, when it is precisely their mourning of Wilde, their acknowledgment of a likeness, that guides them toward that identity.

The verb *read* is a homonym for the color *red*, a word prominent in the Ballad. The poem's title, "The Ballad of *Reading* Gaol," underscores, by macabre exploited coincidence, this homonym, which conflates Christ's blood, communion wine, Wilde's suffering in Reading Gaol, and our reading of the poem. The poem

[31]Ellmann, *Oscar Wilde*, 503–4.

plays with the word: "For none of us can tell to what *red* Hell/His sightless soul may stray" (236); "He did not wear his scarlet coat,/For blood and wine are *red*" (231); "He does not bend his head to hear/The Burial Office *read*" (233); "The grey cock crew, the *red* cock crew,/But never came the day" (240); "God's dreadful dawn was *red*" (242); "In *Reading* Gaol by *Reading* Town/There is a pit of shame" (252). The two meanings, red and read, most palpably intersect here: "The man in *red* who *reads* the Law" (251). Does the man who reads the Law write it, too, or just absently intone what another man has decreed? Wilde discovers the possibility of reading the Law against itself—through reading, opening up a rift within the Law and finding a sexual surprise.[32]

The surprise is Wilde's resurrection: the persistence of his reputation and of the homosexual "type" molded in his image.

> For three long years they will not sow
>   Or root or seedling there:
> For three long years the unblessed spot
>   Will sterile be and bare,
> And look upon the wondering sky
>   With unreproachful stare. (246)

For a mythic three years (Christ died at 33, and Wilde was prisoner C.3.3.), no signs of him will appear above his outcast grave; his legacy will be "sterile"—unreproductive. But then, he predicts his own return; he imagines his revarnished reputation, as well as a new self-designation arising—the ability to choose "outcast" as a pleasing identity. With a new identity comes a new language, an eccentric prison argot at which "the Ballad" marvels:

> I never saw a man who looked
>   With such a wistful eye
> Upon that little tent of blue
>   Which prisoners call the sky . . . (231)

Prisoners, as if perversely, affix the word *sky* to a paltry tent of *blue*—a word infused, at the turn of the century, with gay meanings;[33] outcast men name the objects of their world unconventionally, and it is Wilde's fall and hard labor that gave birth to this new, potentially enfranchising, lexicon.

Here, Wilde describes the "reading" that will sprout from his fall, making it, like Satan's in *Paradise Lost*, fortunate:

> Out of his mouth a red, red rose!
>   Out of his heart a white!
> For who can say by what strange way,

---

[32]The *red* room, in which Charlotte Brontë's Jane Eyre is locked for hitting John *Reed* over the head when he forbade her to *read* one of his books is another exemplary conflation of redness and reading.

[33]See John Addington Symonds, *In the Key of Blue and Other Prose Essays* (London: Elkin Mathews, 1893).

> Christ brings His will to light,
> Since the barren staff the pilgrim bore
> Bloomed in the great Pope's sight? (246–47)

Reading arose: the rose that comes out of his mouth is red, and we must read it. What rises from Wilde's mouth, from Wilde's work, is the possibility of a barren typology—"homosexual"—bringing about new ways of assigning meaning. In *De Profundis*, Wilde said that "everything to be true must become a religion" (154). For gayness to be more than a mere lifestyle or recreational choice—for it to be an encyclopedia, a geography, a wealth of routes and signs—it must acknowledge its own capacious interpretive mannerisms as more than manner, as matter; it must recognize that gay men, at least since Wilde, have known themselves through mourning and cloning—noting a likeness between the plights of two outcasts. Outcast identity is particularly incarcerating, but any identity is a prison—an enclosure, whether fashion or flesh, over which we have little control, but that helps us to read.

I dwell on "reading," of course, because I am a literary critic—interested in styles of interpretation that accommodate readers like myself. My glance at Wilde in Reading Gaol takes place within the limited frame of a revisionary literary critical project. But reading is more than a private traffic with printed matter. It is an engagement, achieved through the imagination, across a distance; a tightly knit affair between a speaker and a listener; a survivor's gesture of reconnaissance and affection toward the past. Reading is mourning—a community forming around a likeness, around a death or a fall. In "The Ballad," Wilde wrote, "The red cock crew": he meant that the cock was red. But I mean something else: the read cock. The cock is Wilde's. And we must interpret it; we must try to read what his cock cries. The read cock—the interpreted penis—elucidated desire—*gay identity as Wilde imagined it*—is something worth reading, interpreting, inventing. If Wilde did not write it, let us write it for him.

Phrases and Philosophies for the Use of the Young

Oscar Wilde

The first duty in life is to be as artificial as possible.

What the second duty is no one has as yet discovered.

Wickedness is a myth invented by good people to account for the curious attractiveness of others.

If the poor only had profiles there would be no difficulty in solving the problem of poverty.

Those who see any difference between soul and body have neither.

A really well-made buttonhole is the only link between Art and Nature.

Religions die when they are proved to be true. Science is the record of dead religions.

The well-bred contradict other people. The wise contradict themselves.

Nothing that actually occurs is of the smallest importance.

Dullness is the coming of age of seriousness.

In all unimportant matters, style, not sincerity, is the essential. In all important matters, style, not sincerity, is the essential.

If one tells the truth, one is sure, sooner or later, to be found out.

Pleasure is the only thing one should live for. Nothing ages like happiness.

It is only by not paying one's bills that one can hope to live in the memory of the commercial classes.

No crime is vulgar, but all vulgarity is crime. Vulgarity is the conduct of others.

Only the shallow know themselves.

Time is a waste of money.

One should always be a little improbable.

There is a fatality about all good resolutions. They are invariably made too soon.

The only way to atone for being occasionally a little overdressed is by being always absolutely over-educated.

To be premature is to be perfect.

Any preoccupation with ideas of what is right or wrong in conduct shows an arrested intellectual development.

Ambition is the last refuge of the failure.

First published in *Chameleon* I: 1 (December, 1894), pp. 1–3.

A truth ceases to be true when more than one person believes in it.

In examinations the foolish ask questions that the wise cannot answer.

Greek dress was in its essence inartistic. Nothing should reveal the body but the body.

One should either be a work of art, or wear a work of art.

It is only the superficial qualities that last. Man's deeper nature is soon found out.

Industry is the root of all ugliness.

The ages live in history through their anachronisms.

It is only the gods who taste of death. Apollo has passed away, but Hyacinth, whom men say he slew, lives on. Nero and Narcissus are always with us.

The old believe everything: the middle-aged suspect everything: the young know everything.

The condition of perfection is idleness: the aim of perfection is youth.

Only the great masters of style ever succeed in being obscure.

There is something tragic about the enormous number of young men there are in England at the present moment who start life with perfect profiles, and end by adopting some useful profession.

To love oneself is the beginning of a life-long romance.

Chronology of Important Dates

1854   Oscar Fingal O'Flahertie Wills Wilde born in Dublin, to William Wilde, an eminent eye-and-ear specialist, and Jane Francesca Wilde, a prolific writer and ardent Irish nationalist who adopted the nom-de-plume of "Speranza."

1864   Speranza sued by a young woman named Mary Travers for libel for denying that Sir William had made sexual advances to her; Lady Wilde loses suit but Travers awarded damages of only a farthing.

1871   Wilde attends Trinity College, Dublin.

1874–78   Enters Magdalen College, Oxford. He leaves with a First in Classics and Litterae Humaniores; wins Newdigate Prize for poetry.

1878–81   Wilde an extravagant presence in London. DuMaurier's *Punch* cartoons lampoon Wilde as "Maudle"; farces staged on the West End parodying Wilde and other aesthetes.

1881   *Poems* published, to a decidedly mixed critical reception. Gilbert and Sullivan's *Patience* premiers, featuring parodies of major aesthetes, including Wilde.

1881–82   Tours America, lecturing on aestheticism, interior design, and himself.

1883   *Vera, or the Nihilists* staged in New York by Marie Prescott; received indifferently. Wilde tours England, lecturing on his lecture tour in America.

1884   Marries Constance Lloyd.

1885–86   Two sons, Cyril and Vyvyan, born to the Wildes.

1886   The year, according to some biographers, of Wilde's first consummated affair with a man, Robert Ross.

1887–89   Takes employment as editor of a fashion journal, *The Women's World*. Begins to publish criticism and fiction in periodical press.

1891   Publishes *The Picture of Dorian Gray* and *Intentions*, a collection of his critical prose. *Dorian* becomes a best-seller and an object of frenzied critical attention as well. Writes *Salomé* and *Lady Windermere's Fan*.

1892   *Lady Windermere's Fan* opens in London, a spectacular success. Meets and begins affair with Lord Alfred Douglas, then a student at Oxford; liaisons as well with young men in London, many of whom blackmail Wilde. Production of *Salomé* planned with Sarah Bernhardt in title role but refused license by Lord Chamberlain's office.

1893–94   *Salomé* published; *A Woman of No Importance* opens in London. Wilde
           spends most of the year with Douglas, the two becoming increasingly indis-
           creet.

1895   *An Ideal Husband* and *The Importance of Being Earnest* open. Wilde con-
           fronted by Douglas's father, the Marquis of Queensbury. Wilde sues
           Queensbury for libel; the defense produces a number of young men with
           whom Wilde had affairs. Wilde immediately arrested for violating antisodomy
           laws and, after two trials, convicted.

1895–97   Two years of hard labor at Pentonville and Reading jails; Wilde's suffering,
           both physical and emotional, is immense. Late in his imprisonment, he writes
           a series of letters to Douglas retelling and meditating on their affair, published
           after his death as *De Profundis*.

1897–1900 After a reconciliation with Douglas and a final separation from Constance—
           who died in 1898—Wilde wanders the Continent, frequently assuming the
           name of Sebastian Melmoth. He writes and publishes *The Ballad of Reading
           Gaol*, another popular success. In Paris, late in 1900, Wilde mysteriously sick-
           ens and quickly dies.

Bibliography

It is fitting that Wilde—prophet of the life as text and of the text as forgery—engenders countless novels and biographies while he awaits a standard scholarly edition of his multiply published, and frequently revised, works. (That edition is due later in the decade.) Two estimable but incomplete editions of Wilde's works are currently available: one edited by Wilde's faithful friend (and, perhaps, first male lover) Robert Ross dates to 1908 and the other, edited by G. F. Maine, was issued in 1945. As far as individual anthologies are concerned, the best are Isobel Murray's *Oscar Wilde* in the Oxford Standard Author's series (1989) and Richard Ellmann's Bantam anthology *The Picture of Dorian Gray and Other Writings* (1982), which includes an introduction by Ellmann, his translation of *Salomé*, and texts of some of the lesser-known plays as well as better known works like *Dorian* and *The Ballad of Reading Gaol*. A number of bibliographies devoted to Wilde are also available: one from Stuart Mason [Christopher Millard] in 1914; one from E. H. Mikhail from 1978; and, most recently, Ian Small's *Oscar Wilde Revalued* (1992), to which I have been much indebted in the production of this anthology.

Wilde's life has produced in its turn any number of reflections, reifications, and responses, some of which even correspond to the facts. Overtly fictional responses begin early and often, from Wilde's own versions of his life (as early as the lectures in America, as late as *De Profundis*) to the contemporary responses of Du Maurier and Gilbert and Sullivan to Frank Harris's posthumous admixture of biographical fact, fantasy, and fiction. More recently, Peter Ackroyd has given us a novel called *The Last Testament of Oscar Wilde* (1983) and Terry Eagleton a play entitled *Saint Oscar* (1989): As their titles suggest, both help promulgate the Wilde-as-martyr fiction that Wilde himself did so much to shape.

The set of fictions that was Wilde's life has been treated by numerous biographies, the most important of which are H. Montgomery Hyde's several volumes (and his compilation of the trial transcripts) and Richard Ellmann's *Oscar Wilde*. Ellmann's biography has not been without its detractors—critics have taken issue on its lack of sensitivity to gay identity politics and its hypothesis that Wilde's physical suffering in life and early death were due to syphillis contracted at Oxford—but it remains the best single biography. More recently, Gary Schmidgall's *The*

Stranger Wilde has reinterpreted Wilde's life from the point of view of his identity as a gay man; polemical and at times shrewd, it is also a bit monochromatic. Far more challenging as a gay male reading of Wilde's life and cultural moment—as well as one that poignantly reflects on the author's stake in this act of literary affiliation—is Neil Bartlett's *Who Was That Man?*

Contemporary critical responses can be found in Karl Beckson's *Critical Heritage* volume. The full entry of Wilde into the canon of literary studies begins with Frank Kermode's *Romantic Image* and Graham Hough's *The Last Romantics*, both of which, however, thoroughly marginalize him. Fine new critical accounts of Wilde's work can be found in Barbara Charlesworth, *Dark Passages;* Epifanio San Juan, *The Art of Oscar Wilde;* and Christopher Nassar, *Into the Demon Universe.* Wilde scholarship owes a substantial debt to Ellmann's critical as well as biographical works; particularly noteworthy is "Overtures to *Salomé*," reprinted in his 1969 anthology, which places Wilde in the context of Oxford aestheticism.

Wilde scholarship in subsequent years has focused powerfully on the question of Wilde's relations, both parodistic and occasionally plagiaristic, with his literary and cultural sources: see especially Kerry Powell's *Oscar Wilde and the Theater of the 1890s.* In the 1980s, Wilde studies entered a different phase with a stress on the relation between the literary and the cultural and economic; the works of Rachel Bowlby, Jonathan Freedman, and Regenia Gagnier center on this problematic. But the most prodigious critical production on Wilde has centered on the questions surrounding his sexuality: The works of Ed Cohen and Eve Kosofsky Sedgwick are perhaps the best examples of these, installing Wilde at the center of a burgeoning inquiry into "queer theory" as well as in the midst of inquiries into aestheticism, consumerism, theatricality, and representation. Which is to say that Wilde remains exactly where he always wanted to be: at the crossroads of thought, speculation, and hope.

ACKROYD, PETER. *The Last Testament of Oscar Wilde.* New York: Harper and Row, 1983.

BARTLETT, NEIL. *Who Was That Man? A Present for Mr. Oscar Wilde.* London: Serpent's Tail, 1988.

BECKSON, KARL. *Oscar Wilde: The Critical Heritage.* London: Routledge and Kegan Paul, 1970.

BUCKLEY, JEROME. "Echo and Artifice: The Poetry of Oscar Wilde," *Victorian Poetry*, 28 (1990), 19–31.

BUCKNELL, BRAD. *"On 'Seeing' Salomé." ELH*, 60 (Summer, 1993), 503–26.

COHEN, ED. *Writing Gone Wilde.* London: Routledge, 1992.

CRAFT, CHRISTOPHER. "Alias Bunbury: Desire and Termination in *The Importance of Being Earnest*," *Representations*, 31 (1990), 19–46.

DELLAMORA, RICHARD. *Masculine Desire: The Sexual Politics of Victorian Aestheticism.* Chapel Hill: University of North Carolina Press, 1990.

DOLLIMORE, JONATHAN. *Sexual Dissidence: Augustine to Wilde, Freud to Foucault.* Oxford: Clarendon Press, 1991.

DOWLING, LINDA. *Language and Decadence in the Victorian Fin de Siècle.* Princeton: Princeton University Press, 1986.

EAGLETON, TERRY. *Saint Oscar.* Lawrence Hill, Derry: Field Day, 1989.

EDELMAN, LEE. "Homographesis," *The Yale Journal of Criticism,* 3 (1989), 189–207.

ELLMANN RICHARD. *Oscar Wilde.* New York: Alfred A. Knopf, 1987.

———. *Oscar Wilde: A Collection of Critical Essays.* Englewood Cliffs, NJ: Prentice Hall, 1969; 1986.

FELSKI, RITA. "The Counterdiscourse of the Feminine in Three Texts by Wilde, Huysmans, and Sacher-Masoch," *PMLA,* 106 (Oct. 1991), 1094–1105.

FREEDMAN, JONATHAN. *Professions of Taste: Henry James, British Aestheticism, and Commodity Culture.* Stanford: Stanford University Press, 1990.

GAGNIER, REGENIA. *Idylls of the Marketplace: Oscar Wilde and the Victorian Public.* Stanford: Stanford University Press, 1986.

———, ed. *Critical Essays on Oscar Wilde.* New York: Twayne, 1991.

GELPI, BARBARA CHARLESWORTH. *Dark Passages: The Decadent Consciousness in Victorian Literature.* Madison: University of Wisconsin Press, 1965.

GILBERT, ELIOT. " 'Tumult of Images': Wilde, Beardsley, and *Salomé,*" *Victorian Studies,* 26 (2), 133–59.

GOODMAN, JONATHAN, ed. *The Oscar Wilde File.* London: Allison, 1989.

HARRIS, WENDELL. "Arnold, Pater, Wilde, and the Object as in Themselves They See It," *Studies in English Literature,* 11 (1971), 733–47.

HOUGH, GRAHAM. *The Last Romantics.* London: Duckworth, 1949.

HYDE, H. MONTGOMERY, ed. *The Trials of Oscar Wilde.* London: Hodge, 1948.

———. *Oscar Wilde.* New York: Farrar, Strauss, and Giroux, 1975.

———. *Oscar Wilde: The Aftermath.* London: Methuen, 1963.

JACKSON, HOLBROOK. *The Eighteen Nineties: A Review of Art and Ideas at the Close of the Nineteenth Century.* London: Grant Richards, 1913.

JOSEPH, GERHARD. "Framing Wilde," *Victorian Newsletter,* 72 (1987), 61–63.

KERMODE, FRANK. *Romantic Image.* London: Routledge and Kegan Paul, 1957.

LEWIS, LLOYD, AND HENRY JUSTIN SMITH. *Oscar Wilde Discovers America*. New York: Harcourt Brace and Co., 1936.

LONGXI, ZHANG. "The Critical Legacy of Oscar Wilde," *Texas Studies in Language and Literature*, 30 (1988), 87–103.

MASON, STUART [CHRISTOPHER MILLARD]. *Bibliography of Oscar Wilde*. London, 1914.

MIKHAIL, E. H. *Oscar Wilde: An Annotated Bibliography of Criticism*, London: Macmillan, 1978.

———. *Oscar Wilde: Interviews and Recollections*. 2 vols. London: Macmillan, 1979.

MOERS, ELLEN. *The Dandy: Brummel to Beerbohm*. Lincoln: University of Nebraska Press, 1960.

NASSAR, CHRISTOPHER. *Into the Demon Universe: A Literary Exploration of Oscar Wilde*. New Haven: Yale University Press, 1974.

PAGLIA, CAMILLE. "Oscar Wilde and the English Epicene," *Raritan*, 4 (1985), 85–109.

POWELL, KERRY. *Oscar Wilde and the Theater of the 1890s*. Cambridge: Cambridge University Press, 1990.

RIEFF, PHILIP. "The Impossible Culture: Wilde as a Modern Prophet," *Salmagundi*, 58 (1983), 406–26.

SAN JUAN, EPIFANIO. *The Art of Oscar Wilde*. Princeton: Princeton University Press, 1967.

SCHMIDGALL, GARY. *The Stranger Wilde: Interpreting Oscar*. New York: Dutton, 1994.

SEDGWICK, EVE KOSOFSKY. *Between Men: English Literature and Male Homosocial Desire*. New York: Columbia University Press, 1986.

SMALL, IAN. *Conditions for Criticism: Authority Knowledge, and Literature in the Late Nineteenth Century*. Oxford: Clarendon Press, 1991.

———. *Oscar Wilde Revalued: An Essay on New Materials and Methods of Research*. Greensboro, NC: ELT Press, 1993.

STOKES, JOHN. *In the Nineties*. London: Harvester-Wheatsheaf, 1990.

WORTH, KATHARINE. *The Irish Drama of Europe from Yeats to Beckett*. London: Athlone Press, 1978.

Notes on Contributors

RACHEL BOWLBY is a Reader in English Literature at Sussex University in Great Britain. She is the author of *Just Looking: Consumer Culture in Dreiser, Gissing, and Zola, Shopping with Freud,* and *Still Crazy After All These Years: Women Writers and Psychoanalysis.*

ED COHEN teaches English at the University of Pittsburgh. He is the author of *Talk on the Wilde Side: Toward a Genealogy of a Discourse on Male Sexuality.*

LAWRENCE DANSON is a Professor of English at Princeton University. He is the author of *Tragic Alphabet: Shakespeare's Drama of Language, The Harmonies of the Merchant of Venice,* and *Max Beerbohm and the Art of Writing.*

RICHARD DELLAMORA teaches in the English Department and the Program in Cultural and Women's Studies at the University of Trent, Ontario. He is the author of *Masculine Desire: The Sexual Politics of Victorian Aestheticism.*

JONATHAN DOLLIMORE is a Reader in English Literature at Sussex University in Great Britain. He is the author of *Radical Tragedy* (1988) and *Sexual Dissidence: Augustine to Wilde* (1992).

RICHARD ELLMANN was, at the time of his death, Goldsmiths' Professor of English Literature at New College, Oxford. His many works include *Yeats: The Man and His Masks, Eminent Domain: Yeats Among Wilde, Joyce, and Pound, James Joyce* (which won the National Book Award), *Ulysses on the Liffey,* and *The Consciousness of Joyce.* He also edited numerous volumes, including *The Modern Tradition,* the *New Oxford Book of American Verse, The Artist as Critic,* in which the essay included here appears, and the *Norton Anthology of Modern Poetry.*

JOEL FINEMAN was a Professor of English at the University of California, Berkeley. He was the author of *Shakespeare's Perjured Eye: The Invention of Poetic Subjectivity in the Sonnets* and *The Subjectivity Effect in Western Literary Tradition.*

JONATHAN FREEDMAN is an Associate Professor of English at the University of Michigan. In addition to *Professions of Taste,* he is the editor of *Hitchcock's America.*

REGENIA GAGNIER is a Professor of English at Stanford University. She is the author of *Idylls of the Marketplace: Oscar Wilde and the Victorian Public,* in which the essay included here appears, and *Subjectivities: A History of Self-Representation in Britain, 1832–1920.*

WAYNE KOESTENBAUM teaches English at Yale University. He is the author of *Double Talk: The Erotics of Male Literary Collaboration*, *The Queen's Throat: Opera, Homosexuality and the Mystery of Desire*, and *Ode to Anna Moffo and Other Poems*.

JOSEPH LOEWENSTEIN is an Associate Professor and Chair of the English Department at Washington University, St. Louis. He is the author of *Responsive Readings: Versions of Echo in Pastoral Epic and Jonsonian Masque* and numerous essays on the literature of the Renaissance.

JEFF NUNOKAWA is an Associate Professor at Princeton University. He is the author of *The Afterlife of Property: Domestic Security and the Victorian Novel* (1994).

EVE KOSOFSKY SEDGWICK is the Newman Ivey White Professor of English at Duke University. In addition to *Epistemology of the Closet*, in which the essay included here appears, she has written *The Coherence of Gothic Conventions*, *Between Men: English Literature and Male Homosocial Desire*, and *Tendencies*.

SUSAN SONTAG is the author of a number of books, essays, screenplays, and novels, including *Against Interpretation*, in which the essay included here appears, *Under the Sign of Saturn*, *Illness as Metaphor*, and *The Volcano Lover: A Romance*.

KATHARINE WORTH is a Professor of Drama and Theater Studies at Royal Holloway College in the University of London. In addition to her *Oscar Wilde*, in which the essay included here appears, she is the author of *The Irish Drama of Europe from Yeats to Beckett* and editor of *Beckett the Shape Changer*.